TRUE FAITH
AND
ALLEGIANCE

TRUE FAITH
AND
ALLEGIANCE

A STORY OF SERVICE
AND SACRIFICE IN WAR AND PEACE

ALBERTO R.
GONZALES

FORMER UNITED STATES ATTORNEY GENERAL
AND COUNSEL TO PRESIDENT GEORGE W. BUSH

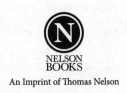

NELSON
BOOKS

An Imprint of Thomas Nelson

Published in Nashville, Tennessee, by Nelson Books, an imprint of Thomas Nelson. Nelson Books and Thomas Nelson are registered trademarks of HarperCollins Christian Publishing, Inc.

Thomas Nelson titles may be purchased in bulk for educational, business, fund-raising, or sales promotional use. For information, please e-mail SpecialMarkets@ThomasNelson.com.

Any Internet addresses, phone numbers, or company or product information printed in this book are offered as a resource and are not intended in any way to be or to imply an endorsement by Thomas Nelson, nor does Thomas Nelson vouch for the existence, content, or services of these sites, phone numbers, companies, or products beyond the life of this book.

Scripture quotations marked niv are from the Holy Bible, New International Version˚, niv˚. Copyright © 1973, 1978, 1984, 2011 by Biblica, Inc.˚ Used by permission of Zondervan. All rights reserved worldwide. www.zondervan.com. The "niv" and "New International Version" are trademarks registered in the United States Patent and Trademark Office by Biblica, Inc.˚

Library of Congress Cataloging-in-Publication Data

Names: Gonzales, Alberto R., author.
Title: True faith and allegiance : a story of service and sacrifice in war
    and peace / by Alberto R. Gonzales (former White House Counsel and former
    U.S. Attorney General).
Description: Nashville, Tennessee : Nelson Books, 2016.
Identifiers: LCCN 2016008306 | ISBN 9780718078874 (hardback)
Subjects: LCSH: Gonzales, Alberto R. | Attorneys general--United
    States--Biography. | Political consultants--United States--Biography. |
    Presidents--United States--Staff--Biography. | Bush, George W. (George
    Walker), 1946---Friends and associates. | Hispanic Americans--Biography. |
    United States--Politics and government--2001-2009.
Classification: LCC KF373.G618 A3 2016 | DDC 340/.092 [B] --dc23 LC record available at
https://lccn.loc.gov/2016008306

Printed in the United States of America

16 17 18 19 20 RRD 6 5 4 3 2 1

To the women in my life who have supported me always: my loving mother, Maria, and my beautiful wife, Rebecca; and to the young men who inspire me: my sons Jared, Graham, and Gabriel.

CONTENTS

A NOTE FROM THE AUTHOR

Many of the events and details I discuss in these pages are controversial and continue to evoke heated debate. Other individuals who witnessed these same events may have different opinions and recollections, but this book reflects my experiences and contains my perceptions of them.

———

This does not constitute an official release of US Government information. All statements of fact, opinion, or analysis expressed herein are those of the author and do not reflect the official positions or views of the US Government. Nothing in the contents of this book should be construed as asserting or implying US Government authentication of information or endorsement of the author's views.

PROLOGUE

ABOARD A CLANDESTINE GOVERNMENT AIRCRAFT, DESTINED FOR LOCATIONS UNKNOWN

Every year, as part of the country's continuity-in-government plan designed to ensure the survival of at least one person in the line of presidential succession in case of a catastrophic event at the Capitol, one cabinet member is asked to be absent from the president's State of the Union address. In 2007, I was *the* designated survivor.

This designation required that I spend the evening on a large government airplane. Although the aircraft did not have all the comforts and technology of *Air Force One*, it was equipped to serve as a flying command center. A senior member of every major federal department and agency accompanied me, each carrying thick binders laying out protocols and classified procedures to advise me in the event I assumed the presidency following a disaster in Washington.

As we departed for places unknown to me, I received a series of classified operational briefings and then I settled in to watch the State of the Union address on a large monitor aboard the plane. As I listened to President George W. Bush addressing the nation, I felt for the first time the full weight of the consequences (as unlikely as they were) of a catastrophic attack. I glanced around the plane at the individuals who would become part of my new team should the unthinkable occur. I wondered momentarily if we would be up to the job of governing a wounded nation in the face of such a horrific nightmare—questions I suspect were shared by every cabinet official before and after me in that position.

As soon as the president concluded his speech and left the Capitol, our plane returned to Andrews Air Force Base. I stood atop the stairs for a moment before deplaning and breathed a sigh of relief. My duty now discharged, I had a whole new appreciation for the person serving as president of the United States.

CHAPTER 1

THE 911 EXPERIENCE

Where were you on September 11, 2001? Ask almost anyone in America who was old enough to remember, and he or she will be able to tell you. It was a day none of us will ever forget.

I awakened early that Tuesday morning and left home around 5:45 a.m., heading to Dulles Airport in northern Virginia, about a twenty-minute drive out of Washington, for a flight to Norfolk, Virginia. I was running late—unusual for me—so I was rushing. But as I was soon to discover, everything about that day would be unusual, except for the fact that it was a crisp, clear, blue-sky morning in America's capital. In front of the airlines' check-in counters, I met Robert Cobb, the White House ethics lawyer on my staff, affectionately known as Moose. A fine lawyer, as well as a strong, competitive athlete with a wry sense of humor, Moose was a good traveling companion.

We boarded United Airlines flight 7223, which was scheduled to take off at 7:20 a.m. As I settled into my seat, I flipped through my speech notes and a White House briefing book outlining my planned events for that day. The speech in Norfolk to a group of government ethics lawyers was merely one segment of a full day of events and meetings. Moose and I were booked to return at 1:00 p.m. Later that afternoon, I was slated to meet with

1

Catholic Hispanic leaders back at the White House, then sit in on another high-level meeting regarding national security; the topic for the afternoon meeting was concerns over Russia and Iran.

After that, I was scheduled to meet with Democratic senators Carl Levin and Deborah Stabenow at the Russell Senate Office Building to discuss Sixth Circuit federal judges from Michigan. Late afternoon, I was to attend a congressional barbeque on the South Lawn. My role was to mingle with members of Congress, hopefully currying favor and goodwill with the legislative branch. I leaned back in my seat and closed my eyes for a few moments. *Just another typical day at the White House*, I thought.

I had no idea.

Moose and I arrived at the Norfolk Waterside Marriott about fifteen minutes prior to my nine o'clock presentation. Officials from the Office of Government Ethics, hosts for the conference, greeted us amiably. As we walked to the hotel ballroom where I was to speak, I received a cell phone call from my longtime assistant, Libby Camp, who was back in Washington. Libby informed me that an airplane had crashed into one of the towers at the World Trade Center in New York. She urged me to get to a television set. Libby was calm, but I could sense a hint of concern in her voice.

In a conference room just off the platform, Moose found a television, and the two of us stared intently at the news coverage of what looked initially like a horrible accident. Reporters speculated that a commuter plane had crashed into the North Tower at 8:46 a.m. Looking at the images on the television, I thought, *How could an accident like that happen on such a clear day?* Something didn't seem right.

It was time for me to speak to the conference attendees so I tried to focus on the audience in front of me. I had no idea that three minutes after I began to speak, another plane, United flight 175, slammed into the South Tower of the World Trade Center. I delivered a relatively short speech and then hustled back to the conference room with the television. The screen filled with aerial shots from a helicopter of the World Trade Center, now with both towers ablaze, confirming my worst fears—this was not a tragic accident; it was overt, insidious terrorism. My stomach tightened and I was momentarily stunned, but this was no time for an emotional response. Indeed, at that moment my first response was not emotional at all; I knew the president was in Florida, but there would soon be many complex legal decisions to be made. I felt compelled to get back to work, back to the White House; I knew I would have an important job to do, and I needed to be there, so I focused on that.

I immediately called Libby. "Get me on the next flight to Washington," I said.

"Yes, sir. I'll do my best, sir," she answered professionally, barely masking the tenseness in her voice.

Moose hailed a taxi and we instructed the cabbie to get us to the airport as quickly as possible. As the taxi raced through the streets of downtown Norfolk, I reached my deputy, Tim Flanigan, on the phone. Tim was already in the White House Situation Room—a relatively small but highly secure room on the basement level of the West Wing.

"What's going on there, Tim?"

He had few details other than the obvious. These were acts of terrorism, and it was believed that al-Qaeda was responsible. President Bush had been in an elementary school in Florida reading to a group of children at the time of the attacks. He was safe and was already on the move—somewhere. Nobody knew if other hijacked aircraft were still in the air or if there were other targets.

There were.

In the fog of such momentous and unprecedented events, when split-second decisions had to be made despite the potential of enormous ramifications, I knew it would be easy to forget protocol, legal authorities, or even logic, leading in the heat of the moment to potential violations of the law. "Tim, listen to me carefully," I said, expecting that our phone connection could be cut off at any moment. "Make sure all major decisions include guidance from the lawyers." At that moment, I didn't know what sort of decisions were in the works, and my mind raced, thinking of the possibilities—whether, for instance, we would have to commandeer certain private resources, such as buses or medical facilities. What if there were terrorist commandoes already on the grounds of the US Capitol or the White House? What legal tools did the president need to deal with attacks upon our citizens, or to have to shoot a passenger jet out of the sky if it were headed toward a nuclear facility or other strategic site? Every decision had to be considered from a legal standpoint as well as concerns for protecting our nation.

A few moments after I hung up with Tim, Libby called back. "Judge Gonzales, the FAA is beginning to shut down all airports and restricting air travel all around the country. Right now there are no guarantees about getting you a flight back to Washington."

"Okay, Libby," I said, my mind already considering alternative methods of transportation.

"And Judge, they say that the volume of cell phone calls is overloading the system, so you may not be able to use your phone much longer."

"Okay, thank you, Libby."

"Judge, one more thing," she said calmly. "The Secret Service has ordered an evacuation of the White House. I have to get off this phone."

"I understand." We hung up, and I didn't hear from Libby again that morning. The Secret Service's precautions were valid. Reports later confirmed that at 9:34 a.m., officials at Reagan National Airport had informed the Secret Service that an unidentified aircraft was streaking through the skies above Pennsylvania, rapidly heading in the direction of Washington, DC.

Near the Norfolk airport by now, my mind raced again through the possible legal authorities the president might exercise to protect America, such as declaring a state of national emergency, restricting travel, taking control of certain industries, and federalizing National Guard troops.

Meanwhile, my wife, Becky, was frantically trying to reach me. Since my trip that morning was a quick jaunt to Norfolk and back, I had not even told her where I was going. Now, on that frightening morning, she simply knew that I had flown out of Dulles Airport. She did not know any of my flight information or my destination. Eventually she reached Libby, who reassured her that I had not been aboard any hijacked aircraft and had arrived safely in Norfolk. Getting home was another matter.

With no information other than what she could glean from television reports and a hurried conversation with Libby, and fearful of another attack, Becky wanted our boys with her. She contacted our oldest son, Jared, who had just started at Emerson College in Boston, making sure he was okay. Then she raced to Spring Hill Elementary to pull our two younger sons, Graham and Gabriel, out of school.

The principal asked Becky to reconsider. She suggested that taking Graham and Gabriel out of the school might signal to other parents that because of my White House connection we knew more than other families. The principal didn't want people to panic.

Becky's maternal instincts trumped the principal's request. She picked up our boys and drove them to a neighbor's house where our sons and the neighbor's children took refuge in the basement, practicing putting sofa cushions over their heads in the event of another attack. Cell phones were out of service by now so Becky continued trying to reach me on our office landline to no avail.

At the Norfolk airport, Moose and I rushed toward our gate, the sounds of our footsteps echoing through the corridor. We passed long lines of stranded passengers, as well as groups of strangers huddled together in the terminal, some crying, others silently staring at the horrific images on the television monitors. The whole place was eerily quiet, with no blaring announcements of flights boarding or gate changes.

The gate attendant saw us coming as Moose and I ran toward her. Before we could utter a word, she shook her head and said, "All flights are canceled." On a nearby television screen, I saw staffers streaming out of the White House gates. On the split screen, shaken journalists were doing their best to describe the mounting calamity, with reports confirming that the Pentagon was now on fire following the third hijacking that crashed American flight 77 into the side of the Defense Department's headquarters at 9:37 a.m. In New York, unwitting cameramen caught images of people falling or jumping to their deaths from the burning floors of the Twin Towers. An unconfirmed report—that later turned out to be false—said that another plane had hit the State Department.

Dear God, I thought. *What is happening?*

I quickly surveyed our surroundings in the terminal, wondering what to do, where to go. I could no longer reach anyone in the White House—a frightening fact in itself—and I had no idea how we might get home. I felt strongly that I needed to be at my post, that I needed to be at the White House when the commander in chief returned. Moose and I decided to rent a car and drive to Washington, if there were any cars still available. As we headed toward the rental car desks, I finally made contact with Tim in the Situation Room. He confirmed that two commercial airliners had crashed into the World Trade Center, decimating both the North and South Towers, with untold numbers of people killed or stranded inside early in the workday. A third plane had been flown into the Pentagon, and yet another plane, United flight 93, apparently had crashed near Somerset, Pennsylvania. Tim wasn't sure, but he feared thousands of people might have been killed in a matter of minutes. He did not know where President Bush was located, but he knew that the president had wanted to return to the White House and had been cautioned against it by Vice President Cheney as well as National Security Advisor Condoleezza Rice.

"We're going to try to rent a car and drive back," I told Tim. I felt more confident knowing that Tim was there at the White House. He was mature and level-headed. As a former senior Justice Department official, I knew he would make sure the right legal questions were being asked, and I trusted his judgment.

While striding through the airport talking to Tim, Moose and I spotted a USO office. We rushed inside, hoping someone there might be able to help us. A naval officer offered to drive us to Norfolk Naval Station, where we would be safe and where the military might have more options.

"Thank you," I said. "Let's go right now."

The officer maneuvered us through the traffic to the base, which by now was transitioning to a state of high alert. All military leaves had been canceled. Military personnel had already erected barricades at base entrances, and armed sentries were posted in strategic locations. The officer explained our dilemma to the guards and we were escorted to the base headquarters, where we showed our credentials to senior officers and asked for help.

Undoubtedly, getting Moose and me back to Washington was not their top priority. Our nation was under attack, and they were trying to secure their base. The last thing they needed was a couple of guys in suits whining about getting back to Washington. The room was tense. The South Tower of the World Trade Center had just collapsed at 9:59 a.m. No one said a word as we watched the television coverage showing repeated images of the crumbling structure, along with hundreds of ghostly, dust-covered people stumbling through the streets trying to get away from the horror.

I understood the officers' uncertainty. After discussing various options, the navy officers suggested the possibility of flying Moose and me back to DC in a navy helicopter if—and it was a big if—they could get flight clearance.

Just then, the television screen filled with more pictures too gruesome to imagine as the North Tower crumbled to the ground at 10:28 a.m. The profound truth did not need words. We all knew that anyone in or around that huge structure moments earlier was now dead. The exponentially magnifying crisis prompted an even greater sense of urgency in me. I had to get back to my post—now.

Several navy officers pursued flight options. "Okay, we think we can get you back by helicopter. Where do you want us to take you in DC?" a senior officer asked me.

"Take us as close to the White House as possible," I replied.

"How about landing on the South Lawn of the White House?" he suggested.

Despite the pressure-packed circumstances, I managed to maintain a modicum of common sense. "No," I said instinctively. "Nobody but the president lands on the South Lawn." I also rejected a suggestion to land near the Washington Monument. I wasn't being humble. There was no need to land there when there were other alternatives. More importantly, I realized that any aircraft other than *Marine One* detected approaching the White House might well be shot down. "Take us to Andrews Air Force Base," I said.

Moose and I waited and waited. Shortly after noon, the navy received clearance to fly us to Andrews Air Force Base. Several enlisted men hustled us to a nearby hangar near the aircraft and issued helmets and life vests to us, quickly giving us the required safety instructions in case of emergencies, all of which seemed ironic on this day dominated by emergencies. Nevertheless, Moose and I nodded in understanding and appreciation.

We boarded a helicopter and a young soldier strapped me in securely. The pilot cranked the engine, but then we sat on the hot tarmac for what seemed like a long time. I was hot and sweaty, and my suit was a rumpled mess. Worried thoughts streaked through my mind. *Are there new reports of hijackings? Is Andrews itself targeted? Are there second thoughts about allowing us to fly into the capital?*

I breathed a sigh of relief when the helicopter's wheels lifted off the ground and we rose into the sky.

On a normal day, a commercial flight from Norfolk to Washington takes less than an hour, but it is a long flight by chopper, especially when you are worried you might be shot down at any moment. Through a headset, I could hear the pilots communicating with someone on the ground, but nobody on board spoke an unnecessary word. Everyone seemed lost in thought. I wondered what I would find when I got back to the White House. Was my family safe? I was irritated with myself for not calling Becky to reassure her. I missed my wife and sons and couldn't wait to get back to them, although at this point I had no idea when that might happen. I knew, now, that my staff of lawyers had been evacuated to a commercial office building in Washington, but I wondered if I had colleagues among the dead.

I thought about President Bush. Where was he? When would he be returning to Washington? Was it even safe for him to return? What was he thinking? What was he feeling? I had come to know George W. Bush well over the years. I suspected that along with a mixture of other emotions, he would also be fighting mad.

From the helicopter, we could see the smoke rising from the Pentagon, and I wondered if my friends and colleagues who worked there were still alive. We landed at Andrews and hurried into a government van for the twenty-five-minute ride to the White House. Along the way, I reached Tim Flanigan and learned that the president had not yet returned, but after making a brief statement from a military location in Louisiana, had been diverted to a more secure location somewhere in the Southwest. All sorts of threat reports were coming in—including, I later learned from Jim Haynes, the general counsel for the Defense Department, concerns about two unidentified planes heading toward the United States, one from Madrid and another from Korea. The Madrid flight was "squawking" hijack.[1] Both planes eventually landed in unanticipated locations outside the United States, and neither plane proved dangerous. But tension levels remained high.

The scene I saw as the van sped through the streets of the capital was surreal. Barricades blocked the entrance to streets close to the Capitol, and capitol police and armed soldiers dressed in black, weapons at the ready, stood on many corners. Apart from the guards, there were hardly any people on the sidewalks, no one strolling the National Mall, virtually no vehicular traffic, and few signs of life. The city looked nearly deserted.

When we arrived at the White House perimeter gates, we were met by Secret Service agents brandishing machine guns—the enhanced security was understandable, but it nonetheless caught my attention. This was in Washington, DC, capital of the land of the free, on the grounds of our own White House. I was also struck by how empty the grounds appeared. Usually, a constant parade of people flowed in and out of the White House compound, with a perpetual buzz of activity, but today it was eerily silent—except for somber-looking agents with their hands near the triggers of their automatic weapons.

We were stopped at gunpoint at several more barricades and asked to produce identification and White House credentials before finally getting to my usual basement door entrance. The West Wing basement seemed ominously quiet. Agents quickly escorted me to a secure underground bunker, the PEOC (Presidential Emergency Operations Center) in the basement of the East Wing, where I found Vice President Cheney and numerous other senior administration officials. I had been to the bunker several times previously for small, private, classified briefings, but today the room was bursting at the seams, crowded with people. The mood in the room seemed heavy, but surprisingly calm. Some officials were on the phone; others were in quiet side conversations around the large conference table that took up the center of the room. The vice president sat at the table, and the activity and attention centered around him.

Glancing around the room, I noticed Transportation Secretary Norm Mineta was on the phone with a serious expression on his face. It was Secretary Mineta's job to make sure air traffic was grounded and all 4,500 planes that had been in the sky earlier that day were accounted for; it was a Herculean task.

I saw David Addington, Vice President Cheney's counsel, and went to him immediately for an update. In quiet but firm tones, David confirmed that the situation at present was stable, and that congressional leaders and cabinet secretaries in the line of presidential succession were accounted for and had been moved to secure locations. Most of the White House staff had been sent home, with essential personnel moved earlier to downtown office buildings. Some of them were already returning to their posts.

I called Tim to let him know I was back and to receive a report on legal issues and an update on the whereabouts of our staff. We still did not know what we might be dealing with from a legal standpoint, so despite the chaos and calamity, we needed as many people as possible ready to work.

Somewhat assured that the counsel's office was functioning as best we could, I stepped away from the crowd. I called home to check on Becky and the boys, and became emotional when she picked up. We talked briefly, and she was relieved to know that I was back and relatively safe, barring an attack on the White House. Neither of us mentioned that possibility.

"I love you, Becky," I said. The words never meant more. "I'll be home as soon as I can." Becky understood that the chance of me getting home soon was really wishful thinking.

Nobody seemed unduly frightened or worried that we were in personal danger. In retrospect, I think we all felt that we had a job to do, and it was incumbent upon us to maintain a sense of professionalism and self-control. I was still working in the bunker later that afternoon when the president convened a teleconference with the vice president and other officials to assess the situation and discuss options for the president's return to Washington. The president was at Offutt Air Force Base in Nebraska. I watched and listened carefully to the president on the secure television monitor in the PEOC. It was reassuring just to see his face. President Bush appeared calm, but I could sense the frustration in his voice. Clearly, he wanted to be back at the White House. He listened carefully to his advisors, weighing the possible risks, and then said simply, "Get ready for me. I'm coming home."

Case closed. No more discussion. The president had emphatically stated during his teleconference that we were at war against terrorism, and ignoring the Secret Service's advice to the contrary, he wanted to direct America's response from the White House.

Despite the Secret Service's concerns about being upstairs in the White House and in the line of fire of another possible attack, I spent much of that afternoon going back and forth between the East Wing underground bunker, the Situation Room, and my West Wing office on the second floor, making sure all the president's legal options were covered. I knew it would be crucial that we consider presidential powers to respond to the threat, as well as to take care of the victims, and to take whatever steps might be necessary to keep the country safe. *What do we need?* was the major question.

Close to 7:00 p.m., I learned the president had arrived at Andrews and was aboard *Marine One*, on his way to the White House, only minutes away. I immediately headed toward the Oval Office. I met Karen Hughes, the White House communications director, in the second-floor hallway, also on her way to the president's office, and we walked down together. She was carrying a batch of papers, a draft of a speech she and presidential speechwriter Mike Gerson had been working on for the president's address to the nation later that evening. I carried with me, as I always did, my pocket edition of the United States Constitution and various briefing papers on possible legal authorities the president might need to exercise in responding to the terrorist attacks.

Dusk was falling over Washington as Karen and I stood quietly, alone on the Oval Office portico, our eyes fixed on the sky, watching for the president. Both of us were immersed in our own thoughts and because we were good friends, conversation seemed unnecessary.

A *Marine One* arrival on the South Lawn of the White House is a spectacular event. Watching that huge green-and-white helicopter with the American flag emblem and the words *United States of America* on the fuselage come into view above the trees against the backdrop of the Washington Monument, one can't help but be overwhelmed with patriotism.

On a normal day, I could hear the sound of the helicopter from my West Wing office. The noise is nearly deafening; the force of the wind from the chopper's giant blades buffets the surrounding trees and always seems to startle visitors. Usually, a roped-off area is provided for families and friends of White House staff, cabinet officials, or members of Congress to greet the president. And there was always a bank of cameras and reporters' microphones to record another moment in history. I'd stood there numerous times myself with family and friends, and I never tired of seeing a presidential departure or arrival in person.

On this night, however, there were no members of the media, no flag-waving well-wishers on the South Lawn. I saw only a single White House cameraman and a cadre of agents—part of the emergency response team—with weapons drawn, forming a protective perimeter around the landing area—and Karen and me.

We stood motionless, a mere fifty yards away, as three huge, identical helicopters appeared in the sky above the South Lawn. For security reasons, two decoy choppers always accompany the president, and not even most of us in the White House are ever certain which helicopter is transporting the commander in chief. At the last moment two choppers peeled away, and the helicopter carrying President Bush swooped in toward the ground, lower and faster than usual, landing perfectly.

Karen and I watched as President Bush hurried down the airstairs, smartly saluted the uniformed marine, and strode across the South Lawn toward us, the anger and resolve evident in his face. *This is why George Bush was elected president*, I thought. *This is his time, his moment to lead our country.*

Karen and I greeted the president somberly and welcomed him home. He acknowledged us with a nod and walked straight into the Oval Office, with Karen and me following him. Inside, there were already large cloth sheets covering the Oval Office floor as movers rearranged furniture in preparation for the televised speech to the nation later that evening. The president, Karen, and I walked through the office and into the private dining room just off the Oval Office.

The dining room is a relatively small square room with, at that time, royal blue carpeting. A three-drawer credenza sits against the east wall, and the south wall has a large window surrounded by floor-to-ceiling white flowered draperies. An ornate wooden table sits in the center, surrounded by six upholstered chairs with royal blue leather seats. On the table sat an arrangement of roses.

The president sat down at the table with his back to the window. Soon Chief of Staff Andy Card arrived, along with Ari Fleischer, the president's press secretary, and National Security Advisor Condi Rice. Andy stood to the president's right, and Ari and Karen sat nearby; Condi remained standing, and I did, too, directly across the table, facing the president.

Each of us reported on what we were doing, answered questions from the president, and spoke briefly about our experiences and impressions from that day. The president stated bluntly that we were at war. He had no hesitation in his voice and no concern about being politically correct; he called it for what it was.

Amidst the myriad issues he faced, the president's immediate concern was for the victims of the attacks and their families. We talked about what he planned to say during his address to the nation to help ease their pain. He seemed to know instinctively that the country needed his courage and his leadership, and in his first nationally televised appearance from the White House since the nightmare began, he wanted to convey a message of reassurance.

When the red light on the television camera came on, it was obvious that the president was in complete control of his emotions and appreciated the gravity of the situation. He spoke slowly and firmly. "Today, our fellow citizens, our way of life, our very freedom came under attack in a series of deliberate and deadly terrorist attacks," he said. At that moment, we still did not know how many people had died; it would be weeks before we settled on the number—2,973 souls indiscriminately annihilated that morning.

So President Bush spoke more broadly. "The victims were in airplanes, or in their offices; secretaries, businessmen and -women, military and federal workers; moms and dads, friends and neighbors. Thousands of lives were suddenly ended by evil, despicable acts of terror."

The president promised America that we would find the terrorists and bring them to justice. And then in one of the most significant statements ever spoken by an American president, President George W. Bush said, "We will make no distinction between the terrorists who committed these acts and those who harbor them." That line would have incredible significance and would come to be known as the Bush Doctrine, a cornerstone in the many complex and controversial issues we would confront in the years ahead. Some of those issues had not been encountered by our country since World War II. Many others had never before confronted Americans.

Sometime around midnight, things began to wind down, so Tim Flanigan and I decided to go home and try to get some rest. Because I had parked in the same Dulles Airport lot in which authorities believed the hijackers of American Airlines flight 77—the plane that had hit the Pentagon—had also parked, my car had been impounded pending further investigation. Tim offered to give me a ride home.

We were both drained, and as Tim drove through the empty streets, it felt as though months had passed since my early-morning flight. I had taken off at 7:20 a.m., just fifty minutes before American Airlines flight 77 was flown into the Pentagon, killing 125 people inside, as well as the plane's crew of six, and fifty-eight passengers, including our friend Barbara Olson, wife of Solicitor General Ted Olson, one of our colleagues in the Bush administration. I couldn't help wondering if I had crossed paths with the hijackers that morning, or perhaps even some of the passengers, whose bodies were still being extricated from the rubble at the Pentagon. I squeezed my eyes tightly shut and tried to dismiss the images from my mind.

Becky was still waiting up for me when Tim dropped me off. I was glad to be home. I stepped inside the door of our home and hugged my wife; we held on to each other for a long time. Neither of us wanted to let go. The boys were in bed so Becky and I talked about all that had happened that day, and what it might mean for our nation. Tears streamed down Becky's face, and I tried to reassure her that everything would work out—as my father often told me, it had to work out.

When we could barely keep our eyes open, we tried in vain to get some sleep. A few hours later, Tim picked me up again, and we headed back to the White House around 5:30 a.m. to confront a brand-new world—a world that is not safe, and may never be safe again.

CHAPTER 2

DREAMING THE DREAM

I grew up in a much calmer environment, or at least it seemed that way. Immigration—and particularly illegal immigration—is and will most likely remain a hot-button issue in America for years to come. In the Gonzales family, immigration was not simply a hot topic we heard discussed on a television program; for my family, it was a deeply ingrained reality. Three of my four grandparents were born in northern Mexico, where they struggled to eke out a subsistence-level lifestyle in farming and ranching communities. They crossed the border into the United States—possibly legally, though probably not, at times—in search of a better life. They were perpetually poor, but they were hard workers, migrating to wherever the jobs could be found, primarily in Southwest Texas, occasionally making their way back home to Mexico, only to be forced back northward when they could not find work south of the border.

Although they lived in the United States most of their lives, my grandparents never lost touch with their Mexican roots. Both of my parents, however, were born and raised in America. My father, Pablo M. Gonzales, was born in 1929 in Kenedy, Texas, a small town with a population around three thousand people located in Karnes County, about sixty miles southeast of San Antonio. A nondescript place, Kenedy is best known in history as the location of the Kenedy Alien Detention Camp, where German, Japanese, and Italian prisoners of war were held during World War II. Some of the people detained in the internment camp were civilians who had been long-time residents of the United States.

The oldest of fifteen children, my father left school before finishing second grade and went to work doing odd jobs in town and around the house to support his family. He never really had a childhood. He never participated in athletic games or pool parties; his life was dominated by hard work. Like the children of so many other migrant workers, from the time he could carry a basket Pablo Gonzales traveled with his family to various parts of the country, picking crops. He worked with a passion, as though his life depended on it, which it did—often pushing his brothers and cousins to work harder in the fields so the family could survive.

As an adult, he worked at various manual labor jobs with construction companies. He was a quiet, serious man, difficult to read or know well, and even his own brothers and sisters had difficulty figuring him out. As the oldest, he was the leader, the one who pushed his siblings to work. People close to him were certain of two things regarding Pablo Gonzales: he worked hard, and he expected those around him to carry his or her fair share of the load. Pablo never sought or accepted a handout.

Maria Rodriguez, my mother, the woman who would most impact my early life, was born in 1932, the fourth of seven children in a poor family in San Antonio, Texas. A shy, introverted little girl, Maria loved to read and enjoyed school. She completed the fifth grade, and had a good start in the sixth grade, when her father took her out of school early in the spring. He packed up the family and carted them off to Michigan to pick crops. They returned to Texas later that fall, but school had already begun, so Maria sat out the remainder of the school term. Migrating to find work was the yearly pattern for her family, preventing Maria from completing another academic year due to her extended absences.

Maria's hopes of returning to school were further dashed when tragedy struck the Rodriguez family. At only thirty-two years of age, Maria's mother died during natural childbirth at home. The child was stillborn. Maria was a mere nine years old at the time. Nevertheless, as the oldest female in the family, she assumed the role of mother and caretaker.

In both Pablo's and Maria's families, any money earned by the children was turned over to the head of the household to help make ends meet. It was, after all, the 1930s and early 1940s, and America was still reeling from the stock market crash of 1929 and the Great Depression that followed. Not surprisingly, during their childhood and adolescent years, neither family had indoor plumbing or telephones. Both grew accustomed to using outhouses, washing their clothes in a creek or a washtub, and cooking their meals on an old-fashioned wood stove.

When Maria was seventeen and Pablo was nineteen, they met in Lorenzo, Texas, where their families had trekked as part of their yearly pilgrimages to pick cotton. It was love at first sight. A few months after picking season, Pablo asked Maria's grandmother if he could have Maria's hand in marriage. Firmly entrenched in family traditions, Pablo did not dare ask Maria to marry him without receiving the blessing of her eldest family members. Grandmother and Grandfather Rodriguez gave their consent, as did Maria's father, but it was two years before the excited couple could marry.

Raised a Catholic, Maria possessed a strong faith in God. Because the church taught that marriage is a sacrament, Maria insisted on a church wedding and Pablo agreed. They married in the Catholic Church in San Juan Capistrano Mission in San Antonio. Not surprisingly, the young Catholic couple had their first child, a daughter they named Angelica, within a year.

I was the second of eight children—first Angie; then me, Tony, Rene, Timmy, Theresa, Christine, and Paul—born to Maria and Pablo Gonzales. As usual, my father had been following the work opportunities, so the family was living in San Antonio, Texas, when Mother gave birth to me on August 4, 1955, at Santa Rosa Hospital. I was the firstborn boy—a position of honor in Hispanic families—and my parents felt it was important that I have a name that reflected my distinction, so they named me Alberto R. Gonzales, the R in honor of my mother's maiden name, Rodriguez, even though they gave me no middle name to accompany the middle initial.

During my first few years, our family moved frequently as my father chased available construction jobs, first to Texas City, then to Beaumont, and eventually settling in the Houston area.

About the time I turned five, my parents purchased a small, undeveloped lot in Humble, a community named for Humble Oil Company (the predecessor of Exxon) on the outskirts of northern Houston. By then, my father was an excellent carpenter, so after work each day and on weekends, he and two of my uncles set about building a small, two-bedroom house for our growing family. I played in the yard as my father and his brothers sawed and set the two-by-four frames, hoisted and nailed the plywood and composition shingles onto the roof, and nailed up the sheetrock for the interior walls. The brothers sank a well in the yard for water and installed a septic tank to collect and diffuse sewage.

They did all the work themselves, without the help of any professionals or subcontractors. Although my father had limited funds with which to build, he never considered asking the government or anyone else for help. He believed in family helping family; his brothers would help him build his home, and then he would return the favor one day. Brother helping brother—that's the way it was meant to be.

The Gonzales brothers built the house, but they included no luxuries. We had a small kitchen, two bedrooms, a living room, and a bathroom, but no hot running water, so we boiled pots of water on the kitchen stove to fill the tub for our baths. We didn't get a home telephone until I was nearly a junior in high school. This was the house in which I grew up, and the entire time I lived at home, I shared a bed with one of my brothers, while two other brothers slept in another bed in the same room. My sisters shared the other bedroom, and our parents slept on a bed in the living room. The accommodations were crowded by the time our family grew to ten members, but our mother filled our home with love, discipline, and great food.

Each morning, my mother awakened me before dawn to eat breakfast with my father. The breakfast was always the same—scrambled eggs and tortillas. While my father and I ate, my mother prepared Dad's modest lunch of beans and tortillas and placed the meager portions in a brown paper bag. That daily routine rarely changed. I stood outside our house and watched him walk up the road and hitch a ride to work at a construction site. I waved until I could no longer see him. Then I went back inside and roused my brothers and sisters from their sleep as Mom prepared breakfast for the rest of the family.

It never dawned on me as a young boy that my parents had set up housekeeping on the poor side of town. Our few neighbors were like us, hard-working, blue-collar families. I noticed, however, that many of the lots around our home remained vacant and unkempt all the years I lived at home. My brothers and I didn't mind. The vacant lots made good sandlot baseball fields, and I loved playing baseball.

Our mother insisted our family attend mass every Sunday, and that each of the children be baptized and confirmed in the Catholic Church. Mother suspected that we probably would not consistently attend church services if the decision were left solely to our father. My dad believed in God and in Jesus Christ as our Savior, but he was not as devoted as our mother.

Almost like a scene out of *Fiddler on the Roof*, my father had reminded my mother, "Maria, I am the head of this family, and *I* will decide if we are going to church." Indeed, he emphasized that he would determine whether my mother *could* attend services.

Surprisingly, my strong-willed mother agreed with my father. "Yes, Pablo, you are the head of the family, and I am required by God to obey you. But just remember, *you* will have to answer to God for this decision, and you will have to account as to why I missed mass."

So we went to church. My father recognized and respected true authority. Indeed, he never again spoke a word in opposition to our family attending church services.

Mother later credited the Holy Spirit for giving her the right words to say in the most appropriate manner. Because of their traditional Mexican upbringing, had she directly challenged her husband's authority and claimed her independent right to attend mass, my father would have undoubtedly balked. But Mother knew that her husband respected and feared God's judgment. And perhaps she also knew a bit of psychology.

My father was a proud man, steeped in our ethnic traditions. He had been raised in the old ways—in the days when women stayed home and tended to the children, and the men went out to earn a living. As the head of the family, my father believed it was his responsibility to provide for his family. My mother never worked outside the home nor learned to drive an automobile until after my father died. To my father, for his wife to take a job outside the home to help make ends meet would be tantamount to saying that he was not adequately providing for his family.

My father's independent spirit was a mixed blessing. His responsible nature and commitment to work made it difficult to challenge his excesses. Consequently, when he wasn't working himself ragged, he sometimes drank excessively—especially on weekends. Despite being a good man with many noble qualities, my father was an alcoholic, and when he drank, he became a different person, often belligerent, caustic, and mean. Sometimes he and my mother had terrible fights, lashing out at each other in vicious verbal sparring. On a couple of occasions, driving while intoxicated, my father wrecked our one family car. It was a miracle he never hurt himself or injured anyone else.

Regardless of his circumstances, which often included a throbbing headache and a heavy hangover, my father got up at five o'clock on Monday morning and set off for work. I don't know how he did it. His dedication and sense of duty to his family were so strong that no matter how sick he felt, he refused to miss work. No doubt his indomitable work ethic helped fuel my own.

It broke my heart to see my father drunk. His alcoholic episodes left an indelible impression and produced in me an irrevocable decision to avoid alcohol. In the military, and during my service in Texas government and eventually the White House, despite the readily available alcohol, I chose not to drink. Not during the long, lonely nights on an isolated air force radar site, not at the many Washington parties and receptions I attended, not at all; any time I was tempted to raise a glass or down a shot of whiskey, images of my father flooded my mind. Those memories were strong deterrents and still are.

Since we had only one car, when one of us kids got sick and needed to go to the doctor, my father dropped off my mother and *all* of the children at the county clinic on his way to work. Mother packed a sack lunch, and we spent the entire day at the clinic until my father returned to pick us up after work. In an emergency, Mother might ask a neighbor for a ride to a bus stop a few miles away. We would then catch a bus to the county hospital. The image of my mother carrying an infant with several kids in tow, hurrying to get medical attention for one or more of her sick children, is forever ingrained in my heart and mind.

For her part, Maria Gonzales thought nothing of it. When I asked her later about her sacrificial spirit, she simply shrugged. "That is what moms do," she said.

During one of our many trips to a clinic that provided free immunizations to poor families, Mother was speaking to us kids in Spanish. A nurse overheard our mother. Whether from prejudice or a sincere desire to help, I would never be sure, she warned my mother, "You better speak English to your children. They are going to have a hard time in school and in life here in America if they can't speak English." Bilingual education did not exist in our area yet, so anyone who did not learn English was bound to have a tougher time in life.

Mom took the nurse's words to heart. My parents continued speaking to each other in Spanish, but thereafter they made a conscious decision to speak only English to their children. Consequently, though I had a rudimentary understanding of the language, I didn't become fluent in Spanish. While friends and relatives questioned the wisdom of our parents' strategy, knowing and speaking English worked to my advantage academically. Many kids in Texas schools who spoke mostly Spanish were erroneously assumed to be poor and academically challenged.

———

As a young boy, I persuaded my parents to let me join the Cub Scouts. Many of the boys in my pack were, like me, from poor families, so the camaraderie we felt from wearing a Cub Scout shirt and neckerchief, our chests decorated with colorful patches we had earned, was especially motivating. One project, however, taught me a lesson I have never forgotten.

Members of my Scout pack were required to carve a canoe from a stick of wood using only a pocketknife. Most of my fellow Cubs chose branches no wider than an inch. Not me. I picked out a piece of wood three to four inches thick and went to work whittling it into something that looked like a boat. After school, day after day, I worked diligently on the project, but as the deadline approached, I realized that at the pace I was progressing, I would not finish in time.

With hope nearly gone, I asked my father for help. He looked at my scarred piece of wood, and we began working together to hollow it out. As I followed his instructions, slowly the branch began to take on the shape of a canoe.

"Dad, do you really think it is going to work out?" I asked.

My father looked at me and smiled. Then with absolute confidence, he said, "Son, it's gotta work out." He harbored no doubts in his mind about the outcome. *It had to work out.*

My father's optimistic attitude, instilled within me, would serve me well over the years, especially when the world was shaking and people all over the earth were wondering whether things were going to work out. During my lifetime, I have had to confront some difficult situations, circumstances that seemingly defied resolution. In those most intense times, I often remembered the simple lesson I learned from my father: yes, there is a solution, and everything will work out if you are patient, have faith, and just stay with it.

I played organized summer baseball, and I was a pretty good player, too, selected as the league's Most Valuable Player in Little League when I was twelve years old, and again in Pony League when I was fourteen. Baseball continued to be my first love, but like many boys in Texas, I also played football. My passion for the gridiron heightened even more when I got a part-time job selling soft drinks at the seventy-five-thousand-seat Rice Stadium on the campus of Rice University, a beautiful, tree-lined setting located just off Main Street in Houston, but seemingly in its own world, tucked away in the shadow of the Houston Medical Center.

To me, the Rice campus was like a heavenly oasis in the midst of the busy city. For several seasons in a row, I worked on Saturdays as a soda-vendor, carrying trays of cold Cokes and Sprites up and down the upper deck during Rice's home football games. Following the game, after cashing out and returning my soft drink trays on Saturday afternoon or evening, I sometimes climbed to the top of the stands and watched the students walking back to their dorms. I dreamed of attending college and wondered what it might feel like to be a student at Rice.

My parents possessed little academic education themselves, so not surprisingly, they didn't see college in their children's futures. Their simple hope was that my siblings and I could graduate from high school and get a job. To my mother and father, earning a high school diploma was an admirable and honorable accomplishment in its own right, for us and for *them*—signifying my parents' achievement in providing a better life for their children.

As a child, I never sensed overt discrimination against me, perhaps because there were so many other Hispanic kids around or maybe it was simply the natural innocence of youth. But as I moved into junior high, I increasingly noticed the differing attitudes toward students with darker skin. Indeed, I sometimes felt embarrassed by my Mexican heritage.

In class one day, my eighth-grade history teacher vividly recounted the historic battle at the Alamo, a major milestone in the fight for Texas independence from Mexico. As the teacher extolled the virtues and heroic acts of men such as Davy Crockett and Jim Bowie, and how they had stood against the tyranny of General Santa Anna and the evil Mexican army, I squirmed in my seat, increasingly uncomfortable about being poor and of Mexican descent. I wanted so much to be one of the good guys, but with my dark skin, brown eyes, and black hair, I looked a lot like the bad guys our teacher had been describing.

School and home remained disconnected worlds for me. Apart from the usual parental demands such as "Get your homework done" at home, my family members never discussed anything about history, math, geography, or government, civics, or politics. We rarely watched the local news, much less national news, and we did not subscribe to either of Houston's two newspapers. Although they were US citizens, my parents never voted during my childhood. Civic involvement was not a priority to my parents.

They focused on making a living and feeding eight kids. Clearly, my later interest in law and government were acquired tastes.

My freshman year at a new school, Douglas MacArthur High School, got off to a rough start, perhaps because of my last name. I was placed in a number of remedial classes, but determined to prove myself, I worked harder. By the end of that year, I had turned things around, earning As and Bs. During my sophomore year, I was also successful on the athletic fields. Although I was relatively small, I was agile and fast, and I had no qualms about tackling the big guys. I earned my position as starting middle linebacker on our junior varsity football team. That same year, I also made the varsity baseball team, playing the shortstop position. My self-esteem rose commensurately with my success in sports, as did my popularity with my peers.

With success in the classroom and on the athletic field, I developed an I-can-do-this attitude. Perhaps equally important, I began asking myself, *Why not me? If others can succeed and make their marks in the world, why not me?* That sounds rather innocuous nowadays, but for a kid with my upbringing, that question was nothing less than transformational.

Like most teenagers, I soon became more aware of material possessions, noting especially what my family and I did *not* have, compared to what other kids seemed to take for granted. I was embarrassed about sharing a bedroom with my three brothers, so I never invited friends over after school or to spend the night on weekends. Whenever I got a ride home from school or football practice, I usually asked to be dropped off at a corner, down the road from my house, so my friends couldn't see where and how I lived. My conduct was foolish and immature, and my father would have slapped me across the back of the head—literally—had he known of my duplicity. But I wanted desperately to fit in with my buddies from school, to not be ostracized because of my family's poverty. It did not occur to me that some of my friends might be hiding their own embarrassment.

I continued to do well academically, and my parents even became more supportive of my athletic pursuits. I was still on the varsity baseball team and was also selected as an All-District strong safety in football.

My senior year began and ended far too soon. In between, I became a member of the National Honor Society, dated the head baton-twirler who motivated me to be better, and I lettered again in football and baseball. By many universities' criteria, I might have been considered a prime candidate for admission or possibly scholarship assistance, but neither my high school guidance counselor nor my parents encouraged me to pursue higher education. While a few of my friends planned to enroll in community colleges, most of my buddies were merely excited about getting out of school, leaving home, landing a job, and living on their own. I assumed that's what I would do as well, since I could not afford to attend college.

My older sister, Angie, and I both graduated from MacArthur High School in May 1973. It was a happy day for the Gonzales family, and our parents beamed with pride. Even my low-keyed father seemed excited. I had graduated with honors—23 out of 389 graduates—but in the midst of the celebration, I felt slightly lost. I had no idea what I was going to do with the rest of my life.

A few days after graduation, I interviewed for various blue-collar jobs I had seen advertised. I was hired by Houston Belt and Terminal Railroad Company, but I didn't really see my future as a track-switcher. Nevertheless, the pay was good, and I managed to save a few dollars working there briefly during the early summer of '73.

Meanwhile, a high school friend and I talked frequently about joining the air force. His father was an air force veteran who often spoke to us in grandiose terms about the benefits of a military career. The more I thought about it, the more the military made sense for me. I could earn a steady paycheck, learn a trade, serve our country, and I'd even receive GI Bill benefits in case I wanted to think more seriously about attending college one day. The armed forces was a siren's call for young men and women like me who hailed from poor, underprivileged families. The Vietnam War was winding down, and although I had never even been aboard an airplane, the air force seemed like a way I could see the world.

Without even consulting my parents, I signed on with the air force for a four-year stint. My enlistment would not take effect, however, until I turned eighteen years of age. Early on the morning of August 23, 1973, the air force recruiter arrived at my home to transport me to the induction center. Apparently, he wasn't taking any chances that I might back out.

He needn't have worried. I had no intention of reneging on my commitment. Quite the opposite: I was excited to begin a new adventure. Having never served in the military, my father eyed the recruiter suspiciously, but he said little about my decision to enlist. My mother, however, was surprised that I had joined the military service. She hadn't expected that of me. Nevertheless, she was supportive and hugged me as we said good-bye. I hugged my father and walked out the door with barely a gym bag full of possessions. I was off to see the world.

CHAPTER 3

SNOW BIRD

I stepped onto an airplane for the first time at eighteen years of age, my virgin flight whisking me from Houston to San Antonio, where I began basic training at Lackland Air Force Base, part of Joint Base San Antonio, which now includes Fort Sam Houston and Randolph Air Force Base. Although I probably didn't think so at the time, joining the military was one of the best decisions of my life. The discipline was good for me, and I learned how to take care of myself.

Following basic training and a short leave, I reported to technical training school at Keesler Air Force Base in Biloxi, Mississippi. I graduated from tech school as a weapons technician/operator about six weeks later and was immediately confronted with what I now realize was one of the pivotal points of my life. It started with some of the best news any airman could ever receive: I was being assigned to duty in Key West, Florida. Wow, beautiful beaches, tropical breezes, and a laid-back, easygoing atmosphere—and they were going to pay me for serving there too.

I was informed, however, that during my four-year tour of duty in the air force, I would have to serve one tour in a remote location, probably for at least a year. I could enjoy working in Key West now, with the knowledge that the more difficult tour would follow, or I could take the harder, remote assignment now, location yet to be determined.

My father had always taught me to do the hard job first. Getting the difficult work out of the way made everything else that followed seem that much easier. That was the more responsible and mature thing to do. My choice was clear. I was my father's son, so I kissed Key West good-bye without even seeing it.

When my new orders came through, I discovered that I had received the remote assignment—one of the *most* remote in the entire air force. I was assigned for one year at a forward early-warning radar site at Fort Yukon, Alaska, located *north* of the Arctic Circle. Only about one hundred men were stationed at the site, and the nearest civilization—a small village of about six hundred Alaskan natives—was nearly a mile away. Fort Yukon was accessible only by air during the winter months, but it could be reached by boat during the summer, traveling up the Fort Yukon River—after the ice had melted. I reported at the end of January 1974.

Despite the bone-chilling temperatures, I loved Alaska. I spent several evenings staring up into the dark northern sky, mesmerized by the awesome greenish-yellow aurora borealis, the northern lights. I watched dashes of red pierce the darkness, along with streaks of blue, or what looked like whirlwinds of green, as the gaseous particles from the earth's atmosphere collided with gaseous particles from the sun. I watched as God put on a spectacular free show every winter night. I had never seen anything quite like it.

As a Forward Early Warning Radar station, Fort Yukon was on the front lines in standing guard against ballistic missile attacks or any air or ground incursions, especially by the Soviet Union, headed toward Alaska and, ultimately, mainland North America. My deployment occurred during the Cold War, so tension and suspicion between the United States and the Soviet Union were still intense. The US/Soviet nuclear arms policies of Mutually Assured Destruction, based on the idea that if the Russians launched nukes at us, we would retaliate in kind—and vice versa—kept the world in an awkward, precarious balance, but there was no denying that a perpetual threat existed.

Our job at Fort Yukon was to maintain a vigilant lookout, especially for missile attacks, but also to keep our electronic eyes open for any aircraft that might be operating in US airspace. If we detected anything unusual, our station sent notice to Elmendorf Air Force Base in Anchorage, where F-4 fighter jets immediately scrambled and took to the air to check out and deter the intruders.

I was a weapons controller technician, so part of my job was to keep my eyes on the radar scope and report to the officer who was in communication with the pilot of a scrambled jet. I calculated attack angles and tracked the armament and the fuel capacity, constantly feeding the information to the controller, to assist the officer as the fighter jet tracked the intruder.

Partly to pass the time, I took on an extra job cleaning the officers' lounge, and as a result I got to know two officers who had graduated from the Air Force Academy. They seemed impressed when they noticed me studying for a correspondence course I was taking from Alaska Methodist University.

"Have you ever considered applying to the Air Force Academy?" one of the officers asked.

"No, sir. Not really."

"You could get an entire college education there for free and become an officer, maybe a pilot."

I had never thought about becoming an officer, and I had no illusions about becoming an air force pilot, so I had never seriously considered applying to the academy. I didn't know much about the appointment process to America's military academies, nor did I know that the acceptance level was low and the candidates for entrance were highly competitive. Each year, thousands of America's best and brightest young men (and eventually women) applied for entrance, hoping to earn their college degrees and officers' commissions. Most of those applicants were turned away. Usually, a candidate was nominated by his or her US congressman or senator. I didn't even know a government official at that time.

Nevertheless, with the encouragement of these officers, I began to think, *Why not? Why not me? Maybe I could become an officer. It is worth a try, and I have nothing to lose.* Perhaps, more importantly, I realized that if I didn't believe in myself, if I didn't think I deserved it, why should anyone else? Sure, acceptance at the Air Force Academy was a long shot, and I had no connections, but the officers informed me that like the other military academies, the Air Force Academy accepted a few candidates each year from its regular rank and file enlisted men. I had a shot.

I decided to go for it.

But it wasn't a one-man effort. In fact, looking back, I'm amazed at how many of my officers and fellow airmen pitched in to help me, flying me to Fairbanks to take the physical fitness test, arranging for me to take the ACT at Fort Yukon, even introducing me to the commanding general of the Alaska Air Command to obtain a recommendation. And then in December 1974, just days before Christmas, I received word: I was ordered to report to the US Air Force Academy Preparatory School in Colorado Springs early in January 1975. It was a conditional acceptance; if I successfully completed a semester of refresher courses in math and English, I would be admitted to the Air Force Academy.

I scrambled to pack up my gear. I had no idea where all this would lead, but if I could get to Elmendorf Air Force Base in time to process out, I could spend Christmas in Texas with my family. I said hasty good-byes to my officers and friends at Fort Yukon and caught the plane to Elmendorf. As the aircraft sliced through the winter haze, I thought back over my choices. By choosing the hard road rather than the duty in Key West, I had discovered an opportunity that might change the direction of my entire life. I breathed a silent prayer and thanked God for guiding my steps.

CHAPTER 4

FROM A FALCON TO AN OWL

The Academy Prep School is located on US Air Force Academy grounds, a few miles from the main campus, where I was welcomed along with seven other midterm "regulars," men who were already in the air force and had likewise been selected. In addition to our academic studies, we maintained a rigorous physical fitness regimen that included long-distance runs, swimming, and other conditioning exercises. I studied hard, and when the grades were posted in early June, I was accepted at the academy, entering on June 30, 1975, as a member of the class of 1979, the last all-male class of approximately four thousand in the cadet wing.

Because of the semester at the prep school, getting acclimated to life at the academy was relatively easy, and I soon fell into a routine, studying and working hard as a cadet. My fellow freshmen in Squadron 33, nick-named "Cellar rats," selected me as their representative to the freshmen class council, where I interacted with the thirty-nine representatives from other squadrons and was subsequently elected as class council president. The council was an advisory group with no real authority in a strictly military environment, but it did provide me opportunities to communicate with and get to know the commandant of cadets.

In both the fall and spring semesters, I managed to make the dean's list—which recognized academic achievement—and the commandant's list—which recognized exceptional military achievement. My success placed me on the superintendent's list, a highly sought-after position among serious-minded cadets. As a reward for making the superintendent's list, I received primo choices for summer electives. I chose to fly gliders.

I was proud to be among a group of men who were committing our lives to serving our country. When I went home for summer break, my parents and siblings seemed proud to see me in uniform. I relished being home for a few weeks, although I was reminded of how much I missed my family and life in Houston. All too soon, it was time to return to another daunting dose of academics and military drills.

Though I still did well, I eased off on the military aspects and focused more on academics during my second year at the academy. I especially enjoyed courses in national security and military history. I loved the intricacies of these courses, especially the military tactics used in famous battles, and I seemed to grasp the class content much easier than my courses in math, engineering, and science.

I even allowed more time for a social life. Once a week, I attended an evening Bible study hosted in a home, which included both military cadets and young women from Colorado Springs and the surrounding area. Not surprisingly, the Bible study proved quite popular among cadets.

One night at Bible study, I met Diane Clemens, an attractive, green-eyed young coed from Illinois, who attended the University of Northern Colorado at Greeley, located just north of Denver. She was visiting with some female friends from Colorado Springs who regularly attended the Bible study, so she came along. Diane possessed a vibrant and devout Christian faith, and she sang and played guitar beautifully. We were immediately attracted to each other and soon began dating. We attended the Bible study together whenever Diane was in town, and I made numerous trips to Greeley as our relationship continued to grow.

As I approached the end of my second year at the academy, another pivotal point regarding my future loomed large. Although I loved being at the academy and learning to fly gliders intensified my interest in becoming a pilot, I wondered if I would qualify for pilot training due to my eyesight, which had begun to degenerate. Moreover, I pondered whether I was meant for something besides a military career. I prayed frequently and seriously about the direction of my life, asking God to guide my steps.

I knew if I continued one day into my next semester at the academy, I would be locked in and would owe the air force a longer service commitment if I subsequently left, even though by now I was close to fulfilling my initial four-year contract. If I were ever going to change course, now was the time.

My childhood dream of attending Rice University returned, but I didn't want to foolishly walk away from a priceless opportunity at the academy. As I considered my options, it seemed as though I couldn't lose. If I stayed on, I could complete my studies and serve my country in the air force. It would be a good life and career—certainly more than I could have expected had I stayed in Humble. On the other hand, if I applied to Rice and was accepted, that would be my answer to prayer, and an indication that I should pursue a different sort of career. As an act of faith, I filled out the required forms for admission to Rice and put the matter in God's hands. I didn't discuss my decision with my parents, nor did I discuss the possibility of leaving the academy with any of my fellow cadets or officers.

On May 13, 1977, I received my answer. The Rice University Office of Admissions accepted me, and I could transfer in as a junior in the 1979 class. Two weeks after my notification from Rice, I withdrew from the Air Force Academy. The air force placed me in the air force reserves with an honorable discharge that would become effective August 23, 1979.

When I returned to Texas at the end of the semester, I informed my parents and siblings that I was home to stay, that I was going to remain in Houston and attend Rice. My mom was thrilled to have me home, but my father wasn't too keen on the idea of my quitting the academy. It wasn't that he wanted me to be a pilot; he simply didn't like the idea of one of his children quitting *anything*. He didn't say much—he rarely did—and I think he was at least pleased that I planned to finish my college degree program. Still, I'm sure the question rankled in his mind: *Why is my son quitting?* Quitting was a foreign concept to my family.

Thanks to a very generous endowment program, Rice is able to maintain a relatively low tuition compared to many other private universities, but the costs were still staggering to me. Of course, that meant I had to earn some money in a hurry.

That summer, my father helped me to get a job sweeping floors at the rice mill where he worked. To some people, the idea of sweeping floors might seem demeaning. After all, I had just completed four semesters on the dean's list at the Air Force Academy, and I was soon to begin classes at one of the most prestigious and elite universities in the country. But to my father, any job that was not immoral or illegal was noble. I sucked up my ego and went to work. More than the income I earned, the job reminded me of the hard work and sacrifices my parents had made for my siblings and me. As a small concession to my pride, I placed a Rice University sticker on the windshield of my car. I wanted my coworkers at the mill to know: *I may be sweeping floors, but I am a college student!* At Rice, no less.

The Rice Institute was the brainchild of William Marsh Rice, a wealthy entrepreneur who made a fortune in the cotton trade and other businesses. Rice envisioned a world-class university created for the advancement of science, art, and literature. At his death in September 1900, per his wishes, much of his wealth was placed in a financial trust established to provide a tuition-free education to academically excellent *Caucasian* students—Hispanics, African Americans, and other nonwhites were excluded. For more than sixty years, the university operated on that basis. In 1965, the Rice Board of Trustees filed a lawsuit seeking to allow Rice to admit students without regard to race. Because of William Rice's stipulations, the only way to do so was to break the financial trust. The board chose racial equality over the money, resulting in Rice University charging students tuition, but students who looked like me could now attend.

The campus itself is comprised of magnificent Neo-Byzantine architecture with red-tile roofs atop buildings of rose-hued brick. It is situated on 285 acres of land next to the Houston Medical Center in the heart of the city. Yet because the campus is entirely enclosed by hedges and a double row of oak trees, students often refer to "life within the hedges." I loved walking through the beautiful tree-lined campus. Stepping inside the hedges felt almost as though I were visiting an exotic location in another part of the country.

Rice is known as a top-notch engineering school, and the curriculum is loaded with math- and science-related subjects. With those courses not my strongest suits, I was grateful when I learned that during my two years at the Air Force Academy, I had already satisfied my math and science requirements, so I was free to explore other areas of interest at Rice. I chose a political science major because I was fascinated by comparisons between the American system of government and those of other countries. Although Kent State, Watergate, and the Vietnam War continued to cast long shadows over many American college campuses, I refused to buy into the cynicism shared by many of my fellow collegians and professors. On the other hand, I did not feel it was incumbent upon me to rally the troops to help save the republic. Perhaps because I was a few years older than many of the other students, having already served in the military, I didn't get caught up in much of the student activism that was rampant in academia. For the most part, I steered clear of campus controversies and focused on my studies.

By the end of my first year at Rice, I was convinced that law school was for me. In the fall of 1978, I applied to six law schools, including Harvard and Yale. *Why not?* I thought. I believed by now that anything was possible. Moreover, I felt fairly sure that I would be an attractive candidate for law school. After all, I was an air force veteran, an honors student at a prestigious university, and a Hispanic from a southern state. Besides, what did I have to lose?

By March 1979, I received my first acceptance letter. And then another. And another. Before the end of May, all six schools—including Harvard and Yale—responded positively, not only accepting me to their law schools, but offering generous scholarship and loan packages as well. I now faced another potentially life-changing decision, with few close advisors to whom I could turn for wisdom.

During that school year, I'd worked as a messenger at Hutcheson & Grundy, a respected medium-size downtown law firm in Houston. In conversations with some of the attorneys there, I asked for their advice.

"I've been accepted at both Harvard and Yale," I said. "If it were you, which would you pick?" The attorneys looked at me as if I were joking.

What? The messenger boy? Accepted at Harvard and Yale? Most of the lawyers working there had not graduated from Ivy League law schools.

Once I convinced them that I had, indeed, been accepted at both storied schools with distinguished law pedigrees, the attorneys usually concurred: mine was an enviable position, and I couldn't go wrong, regardless which school I chose. That didn't help a bit, but I appreciated their input. Nor could my parents offer much insight about my decision, as neither one of them had finished high school, much less gone to college.

I had never visited either of my two front-running schools, so I was excited about attending school in a new environment. I was attracted to the relatively small size of Yale's student body, but something about living in the Cambridge/Boston area appealed to me even more. I made my decision based not on academics or esteemed faculty members, but primarily on geography. I felt living in Boston for three years would be more enjoyable than living in New Haven, Connecticut, so I said yes to Harvard's offer with the full intention of returning home to Texas to practice law. In the meantime, I would be a Harvard man.

A few months later, I received my bachelor of arts degree from Rice, graduating with honors in my political science major. My parents attended my graduation ceremony, the first time either of them had ever set foot on a college campus. My father was uneasy with all the pomp and circumstance, but my mother beamed with pride. Her son had not only graduated from high school, here I was graduating from a university. "I could never have imagined this!" she said quietly over and over. And to top it off, I was going to law school—not just any law school, but Harvard Law School. My mother had loved school as a little girl, and although she had no real concept of what it meant to attend Harvard, she knew it was a big deal. I was proud to be her son. It was my graduation, but in many ways, it was *her* day.

Years later, I often watched with amusement as reporters asked my mother what it was like to have one of her children escape poverty, grow up to attend Harvard, and become the attorney general of the United States. "Aren't you proud of your son?" the reporters probed.

"I'm proud of all my children," my mother responded.

That's a mom.

The reporters always nodded in agreement at Mom's perfect response.

CHAPTER 5

CRIMSON PRIDE

Diane and I had become more serious in our relationship during my last semester at the Air Force Academy, so when I moved back to Houston, she soon followed and got a job there. Shortly after I graduated from Rice University, Diane and I married in a small Protestant ceremony at a church in north Houston.

We had barely returned from our honeymoon when it was time to pack up a U-Haul trailer hitched to Diane's old Pontiac LeMans and make the 1,800-mile drive to Cambridge, Massachusetts, in August 1979. After days of fruitless searching for housing, we arrived at a low-income government high-rise known as Rindge Towers at Fresh Pond, a dirty, roach-infested residence. Trash littered the halls and the parking lot. But Diane and I were out of options and begged the manager to allow us to live there for a year. The landlord must have seen the looks of desperation in our eyes, because he finally relented and agreed to lease an apartment to us.

Diane got a job as a paralegal in a small Boston law firm, so she drove the car to work, while I rode a ten-speed bicycle her parents had given us. As I pedaled my bike up the tree-lined sidewalk and stopped for the first time in front of the steps of Langdell Hall, the majestic law library on the Harvard campus—replete with old stone columns, huge paneled windows, and ivy growing up the walls of the stately building, just as I had seen it in photographs—the full force of the miracle of my being there suddenly struck me: *I am going to Harvard Law School! Unbelievable.* It was a moment I have never forgotten.

I had read Scott Turow's book *One L*, in which he chronicled his first year of law school, and I had watched the movie *Paper Chase*, about a first-year law student at Harvard, so I thought I knew what to expect. But nothing could have prepared me for going to class in Harvard's historic Austin Hall, a red-stoned building built in a Romanesque Revival style, the initial home of Harvard Law School. I enjoyed learning the law in the old-fashioned Socratic method, a style of teaching in which, rather than lecturing, the professors asked evocative questions that stimulated debate and demanded critical thinking. Students were expected to be prepared, ready with meaningful and correct answers to the professor's questions, based on their reading of legal cases involving the subject matter.

Shortly after moving into Rindge Towers, we awakened one morning to discover that somebody had stolen our car, parked outside the apartment. We were disappointed but not entirely surprised, considering the environment in which we were living. We couldn't afford to buy another car, but Boston has a good mass transit system, so Diane rode the bus and then the train to and from Harvard Square to work, and I continued riding my bike to and from campus.

Harvard provided me with a helpful financial package of scholarships and loans, and part of my tuition and other expenses were defrayed by my GI benefits, but we still fell far short of what we needed. After my first year, I got a summer job clerking at the regional Environmental Protection Agency headquarters in Boston. When classes resumed, I continued to work part-time at the EPA.

Many of my fellow Harvard Law School students had sufficient financial resources that they did not have to work. I didn't, so I was glad for the job. It was difficult to balance my studies—law school demands so much reading—along with marriage and working a part-time job, but I felt it was worth it. Diane and I were young and we believed that our temporary sacrifices would lead to long-term success, so we did whatever we had to do to make things work.

Maybe because we were so busy trying to survive, we allowed our church attendance to take a backseat. We dropped into services occasionally, but church was less of a priority; we made little effort to improve our lives spiritually and engaged in few spiritual activities with friends in our social circles. That was a mistake. Although we didn't recognize it at the time, neglecting our spiritual lives starved essential elements of our relationship that had attracted us to each other in the first place.

Rather than becoming involved in a local church congregation, our closest friends were fellow male Harvard students and their wives. Fortunately, they were mostly salt-of-the-earth types, Midwesterners who planned to return to their home states after earning their law degrees. Few of these friends confessed to having aspirations to become involved politically, nor did I. Most of us simply wanted to return home and stake out a comfortable career in law. Had someone jokingly suggested, "Can you imagine Al Gonzales as the White House counsel, or the attorney general of the United States?" it would seem improbable.

Diane and I enjoyed doing things together with other married couples, as well as going to Red Sox baseball games at Boston's famous Fenway Park, a childhood dream come true for me. We loved touring the many picturesque and historic sites in the Boston area, and after a year of living in Rindge Towers, we were excited to find a nice, one-bedroom apartment on Concord Avenue near the Radcliff Quadrangle, which was home to three upperclassmen residence buildings. This quad was between Harvard and Porter Squares, surrounding a beautiful lawn where students often studied or simply relaxed outdoors in warm weather. I was glad to be closer to campus, and both Diane and I were relieved to be out of the low-income housing in which we had been living.

Diane remained working in Boston while I went back to Houston during the summer following my second year of law school so I could work at jobs clerking for two blue-blood Houston law firms. We hoped to return to Houston after I graduated.

I began my last year at Harvard in the fall of 1981. I used my spare time to fill out job applications for law firms back in Houston. I was pleased when I received an offer for a full-time position as a transactional lawyer with Vinson & Elkins, one of the most prestigious law firms in Houston; I had clerked for them the previous summer. I still had six months of law school to complete, but I accepted the opportunity at V&E, so we knew where we'd be going once I graduated.

I was back in school on Friday afternoon, January 22, 1982, and Diane and I were about to go out to dinner when we received a call from my sister Angie in Houston. My father and a coworker had been working on the roof of a fifty-foot-high rice silo when my dad slipped and lost his footing. He plummeted to the cement-surfaced parking lot below. His buddies raced to his aid and found him still alive, but with multiple critical injuries, including what doctors would later describe as several broken bones and a fractured pelvis.

When medical help arrived, they immediately called for a LifeFlight helicopter to transfer my father to the hospital. Whether on the ground or in the chopper, I don't know, but my father's injuries caused him to experience heart seizures.

While the medical team attended to my father, a representative from the rice mill company called to inform my mother, picked her up, and then raced across town to the hospital. My father was still breathing when Mom arrived, but he had already been taken into surgery, so she didn't get to see him or talk with him.

My father passed away on the operating table, without even an opportunity to say good-bye. He had died the way he had lived—working hard to provide for his family.

I hung up the phone, stunned. It was hard to fathom that my dad—strong, healthy, vibrant, and vigorous at fifty-two years of age—was no longer alive. I wanted to reach out to him, to talk with him, to tell him that I loved him. But he was gone. There was so much we had left unsaid, so much I wanted to know about him, so much I had hoped to share with him about me, so many conversations we'd never have. A heavy sadness fell over me like a soaking wet blanket, weighing me down. Diane tried her best to console me, but this was new territory for both of us. After a while, I forced myself to straighten up, and as quickly as we could catch a flight, Diane and I flew home to Houston for the funeral.

Staring at my father in the casket, I was most struck by his hands. They were the hands that had held me as a baby; hands that had helped me carve a model canoe out of a tree limb; hands that could build anything. They were callused, strong hands, full of grace and character.

A number of my father's coworkers attended the funeral. Similar to my father and mother, most of them were poor, yet they collected several hundred dollars and presented the money along with their condolences to my mother. The man who had been working alongside my father when he fell literally wept at the graveside; he was so distraught that he had been unable to save his friend.

All of my siblings except for our brother Rene were there for the funeral. Rene had been killed in a hit-and-run accident when he was eighteen. Rene had struggled with alcohol and drug problems and had dropped out of high school. Prior to the tragedy, we had not heard from him in a while. We only learned about his death when the newspaper printed a sketch of his face and asked the public for help identifying this unknown person.

I pondered then and many times afterward on what had made the difference in my brother's life and my own. Rene had a bright smile and was fiercely competitive on the baseball field. We both had the same DNA, yet we had made different choices. Perhaps my father's drinking influenced Rene's life in different ways than it had mine.

Diane and I stayed in Houston for a few days following my father's funeral, talking with my siblings and making sure my mother would be well cared for. Because it was a work-related accident, she would receive workman's compensation, but we were still concerned about her financial well-being. Our older sister, Angie, chose to stay at the family home with Mom. We tried to cover as many details as possible in a short period of time, but knowing that I would soon be returning to Houston to practice law helped ease my concerns for how Mom would survive.

I tried to encourage my mother as Diane and I headed to the airport:

"We'll be back in a few months, Mom." She hugged me good-bye and tried to smile. She was a strong woman, strong in her faith and strong in her love for family.

We returned to Cambridge, and I threw myself into my studies, anxious to complete my academic education and get back home. More than ever, the lessons I had learned from my father propelled me to pursue my dreams. It had been a good experience at Harvard, but I was excited to start a new adventure, practicing law and hopefully earning a good income.

My brother Paul and sister Christina flew to Boston to visit and helped Diane and me pack up our belongings once again, prior to the long drive back to Texas. I graduated from Harvard Law School in the spring of 1982. I was so glad to be going home, I did not even stay to attend my graduation ceremony. Twenty years would pass before I returned to campus as the Harvard Law School "Class Day" speaker and to receive the Harvard Law School Association Award, the group's highest award given to a Harvard graduate.

CHAPTER 6

A PARTY TO CALL HOME

Vinson & Elkins boasted a distinguished reputation for excellence in law and business circles. Long before law firm mergers became commonplace, V&E employed hundreds of lawyers with multiple offices in Texas, Washington, DC, and a few foreign countries.

I joined the firm as part of the business/real estate/energy group, working on business mergers and acquisitions, the purchase and sale of stock or assets of companies, commercial real estate leasing and sales, and corporate and partnership transactions. The ventures with which I was helping often involved millions of dollars and allowed no room for mistakes. The work was fascinating but demanding. We worked long hours—my first week on the job, we were closing a large transaction, so I didn't get home until the wee hours of the morning every single night—but the diversity of challenges and the talent of the V&E legal team made my chosen career more fulfilling than I had imagined.

Diane and I lived in an apartment during our first six months back in Houston. Once I settled in at my new job, we bought a house in west Houston, in a Spring Branch neighborhood. I also bought a brand-new silver Mazda RX-7 sports car, the first new car I ever owned.

For the next few years, I poured myself into my career. I enjoyed my work, did it with excellence, and I soon attracted the notice of my superiors in the firm. Before long, I set my sights on an even loftier goal—that of partner.

Vinson & Elkins had never invited a person from a minority ethnic background to be a full partner in the firm. It wasn't so much that they were prejudiced; like many other law firms in Houston at the time, they simply did not make diversity a priority, especially when it came to promoting members of the firm. In fairness, the number of highly qualified minority attorneys at that time was relatively low, but the legal workforce was changing along with the rest of the nation in that regard. I was determined to become the firm's first-ever partner to hail from a minority background. I didn't do so by staging protests or playing the race card; I decided to let the quality of my work become my platform for change.

I also began to seek out other opportunities to become involved in our community. Although V&E did not emphasize diversity, the firm encouraged its members to promote our profession through service in local, state, and national bar associations, as well as volunteer organizations within our city. I looked for groups that wanted to promote Hispanics, and those that shared my values. I served on boards of directors for several organizations and provided pro bono legal work for others, as well as serving as president of the Houston Hispanic Forum and Houston International University. My community service filled a void in my life that the legal work could not. I felt that I was giving back to help others like me.

I noticed, of course, that many of the Hispanic community leaders in Houston were Democrats, but in almost every Hispanic group with whom I volunteered, I encountered a number of strong Hispanic women who were Republicans, and they made an impression on me by the way they got things done. The Republican Party was on the rise in Texas after a long period of Democrat dominance, owning every statewide office since 1872. In 1961, Republican John Tower was elected to the United States Senate, and change was in the wind.

Partly because of an influx of transplants moving to Texas from various parts of the country, Republican influence continued to grow stronger. Then in 1978, Bill Clements, an outspoken, colorful figure and an owner of an offshore oil drilling company, became the first Republican governor of Texas since Reconstruction. Even heavily Democrat-leaning Houston became invested in more conservative candidates, most notably George H. W. Bush. The former oilman had successfully run for a seat in the United States House of Representatives, later becoming ambassador to the United Nations, chairperson of the Republican National Committee, and eventually served as our nation's CIA director. Although Bush failed to become the party's candidate for president in 1980, Ronald Reagan recognized his value and invited him to run as his vice presidential candidate. The tandem made for a powerful team, handily defeating Jimmy Carter and Walter Mondale.

Although it was still not fashionable to be a Republican in Texas, especially a Hispanic Republican, by the time I signed on at V&E, we had a Republican from Texas serving as vice president of the United States.

———

Up to that point in my life, I had been apolitical, but as I looked at the political landscape in Texas, I felt inclined toward the Republican Party. First, I liked the Republican's view of limited government. My father had taught me the importance of self-reliance and taking responsibility for my own life. He disdained government interference in our daily lives and believed intensely that ultimate authority and the determination of right and wrong derived from God, not government.

Granted, government could provide a hand up to people in dire need. People who have experienced an unusual or unexpected setback—such as a prolonged, serious illness or a family tragedy, some natural disaster, or even a temporary period of unemployment—may need government help for a season, but not for a lifetime. Our community had many needs, but I didn't believe that more government involvement was the answer. Instead, I felt we would be much better off by strengthening the extended family and helping and encouraging businesses, churches, and private nonprofit organizations take a more active role in meeting community needs.

I was attracted also to the outspoken faith in God that I heard and witnessed in the lives of many Republican leaders. That resonated with me, because even though I had not been actively involved in church life in recent years, most of my core values were based on my faith in God. Certainly, a few Democrats seemed unashamed of mentioning Jesus Christ, but I found a more open atmosphere to express genuine, vibrant, Christian faith within Republican circles.

I also liked the Republican emphasis on taking pride in America and the importance of a strong national defense. I recognized that although our country provides unparalleled liberties and economic opportunities, our prosperity cannot be enjoyed without security. Moreover, even though I had never been ordered into combat, I was still a soldier at heart, and I believed that those men and women who wore our military uniforms deserved our unqualified support. They should never be denigrated or pressured because of policies put in place by their superiors. Moreover, we should honor and care for our veterans. While some of my Democrat friends publicly expressed similar regard for our soldiers, that support did not always translate into public action. Too often, they were quick to look at the national defense budget as the place to cut anytime our nation needed money—which we always did.

I didn't agree with everything the Republican Party espoused, but increasingly my views about family, faith, and country moved me into Republican circles. The party leaders in Texas, excited to attract men and women of Hispanic and other minorities, welcomed me enthusiastically. I poured myself into party activities and soon became the chairman of the Harris County Republican National Hispanic Assembly, the Houston branch of the national organization, promoting the truth as I saw it that the Republican Party better represented core Hispanic values.

———

As I climbed the ladder to greater recognition and prestige in my career and within the local Hispanic community, I left one person behind—Diane. We were both busy with work, so our time with each other was increasingly limited. For six years, as our careers grew brighter, our relationship did not.

Perhaps, more importantly, we continued to place the spiritual aspects of life on the back burner, so I guess we shouldn't have been too surprised when the flame in our relationship began to flicker, and eventually went out. We divorced in July 1985.

Since we had a relatively small amount of mutual property and no children, the divorce was amicable. But it was not without pain. No divorce is. As Diane and I tried to maintain a sense of civility and normalcy throughout that period of our lives, it was nonetheless difficult to tear apart our marriage. Following the divorce, Diane decided to move back to the Midwest, which eased some of the awkwardness between us, since we no longer bumped into each other in Houston circles. After a while, since we had no children, we had no further reason to stay in touch, so we didn't.

The dissolution of our marriage discouraged me. I felt a sense of disappointment and failure. I knew that I wanted to be in a relationship, but I thought it might be wiser to keep things casual so I could focus on my career and community activities.

For the next several years, I threw myself into my job and my activities with various charitable organizations. At work, I focused more intensely on my goal of making partner at my law firm. In addition to my full-time legal job, I was also busy teaching law classes at the University of Houston. I sold my home and moved into an apartment at the downtown Four Seasons Hotel, a block from my office. Yet I missed being in a meaningful relationship.

And then God smiled on me. I had met Rebecca Turner when she was sixteen and in high school, and I was a junior at Rice. Becky had been raised in a large air force family and had moved numerous times during her childhood. She eventually married a childhood friend of mine, though they later divorced. Becky and I had remained friends through our respective marriages. She was a successful banker and single mother raising her young son, Jared. She was beautiful and bright, and I was in love. I was happy to learn that she loved me too. We were young and full of hope and wonder— although we could not imagine the adventure ahead of us.

Meanwhile, in 1988, one of Houston's adopted sons, George H. W. Bush, became the forty-first president of the United States. Within months,

I received an invitation from the new administration to consider a job in Washington.

I traveled to the nation's capital and met with various members of the Bush administration. Although I was a Texan at heart, I loved the majesty of Washington, and the possibility of working there was intriguing. Nevertheless, I had my sights set on making partner at my law firm; after that, I felt I could punch my own ticket. I was optimistic that my goal of becoming a partner was nearing reality, so I turned down the offer to work for President George H. W. Bush. It was a potential turning point in my life, and in saying no, I wondered if I would ever have another chance to work in Washington.

In 1990, President Bush designated my alma mater, Rice University, as the host for the Economic Summit of Industrialized Nations, a three-day gathering of leaders from eight of the world's leading industrialized countries to discuss diplomatic, environmental, and human rights issues, as well as economic development. Because of my community involvement, I was recommended to help with the legal work for the host committee. The summit raised my visibility, especially with prominent local and national Republican leaders.

A few years later, when the 1992 Republican National Convention was held in Houston, the new host committee came calling for my legal services once again, which I happily provided. The relationships I forged through serving would greatly influence my future.

In the autumn of 1990, I was elected to the partnership of Vinson & Elkins. My selection, along with a Hispanic woman elected at the same time, marked the first time in history that V&E boasted minority partners. Not everyone at the firm, however, was thrilled that I had made partner. Shortly after the announcement, one of my partners cautioned me to watch my back because there were still some at the firm who wanted me to fail. Undeterred, I was determined to prove them wrong.

Mixed in with all the tremendous excitement and success I was experiencing, in 1990, I received sad news. My former wife, Diane, had been traveling on a business trip when she was killed in an automobile accident.

Although we had not seen each other in several years, her passing nonetheless grieved me. We had lived an important part of our lives together. The pain I shared with her family and friends helped put my own life in perspective as I pondered the fragility of life and how quickly it can be snatched away. Diane's death reminded me of my own mortality, too, and caused me to think more seriously about what really matters.

In 1991, after attending a wedding of dear friends in France with Becky, I asked her to marry me. She was my best friend and I wanted her by my side. Because we both were married previously, we didn't want a large wedding. I asked Becky to marry me on a Tuesday afternoon, and by Saturday we were standing in front of a preacher. She was thirty and I was thirty-six. The wedding was at a picturesque, white church in the forest outside Kingwood, Texas. The guest list was short, with only Becky's bright young son, Jared, a few family members, close friends, and many nieces and nephews, and children of friends.

That fall, Becky and I bought a beautiful home in West University, a small, affluent neighborhood with picturesque trees and lovely homes bordering the Rice campus in Houston. The following year, 1992, God blessed us with the birth of our son Alberto Graham Gonzales. I was now a full-fledged partner at V&E, and Becky loved being a full-time mom and part-time student. Life was good, and Becky's dream of settling down and living in one place was coming true. I had a great job making a good income with a promising future, but I wanted to do more. I could have remained in my comfort zone, yet for some unexplainable reason, I felt restless . . . and then I met George W. Bush.

CHAPTER 7

BECOMING A BUSHIE

I liked George W. Bush immediately. Becky and I had first met Bush back in the late 1980s at a campaign event held at a hotel in Houston, when the elder Bush was running for president. "We love your mom," Becky said to the younger Bush.

A Midland, Texas, oilman and part owner of the Texas Rangers Major League Baseball team, George W. Bush possessed a casual, youthful flair and a full head of brown hair. His bright blue eyes twinkled as he twisted his mouth into the playful, pursed-lips grin for which he would soon become well known. "Everybody loves my mom," he replied, nodding whimsically. "She's my dad's secret weapon."

In late 1993, when I next spoke with him, George W. Bush was the son of a *former* president. In what most Republicans had considered a certain victory following the stunning American military performance in Iraq during Desert Storm, Bush's dad had suffered a surprising defeat to Arkansas governor Bill Clinton.

Now, with the Texas gubernatorial election still more than a year away, George W. Bush had boldly announced that he hoped to unseat the popular, incumbent Democrat—Texas governor Ann Richards—in 1994.

Well known for her acerbic tongue, Richards had gained national notoriety during the 1988 Democratic National Convention when she attempted to skewer candidate George H. W. Bush. "Poor George, he can't help it," she said. "He was born with a silver foot in his mouth." The comment may have endeared her to Democrats on the national scene, but many folks in Texas found her remark disingenuous. Republicans saw an opening.

A lawyer with whom I had worked closely during the 1992 Republican National Convention asked me to help host a meeting with minority members of the Houston legal community so they could meet Bush. I was happy to do so, and a group of fifteen to twenty attorneys gathered at my law firm to hear the upstart challenger.

During his presentation, George W. Bush was energetic and engaging. He spoke in realistic terms about his positive vision for Texas. He warmly reached out to the Hispanic community in his comments and then took questions from the crowd, fielding them adeptly and honestly.

I liked him, I was quite impressed by him, and I planned to vote for him, although I didn't believe he stood a chance of beating Ann Richards in the election.

I watched the campaign with interest over the next year and spoke only briefly with Bush at two separate events. He acted as though he knew me, but I wasn't so sure. Good politicians always act as though they know their constituents; few actually do. Nevertheless, Bush's campaign theme piqued my interest: "What Texans can dream, Texans can do."

I was wrong about Bush's political potential. Bush defeated Richards handily.

Following the election, I sent Governor-elect Bush a brief letter congratulating him and expressing my willingness to serve Texas and his administration any way possible. At best I was hopeful for a high-profile appointment to a board or commission so I could keep my law partnership. I didn't really expect a response, so I was surprised when on November 17, 1994, I received a phone call from Bob Whilden, one of the senior partners in V&E's corporate law department and a member of the firm's management committee. "The governor-elect just called," Bob said, "and he asked whether you might be interested in joining his staff as general counsel."

"What?" I asked, unable to conceal my interest.

"Yes, he says that the appointment would be great for you and good for the firm."

My curiosity was piqued. "Thank you, Bob." I could tell by the tone in Bob's voice that he was amenable to my accepting the offer should it come.

"He'll be giving you a call in a few days."

"Okay; thanks, Bob." I hung up the phone and stared at it for a few seconds, wondering what had just happened.

Don't misunderstand, I was happy at the firm and had established myself in a position that could only expand my influence and income. I served on multiple boards for organizations within our community and was active working with various Hispanic groups. These volunteer activities presented a fulfilling diversion from my day job. Yet something was missing; there remained that subtle restlessness in my heart and mind. I couldn't describe it in specific terms, but it was there. Becky recognized my restiveness and felt there was something greater for me to do. At the time, she believed it might involve some manner of serving in our community, or in a local position with city or countywide influence. I wanted to do something more meaningful with my life and, as I recognized at that moment, perhaps this opportunity with the new governor held that potential.

Although I was intrigued by the possibility of working with George W. Bush, I kept the information to myself that entire workday. I didn't even share it with Becky immediately, waiting until I had time to think through the implications. My wife was happy with our life in Houston; she was taking classes at a local university to complete her college education, we had two wonderful young sons, and she was pregnant. Accepting a job with Bush would entail moving to Austin, and I saw no need to rock the boat if we weren't taking a ride.

Later that evening, after weighing the pros and cons, I broached the subject with Becky: "The governor-elect has offered me a job as his general counsel." I could see the anxiety spring into her eyes as she instantly recognized the radical transition that my accepting a position in the governor's office might make in our lives. After moving several times as a child in an air force family, Becky had hoped for roots and stability. Her dream had come true, and she did not relish the idea of moving again.

"I love our home, I'm back in school, and I am pregnant," Becky said.

"Well, it's just a few years," I answered. "We could move to Austin, and then we'll come back and I'll go back to work at Vinson & Elkins, and our life will return to normal." My wife's feelings mattered to me, and I wanted to avoid upsetting her. Yet I also knew that Becky could be happy anywhere, as long as we were together.

Becky voiced all of the concerns that I had considered, plus one more: the salary. Although we were not yet sure what the position of counsel to the governor paid, we knew that it would be less than my income at V&E. When we married, Becky had given up her career as a bank loan officer to raise our children and finish her education, so money would be an issue. We decided to forgo making a decision about the matter until we knew more information about the potential move.

I had been selected as a member of the Houston chapter of the American Leadership Forum, so the following day, I was attending a daylong seminar with that group when the governor-elect called me. He began the conversation casually, "Hey, big guy. How are you doing?"

Bush's informality put me at ease immediately. He chatted amiably about his plans and indicated that he wanted me to serve in an important position within his administration. "I'm traveling right now, but would you be willing to meet with Harriet Miers and me and possibly a few others when I get back to Texas? Harriet is my general counsel during the transition from Governor Richards's administration to ours."

"Of course," I replied. "I'll be glad to meet."

"Would you be interested in being the governor's general counsel?" he asked.

"I could be very interested," I responded enthusiastically. "I'm willing to serve if I can find a way to afford being away from my law practice for a few years."

The governor-elect seemed surprised and pleased that I would be willing to leave a lucrative law practice to serve with him. "Okay, then," he said. "Consider it a done deal, pending our meeting."

We discussed several meeting dates, and the call concluded with me thanking Bush for the opportunity.

When I hung up the phone, I felt my stomach churning. *What have I gotten myself into?* I thought. I had no idea where this would take me, but I was excited about the possibilities.

Over the next few days, I spoke several times with Harriet Miers about Bush's job offer and what it entailed. I knew Harriet fairly well because I had served on the board of directors for the state bar of Texas, of which she was then president. She was one of the most prominent attorneys in Texas, George W. Bush's personal lawyer, and a former member of the Dallas City Council. She was bright, tough, and most of all, I quickly discovered, she was intensely loyal to George W. Bush and expected the same true allegiance from her colleagues.

Since I had no real relationship with the governor-elect, I wondered how he worked with lawyers, and about my responsibilities as his counsel. Harriet explained that my role would be that of a legal troubleshooter, dealing with all sorts of issues, everything from legislation to litigation to overseeing clemency issues related to the executions of convicted criminals. I'd also be reviewing and advising on the governor's policies and any ethical issues that affected our state or the governor's office.

My conversations with Harriet inspired me. If I took this new position, I would no longer simply be helping a client buy or sell a business; I would be working for the people of Texas. Whether it was God's leading, or my own inner contentment, or a combination of both, I felt great faith and peace about this new direction I was considering, confirming to me that this was what I was meant to do with my talents, my life—at least for a season.

I became so enthusiastic about the opportunity that one afternoon I drove from Houston to downtown Austin—a distance of more than 160 miles—just to view the Texas capitol up close and to scout out the area. I walked into the lobby of the Sam Houston Building, a nine-story complex adjacent to the majestic Texas capitol, where Governor Richards's counsel's office was located, and where I assumed that my office would be located as well. The Sam Houston Building was located directly across the courtyard from the Texas Supreme Court. Standing on the capitol grounds, I began to realize the full implications of my potential move. I could barely believe that I might have the opportunity to serve my state surrounded by such august beauty.

Over Thanksgiving dinner at my mom's house, the home in which I had grown up, Becky and I told my entire family about the new job offer. All of my siblings and their spouses were there.

My family members were thrilled at my new opportunity, and Mom especially was proud, although she became less enthusiastic when I told her that the job required a move to Austin. Nevertheless, she was happy that I was happy. My mom prays every day for each of her children and our spouses, and everyone knows that God pays special attention to a mother's prayers. He sure has done so to mine.

On December 1, 1994, I arrived at Governor-elect Bush's transition office, located in the Vaughn Building on Brazos Street in Austin. There I met with Joe Allbaugh, Bush's campaign manager, a quintessential behind-the-scenes sort of guy. A broad-shouldered bear of a man whom I guessed to be slightly older than me, Joe was about six foot four, with large glasses and a slightly receding hairline that he wore in a flat-top crew cut. Joe looked intimidating—and he was. He didn't waste words; instead, he spoke straightforwardly in a gruff voice, lacing statements with language so colorful there was no question about what he meant. Yet he also had a quiet, softer side. An Oklahoma cowboy with midwestern roots and values, Joe exuded a strong, calm confidence. But no one had any doubt about who was in charge.

The governor-elect had asked him to serve as his executive assistant, basically a chief of staff position, so he was somebody I would be working with regularly. As we talked, I appreciated his insights, his discretion, and his loyalty to his boss. I left our meeting anticipating that Joe and I would become not only close colleagues but good friends. And we did, as did our spouses, Diane and Becky. Joe is a good man; he was later appointed director of FEMA.

The next morning, I met privately with George W. Bush for the first time. He seemed relaxed yet energetic, as though he was raring to get started as governor. His background was the polar opposite of mine. He was the ultimate insider, a man who grew up as the privileged son in a patrician family, wealthy and politically well connected. I was an outsider who grew up in poverty, whose father had never even voted. But we shared many of the same values, so we hit it off. Down to earth, with no ostentatious, pretentious inclinations to formality, he was self-confident and, contrary to impressions later perpetuated by the media, he had an amazing command of important issues. In a face-to-face conversation, it was nearly impossible not to like him. I certainly did. I liked him as a person and I liked what he stood for. Looking back, I realize that it wasn't about politics. I would have supported George W. Bush had he been a Democrat.

Bush was engaging and focused. He looked me right in the eye during most of our conversation. He discussed candidly what he expected of me and I explained what intrigued me about the position. When I asked about my role and access to him, Bush picked up a marker and drew nine x's on a whiteboard near his chair. He then wrote a G above the center x. Tapping the G with his finger, he said, "This is me." Then he pointed at the center x and said, "This is Joe. Joe will be the first among equals, but I want every member of our senior staff to have direct access to me." He made it clear that although Joe would function as chief of staff, the governor-elect did not want filters, so his top staff—which included me—could walk into his office at any time to discuss with him anything we regarded as important. "My father was ill-served," he said, "by the gate-keeping role played by White House chief of staff John Sununu." John might have meant well, attempting to allow only the most important matters to reach the president, but that was not the process the governor-elect wanted.

I was pleased by what I heard, so as our meeting drew to a close, I felt free to pose a personal question. "Why me?" I asked. I knew Bush could have invited any number of highly qualified Texas lawyers to serve as counsel. "You don't know me. Why have you offered this job to me?"

Bush's eyes twinkled and he chuckled. "Because you turned down a job offer with my old man, that's how you got on my radar screen," he said. He was right, but I was surprised that he knew the story. This was the first of many incidents when I would discover that his laid-back style did not imply a lack of knowledge or preparation.

I smiled and again thanked the governor-elect for giving me the opportunity to serve.

As we said good-bye, Bush extended his hand and shook mine. "Welcome aboard. I know you and your family are making a big sacrifice to serve on my staff," he said, "and I will make it worth your while." As I left that day, I appeared calm and collected, but inside, I was tremendously energized. The only minor concern I carried away from our meeting was a Bush comment about the sitting attorney general, Dan Morales, a Democrat. Bush had warned me to keep an eye on Morales, a man with whom I would have to work closely as counsel. Nevertheless, in the weeks to follow, I threw myself into preparing and learning about the job. It was an adventure I wanted to live to the fullest, because, after all, I had promised my wife that I would step away from my legal practice to work in government circles for only a few years.

I had no idea how inextricably linked our destiny would become to that of George W. Bush.

CHAPTER 8

THE DEATH CASES

At the beginning of the year 1995, I began traveling back and forth from Houston to Austin for more than a month during the transition, living out of a suitcase. Leaving Houston permanently, however, and in particular, leaving my job at V&E, was difficult. For more than a dozen years, I had enjoyed working with a prestigious law firm and earning a lucrative income. Following my meeting with Joe Allbaugh, I now understood that walking away from such security and accepting a job as Governor Bush's counsel meant taking a nearly two-thirds cut in pay. While Becky and I were not overly materialistic in our lifestyles, we had acquired the accoutrements and the associated expenses of a young, successful lawyer's family.

Because I began working with Governor Bush before Becky and I had time to buy a home in Austin, I rented a small apartment a few minutes drive from the capitol. Becky, Jared, and Graham joined me in Austin for the governor's inauguration on January 17, 1995. A few days later, Becky returned to Houston with our sons to handle the myriad details involved in the transition to life in another city. Complicating matters further, Becky and I were expecting another baby in June.

After our third son, Gabriel, was born, we bought a home in Austin. Shortly after that, Becky put school aside, knowing that she needed to go back to work. With the reduction of our income, and an additional child, our choice was not whether she would reenter the workforce; truth is, we needed the money. Becky took a job in the Texas attorney general's office, handling financial matters for the Sexual Assault Prevention and Crisis Services division, while her mom helped with our boys until they were old enough to attend daycare.

———

"Always return one another's phone calls first," Governor Bush instructed his senior staff members during the first formal meeting of his administration. His statement initially struck me as odd, but I quickly realized his logic. As a former owner of the Texas Rangers baseball team, Governor Bush did not merely want employees; he wanted team members who valued one another. Looking around the room, I could tell he had assembled some excellent teammates, with Joe Allbaugh as captain. Karen Hughes, who had also worked with George W. Bush during his gubernatorial race, was in charge of communications. Media savvy and perpetually searching for the positive, human-interest aspects of any story, Karen modeled a joyful yet realistic glass-half-full attitude that sprang from her Christian faith. Margaret LaMontagne (soon to be Spellings) headed up public education—an important job, since the governor was unhappy that Texas school districts received funds based on property taxes of homes and businesses. He felt the system was unfair, especially to minority students living in poorer districts. He wanted to change the way Texas schools were funded, though he knew it would be an uphill grind and Margaret would have her hands full. But she seemed up for it. We were also joined by Dallas businessman Clay Johnson, the governor's former Yale roommate and longtime friend who would run the appointments office. Karl Rove, while technically not part of the staff, was a frequent visitor and focused primarily on political matters.

Governor Bush had gathered a fantastic team of coworkers, and from day one, we established and maintained a cooperative spirit and a healthy work atmosphere. All of our jobs were made easier by one of our boss's greatest strengths: the ability to ask open-ended questions that seared right to the heart of a matter. His keen insight allowed him to sort out opinions and reduce an answer to its core. I marveled at his ability to make good decisions.

The governor quickly and purposely forged a strong relationship with Lieutenant Governor Bob Bullock and House Speaker James (Pete) Laney—both highly respected, influential Democrats. Bob Bullock's brash, intimidating personality was legendary in Texas political circles. He was smart and cagey, and only a few years earlier, Karen had referred to him as "Archie Bunker Bob." Bush and Bullock butted heads at first, but then both men said, "We're going to do what is best for Texas."

Speaker Laney was a farmer, who was always ready to go home to West Texas and ride a tractor at the end of a week fighting legislative battles. His down-to-earth, understated manner made him particularly effective as a legislator and a leader.

Bush, Bullock, and Laney essentially laid aside political differences to get good things done for the people of Texas. Bullock and Laney liked and respected Bush, and Bush genuinely liked and respected them. They didn't always agree with one another, but they were willing to compromise and put the needs of the people ahead of their own political allegiances. They were true leaders whose top priorities were to serve the people of Texas.

A few years later, when Governor Bush ran for reelection in 1998, Bob Bullock made it clear to Texans that he supported the Republican incumbent, George W. Bush. This was even more astounding given the fact that Bullock was the godfather to one of the children of the opposing Democrat candidate.

As general counsel, my job was to provide prompt and accurate legal advice to the governor and his staff on a wide variety of issues ranging from ethics to criminal justice. It was an enormous responsibility, and fortunately, I had a team of six lawyers to help me. I had also talked at length with David Talbot, who had served as counsel to Governor Ann Richards. David was gracious with his time, tremendously helpful to me, and his advice was right on target. Many of the processes I implemented as Governor Bush's counsel were similar to those David had used to serve Governor Richards.

In Texas, the state's chief legal officer, the attorney general, is not appointed by the governor but is elected by the public. Dan Morales, a Harvard-educated Hispanic, had been elected attorney general in 1990, five years earlier.

Early in the Bush administration, the governor met with Morales; Jorge Vega, his first assistant, with whom I had played intramural softball and football at Harvard; Jay Aguilar, one of his top litigators; and me regarding an important litigation matter concerning prison overcrowding. As I looked at the men gathered in the governor's office, I marveled at the sight. Here was the new governor, the son of a former president of the United States, being advised by four Hispanics, all of whom had risen from humble circumstances to become Harvard-educated attorneys. *How ironic*, I thought. At a time when Hispanics were making slow progress in cracking the partnership ranks in many Texas law firms, four Hispanics were helping to guide the governor on major legal decisions that affected our state.

George W. Bush did not merely talk about diversity. He modeled it. To him, skin color, race, or gender were nonissues. If a person was qualified for a job and could do the work with excellence, that's all that mattered to Bush. Nor was he reluctant to have strong women on his staff, as evidenced by Karen and Margaret, neither of whom were the wallflower type.

Soon after I began, I was confronted with one of the job's most difficult and controversial tasks—dealing with the death penalty and its application to inmates who had been found guilty and deserving of death by a jury of their peers. Part of my duties involved the heavy responsibility of making recommendations regarding clemency decisions, based on applications to the governor presented on behalf of men and women on Texas death row. I understood that each request represented a real person, so we painstakingly reviewed every case. Virtually all of these requests were denied, not because of any lack of compassion, but because of Governor Bush's faith in the Texas criminal justice system.

At the time I became counsel, Texas had executed 464 inmates since 1974. Several more executions were scheduled to happen early in Governor Bush's watch, the first on January 31, 1995, less than two weeks into the governor's term.

Unlike the United States president and the governors of some states, the governor of Texas cannot unilaterally pardon or commute the sentence of a

convicted criminal. Due to a scandal that exposed a previous governor selling executive clemency, Texas instituted a policy that gave the state Board
of Pardons and Paroles power to check the governor's discretion to issue a
pardon or commute a death sentence. The Texas Constitution provides the
governor authority to grant a one-time, thirty-day reprieve to a death-row
inmate seeking clemency. Any other form of clemency, such as a pardon or
commutation of a sentence, requires a concurring recommendation by the
eighteen-member Board of Pardons and Paroles.

As such, prior to execution, every death penalty case was thoroughly
reviewed by the governor's office, and that responsibility fell to my legal staff
and me. Ordinarily, the Texas attorney general's office notified me several
months in advance of a scheduled execution. I assigned each case to one of
the lawyers in our office, and that attorney studied it and prepared a summary for my review and the governor's.

I knew that Governor Bush supported the death penalty for heinous
crimes involving loss of life. He had campaigned on a law-and-order platform, and I had heard him discuss his confidence in the criminal-justice
system to weigh evidence and determine guilt or innocence. He did not
believe the governor should second-guess juries or judges. I quickly learned
that if there was no doubt about an individual's guilt, and the courts had
decided all the legal issues, unless there was some compelling new information such as DNA evidence that the courts had not considered, the
governor was unlikely to grant clemency. Nevertheless, Bush wanted to
make absolutely certain that only those guilty of the crimes for which they
were convicted were executed. In later years, the media portrayed him as a
calloused, uncaring, coldhearted tyrant who was indifferent about allowing
executions to go forward. Nothing could be further from the truth.

Early in the administration, although I knew it would be gut-wrenching,
I went to the state's death chamber in Huntsville, Texas, to witness an execution. During my three years on the governor's staff, I supervised clemency
requests relating to more than forty-five death-penalty cases, and I witnessed three executions.

Why would I feel the need to witness an execution? First, I thought it important to understand fully the procedures and mechanics of this very significant and solemn government duty. Second, I wanted to experience—to the extent possible—the gravity of these proceedings, to feel the emotion in relation to the execution of a human being. This was serious business, and I wanted those images from the death chamber firmly in my mind every time I reviewed one of these cases.

One of my most wrenching visits to the death chamber took place in 1995, when I went to Huntsville to witness a midnight execution. The inmate had been convicted of killing a young woman in San Antonio nine years earlier, shooting her twice in the head with a .22-caliber pistol. I watched as he was fingerprinted one final time to confirm his identity just prior to his execution. He appeared smallish and I noticed his hands. The victim had been with her boyfriend on her way to a nursing aide school when the inmate, a paroled murderer, grabbed her in a headlock with those hands and dragged her for two blocks at gunpoint.

I met with the prison chaplain, who was about to retire after having counseled nearly one hundred death-row inmates. After a final conversation with this particular inmate, the chaplain and I found ourselves alone for a quiet talk. I was curious about this chaplain and about the strength of his faith, so I asked him whether he was comfortable with the taking of a life, even when demanded by the state of Texas.

He looked at me intently for a moment and in a whisper revealed that as the hour of death approached, most inmates he had counseled had confessed—sometimes in graphic detail—to the crime for which he or she had been sentenced to die. In the twilight of life, they prayed for forgiveness, he said. "Nothing compares to listening to a killer describing his feelings as he killed his victim. One inmate," he said with a sad sigh, "confessed to killing a woman just for the feeling of the kill."

And then he revealed something that bothers me to this day. He told me that many of these midnight confessions were not limited to the crime for which the convicted criminals were being executed. These confessions sometimes included other killings and other crimes. I asked what he would do with this information, and he shook his head. "Nothing," he said as his shoulders sagged, the sanctity of confession preventing him from disclosing what he learned. The chaplain's face was filled with deep creases formed undoubtedly over the years by the weight of the confidential burdens he bore.

I thought then about the many families of the victims living in heartbreak who would likely never know closure. How many of their prayers had gone unanswered? At that moment I said a silent prayer for those families, and I thanked God that I had been spared the burden of shouldering the loss of a loved one and not knowing how or why.

In my years of service, I have often spoken to God in prayer. I prayed to not have to endure certain challenges, and there were many times I asked for wisdom to help me accept, if not to understand, that which seemed totally unfair or utterly incomprehensible. Yes, the privileges and perks from my service in Austin were enjoyable, but the burdens were sometimes staggering.

Later, after his retirement, I heard that the chaplain spoke out against the death penalty. His change of heart and assertion that the system is flawed did not affect my belief in the death penalty. I supported the people's will that the death penalty be available as a punishment. His change of heart did, however, intensify my support of procedures to ensure that we apply the death penalty only for those who are truly guilty, who are mature and of sound mind, and who are cognizant of the consequences of their crimes.

When Governor Bush first took office, executions were conducted at midnight, but early in his first term, the state legislature changed the execution time to 6:00 p.m., to defray the cost of overtime for the wardens and prison officials. A member of my staff normally met with the governor and me the evening before or the morning of an execution to discuss the case and the application for clemency. The governor usually made his decision regarding clemency during those meetings, but would not announce it if there were legal appeals pending. After all legal appeals were exhausted, and the execution was about to begin, I communicated the governor's decision by telephone to the warden in Huntsville and then stayed on the line as the condemned criminal was led to the death chamber. I remained on the telephone with the warden right to the end, just in case there was some last-moment reason to halt the execution. When the execution was over, I called the governor's residence and usually left word with a member of his security detail, providing the time of death and any other important details he should convey to the governor.

One of the most highly publicized cases with which we dealt was that of Karla Faye Tucker, who had brutally murdered two people with a pickax and had boasted about how she had enjoyed doing it. The jury convicted her and she was sentenced to die. Years later while in prison, Ms. Tucker became a born-again Christian. She even married a prison chaplain while incarcerated.

The district attorney notified our office the week before Christmas that Ms. Tucker's execution date was set for February 3, 1998. A few weeks earlier, Governor Bush had appointed me as Texas secretary of state. My successor was Margaret Wilson, a seasoned litigator and former colleague of mine at Vinson & Elkins. Since she was relatively new, I continued to support her during the transition by discharging many duties ordinarily the responsibility of the general counsel until Margaret was ready.

The Tucker story made headlines all around the world. Catapulting the case above others was the fact that no woman had been executed in the United States since 1984, and Texas had not executed a woman in more than one hundred years. I expressed my concerns to the governor that he and Texas might reap a whirlwind of negative press for executing a woman. Gender, however, was not the paramount issue to Governor Bush; he insisted that the same standards of justice be applied to all. Communications director Karen Hughes reminded reporters, "The gender of the murderer did not make any difference to the victims."[1]

Nevertheless, the public rallied to Ms. Tucker's side, with many supporters calling for the commutation of her sentence. Anti-death-penalty protesters held vigils outside the gates of the governor's mansion, and many evangelical Christians protested that this repentant and remorseful person should not be executed. Pat Robertson, founder of the Christian Broadcasting Network, called the governor's office personally—and Robertson's lawyer made a similar call to me—asking for mercy for Tucker, based on her changed life as a Christian. She was a model prisoner who worked tirelessly to support and minister to other inmates. She had already been on death row for fourteen years as various appeals were filed on her behalf.

My legal team had thoroughly reviewed the case and had concluded we had no basis on which to recommend clemency, but I wanted to make sure. At home late one night, I watched a videotape of the grizzly crime scene. It was revolting. As I viewed the tape, Becky unexpectedly came into the room, and when she saw the screen, she gasped.

"Al! What is that?" she cried.

"It's the police video of the Tucker crime scene," I told her. The images were disturbing, and she quickly left the room.

In December 1997, the chairman of the parole board and I visited with Ms. Tucker on death row because I knew the governor would ask me about the authenticity of her spiritual conversion. Many death-row inmates grow quite religious and find faith as their execution dates draw nearer. Some claim to be changed as a result of meeting God and now worthy of clemency consideration. Not all of them are sincere. But as I visited with Ms. Tucker, I was convinced of her conversion. She no longer blamed her mother for trying to turn her into a teenage prostitute, nor did she make excuses that she had been high on drugs during the murders, both of which had been part of her previous defense. She did not try to dodge responsibility in any way; she admitted her guilt and that her trial and appeals had been fair. She had repented in tears, and her only hope was that the governor might allow her to live out her life in prison where she could help other young women turn their lives around.

We talked for quite a while, and I was convinced that Karla Faye Tucker was a changed person, but she had admitted to committing a heinous crime and there were no grounds on which to commute her sentence or grant a thirty-day reprieve. I knew that given the governor's standards, it was highly unlikely that he would grant clemency; there was no question about her guilt, and there was no new evidence that had not been considered by the courts.

As I rose to leave Ms. Tucker, I thanked her for seeing me and said, "I think we have all the information we need."

Ms. Tucker looked at me and with an almost desperate sound in her voice, asked, "Is that all there is? Will I see you again?"

"I don't think so," I replied solemnly. As I left, I felt deep sadness.

I returned to Austin and shared my impressions with Governor Bush. The Texas Board of Pardons and Paroles voted sixteen to zero with two abstentions that clemency be denied; the US Supreme Court reviewed the case and also denied a request to halt the execution.

The morning of the scheduled execution, I arrived at the office at 7:00 and met briefly with Governor Bush before he left for a planned event in north Texas, where he was announcing the restoration of the home of legendary Texas Democrat and US congressman Sam Rayburn, who had served as Speaker of the House for more than twenty years. Unless something extraordinary and unexpected happened, the governor was not going to grant a thirty-day reprieve to Karla Faye Tucker. By the time Governor Bush returned late that afternoon, the media was in a frenzy, ready to report on every detail of the Tucker execution.

Around 5:00 p.m., I called Ms. Tucker's attorney, David Botsford, who told me he wanted to file more appeals with the Texas Court of Criminal Appeals, which he did. Less than an hour later, we learned that the federal courts also denied the requests. Shortly after that, Botsford called again, informing me that he had nowhere else to turn, and he would not file any further appeals. As a last-ditch effort, the Tucker lawyers asked Governor Bush to postpone the execution for thirty days. The decision was now up to the governor.

As Governor Bush went on live television to tell the press and the people of Texas his decision, he was emotional. He briefly reminded everyone of his oath to uphold the law and his concern that justice be applied fairly. He acknowledged, "Like many touched by this case, I have sought guidance through prayer." He told the reporters that the case had been reviewed by the Texas courts as well as the US Supreme Court, and then he concluded, "Therefore, I will not grant a thirty-day stay."

His voice cracked a bit and his eyes were moist as Governor Bush said, "May God bless Karla Faye Tucker, and may God bless her victims and their families." He immediately left the pressroom and returned to his office, where Joe Allbaugh, Clay Johnson, and I were waiting. He looked melancholy, as though he carried a heavy weight on his shoulders.

For the next twenty minutes or so, we sat together quietly while Margaret Wilson and Deputy Counsel Donna Davidson, in the counsel's office, stayed on the telephone line with the warden in Huntsville and relayed reports from the prison. Donna's strong voice repeated the warden's words: "6:25, prisoner led from cell . . . 6:35, lethal dose administered . . ." and then somberly Donna gave the final report.

At 6:45 p.m. on February 3, 1998, with nearly a thousand people outside the prison—some praying, some protesting—inmate number 777, Karla Faye Tucker, became the first woman executed in Texas since 1863.

Every execution was heart-wrenching, and Ms. Tucker's was especially so. The governor sighed and prepared to leave. Before going out the door, he turned to me. "Thank you," he said quietly. "You did a good job."

Maybe so; I knew we had done the right thing for the right reasons, but it was still one of the most difficult and emotional days of my service.

CHAPTER 9

TEXAS CAMELOT

O ne of the more memorable highlights during my tenure as governor's counsel was the celebration of George W. Bush's fiftieth birthday in July 1996, on the grounds of the governor's mansion. Dozens of family members, friends, government officials, and other well-wishers attended, all in a festive Fourth of July mood. It was a casual event, and the governor was in a jovial spirit as we all chowed down on Texas barbecue and fried chicken.

It had already been a great day when Lieutenant Governor Bob Bullock rose to offer a toast to Governor Bush. Although a staunch Democrat powerhouse, Bullock lavished sincere praise upon his Republican governor, then concluded his remarks as he raised his glass and said, "And I believe we are standing in the presence of the next president of the United States!"

Whooom! It was a pivotal moment. Bob Bullock's toast expressed publicly what many people in Texas and elsewhere were saying privately. The birthday celebrants cheered wildly, and Governor Bush smiled and nodded in appreciation. Becky and I cast knowing glances at each other. We might not be relocating home to Houston anytime soon. We had the feeling again in November 1997 at the dedication of the George Bush Presidential Library and Museum at Texas A & M University in College Station, for the governor's father. The event was celebrated by former president George H. W. Bush and his wife, Barbara, along with the entire Bush family, as well as former presidents Gerald R. Ford and Jimmy Carter. President Bill Clinton spoke at the ceremony. Former staffers and friends reminisced about wonderous achievements, while the governor's staff and friends dreamed of what might be. As I watched the scene unfold, I thought, *This is like a Texas Camelot.*

In December 1997, Governor Bush appointed me Texas secretary of state. I was especially honored because the position was the only statewide constitutional office for which individuals did not run for election. Under the Texas constitution, the secretary is appointed by the governor.

I moved into a spacious and beautiful office on the first floor of the capitol and directed a staff of more than 250 people. As secretary of state, I was the chief state elections officer and the custodian of all state business records, as well as chief protocol officer, so part of my responsibilities included entertaining foreign dignitaries who visited Texas. Becky and I loved the cultural and diplomatic aspects of this new position. As the son of a former president and a successful governor, George W. Bush was already being viewed as a potential presidential candidate, so the number of high-profile foreign visitors increased each year he was in office. Becky and I interacted with diplomats and business leaders from various countries around the world.

Governor Bush also designated the secretary of state as the chief liaison between Texas and Mexico, dealing especially with border matters. That responsibility thrust me headlong into grappling with many complex immigration issues, and balancing our state's compassion with the need to protect our borders. The increasing flow of illegal immigrants taxed Texas resources, and while Governor Bush had a heart for Hispanics, he was also committed to upholding the law. As a person of Hispanic heritage, I well understood the controversies and sometimes felt torn. My first allegiance, however, as a lawyer and a state official, was with the law and Texas.

In March 1996, Texas attorney general Dan Morales boldly sued several of the national tobacco companies in federal court in Texarkana, Texas, to recover Medicaid costs related to smoking. Morales hired five well-known and experienced Texas trial lawyers to represent the state on a contingency fee basis. The trial lawyers agreed to bear all the costs, as well as all the risks, of the litigation. If successful, they would be entitled to an amount equal to 15 percent of the award to the state. If unsuccessful, they would receive nothing. The case settled in January 1998, and ultimately, the tobacco companies agreed to pay the state $17.3 billion, which meant the five trial lawyers stood to make a whopping $3.2 billion, or $640 million each!

Some legal ethics experts and Texas conservatives, including Republican John Cornyn, who was running for Texas attorney general, questioned the enormous size of the attorneys' fees. Although he believed in the sanctity of contract, in February 1998, Governor Bush decided to intervene in the case, to hopefully recover a portion of the legal fees for the people of Texas. The governor believed the lawyers were entitled to be reimbursed for their expenses and reasonably compensated for their work, as well as rewarded for assuming the risks of the litigation. These fees seemed excessive, however, and, we believed, included money that could be used by the state to help address costs related to smoking. Governor Bush instructed me to work with his general counsel, Margaret Wilson. The response from Morales was immediate and personal. He bitterly—and publicly—resisted the governor's attempted intervention in the litigation, and we found ourselves in the unusual position of being at odds in a very high-profile case with our own attorney general.

In addition to my constitutional and statutory duties, a significant portion of my thirteen months as secretary of state was devoted to negotiating with the trial lawyers to resolve the fee dispute without jeopardizing the substantial award to the state. Our strategy was to sever in court our dispute over the legal fees from the state's award. Morales and the trial lawyers initially resisted our efforts to sever, knowing that our fear of losing the state award was a powerful leverage against the governor. That the outside counsel would hold hostage the state's award to protect their own fees raised eyebrows that they had breached their fiduciary duty to their client.

The interaction between the players was fascinating to me. Conversations were usually cordial, but at times they grew tense. I spent countless hours in meetings and discussions with the trial lawyers and the attorney general's office attempting to find a solution. There were several hearings in federal court, multiple conferences in the judge's chambers, and clandestine meetings with individual trial lawyers—all without success. Eventually the governor, seeing little progress, agreed to allow the issue of the legal fees to be arbitrated. Even reaching that agreement was complicated by the emergence at the eleventh hour of a lawyer named Mark Murr.

Murr was a friend and former colleague of Morales. Morales claimed that Murr had been a close advisor to him in the tobacco litigation and was thus entitled to a percentage of the legal fees. The trial lawyers became angry and suspicious when Morales produced engagement contracts with Murr for the first time; in fact, the trial lawyers contended that they had never heard of Murr! I, too, was surprised and had doubts, having never met nor spoken with Murr. Even after a majority of the trial lawyers told me they were willing to move forward and resolve the dispute over the fees, Morales continued to refuse to approve any agreement between the governor and the trial lawyers over severance or the fees unless Murr was also paid.

As we approached the fall 1998 elections, the governor wanted this matter resolved. The issue of the fees was serious but it was also a distraction, and Governor Bush was simply more comfortable allowing other state officials, particularly incoming attorney general John Cornyn, to carry on the fight.

Eventually Murr received an award through an arbitration panel, but questions about the legitimacy of his claim continued. As the scrutiny intensified, Murr walked away from his award. The questions, however, remained.

Following federal and state investigations, Morales was arrested, tried, and sentenced to four years in a federal prison for mail fraud and tax evasion. An indictment to which Morales pleaded guilty said he tried to steer more than a million dollars in *unearned* legal fees to Murr, who had previously admitted his role in the scheme and received a six-month prison term.

The trial lawyers eventually got their big payday following arbitration, and over time the state received its money, although some experts question whether the successful litigation truly affected the behavior of the tobacco industry, or whether the monies from the award intended to educate the public of the dangers of smoking made a difference.

For me, the "tobacco war" was an interesting experience involving huge egos, corporate liability, political fortunes, criminal wrongdoing, and ethical improprieties, all with billions of dollars at stake. I learned a lot about greed, power, and human nature. I also learned that I was a pretty good negotiator, a skill that would serve me well in the years to come.

———

After serving as secretary of state for ten months, on September 30, 1998, news broke that Justice Raul Gonzalez of the Texas Supreme Court, and the only Hispanic on the nine-member body, was stepping down. Raul was a socially conservative Democrat, and the assumption was that Governor Bush would replace him with a Republican. Bush understood Hispanics, and they trusted him. In budget meetings, the governor sometimes lamented spending more money for prisons when we were spending comparatively little for schools to educate Hispanics along our border with Mexico. He made it clear that he wanted a Hispanic on the court. Racial diversity was important to the governor, and with Justice Gonzalez's retirement, our court was devoid of diversity. That turned the spotlight on me.

The following morning, I attended a breakfast for the energy minister of Mexico held at the governor's mansion. As the secretary of state, it was not unusual that I should be included at the event, and following the minister's departure, Governor Bush nodded to me and said, "I need to talk with you. Come on upstairs to the residence."

I followed the governor upstairs and almost as soon as we sat down, he looked me in the eyes and asked, "Do you want to go on the Supreme Court?"

Even though I understood the circumstances, his question still surprised me and threw me off guard slightly. "Do you want me to go on the court?" I asked.

He looked at me in surprise, as though saying, "It's not what I want; what do you want?"

I had never aspired to be on the court; indeed, I worried that my legal experience might not be broad enough. I had worked quite successfully as a transactional lawyer, handling business deals worth millions of dollars, but I was not a litigator who argued cases in front of a judge or jury. Nor had I ever been a trial judge. That didn't seem to matter to Governor Bush.

"Can you give me some time to think about it?" I asked.

"Sure, take the time you need," the governor responded.

I talked to Becky about the pros and cons of the position. Unlike the United States Supreme Court justices who are appointed for the remainder of their lives or until they choose to retire, justices in Texas serve six-year terms and then must run for reelection. Although Governor Bush would appoint me to fulfill the final two years of Raul's term, I would have to stand for election in 2000, and I wasn't sure my heart was in that. I loved my job as secretary of state. Besides, what would we do if I *lost?* I talked with several other people whose advice I highly respected, and they suggested that besides being a great honor and an important way to serve our state, going to the Texas Supreme Court would be a worthwhile career move for me. Becky and I concluded that our advisors were right. I accepted the appointment and took a seat on the court in January 1998.

Some of the most difficult cases I faced as a supreme court justice were a series of parental notification cases involving a controversial piece of legislation allowing young women under the age of eighteen to have an abortion in Texas without notifying their parents if they had the permission of a state judge—known as a judicial bypass. If there was a preponderance of evidence that the minor was mature and sufficiently well informed to make the decision to have an abortion; or if parental notification was not in the best interests of the minor or, if notification might lead to physical, sexual, or emotional abuse of the minor, in such cases, Texas legislators had decided that a minor relying on a judicial bypass need not notify her parents before having an abortion.

At issue was not the question of whether Texas would *allow* or *disallow* abortions. That issue had already been decided at the federal level in *Roe v. Wade* in 1973, although it troubled me that unelected judges had recognized the existence of a new fundamental right that simply was not reflected in the words of the Constitution. I considered the exercise of such judicial power arrogant and dangerous in our constitutional scheme. While I regard the right to privacy important, the scope of this right is one that should be left for the people to decide through the constitutional amendment process.

No, these parental notifications cases, in my view as a judge, were not about abortion; they were about discerning the intent of the Texas legislature when it passed the parental notification statute. The Texas legislature obviously intended to permit minors to get an abortion without parental consent if certain conditions were met. Our job as judges was to determine legislative intent with respect to these exceptions. When is a minor sufficiently well informed to make the decision to have an abortion? What circumstances threaten the best interests of the minor? What level of physical, sexual, or emotional abuse would be necessary to trigger a judicial bypass?

Some of the more conservative members of the court appeared to want to interpret the statute in a manner that would make it very difficult, if not impossible, for any minor to get a judicial bypass. I believed my colleagues wanted to impose obstacles that simply were not written into the statute and that would in essence remove the exceptions that the state legislators had voted to establish.

To be sure, I was unhappy with the Texas legislature. They had passed a law with broad, general wording (which was probably necessary to secure the votes for passage and to make the law constitutional), with the likely expectation that the all-Republican Texas Supreme Court would fill in the details with tougher conservative standards. *That* I was not willing to do because that was not my job as a judge.

The legislature had passed a law allowing for exceptions to parental notification, and I did not believe it was my role as a judge, nor within the purview of the judicial branch, to legislate from the bench and to rewrite the law to narrow or eliminate the exceptions. If the standards were to be changed, the legislature would have to step up, amend the statute, and be accountable at the ballot box.

While I was on the court, we decided a handful of these parental notification cases. In every case but one, I voted to deny permission to the minor to have an abortion because the minor had failed to satisfy the statute.

Although I knew Governor Bush to be pro-life, he did not try to influence my opinion in any way, nor did he weigh in on the discussion of parental notification. He never asked about the cases or even hinted to me his feelings about it—which would not have been proper—prior to the supreme court decisions.

I received not-so-friendly-fire from pro-life groups such as Focus on the Family, led by Dr. James Dobson, after I staked out my judicial positions on the parental notification cases. The critics' contention was that I had paved the way for a minor to have an abortion without her parents knowing about it. Not true; the legislature had done that. I understood the critics' concerns and even sympathized with their position. If I were the parent of an underage daughter seeking an abortion, I would want to know. I did not like the Texas statute, but I would not let my personal views influence my interpretation of the law.

I knew my votes on the court would cost me votes in the upcoming Republican primary election. Indeed, several of my former supporters abandoned me. I discovered that while many conservatives claim to support judicial restraint, not wanting judges to legislate from the bench, they don't always mean it when considering issues they consider fundamentally important. Unfortunately, although I was considered a Bush insider, my votes on the parental notification cases forever marked me as an untrustworthy outsider to social conservatives, among whose ranks I counted myself.

CHAPTER 10

THE SEND-OFF

As early as 1997, opinion polls reflected that many people assumed George W. Bush would run for president of the United States. Few of us who were close to him in Austin doubted that he would run, but we understood that he did not wish to announce his candidacy until after the gubernatorial elections in 1998. When Governor Bush was reelected for a second term in a landslide, capturing nearly 69 percent of the vote, some of his closest associates began mentally packing their suitcases.

I did not—especially after he appointed me to the Texas Supreme Court. I loved my new job, so even if Governor Bush ran for and won the presidency, I was not certain I wanted another transition. Becky had already been forced to accept a different state job, having to leave her position with the Texas attorney general's office to avoid a conflict of interest due to my now being on the court.

In June 1999, I went out to Austin-Bergstrom, our city's largest airport, to see off George Bush for the initial Iowa and New Hampshire presidential campaign tour. More than one hundred journalists were already boarding the plane, and a large crowd of Bush supporters had gathered as well. As he was moving through the crush, Governor Bush saw me and motioned toward me with his finger, "Come here." I stepped through the crowd and made my way to the governor.

"I'm really proud of you," I told him.

He seemed pleased to see me at the send-off, and for a moment, I thought he might be overcome with emotion. He said a quick good-bye and jetted off to win, he hoped, the presidency.

When Governor Bush announced he was running for the presidency and began campaigning, Becky and I watched the political scene more carefully because my name was on the ballot with that of Governor Bush in 2000. When it came time for me to run in the Republican primary, although I had been selected by Governor Bush as his counsel and appointed to two statewide offices, I quickly discovered that my Spanish surname stirred suspicions in certain Republican strongholds that I was a closet Democrat. That created challenges during the Republican state primary election. Governor Bush indirectly came to my rescue by allowing my campaign to use segments of his speech at my supreme court investiture ceremony to create a moving television ad, using his words to endorse me as a member of the court. I did no other major advertising during my campaign.

Still, I campaigned hard, knowing that I was in an uphill battle. *Gonzales* was not a name that Republicans were accustomed to seeing on their primary election ballots. Texas is a huge state, and many Republicans outside of the major metropolitan areas were unfamiliar with me. Making matters even more unpredictable, my opponent was actually a Democrat running in the Republican primary. Texas Democrats had kept a strong grip on the Hispanic vote, and despite George Bush's best efforts, many Hispanics were slow to leave their traditions. So it was not a given that I would win my primary election.

Our campaign focused on six main metropolitan areas—Austin, Houston, Dallas, San Antonio, Fort Worth, and El Paso—where we ran my television ad. I carried every county where we aired the ad and lost virtually every county where I had no television ads. Fortunately, I had the endorsement of every major Texas newspaper and of every statewide public official, and I won my primary election.

On election day, the first Tuesday in March when seven states conduct primary elections, the state Republican party asked me to be on stage with

Governor Bush and other statewide Republican officials at an election cele-bration and rally that night. I met the governor in the hallway on the way to the stage, and he hugged me in front of several other state officials. "I told my daughters to vote for you," he said. I knew the Bush daughters were vot-ing for the first time. "Thank you, governor," I said with a smile.

In the general election, I was opposed by a Libertarian candidate, so my Republican supporters and I felt confident that I'd have no trouble winning that race. Nevertheless, I continued to campaign on a small scale, simply to maintain a presence with voters.

From the time Governor Bush set up a committee to explore the prospect of running for president, Becky and I knew in our hearts that if he won and he wanted us to go to Washington along with him, it would be difficult to tell him no. Soon we started seeing new faces in the Bush circles. Consultants and policy experts such as Condoleezza Rice, former provost at Stanford University, visited frequently. Ari Fleischer came aboard as campaign press secretary; Josh Bolten came to help with the campaign. Andy Card, who had served in George H. W. Bush's administration and was a trusted Bush advi-sor, also made frequent visits. Karl Rove, of course, had been researching a potential presidential run for several years. Our state staff continued working for Texas, but everyone knew there was a possibility they might not complete the term.

By the middle of July, after George W. Bush had clinched the Republican nomination, people began to wonder who his vice presidential running mate would be. Many insiders bandied about names such as Tom Ridge, John McCain, Colin Powell, and Dick Cheney. Because I knew the governor val-ued loyalty so highly, I immediately ruled out John McCain. A war hero who had survived being tortured in Vietnam prisoner of war camps, McCain understandably was his own man. Powell, too, might not relish being num-ber two, since he was a four-star general and a former chairman of the Joint Chiefs of Staff, and used to being in charge. Dick Cheney had served in Governor Bush's father's administration, but he was much older than the governor. If I were betting, I would have put my money on Tom Ridge, the former governor of Pennsylvania.

"I think it will be Cheney," Joe Allbaugh confided to me. Joe felt the governor resonated with Cheney's direct, no-nonsense approach to matters.

I was wrong and Joe was right. On July 25, 2000, at a festive campaign event held at Austin's Erwin Center, the largest arena on the campus of the University of Texas, Governor Bush announced that Dick Cheney would be his running mate.

It was at that event that I first met Josh Bolten. A graduate of Princeton with a law degree from Stanford, Josh had worked in the legal offices of Goldman Sachs before signing on with George W. Bush. "I've heard a lot about you. The governor has spoken often of you," Josh said as we shook hands.

"Oh, that's nice to hear," I responded. "I'm glad people are saying nice things about me."

"I didn't say that he said anything nice about you." Josh held a serious expression for a moment and then broke into a broad smile. That was my first experience with Josh's sardonic sense of humor, and as I was soon to discover, it was typical of his personality. We both laughed aloud. I knew immediately that Josh and I were going to get along just fine. I grew to really admire Josh and value his counsel.

I also met Dick and Lynne Cheney for the first time that evening. Cheney brought a wealth of experience to the campaign. He had been a CEO with Halliburton, a Fortune 500 company, and had served as the White House chief of staff for President Gerald Ford; he was a former congressman from Wyoming and a member of the House Intelligence Committee during the Reagan administration, and had served as secretary of defense during the administration of George H. W. Bush. At nearly sixty years of age, it was unlikely that Cheney would be running for office again in four or eight years, so Governor Bush could count on his honest, straightforward insights. The way Dick and Lynne Cheney carried themselves, as well as the gracious manner in which they interacted with people, was impressive. I began to understand why Governor Bush had selected Cheney over the others, and I felt pleased with his choice. Becky and I had dinner with Joe and Dianne Allbaugh after the event, and Joe was elated about our vice presidential candidate.

Governor Bush sent Becky and me an invitation to the National

Republican Convention, one of the privileged few that he offered to people around the country. We were especially honored because the governor had included us in his "friends and family" invitations, which gave us greater access to the Bushes and VIP treatment at the convention. We enjoyed the social events, entertainment, and the many speeches.

The last day of the convention, I saw Joe Allbaugh in the hotel lobby. He waved and said, "Congratulations." I had no idea what he was talking about. Later that afternoon, I received a telephone call informing me that I had been selected to serve on the escort committee; I was one of a small group to meet Governor Bush when he arrived for his acceptance speech that evening. It was a tremendous honor.

Becky and I arrived at the convention around 6:30 p.m. Becky went inside while I went back to the tunnel where Governor Bush was scheduled to arrive. Members of the escort committee formed a receiving line, and while television cameras covering the event zoomed in on us, we greeted the Cheneys as they arrived. Governor Bush and his entourage arrived shortly thereafter, Bush shaking hands with everyone as he made his way down the line.

When he got to me I said, "I'm very proud of you, sir."

He smiled broadly and said, "I'm ready to go!" He continued on into the convention center holding room as the emcee announced to the euphoric delegates and guests that Governor Bush had arrived and had been greeted by the escort committee. The crowd roared in anticipation. Bush officially received the party's nomination that night and gave a magnificent acceptance speech, setting the tone for the exciting campaign ahead. We all knew that Vice President Al Gore would be a formidable opponent, but everyone in the arena had total confidence that George W. Bush would be the next president of the United States.

Becky and I returned home to Austin, excited about the possibilities, and wondering how a George W. Bush presidency might impact our future.

CHAPTER 11

WEST WING POSSIBILITIES

ack home, I received a deluge of requests for interviews regarding Governor
Bush and his presidential aspirations. Although I had to be circumspect
because I was a sitting Texas Supreme Court justice, I told the reporters about
the man I knew—a George W. Bush who genuinely cared about helping people,
and a man with a good heart. I spoke of his passion to help those less fortunate,
and his concerns to improve the educational and vocational opportunities for
all Texans, especially for Hispanic children. "One of the best things the governor has done," I said, "was to inspire hopes and dreams in Hispanic kids." He
had certainly accomplished that goal in my family.

Earlier, Governor Bush had decided that Clay Johnson would lead
the transition team. Dick Cheney would be in charge of the vetting process. Although the election was still more than three months away, it was
important for the new administration to hit the ground running, to be ready
to start governing the day the new president took office. So even though
nobody was certain of the election's outcome, the governor had to assume
that he would win, and he had to begin gathering a strong team around him,
as he had done when he moved into the governor's office. Now, of course, the
transition issues were more complicated, since he needed talented people he
trusted, and who were willing to live in Washington, DC.

Known affectionately as "the icebox" because he was big, white, and sometimes coldly efficient in making appointment decisions, Clay Johnson, with his no-nonsense demeanor, was perfect for the job. A successful businessman who had known Governor Bush longer than any of us, Clay understood his friend's strengths and weaknesses and was determined to surround him with only the best people.

I made no overtures to Clay during the campaign regarding any possible positions for me in the new administration, but other insiders had told me that they believed I would be under consideration. Maybe that's why I wasn't totally surprised when Clay called me the morning of September 6, 2000, and said he wanted to come by my office to pick my brain about something.

I had been up all night working before spending a full day listening to oral arguments featuring the noted Harvard Law professor Laurence Tribe. So by the time Clay arrived later that afternoon, I was wrung out. Nevertheless, I perked up when he indicated the purpose for his visit.

"I was talking to a legal expert," Clay began, "about what factors are most important for the position of White House counsel. The expert said, 'loyalty to the president is the number one ingredient.'"

Clay sat back in his chair as though contemplating. "So I began thinking of all the lawyers I know in America. And I cannot think of anyone who is more loyal to George W. Bush than you."

"Me?"

"Yes, you, Al." Clay leaned forward in his chair. "The ideal person is tough and smart, someone that the governor knows well and trusts. That's you too. The more I thought about it, the more convinced I became that you are the right person for the job. The governor is comfortable with you and has confidence in your judgment." Clay paused and his forehead wrinkled, as though he was thinking about something. "But then I crossed you off my list because you are running for reelection, and it wouldn't look right to win an election and then leave office."

I nodded. People had donated money to my candidacy for supreme court justice, and we had raised more than $800,000 to win the primary election. We weren't spending much during the summer because the Democrats had not run anyone against me and there was only token opposition in the general election from the Libertarian candidate. Still, I understood Clay's concern about asking donors for money and then not serving.

Clay continued, "I had lunch with Karl the other day and I told him that you would be perfect for the job, but gosh, it's too bad that you couldn't be considered."

I nodded again and remained silent.

"But Karl said you should not automatically be out of the running."

"Really?" I replied, feigning only mild interest.

"That's right. Karl said that the real race for supreme court justice took place during the primary. And you won that for us. So people would not be upset about you leaving office to continue serving the governor." He paused. "When I took this job, I understood that you wanted to stay on the court, that you did not want to go to Washington."

Now it was my turn to lean forward. "That's not quite correct, Clay. I said that I would gladly stay on the court and serve, but I did not want to automatically be taken off the Washington list."

Clay chuckled. "I guess I'm the only one who had not thought about you going." I smiled as Clay continued. "I have not talked to the governor about this yet, but I wanted to feel you out and hear what you are thinking."

"To be honest, Clay, I have no burning desire to go to Washington. I have a great job and I love Austin. But if there is an opportunity to work closely with the governor, helping him in some way, I would consider it."

"What jobs would interest you?"

"Something in the White House or the Justice Department," I replied. "As long as I'm working directly with the governor. If I was not working with him, I'd rather stay right here."

"Well, there's no question on how he feels about you," Clay said. "If the governor were going to climb a mountain and could only take along six or seven people, you would be one of those."

I thanked Clay for the comment, all the more meaningful to me because of Clay's track record as a straight shooter, not to mention his own closeness to the governor.

"If you were White House counsel, you would have a very close working relationship with the governor," Clay said. "No question about that."

We talked further about the job, and Clay mentioned that he had some books and materials about the White House operations and the transition. "If you'd like to look at any of those materials, I'll be happy to send them over."

"Thanks, Clay. Yes, I would be quite interested."

"Great. I'll have the materials brought over to you."

After we concluded our meeting and Clay departed, I sat back in my chair and took a deep breath. I had no idea if anything would come of our conversation, but I felt good hearing Clay's assurance that the governor regarded me as one of his closest advisors. I allowed my imagination to roam, thinking about what might happen if the governor won the presidency. I shook my head and snapped back to reality. I tried not to dwell too much on the possibilities. Then Clay's books and materials about the White House were delivered. *This is getting serious*, I thought.

I talked with Becky about the possibility of another potential transition in our lives—a possible move to Washington, DC. We both agreed that while we loved our life in Austin, if Governor Bush asked us, we would welcome the new opportunity. In mid-September, I communicated to Clay that I was willing to serve.

"Great," Clay responded. "I'm going to talk to the governor about it this weekend." I began gathering more information about the positions of White House counsel and attorney general. Because the counsel works closely with the AG, I was curious about whom Governor Bush was considering.

Becky and I followed the 2000 presidential campaign involving our friend even more closely now. Certainly, we wanted Governor Bush to lead our country. Although Vice President Gore had eight years of Washington experience, we had seen firsthand Governor Bush's ability to put aside partisan politics to do what was best for the people. We could only imagine how his positive approach could help revive a sick Washington after the scandals of the Clinton administration. As the summer progressed, Bush's message of unity and bringing dignity and honor back to the office of the president seemed to be resonating with the public.

The evening of November 2, 2000, mere days before the November 7 election, an incident surfaced in the news that threatened to unhinge our hopes. Twenty-four years earlier, George W. Bush had been arrested for driving too slow and slapped with a DUI charge in Kennebunkport, Maine. When news of the DUI suddenly surfaced, Karl Rove and several other key advisors feared accusations of a cover-up that would cost Governor Bush the presidential election.

The incident had never been covered up, though neither was it widely broadcast. Bush had been called for jury duty in Austin in 1996 for a driving under the influence case. In a DUI case, potential jurors would almost certainly be asked if they had any similar prior offenses. When the governor arrived for jury duty, I went with him and engaged in what one publication later described as some "canny lawyering."[1] First, I assured the defense attorney, the prosecutor, and the judge that the governor was present and willing to serve. Then I subtly reminded the defense attorney that should his client be convicted by a jury that included a sitting governor, it would be unlikely that he would ever receive a pardon for the offense from another governor.

The defense lawyer replied that he had already considered this possible conflict, and he planned to strike Governor Bush during *voir dire*, the questioning of potential jurors. Later, in the judge's chambers, the prosecutor said that he had no objections to striking the governor. When asked by the judge, I reiterated that Bush was there ready to serve. "But why waste time going through that process if the lawyers know they are going to strike him anyway?" I asked.

A few minutes later, in open court, the defense attorney presented his motion to strike the governor, and with no objection from the prosecutor, the judge granted the motion. I was glad that our conversations resulted in having the governor dismissed, thus avoiding the disclosure of the DUI before Bush could inform his daughters—both of whom were teenage drivers at the time the news finally broke.

Obviously, I had known about the Bush DUI for some time. When news of it became public, I immediately called Dan Bartlett in the governor's campaign office and relayed what I knew. Governor Bush had admitted that in the past he sometimes had too much to drink, and he chose to play down the matter because he did not want to be a negative role model. The fact that he had not voluntarily disclosed the DUI previously did not play well in the media, but Joe Allbaugh and Dan Bartlett put out fires as best they could from the campaign office, and Karen Hughes helped deal with the press out on the road. Since I was on the supreme court, I said nothing about the issue and stayed out of the public discussion of it. That same day, after his next campaign event, Governor Bush addressed the media, accepted blame, said he was sorry, and answered questions about the DUI. "I've oftentimes said that years ago I made some mistakes. I drank too much, and I did on that night," the governor said. "I regret that it happened, but it did. I've learned my lesson." His wife, Laura, was by his side.

It was a few days before the presidential election. There was nothing left to do but to wait and see how the public responded.

CHAPTER 12

WHITE HOUSE BOUND

A few days before the election, Clay Johnson told me, "The governor is going to call you the day after the election and offer you the job as counsel."

I thanked Clay for letting me know. Although the polls showed the presidential race was tightening, Becky and I remained optimistic that our lives were about to take a dramatic and historic turn. No Hispanic had previously advised the president of the United States as his chief counsel.

The night before the election, Governor Bush came home from his last campaign trip, landing at Bergstrom airport in Austin. Becky and I went out to meet him and joined in the celebration at a private hangar at the airport. A loud and excited crowd of friends and supporters greeted him, and the air was electric at the conclusion of a long campaign. As the event concluded, Governor Bush shook hands with well-wishers.

In the crowd of people, the governor found Becky and me clapping. He walked over close to us and said, "I'm going to call you tomorrow."

I smiled, nodded, and continued clapping.

On Election Day, Becky and I took our two youngest sons along with us to the voting booths, located at an elementary school near our home. I wanted our sons, Graham, age eight, and Gabriel, age five, to see me cast my vote for Governor Bush as president and for me to remain on the supreme court. It felt surreal voting for myself, but Becky and I did it with pride.

That evening, as the news media covered the election returns, the Texas secretary of state's office hosted an election watch party in the capitol suite, where elected officials and friends of the governor and secretary of state could watch the returns together, according to custom. Becky and I attended. It was a fun place to gather with friends and watch the most current and accurate returns in Texas, as tabulated by the secretary of state's office. The mood was festive and optimistic, and it felt good to be back in my former offices.

About one hundred yards to the south of the capitol stood a large stage at Eleventh and Congress. The Austin fire department estimated that a crowd of more than twenty thousand people had squeezed into the area in front of the stage, in anticipation of receiving a new president-elect. It had been a cold, wet day in Austin, but nothing seemed to dampen the crowd's enthusiasm. Indeed, from the windows of the secretary of state's office, we could see that despite the inclement weather, the crowd was growing larger throughout the evening.

Since the Democrats did not run anyone against me in my contest to remain on the supreme court, I was declared the winner early in the evening, with 82 percent of the vote. People at the party enthusiastically congratulated me on the landslide victory, bolstering our spirits even more.

But then, just prior to 7:00 p.m., several television networks called Florida for Vice President Gore. Given Florida's demographics and its large number of electoral votes, and the fact that Governor Bush's brother Jeb Bush was the current governor of Florida, the Gore announcement was both surprising and disheartening. With further projections of a Gore victory in Pennsylvania and Michigan, the party grew quiet as the tension mounted. It looked like it might be a long night.

Close to 9:00 p.m., CNN pulled Florida from the blue column to the yellow—undecided—category. Apparently, the exit polls and the television networks that had forecasted Florida for Gore were wrong. Florida, the pundits now said, was too close to call, as the votes were still being counted. The mood in the capitol brightened, but nobody was lighting cigars yet.

We waited and watched . . . and waited. Finally, at 1:17 a.m. (Central time), the networks projected Florida for Governor Bush, which meant George W. Bush would be the next president of the United States. The room erupted in cheers. Around 1:30 a.m., Al Gore called Governor Bush to concede.

Becky and I grabbed our coats and, along with a number of other people, hurried outside to the stage and joined the huge crowd that had gathered on Congress Avenue, the main street in front of the capitol, to await President-elect Bush. The celebration was already in full swing, with people singing and cheering, shaking hands, and taking photographs of this historic moment. The crowd roared its approval every time the Jumbotron television screen showed video footage of the president-elect.

But then the unthinkable happened: Al Gore called Governor Bush a second time, this time to retract his concession. *What? Who concedes a presidential election and then retracts the concession?*

Apparently the vice president planned to contest the election results in Florida. Disappointed and somewhat confused and dejected, Becky and I headed home, cold, wet, and unsure of what might happen next, and concerned about what these highly irregular twists meant for our nation, and for us.

The banner atop Wednesday's edition of the *Austin American Statesman* trumpeted the news: HISTORY ON HOLD. That headline summed up how Becky and I felt, as did, no doubt, many other Americans. Any hopes that a new day would bring the election to a close were dashed when the Gore campaign manager, Bill Daley, gave a press conference announcing that the vice president's campaign would be requesting hand recounts of ballots in Palm Beach, Miami-Dade, Volusia, and Broward counties, all Democrat strongholds. Moreover, Daley hinted at something sinister when he said the Gore campaign was "still collecting other irregularities," an ironic description considering Daley's family history in Chicago. The recount promised to be historic and bizarre at the same time, so we stayed close to the television throughout the day, grasping at any bit of news that might give us a hint about our future. Nothing did.

That afternoon, despite the long, tumultuous night, Governor Bush called me. In typical form, he began by congratulating me on my victory.

"We each now have had a close contest and a landslide win," he quipped, referring to my close election in the primaries and his whopping victory, compared to my sweep in the general election, and his close race that he unofficially led by a mere three hundred votes, with absentee ballots still being counted. He seemed pleased that I had won a six-year term to the supreme court in 2000, becoming only the second person of Hispanic background ever to be elected statewide in Texas as a Republican.

The governor's voice sounded tired as he and I talked briefly about the election returns. "It was a rough evening, without much sleep," he said. "Don't worry about this recount. It will all be resolved within a few days."

I appreciated his optimism. Legal experts and the media, however, might not have concurred.

"And when it is over," Governor Bush said, "I want you to join me in Washington as the White House lawyer." He told me that Andy Card would be his chief of staff, Condi Rice would be the National Security Council advisor, and Karen, Clay, and Josh Bolten would all be part of the team.

"Thank you, sir," I replied. "It would be an honor to serve in that capacity, and I would enjoy working with you again. Will I have the same sort of access to you as White House counsel as I had when I was your general counsel here in Texas?"

"Absolutely," the governor assured me. "You'll have direct access, as will the other people I mentioned. You will be dealing a lot with the attorney general, but I'm not yet certain who that will be." He mentioned Senator John Ashcroft, former US trade representative Carla Hills, former senator John Danforth, and Montana governor Mark Racicot as possibilities.

"Well then, let me talk with Becky and I will give Clay my answer in the morning."

"Good, and call Andy Card tomorrow and he will bring you up to speed on everything."

"Thank you, sir. Good luck."

During the next few weeks as the legal wrangling continued in Florida, I worked diligently to complete my tasks at the Texas supreme court should I have to resign, and at the same time, I began preparing for the challenges in

Washington. I had a million questions for Clay, and Clay had few answers. "This is all new territory," he said as he rolled his eyes and laughed.

A few days later, I met with Andy Card at the governor's office. We talked for more than an hour on a wide variety of issues. "Your job will be the most important in the White House," Andy told me. "You will represent the president, the presidency, and the White House. You should plan to hire a staff of ten to twelve lawyers and view the counsel staff as the best law firm in the country." Andy described the type of experienced, hard-charging attorneys who might do well. He also told me that my new job would mean a nice increase in my salary, but given the much higher costs of living in Washington, it might actually be a net reduction in pay.

I expressed to Andy my concern that I have time to complete the legal opinions on which I was working at the supreme court. Unlike Clay, who felt that I needed to head for Washington immediately, Andy did not think it critical for me to start work yet. "The only thing to do early on," he said, "is to get our people cleared by the FBI, so you won't be able to do much until January." That gave me a few weeks to breathe.

I left my meeting with Andy encouraged. He seemed down-to-earth, kind, and strictly ethical. Over the next four years, he would become a close friend and ally in the White House.

A question arose as to whether the governor and I should resign. I told Clay that I didn't think it wise to resign our Texas responsibilities while the national election remained up in the air. Clay agreed. "Gore may steal the election, but he will not steal the governorship." I decided that I should not resign my seat on the supreme court until all doubts about the presidential election results were settled.

In the meantime, I talked further with Andy Card, who indicated that Dick Cheney would be actively involved in the transition, and that Cheney's incoming counsel, David Addington, would help with the FBI clearances. Andy also put me in touch with Fred Fielding, a respected lawyer who had served as White House counsel with President Ronald Reagan. Fred would help with the transition, and over time, he became an invaluable advisor to me.

I didn't speak to the governor during the recount in Florida, although

Becky and I closely followed the legal proceedings and the many news conferences. We watched images of officials counting chads, and we listened to the audio coverage of the arguments in the US Supreme Court.

During the recount, several people from the governor's staff went to Florida, but as a supreme court justice, my first allegiance was to the rule of law, so I could not go. I tried to focus on doing my job as a justice. We needed our best hands on deck, too, as the Gore campaign presented one argument after another, to the point of even trying to disqualify many of the absentee ballots cast by members of the US military stationed overseas, many of whom, history suggested, would have voted for George W. Bush.

While we tried to allay our concerns, we all felt uncertain whether Governor Bush would ultimately win. The big question for most of us serving in Austin was what would happen if he did win. Transitions from one presidential administration to another are notoriously difficult under the best of circumstances with the maximum amount of time. We would have neither.

We were decorating our family Christmas tree when I heard the news that the US Supreme Court had ordered that Florida stop counting the ballots. I was somewhat surprised that the Supreme Court would overrule a state supreme court and order that the counting of votes stop, but considered it good news for Governor Bush. Then on Tuesday, December 12, the television networks reported that the Supreme Court had turned down Vice President Gore's request for further manual recounts. The election seemed to be finally drawing to a close.

The following day, Vice President Gore conceded the election—again—this time in a reluctant but gracious nationally televised speech from his White House office. He noted that he had telephoned the president-elect to offer his congratulations. "And I promised that I wouldn't call him back this time," Gore said.

About an hour later, Governor Bush addressed the nation for the first time as president-elect. Becky and I hurried to the floor of the Texas house chambers for the hastily arranged gathering.

Along with many other Bush supporters, we listened as President-elect Bush spoke in heartfelt terms of national unity, healing, and reconciliation.

Now that the election was decided, our nation "must rise above a house divided," he said. He emphasized his desire to serve everyone, not simply Republicans, saying, "I was not elected to serve one party, but one nation." Despite the contentious election campaign and the thirty-seven-day post-election challenge, our government system had worked and the president-elect clearly hoped to bring the nation together. It was a mere ten-minute speech, but it encapsulated George W. Bush's dreams for America's future greatness.

Somewhere in the celebration events to follow, it hit Becky and me full-force: *This is real!* Of course, we had known for a couple months that if Bush were elected president, I would be leaving the court and we would be moving to Washington; but because the governor had not yet announced anything regarding me, I had made no public statements regarding my resignation from the court. Suddenly, the reality of those choices poked holes in the balloons of our idealism. We had a lot of work to do.

The president-elect initially mentioned our plans to my close friend, Chief Justice Tom Phillips, at a dinner party we were attending in Austin. Tom was delighted by the news, but disappointed that I would be leaving. News of my appointment soon began to leak and the press picked up on it, but I said nothing other than to confirm that the president-elect and I had talked.

On December 17, 2000, Becky and the boys joined me at the governor's mansion for a special announcement by the president-elect. It was the only time our boys had been to the mansion, other than to attend Halloween parties held for children of the staff and friends. I smiled as I saw Graham and Gabriel gawking at the cameras in the majestic setting of the governor's mansion.

In a brief event, President-elect Bush announced that Condoleezza Rice would be his national security advisor, his longtime friend Karen Hughes would be the communications director, and that I would be the White House counsel. Bush had announced Colin Powell as secretary of state the previous day.

Covering the event, the editor of the *Dallas Morning News* wrote, "To George W. Bush, Al Gonzales' rags-to-riches story represents the best in America . . . And now he's going to be sitting at the right hand of the president of the United States. Mr. Bush said, 'That really explains what America can and should be about.'"[1]

The morning of December 22, I received a call from Andy asking me if I could be present at the announcement of the president-elect's selection for attorney general—former US senator from Missouri John Ashcroft. I had just left my dentist's office and the left side of my face was still numb from Novocain, but I said, "Sure, I'll be right there."

John Ashcroft had been defeated for the US Senate in the November elections by the late Missouri governor Mel Carnahan. The governor and his aide had been killed in a tragic plane crash in mid-October, and because his death had occurred three days after the deadline for making changes to the ballot, Governor Carnahan's name remained on the ballot as Missouri voters stepped into the voting booth. Carnahan's replacement, Governor Roger Wilson, who had served as lieutenant governor under Carnahan, made it clear that he would appoint Carnahan's widow, Jean Carnahan, to the Senate seat if voters elected her deceased husband. In a hotly contested and controversy-ridden election, the incumbent Ashcroft lost to the sympathy vote for Carnahan.

News about President-elect Bush's appointment of John Ashcroft as attorney general probably generated joy among conservatives and anger among some liberals and so-called civil rights advocacy groups. I was glad to finally meet Ashcroft since I'd heard a great deal about him in recent weeks.

Unfortunately, at our first face-to-face encounter, my cheek looked and felt more like that of a chipmunk. With my Novocain-loaded, still-numbed mouth, I had some difficulty speaking clearly, and I consciously guarded against drooling. While I had a hard time reading John, his first impressions of me must have been hilarious.

In time, I came to regard John Ashcroft as an interesting contradiction of qualities. He was fiercely proud of his conservatism, yet one of the humblest men I have ever known. He readily admitted to not being a legal scholar, yet in defending the president's policies, John was a warrior, always willing to take arrows for the administration—and he took a lot—for which I admire him greatly.

By the time my successor on the Texas Supreme Court was named, I was already in Washington, but I returned for the investiture ceremony. My emotions nearly overwhelmed me as I said good-bye to my colleagues. I hated to leave, but I had been called to other service—to work in Washington with the newly elected president of the United States.

CHAPTER 13

TRANSITION TO POWER

My family and I had a bittersweet Christmas in 2000. We were excited about the upcoming changes, but sad about leaving Austin. The day after Christmas, Clay Johnson and his wife, Ann, went with Becky and me to the Signature Air private terminal at Austin-Bergstrom airport. Clay and I kissed our wives good-bye, and then along with other "Bushies," we boarded a chartered jet for Washington. I carried with me only a briefcase filled with notes and a suitcase full of clothing. I left Becky, once again, with the responsibility to sell our home and find somewhere for us to live in the Washington area. She and the boys would join me for the inauguration, and then not again permanently until after school dismissed in June. I felt sad at leaving my family, but I knew Becky would handle everything in her usual meticulous fashion. I loved my wife and I wanted her with me. She tried her best to smile as she waved good-bye.

As the plane whisked us toward Washington, everyone seemed in good spirits; a bit anxious, perhaps, but nonetheless excited to get started. Soon, the pilot announced that we were beginning our descent into the nation's capital. I gazed out the window as the jet headed toward Reagan National Airport, a short distance from the White House. There was snow on the ground, and I couldn't help thinking that despite its majesty and history, the city looked dreary and cold. I had no idea just how cold Washington could be to outsiders.

Some people assume that when a new presidential administration comes to town, the government pays for the transition—at least for senior staff members. Not so. We received a small moving stipend from the presidential campaign to help defray moving costs from Austin to Washington. By the time Becky and I finally found a house, the stipend was long gone and we were spending our own money. One of my lawyers offered to let me stay in his family's basement until I found a place. I gladly accepted. During the time I was living there, a problem occurred with the furnace emitting carbon monoxide. The repairman told the homeowners that they should not allow anyone to sleep in the basement because the levels of carbon monoxide could kill someone. I had already been sleeping there for several weeks! I quickly rented a small garage apartment in Georgetown and called it home until my family could move to Washington.

The president-elect's transition office was located at 1800 G Street, a few blocks from the White House. My office was a tiny space with a window that faced a brick wall, but I didn't mind. I was in Washington, working for my friend, the soon-to-be-inaugurated president of the United States. When Clay first saw my office, he was embarassed that the counsel to the president should be assigned to such a location. "Don't worry about it," I told him. "I don't mind. It's only temporary, and in a few weeks, I'll be moving into an office in the West Wing."

Soon after arriving in the transition office, I met with David Addington, who was assisting Fred Fielding with transition issues. David, a graduate of Duke Law School and former defense department general counsel, would serve as general counsel and later as chief of staff to Vice President Cheney. David cut an imposing physical presence. His personality was very direct, and I felt sure he would be a strong ally. "You will have the finest law firm in the world," he told me. "Everybody wants to work for the counsel."

David's careful nature surfaced in our initial conversation. "OLC is available to help," he said, "but you might want to keep things in house that you don't want others to know about." The OLC, the Office of Legal Counsel, is relatively unknown to the general public, but is one of the most important offices in our government, since it is basically the attorney general's law office and counsel. I had no reason to be unduly suspicious or secretive, so I was a bit puzzled at David's caution, especially when compared with everyone else's optimism. When I later asked Clay Johnson about David, Clay described him as a tough, knowledgeable lawyer who would run through a brick wall to solve a legal problem. I soon discovered that Clay had understated the matter. There was nothing subtle about David. He was smart and opinionated, someone you wanted next to you in a foxhole.

Fred and his small team of volunteers handled many of the legal issues during the early days of the transition as I put together my staff. Due to the Florida recount, we had only a matter of weeks to actually assemble a team to help the president govern the country. While Andy Card, Clay Johnson, and others had been informally interviewing potential staff members, and Dick Cheney and his staff had been putting out feelers since mid-November, until the election was finally settled, no one could extend firm job offers. Decisions that normally could be made between Election Day and Inauguration Day—filling some of the most important positions in the United States government—now had to be made in a compressed transition period. Consequently, we worked extra hard to identify and interview extraordinarily talented people to serve in the executive branch.

Fortunately, because the Clinton administration had been in office for eight years, an army of talented conservative lawyers had been patiently waiting for an opportunity to work in the White House. The array of outstanding legal minds President Bush attracted was impressive, even by Washington standards.

Although I had a close relationship with George W. Bush, I had no federal experience and limited Washington connections, so I decided to balance my strengths by hiring a team with proven federal experience and who were well known in Washington legal circles and conservative political groups. I hired as my deputy Tim Flanigan, a former assistant attorney general for the Office of Legal Counsel (OLC) and former clerk for US Supreme Court justice Warren Burger. Tim was very bright and possessed the wisdom and patience one needs as the father of fourteen children—which he was.

I also hired Brett Kavanaugh, an outstanding attorney who had worked for independent counsel Ken Starr and had clerked for US Supreme Court justice Anthony Kennedy. Brad Berenson, another former clerk for Justice Kennedy and a partner at Sidley & Austin, also joined our team. Courtney Elwood had been an attorney with Kellogg Huber and was a former clerk for US Supreme Court chief justice William Rehnquist. Noel Francisco was an associate with Cooper Carvin and had clerked for US Supreme Court justice Antonin Scalia; Helgi Walker was the senior legal advisor and chief of staff to commissioner Harold Furchtgolt-Roth of the Federal Communications Commission, and had clerked for US Supreme Court justice Clarence Thomas. Stuart Bowen was a former deputy counsel to Governor Bush and the first lawyer I had hired in the governor's office. Rachel Brand was a former associate with Cooper Carvin, who would go on to clerk for Justice Kennedy. Chris Bartolomucci was the former counsel for the Senate Whitewater investigation committee and was a former partner at Hogan & Hartson. Robert Cobb was the ethics advisor, and John Bellinger was the principal National Security Council legal advisor, a dual-hatted and key assistant to both Condoleezza Rice and me. The lawyers I had assembled were smart, tough, and loyal to the president and to me, with a clear understanding that our first true allegiance was to the United States Constitution, after which our top priority was protection of the constitutional prerogatives of the presidency.

In addition to this remarkable array of talent—a group that many legal eagles in Washington referred to as the "Dream Team" of lawyers—David Addington also sat in on many of the meetings held in my office, offering strong opinions that I knew reflected the views of his boss. We met every morning at 8:15 a.m. to discuss assignments, priorities, and pending deadlines. In a room filled with overachievers, there was never a dull moment, with plenty of good-natured banter about one another's performances, opinions, and politics.

As my legal team came together, I increasingly assumed more responsibility from Fred Fielding for the legal issues during the transition. Much of the transition planning occurred in meetings with the vice president-elect

Dick Cheney and other senior staff. I made only one visit to the White House to meet with President Clinton's counsel. It was a brief meeting that offered little insight into the job. Nevertheless, I quickly grew comfortable with my role, thanks to some excellent advice I received from former White House counsels from both parties, including Lloyd Cutler, A. B. Culvahouse, Boyden Gray, and my new friend Fred Fielding. All were gracious with their tips and helped reduce my learning curve. On one point, all of the former counsels concurred. "This job will be the most difficult and the most rewarding of your career," they said. They also agreed that there was nothing they could say that could adequately prepare me for the enormous responsibilities and the wide-ranging issues I was sure to encounter.

I never could have imagined how correct these advisors would be.

Inauguration week began for me on January 17, 2001, when my wife and three sons arrived in Washington. Although our younger sons, Graham and Gabriel, seemed excited about the events, I wasn't sure how much they truly understood about their daddy going to work in the White House, or how much their lives were bound to change. None of us did.

Washington buzzed with excitement as Republicans from all over the nation—including an especially enthusiastic bunch from Texas—descended on the city, swamping the hotels and restaurants and having a good time. Those of us involved in the presidential transition, however, continued to prepare for the transfer of power. On January 17, 2001, we had our last transition meeting with Vice President-elect Cheney. The following day, we began our senior staff meeting at 7:30 a.m., as we would every work day after George W. Bush took office. Unlike President Clinton, Bush was known for his punctuality. Meetings always began on time and often ended early.

Even before we officially got rolling, meetings dominated my day. On Friday, January 19, the day before the transfer of power, I completed a series of meetings and interviews with Ted Olson as solicitor general and John Manning and Doug Cox for the position of assistant attorney general for the Office of Legal Council.

At 3:45 p.m., I attended a meeting at Blair House, the elegant, official presidential guest house located across the street from the White House. At the meeting were President-elect Bush, Josh Bolten, Vance McMahon, John Bridgeland, Harriet Miers, Karl Rove, and Gary Edson. I had only visited with Bush a few times during the transition, so I was interested to see how he was faring through it all. In less than twenty-four hours he would be the leader of the free world, yet he seemed remarkably relaxed and calm.

I reported on some of the memos our office was preparing, and we agreed to meet immediately after he took office to discuss the matter of presidential succession in the case of emergency or vacancy.

The night before the inauguration, Becky and I, along with our family, attended a number of inaugural events including a candlelight dinner billed as a black-tie and boots gala appropriate for Texans in the mood to celebrate. That same evening, we attended the Hispanic Presidential Inauguration Gala. I was weary from working all day and drained from doing interviews with various media, but how often do you get to experience presidential inauguration activities from the perspective of an insider? We wanted to experience it all, everything we possibly could squeeze into our inaugural week schedule. As a senior member of the incoming Bush administration, I also felt an obligation to attend as many functions as possible to meet the president-elect's friends and supporters. Moreover, as the most senior Hispanic White House appointee, I sincerely wanted to represent our heritage at these historic events. So, weary or not, Becky and I dressed to the nines and went out to party.

Inauguration Day, January 20, 2001, dawned as another wintry cold, wet, downright miserable day weather-wise, but nothing could dampen my excitement and pride. For the midday ceremony, Becky and I sat in the VIP section with members of the Bush family, friends, and cabinet members, each strategically positioned on the platform temporarily located on the Capitol steps. Although the drizzle was incessant, the temperatures were in the low twenties, and we wore ponchos to keep dry, we were witnesses to history—and we loved it.

As I sat among that distinguished group and watched my friend take the oath of office as the forty-third president of the United States, I thought about my mom and dad picking cotton in West Texas. I thought about my brothers and me playing baseball in our backyard. I thought about selling the trays of Cokes and Sprites at Rice University football games. I thought about my decision to risk leaving my old law firm and go to work for Governor Bush. As I sat watching history unfold before my eyes, even in the cold, misty weather, I thought back to the promise by Governor-elect Bush that he would make it worth my while. He was right. I thought, *It has been worth it all!* And I thought about how much I genuinely loved America.

By now Becky was freezing, so after the ceremony we were happy to go inside the Capitol to a pre-inaugural parade reception. Later we settled into our seats on the reviewing stand along with the president and the First Lady and watched the inaugural parade coming up Pennsylvania Avenue. Occasionally I had to step out to field phone calls regarding some last-minute clearances for a couple of cabinet nominations. In the years to come, Becky would become quite accustomed to me getting up in the middle of an event or one of our boys' soccer games to take a call related to work. My normal habit was to pace as I talked, and then when the call was complete, I would return and act as though nothing had happened and that I hadn't missed a thing. Of course, I missed a lot.

That evening, Becky and I got dressed up again and attended the Texas-Wyoming Ball, followed by the Fiesta Americana Inaugural Ball. As the night grew late, the events filled with happy revelers seemed to blur together, and we finally returned to our hotel room at the Westin exhausted but ecstatic. What a day—what a night—what a country!

———

Andy Card had given instructions to the White House staff that we need not arrive at the office before noon the day following the inauguration. Nevertheless, I got up early and headed to the White House to scout out our space in the West Wing, as well as the offices in the Old Executive Office Building (OEOB) next door to the White House, where a number of my lawyers and staff members would be located. I showed my new White House photo identification card, and the guard waved me into the complex. Security was daunting and impressive, but nothing like it would be nine months later. I drove past several heavy steel gates and showed my ID again at each one.

I parked on West Executive Drive and entered the White House through the basement door, where a guard at the desk checked my ID again and then helped me find my office, situated in the southwest corner on the second floor of the West Wing. Traditions are highly respected in Washington, and my office was the one traditionally assigned to the president's counsel; it was the same office that Fred Fielding had occupied during his tenure with President Reagan.

The office itself was fully paneled with dark wood and had several large windows, although a balcony, built in part to provide additional security, obscured my view of the South Lawn and to the west. The furniture in the room included a stand-up writing desk and a built-in desk against the wall. Adjacent to the counsel's office suite was an embarrassingly small office for the deputy counsel, and an outer lobby area where we stationed three assistants. The remainder of my staff would work out of a group of large offices in the massive OEOB, overlooking Seventeenth Street to the west of the White House. Many of the offices in the OEOB contained fireplaces and were huge compared to the older, smaller West Wing offices, where space was at a premium.

When I arrived at the White House, cleaning crews were still hard at work cleaning up debris left over by the Clinton White House. Tech crews were installing new computers, phones, and communications equipment, and other crews were changing out furniture.

The sights that I first encountered were surprising. Although the cleanup crews had begun working the day before, immediately after the Clinton crew moved out, the place was still a mess. I was surprised at how much debris was strewn around the offices, especially those in the Old Executive Office Building. More surprises abounded, including the discovery of trashed offices in the White House and keyboards with the *W* scratched off, apparently a childish insult perpetrated by outgoing Clinton/Gore personnel.

The clutter and debris was so bad most of my staff of lawyers could not even work in their offices that first day on the job. Undoubtedly, part of the mess was the result of normal wear and tear, and the type of clutter that might occur when hundreds of people leave an area all at once. Additionally, there was furniture stacked upon furniture, perhaps because it had taken so much extra time for the moving men to do their work, making it even more difficult for a bunch of lawyers to negotiate the territory strewn with junk. Nevertheless, I was truly surprised to see the mess that morning.

At two o'clock, the White House opened to family and friends for informal tours. It was a fun, festive, and inspiring afternoon, although we took special pains to prevent visitors from seeing the still disheveled OEOB. When the tours were completed, Andy Card led a short senior staff meeting. Tomorrow was our first full day of work, and we were already expected to be ready to roll.

On Monday, January 22, all staff members and commissioned officers were sworn in during a ceremony in the East Room. Immediate family members were able to attend. In a simple, down-to-earth talk—it really couldn't be called a speech—the new president asked all of us to maintain the highest standards of ethics, and to serve the American people with respect and humility. He noted, "I want it said of us at the end of our service that promises made were promises kept. On a mantelpiece in this great house is inscribed the prayer of John Adams, that only the wise and honest may rule under this roof. He was speaking of those who live here, but wisdom and honesty are also required of those who work here. I know each of you is capable of meeting that charge."

Following the ceremony, I said good-bye to Becky and the boys, and they headed back to Austin. I wouldn't see the boys on a regular basis again until summer.

CHAPTER 14

THE CALM BEFORE THE STORM

With the festivities now concluded, and my family safely on their way home, I went back to work, ready to focus fully on the tasks ahead. My responsibilities as counsel entailed a unique combination of law, policy, and politics. One of the first issues with which I needed to speak with President Bush was an awkward one—the matter of succession, reviewing the Twenty-Fifth Amendment to the Constitution, the plan for what must happen should the president become physically or mentally incapacitated, or otherwise unable to discharge the duties of his office. This concerns more than life or death situations; it also pertains to a potential sickness or medical operation in which the president is in a coma or under anesthesia for a period of time.

Adding to the seriousness of our discussion was the fact that Vice President Cheney had a history of heart problems. He had experienced an incident as recently as November during the Florida recount, in which he was rushed to George Washington University Hospital, seven blocks from the White House, where doctors inserted a stent into one of the vice president's arteries that was 90 percent blocked.[1] So as uncomfortable as it was talking about such matters, we all had to be on the same page should something happen that would result in the president being unable to discharge his duties. We also had to ask, "What happens if the vice president becomes ill or incapacitated and can no longer perform his duties? Who should be notified and what steps should be taken to make sure the United States government is not decapitated and left devoid of leadership in case of an attack or some natural disaster?"

My legal team and I were immediately immersed in a wide variety of issues, everything from requests for clemency to reviewing presidential pardons. President Clinton had granted more than one hundred pardons in the final days and hours before he left the White House. Included was a last-minute pardon for Marc Rich, still an at-large fugitive who had been indicted for tax evasion and illegal dealings with Iran; as well as pardons for Roger Clinton, the president's brother, and Susan McDougal, notorious for her associations with the Whitewater scandal.

We also had to make immediate decisions regarding the current ninety-three US attorneys. When President Clinton took office, he fired all ninety-three US attorneys—which is a president's prerogative to do for any reason other than to obstruct justice—but we felt the country would be better served by keeping all but twenty-nine of them in place for a while, and even giving those we would ask to leave a thirty-day notice. Rather than a massive upheaval, we decided we would replace others as their successors could be appointed. With the Republicans in power in the Senate, few people paid much attention to our decision regarding the US attorneys in 2001, but when we removed seven US attorneys at once six years later, with the Democrats wielding the reins of the Senate, I was criticized for playing politics and potentially interfering with ongoing investigations. This was just one of too many examples of hypocrisy in Washington that still amaze me to this day.

President Bush informed me early in the transition that one of my most important responsibilities was to help identify and interview candidates for possible federal judicial appointments, as well as US attorneys and US marshals. In response, I chaired a White House group called the Judicial Selection Committee, which included the attorney general and senior members of his staff; Andy Card; Nick Calio or his representative from White House legislative affairs; Karl Rove; and my entire team of lawyers.

We met every Wednesday at 4:00 p.m. in the Roosevelt Room and kept an ongoing list of potential appointments. When we were notified of a vacancy or an impending vacancy, our committee worked to find the right, qualified person to fill that spot. Recommendations might come from home-state senators, members of Congress, a governor, political groups, or interested citizens. Once the committee had at least three suitable candidates, we invited them to the White House for interviews. The person interviewed had to pay his or her own expenses for these trips, but no candidate that I know of ever turned down the opportunity to interview in the West Wing for a federal position because of money.

During the early months of the administration, I worked seven days a week, and some of these interviews often ran until 9:30 at night. In the office by 6:00 a.m., I worked such long days that the wisdom of keeping Becky and the boys in Austin until school dismissed for the summer was apparent. It was Jared's senior year, Graham was in second grade, and Gabriel was in kindergarten. I knew the best decision was for them to stay in Austin, but I missed my family. Those feelings were exacerbated even more when Becky sent me a hand-drawing colored by Graham. On the paper, along with his tearstains, Graham had written, "Come home, Daddy." Then, just to make sure I did not forget, Graham included our home phone number. I felt some tears in my eyes as well.

On my first trip back to Austin, I went directly to Graham's school and found him in the cafeteria. He spotted me and came running, practically leaping into my arms. "Daddy, I'm so glad you are home!" he said. I knew I'd only be home for the weekend, but I was glad to hug my son. I eventually framed Graham's handwritten note, and I keep it in my office to this day.

As I continued working to identify nominees, President Bush repeatedly encouraged me to find more qualified women and minority candidates. I knew diversity mattered a great deal to George W. Bush, and he wanted to see judges reflect the diversity of our nation, so I strove to comply with his request.

After the president approved a candidate, the FBI ran extensive background investigations that often took six to eight weeks. Meanwhile, the

Justice Department continued to evaluate the candidate's writings or speeches while questioning friends and colleagues. It was not an easy process for a potential federal appointee to navigate.

Nominations for federal judges are evaluated by the powerful Senate Judiciary Committee. A longtime, albeit rather outdated, Senate tradition provides a home-state senator a way to quietly support or oppose a nomination through the long-recognized custom of returning a "blue slip." If both home-state senators return a positive blue slip to the committee, the nominee is normally given a green light to proceed for a hearing. If both home-state senators return a negative blue slip, the nominee will probably not even get a hearing. Negotiations become complicated when the home-state senators disagree on their blue slips, although traditionally, deference is given to the state's senior senator.

Prior to President Bush's announcement of his first judicial appointments, I discovered how powerful those blue slips were. Senate Democrats in California and Maryland declined to return positive blue slips for several excellent potential judicial nominations, thus preventing them from even receiving a hearing before the Judiciary Committee.

Occasionally, home-state senators attempt to manipulate the process. When Republican senator Arlen Specter once brought forth recommendations for judges in his home state of Pennsylvania, one of whom had actively campaigned against Bush for president, I balked. I knew the president wanted conservative judges, and I reminded Specter of that. Specter was the ranking Republican member of the Senate Judiciary Committee, so his support was important in getting our judges confirmed. He boo-hooed about keeping his constituency happy, and I understood that, but after I talked with the president, we laid down some ground rules. I said to Specter, "Respectfully, we'll work with you on this nomination, but don't do this again. You can recommend someone who is less conservative; you can even suggest someone who is a Democrat, and that person will get a fair shake. But, sir, don't ever again recommend someone who actively worked against the president. That just isn't going to happen." Specter grumbled but went away happy.

In addition to identifying potential federal judges, I was busy on numerous other fronts. I attended every meeting of our National Security principals committee, which included Vice President Cheney, Secretary of State Colin Powell, Secretary of Defense Donald Rumsfeld, the chairman of the Joint Chiefs of Staff, General Hugh Shelton, CIA director George Tenet, Chief of Staff Andy Card, and, along with other White House staff, National Security Advisor Condoleezza Rice, who set each meeting's agenda. When the principals met with the president, the group was known as the National Security Council. From the beginning of the Bush administration, discussions in those early-morning meetings covered concerns about Russia, China, North Korea, and the Middle East, including Israel and Iraq. Violations of the no-fly zone in Iraq put in place after Desert Storm were of special concern because they posed grave danger to our military, especially to our pilots patrolling the skies above Iraq. Discussions ranged from how to impose additional financial constraints on Iraq to how we might provide more humanitarian aid.

It was an exciting time that tested my talents and satisfied my desire to do a job of consequence.

———

On a breezy, cool, clear-sky morning in early April 2001, my friend was showing me around his elegant new home, replete with historic paintings and famous furniture. As we completed the tour of the upstairs, we stepped outside onto a beautiful balcony overlooking a panoramic view. We both stood silently, staring at the scene before us.

I broke the silence. "Well, what's it like to be president?"

With his eyes twinkling in the bright sunlight, the forty-third president of the United States cocked his head and chuckled. "It's really cool."

We both laughed.

We returned to the sights in front of us—the perfectly manicured South Lawn of the White House below us, the Washington Monument in view straight ahead, and beyond that, the Jefferson Memorial. Standing on the Truman Balcony with President Bush, I was struck by a mix of emotions.

On one hand, I was happy for my friend. This man I had known from Texas was now the most powerful person in the world. I was thrilled for him and proud that he had asked me to be there with him. In the history of America, nobody who looked like me or who had a Hispanic background or a name like Gonzales had ever been chosen to give daily legal advice to the president of the United States. I realized that whether I wanted to be or not, I was a role model to millions of Hispanics in America and around the world.

On the other hand, I felt an inexplicable, uncharacteristic twinge of sadness. I knew that with our new positions and responsibilities, these kind of moments were going to be rare for us.

When I worked with him in Texas, at the end of a busy day, I sometimes dropped by his office and we talked about a raft of subjects—everything from politics, to policy, to people, to baseball. Especially baseball. Then governor Bush knew that I was a fan of the game, particularly the Houston Astros, and as a former Major League Baseball team owner, he possessed all sorts of inside information and frequently told stories about some of my heroes of the diamond.

Now, however, looking out at the majesty before us, it seemed hard to imagine simply dropping by the Oval Office to talk baseball. Moreover, Andy Card set the standard early in the administration. "If you *need* to see the president, you get to see the president," Andy said. "But when you simply *want* to see the president, you don't get to see the president."

Andy was not being overly protective. Time in the Oval Office is too precious to be wasted. Every minute counts.

So as President Bush and I gazed at the city before us, I knew that moments such as these were to be cherished, because they would be rare in the days ahead.

————

From the first announcement that I was going with Bush to Washington, there had been speculation about me going to the US Supreme Court. While the rumors were flattering, they were also embarrassing, and I was uncomfortable about them. I felt that I was part of a team, and I worried that the media attention I was receiving might cause jealousy among members of the staff. The press stories also painted a bull's-eye on me for the president's critics—and to my surprise, some of his supporters.

I had barely been in Washington a few months when I learned that the *National Review* was preparing a story about me that would question my conservative credentials. I talked to Tim Flanigan about it, and he indicated that he would encourage his friends within the conservative community to defend me. I appreciated Tim's help, especially since I was not part of the Washington legal establishment, nor was I a member of the Federalist Society, an organization that included well-known conservative lawyers, judges, and legal thinkers. Although I was thrilled to be part of the Bush administration, I was surprised that I was booed at a speech in front of a conservative group when I said that the Supreme Court tells us what the Constitution means, which is why it is so important who is on the court. *Welcome to Washington.* It seemed the audience was suspicious of my conservative values and worried that President Bush might someday appoint me to the Supreme Court. It was a concern among conservatives that I would never overcome, despite my selection of strong Federalist Society staff lawyers and my support for conservative policies and judges who shared a conservative judicial philosophy.

If President Bush knew about the rude reception I had received, he didn't let on. On April 9, 2001, he and I had lunch together in his private dining room located behind the Oval Office. While having lunch with the president of the United States is impressive, that day was most memorable to me because we had peanut butter and jelly sandwiches—a Bush favorite. There was nothing pretentious about this president.

During lunch, he asked me, "Have you ever ridden aboard *Air Force One* or *Marine One?*"

"No," I said, "but I'm ready whenever you are."

"I'll be going back to Texas for Easter. Why don't you ride along?"

He didn't have to ask me twice.

The next morning, I arrived at the White House around 6:00 a.m. as

I usually did and then slipped into the Oval Office prior to the senior staff meeting scheduled at 7:30 a.m. As one of the senior staff who could stop in to see the president without an appointment, I had learned that the best time to catch him was between 7:00 a.m. and 7:30 a.m. Usually, this was unscheduled time for him and he was fresh and attentive, sometimes having just read a portion of Scripture and praying. Occasionally Andy Card joined us, but frequently it was just the president and me in those quiet, early-morning conversations.

On this particular morning, I wanted to discuss federal executions with him, since one was scheduled in the weeks ahead. We reviewed our standards for clemency, just as we had in Texas. The president then expressed a refrain he would repeat often to me: "I'm concerned about the number of blacks and Hispanics in federal prison as compared to the number of whites."

"Yes, sir. So am I." Inequities in our criminal justice system would be an ongoing issue throughout Bush's presidency, but one on which we made little progress.

We were already dealing with major issues when the atmosphere in the White House intensified during the first eleven days of April 2001, because of a confrontation with China. An American plane, a large, propeller-driven EP-3 carrying twenty-four crew members, had been conducting a routine reconnaissance mission in international airspace about seventy miles off China's shores.[2] The American plane was intercepted by two Chinese fighter jets, one of which struck one of the EP-3's propellers, shearing off the plane's nose cone and causing the American plane to plunge toward the ground. The Americans entered Chinese airspace and made an emergency landing on Hainan Island, desperately trying to destroy sensitive intelligence information before they hit the ground. The Chinese plane crashed as a result of their pilot's miscalculation.

Chinese soldiers captured the American crew and interrogated them long into the night. China launched a false campaign in the media, contending that the US plane had rammed its fighter jet, causing the crash and death of its pilot. China held our airmen hostage and demanded an apology, even though they knew that their pilot had caused the incident.

Clearly, China was testing America's new president. Bush recognized that the Chinese were not our friends, but he did not wish to alienate them either. As negotiations with China ensued, the National Security Council met repeatedly regarding this issue over the next ten days to determine how we would respond. Opinions varied. National Security Advisor Condi Rice and Secretary of State Colin Powell leaned toward apologizing to the Chinese to dispel the tension between the two countries and to get our airmen and plane back as quickly as possible. Secretary of Defense Don Rumsfeld did not favor apologizing because the "Chinese knew they were in the wrong."[3]

President Bush refused to issue an apology for an incident that had not been our fault. Eventually, we put out a statement regretting the loss of life and emphasizing the need to prevent further incidents.[4] Perhaps recognizing it was the best they were going to get from President Bush, the Chinese relented and released our airmen the morning of April 11, 2001.

I was in the Oval Office along with Condi, Dan Bartlett, Ari Fleischer, Karen Hughes, and Harriet Meirs when we received word that the Chinese had backed down from their demands. "There will be no gloating," the president said. "No victory dance." His were not the actions of an arrogant man, nor were they the response of a president looking for an opportunity to apologize for the United States, especially when we were not at fault.

He was glad the incident had concluded peacefully without further loss of life. It would be more than a month, however, before we got our reconnaissance plane back, after the communists had studied it and learned all they could from it.

The day following the pilots' release, after my assortment of scheduled meetings, an official White House driver transported me to the Pentagon to board *Marine One*, the president's helicopter that would take us to Andrews Air Force Base to board *Air Force One*. Ordinarily, *Marine One* lands on the South Lawn of the White House, but the lawn was being prepared for President Bush's first Easter egg roll. I had worn my cowboy boots for the trip home, and the president noticed them and nodded his approval. At 3:30 p.m., we took off for the short ride over to Andrews. "Look out the window," the president said as he pointed out various monuments along the way.

Washington is always a majestic sight, but even more so from the windows of *Marine One*.

We bounded out of the helicopter and up the stairway leading to the president's plane, the president sharply saluting the marines standing at attention as we passed by. We quickly settled in, and at 4:00 p.m., *Air Force One* took off from Andrews and headed to Fort Hood, in Killeen, Texas, about a three-hour flight and a short sixty-mile drive to my home in Austin.

The plane was spacious and majestic, a worthy symbol of American prestige and power. The president encouraged me to look at his suite, which included a bedroom and an office. "What do you think of *Air Force One?*" he asked. I smiled at him and nodded my head. "It is a fitting plane for the president of the United States," I replied. He laughed and went back to work.

The flight was relatively uneventful, and I was excited—I had not seen Becky and the boys for several months. We squeezed every moment out of the weekend and celebrated a wonderful Easter together as a family. Being reunited for a few days reminded me how much I missed my family and how I was looking forward to them joining me in Washington. All too soon, it was time for Becky and the boys to drive me back to Killeen.

I kissed my wife and sons good-bye, and at 4:35 p.m. Sunday afternoon, *Air Force One* roared down the runway, pointing us back toward the nation's capital. On board, the president looked tanned, as though he'd been out in the warm Texas sunshine over the weekend, and he seemed rejuvenated—yet the mood on the return trip was rather subdued. It seemed I wasn't the only one who missed Texas. I spent most of the flight studying the judiciary committee transcripts of the Clarence Thomas Supreme Court confirmation hearing from ten years earlier. I felt sure that we would soon be embroiled in confirmation hearings of our own, and I'd be right in the middle of all that, one way or another. I wanted to be prepared.

The media continued to report that I might be nominated in the case of a Supreme Court vacancy. Everyone knew that George W. Bush wanted to have a diverse court, and I had done more than a dozen interviews with reporters from the *Washington Post*, the *National Journal*, *US News and World Report*, the *Los Angeles Times*, and others. All had hinted that my name was in the mix. It was crazy; I'd been in Washington less than five months, but the more my name was in the media, the more talk there was about nominating a Hispanic to the Supreme Court. I continued to worry about the press attention, but eventually got more comfortable with it, believing that perhaps the anticipation that President Bush might make a historic pick would resonate with Hispanic voters and help Republicans in future elections.

During my service in the Bush administration, I was often asked to introduce the president at Cinco de Mayo events. Held in the Rose Garden or in the East Room, the ceremony usually featured mariachi performances and a Hispanic music artist, and then I introduced the president, who welcomed the guests. I was overwhelmed with pride in my Mexican American heritage and a sense of awe that here I was introducing the most powerful person in the world. The president usually spoke about immigration issues, but more so about inclusion, tolerance, and the importance of education as the key to all of our success in the world. He seemed to especially enjoy being with the Hispanic groups, and they related to him and his values.

On May 9, President Bush presented to the Senate his first group of nominees for the US Circuit Courts, a list that my team of lawyers and the DOJ lawyers had been working on for months. The nominees were a diverse group of first-rate legal minds, such that Democratic senator Patrick Leahy publicly noted that he thought them impressive. Apparently that meant nothing. Getting the nominees confirmed by the Senate would prove a long, exasperating process in which Democrats stonewalled many nominations. Some of the nominees would never be confirmed.

Meanwhile, Becky and I closed on a home she had found in Vienna, Virginia, about twelve miles west of Washington. It was an older mid-century-era house, but Becky saw potential. "Just imagine if this room didn't have foil wallpaper, and we painted the walls a creamy coffee color," she'd say, showing me another paint sample. A few weeks later, the movers arrived, along with Becky's dad, our sons, our dog, Sasha, and our parakeet, Turquoise, and we began a new adventure in our lives. Unfortunately, I wasn't much help in the moving-in process, as I was busy at work dealing with the highly publicized execution of Timothy McVeigh.

Along with his accomplice Terry Nichols, McVeigh had callously murdered 168 people, including 19 children, in April 1995, when they bombed the Federal Building in Oklahoma City. McVeigh's execution, scheduled for June 11, 2001, would be the first federal execution in forty years.

Four days prior to the execution date, I met with the president to discuss the details and any pending clemency requests. There was no question about McVeigh's guilt, nor were there any new issues that had not been reviewed in the courts. The president saw no reason to delay justice. At 7:52 a.m. on June 11, I informed the Department of Justice that the president had reviewed the matter carefully and saw no basis for clemency; therefore they should proceed with the execution. Timothy McVeigh was pronounced dead at 8:14 a.m., and at 8:15 a.m., I informed the president. An ugly, heart-rending chapter in American history came to a close.

———

It was an exciting time for Becky and me, yet also a stressful period in our marriage. For instance, the second day after Becky arrived, she was still unpacking boxes when I called her from the White House around one o'clock in the afternoon. "Please stop whatever you are doing, and get ready. We have to be at Vice President Cheney's home at five o'clock for dinner."

"What! Are you kidding?" Becky said. "I haven't even found the box with my clothes in it yet." Nor did she know where the vice president lived or how to get there. But she made it on time to the Naval Observatory, the home of American vice presidents since Walter Mondale first lived there in 1977.

The event was to honor and recognize some American artists. We met many new friends that evening, including Bill Coleman, who became a marvelous mentor to me. Bill was one of the first black fighter pilots in World War II, and later became a clerk to Supreme Court justice Thurgood Marshall, and then transportation secretary under President Gerald Ford. Over the years, Bill and I had many conversations about the law, and he expressed hopes for me to eventually move onto the Supreme Court.

Besides the great privilege of working in the White House, I enjoyed the opportunity to participate in other, less stressful activities with the president. For example, we occasionally played golf together on the South Course of Andrews Air Force Base. Always competitive, the president wanted to win—and so did I! But even on the golf course, work was never far from mind. Walking off a green after putting on July 3, 2001, the president told me that he had decided to appoint Bob Mueller as the new director of the FBI. Bob would take over the bureau in early September.

On our first Fourth of July in Washington, First Lady Laura Bush hosted a festive birthday party for the president at the White House. Although George W. Bush's birthday is on July 6, Mrs. Bush decided to combine the celebrations. This annual celebration at the residence would become a favorite for Becky and me during our time in Washington. My family and I attended the warm, personal affair, replete with Texas-style food. After dinner, the party moved out to the Truman Balcony overlooking the South Lawn, which by then was crowded with more invited guests. As the president and First Lady stepped out onto the balcony, the crowd on the grass below cheered and then spontaneously began singing "Happy Birthday."

As if on cue—and perhaps it was—a majestic fireworks display commenced over the Washington Monument. It was one of the most impressive sights I have ever witnessed.

When Congress recessed for the summer on August 4, the business aspects of the White House slowed down slightly. Nevertheless, I was surprised one day when the president tracked me down by phone. Thinking that some new crisis had arisen, I grabbed a pad and pen. "Hey, Fredo." The president used his favorite nickname for me. Bush had endearing nicknames for almost all of the people close to him.

"Yes, sir."

"Fredo, do you want to play horseshoes this afternoon? My brother Marvin is here, and we can get Andy Card; should be good."

"Of course."

At 5:30 p.m., the president, his brother Marvin, Andy, and I met at the horseshoe pit that had been installed near the White House swimming pool during Bush 41's administration. Marvin and I teamed up against the president and Andy, and the competition was intense. I played surprisingly well, and Marvin and I won the first two matches easily.

"Have you been practicing?" President Bush asked me several times.

I could tell the president's strong competitive nature was surging, so Marvin and I concentrated even harder on every shot, barely pulling out victories in the final two matches.

As we left the horseshoe pits, the president slapped me on the back and said, "Yes, sir, Fredo, you really showed me something today with your play."

I smiled and simply said, "Thank you, sir."

When the president left for a few weeks of vacation, the daily pace at the White House slowed even more. I took advantage of the lull by inviting some of my staff lawyers to join me in playing doubles on the White House tennis courts. Although it was sweltering hot with oppressive humidity, the lawyers did not want to miss the rare privilege of playing at the White House.

Despite these occasional light moments, the summer was anything but stress-free. Terror threats had been ramping up all summer long, and nearly every government agency in Washington was on heightened alert. As far back as the beginning of the Clinton administration, the United States government was wary of the al-Qaeda terrorist group and its leader, Osama bin Laden. That was part of the reason Bush had carried over from the Clinton administration two key players—Richard Clarke, counterterrorism advisor under Clinton, and George Tenet, director of the Central Intelligence Agency (CIA). Both Clarke and Tenet regarded threatened attacks on American interests as real. And terrorism threats were part of the president's daily briefing. Who could forget the 1993 bombing of the World Trade Center or many other acts of terrorism in recent years? These included the al-Qaeda bombing of Khobar Towers in Saudi Arabia (which killed nineteen US Air Force service members in 1996), the bombing of the American embassy in Nairobi in 1998, and the attack on the USS *Cole* that killed seventeen Americans as their ship sat docked in Yemen a year before we took office.

An open, gregarious, wonderfully likable fellow who cared about his agents, George Tenet was not given to exaggerations. As early as February 2001,

Tenet was sounding alarms. He told the Senate, "The threat from terrorism is real, it is immediate, and it is evolving . . . Usama Bin Laden [sic] and his global network of lieutenants and associates remain the most immediate and serious threat . . . He is capable of planning multiple attacks with little or no warning."[5]

By Memorial Day, Tenet was even more emphatic, reporting to the president that he was worried about increased chatter the CIA was picking up from terrorist groups around the world regarding something big happening soon. He had received information that a notorious al-Qaeda facilitator, Abu Zubaydah, was developing an attack plot, but the threat was thought to be overseas against American interests or against Jordan, Saudi Arabia, Israel, or Italy, the site of the G8 summit just two months away.[6]

By July, according to Tenet, Attorney General John Ashcroft had been briefed by senior counterterrorism officers who told him "that a significant terrorist attack was imminent and that preparations for an attack were in the late stages or already completed."[7] Sitting in the National Security Council meetings and the meetings with the principals committee, I was convinced that al-Qaeda was a serious threat, but no one was pointing to any plots or attacks within the United States. The assessment remained that the targets were likely to be overseas, rather than on our homeland. The threats continued to be troubling, but lacked specificity throughout the summer.

The Labor Day holiday marked the end of summer and the return to normal within the White House. On September 5, 2001, President Bush welcomed his friend Mexican president Vicente Fox and his First Lady, Marta Fox, to the White House. The two presidents had met previously in Mexico at San Cristòbal, Fox's family farm, and both shared real hope that they could carve out new immigration reforms and improve relations between our countries. Becky and I attended the arrival ceremony on the South Lawn, and it was a proud moment for all Mexican Americans. As I looked out at the large audience of Mexican Americans, I couldn't help feeling a sense of personal pride in my heritage. Later I attended the private meeting between the presidents in the Oval Office, and that evening Becky and I attended our first official state dinner, the first of the Bush presidency.

That alone made it special. Bush had invited an eclectic assortment of guests that evening, including Clint Eastwood, Alan Greenspan, Plácido Domingo, William Rehnquist, and Emilio Estevez, as well as politicians such as John McCain and Joe Biden. After dinner, fireworks filled the skies above the Washington Monument. This was no small demonstration—the fireworks were supposed to last for ten minutes but continued longer than twenty, after which "the sky was so bright you could barely look at it," as Karen Hughes later recalled.[8] Condi quipped, "We were testing the new missile defense system." Andy Card later described the first state visit as "a fairy-tale day." I found it inspiring that such an occasion was held in honor of the president of Mexico, given our country's rich Mexican heritage.

President Fox gave a speech in the US House chambers the following day, the first Mexican president ever to address a joint session of Congress. He was received warmly by both Democrats and Republicans. Later that afternoon, President Bush and President Fox flew to Ohio, where they spoke at the University of Toledo about immigration and the shared interests between our two countries. In his comments, President Bush said, "Fearful people build walls; confident people tear them down."[9] President Fox later commented that he firmly believed George W. Bush "had the opportunity to become the Latino Lincoln—giving hope to 12 million Mexican immigrants and, not coincidentally, realigning Hispanic voters into the Republican Party for a century."[10]

My work schedule on Monday, September 10, was relatively routine. I began the morning with the usual senior staff meeting, following my counsel's office staff meeting. During the day, I met with the president of the American Bar Association, chaired a strategy session with the lawyers on my staff regarding judicial nominations, and I participated in a meeting with White House and Justice Department officials concerned about an antitrust policy issue. I put some finishing touches on a speech I was to deliver the following morning in Norfolk, Virginia. My last meeting of the day was in the Situation Room on the basement level of the West Wing; the gathering discussed national security issues relating to North Korea. Routine. Nothing exceptional. Just another day in the White House.

It was dark by the time I finished, and as I left the West Wing that evening and walked to my car parked adjacent to the White House on West Executive Avenue, I could not imagine how my life was about to change—indeed, how every American's life was about to be affected—within the next twelve to fourteen hours.

CHAPTER 15

THE NEW PRIORITY: DEFEATING TERRORISM

The headlines and photos in the morning papers on September 12, 2001, told the horrendous and sobering story. President Bush had stressed the night before that our priorities had changed and defeating terrorism was job number one. That didn't mean that my lawyers and I could stop our other work to focus on terrorism; we were still responsible for counseling the president on judicial appointments, legislation, and a wide range of other issues, but everyone understood that we were now advising a wartime president. We also worried over the very real threats of imminent attacks, that our nation could be hit again with a follow-up attack. Preventing further terrorist attacks became a perpetual preoccupation for all of us.

Beginning with our senior staff meeting at 7:30 a.m., I attended one meeting after another, the first being the principals meeting in the Situation Room. The meeting that Wednesday included—as it frequently would from then on—CIA director George Tenet, Attorney General John Ashcroft, Treasury Secretary Paul O'Neill, and the recently appointed FBI director Bob Mueller, who had been on the job little more than a week. A meeting of the full National Security Council followed at 9:30. Tenet confirmed what we all suspected: Osama bin Laden's terrorist organization, al-Qaeda, was behind the attacks. Tenet's threat report was daunting. Any hope that we could lower our guard, that the final attack had been delivered, quickly dissipated as the principals listened intently to the CIA director's intelligence concerns.

Every meeting raised a raft of legal issues with which our lawyers had to grapple: What were the rules of engagement against a terrorist organization? Did the doctrine of self-defense define how imminent or dangerous a threat had to be before force could be used?

Some of our lawyers suggested that President Bush should publicly state that we were at war. Others urged caution because a declaration of war triggers all sorts of domestic statutes and international treaty obligations. To note just one, a formal declaration of war allows the president to collect "signals" intelligence—which could include radio, television, telephone, Internet, cell phones, and computers—outside the provisions of the Foreign Intelligence Surveillance Act (FISA) for a period of fifteen days. Collection of such data would become a major issue in the years ahead, and it was already on our radar that first Wednesday following the attacks. Everyone recognized that being able to obtain accurate and timely intelligence would be key to protecting our nation from further attacks.

Internationally, if the United States declared war, that would trigger obligations on the part of our allies to also join in a declaration of war against the enemy. That's what allies do—or are supposed to do, anyhow. Domestically, many contracts have an exclusion clause pertaining to "acts of God" or "conditions of war" that might cause some businesses to deny services or cease performing according to their prior agreements. So using the phrase *declaration of war* mattered greatly.

Perhaps, the lawyers pondered, it might be better to declare that the terrorists had attacked our freedoms or that we had suffered a terrorist assault, and the United States would wage war against terrorism.

The enormity of our legal tasks became apparent as we debated the domestic and international implications of a declaration of war by our Congress. We discussed whether the United States had ever declared war against a non-state actor, since al-Qaeda had no sovereign territory to attack.

What precedents did we have involving other nations? What legal questions surrounded the targeting of non-state actors? Would a congressional resolution authorizing the use of military force be sufficient, or did we need a declaration of war? One question led to another, with few easy answers.

In the Oval Office after another of many meetings, with these issues in mind, I attempted to caution the president about prematurely saying that we were at war, or even using phrases containing the word *war*, before knowing the full legal implications. Bush was having none of that. "You lawyers can call it whatever you want," he said. "As far as I'm concerned, we are at war."

At 11:30 a.m., the president met with congressional leaders from both parties in the Cabinet Room at the White House. I sat on the back row, in my usual spot, with my back to the Rose Garden just behind and to the right of the president. Bush was at his best, strong and forceful, and definitely not parsing his words. "These guys are like rattlesnakes," he said, speaking of al-Qaeda. "They strike and go back in their holes. We're not only going to go after the holes, we're going after the ranchers." He explained that the United States would punish anyone providing haven to terrorists, as well as the terrorists themselves. "This is a different type of war than our nation has ever fought," he said. "We will use our resources to find the enemy, we will rally the world, we will bring patience and focus and resources . . . we will not let them win the war by changing our way of life. This is more than a particular group, it is a frame of mind that threatens freedom—they hate Christianity, they hate Judaism, they hate everyone who doesn't think like them."[1]

At that meeting, the congressional leaders were eager to give the president the tools he needed to defend the country and to punish those responsible for killing innocent Americans. Although we had not yet prepared a formal document, they expressed bipartisan support for a congressional resolution authorizing the president to use all necessary force to defend our country. Speaker Dennis Hastert promised he would guide financing bills through the House of Representatives to help cover the anticipated additional costs of military action. Senate majority leader Tom Daschle asserted that Democrats would support the president, but emphasized that he expected consultations by the White House.

One touching moment occurred when aging Democratic senator Robert Byrd reminded everyone that he had served under eleven presidents, as far back as John F. Kennedy. He looked directly at President Bush and said, "I congratulate you on your leadership in this very difficult, unique situation . . . There is still an army who believe in this country, believe in the *divine* guidance that has always led our nation. Mr. President, mighty forces will come to your aid."[2]

The meeting with congressional leaders ended on a positive note, with members of both parties encouraging the president to address the American people in a joint session of Congress as soon as possible. Bush agreed; that was definitely something he wanted to do—when the time was right.

As chief of staff, Andy Card guided all of us during the awkwardness of our "new normal." The United States was the most powerful country on earth, yet we had failed to prevent an attack by a group of Islamic radicals, many of whom had trained in bin Laden's terrorist camps in Afghanistan, one of the poorest nations in the world, and some of whom had been operating unimpeded in the United States for months. So reflecting the adage that we simply did not know what we did not know and that almost anybody could be suspect, Andy instructed senior staff to inform our people to behave as though we were at war. "Exercise extra care to prevent the leaking of classified or sensitive information," he said. Even the distribution of the president's schedule would be limited. All West Wing tours were canceled indefinitely. "And exercise care in talking about sensitive information on the telephone. Shred all classified and sensitive papers. Assume that the enemy is monitoring our trash." We should be cautious even around the White House cleaning staff and others who moved through the building performing services and doing chores; they might have ulterior motives. "Do not allow any sensitive or classified paper to lie on your desk unless you are in the room," Andy instructed. His bottom line was obvious: trust no one.

Andy also asked us to encourage staff members to take advantage of stress counseling provided by the White House. While most of us seemed to be functioning fairly well without a pervading, pernicious sense of fear, the trauma all around us with which we were dealing at work and at home was real. I didn't engage with the counselors myself, but I appreciated the concern.

The White House also provided home-to-work-and-back government transportation for senior staff for a while. Both Andy and the president had been frustrated on 9/11 when they could not reach key staff members. Moreover, Andy wanted to ensure we had access to transportation in the event that we needed to move to a secure location at a moment's notice.

As we worked through security issues, access to the West Wing became much more limited, with the guarded perimeter outside the grounds increased. Anyone not working in the White House had to be accompanied by someone authorized to be in the West Wing. That meant that even my team of lawyers working across the street in the Old Executive Office Building could not come to see me unless accompanied by someone authorized to be in the White House. The new rules were inconvenient at times, but everyone understood their necessity.

Without anyone formally saying so, workdays at the White House stretched on a regular basis from already exhausting fourteen-hour days to eighteen-hour days. Many of us were sleep-deprived so it was not uncommon for somebody to yawn or nearly nod off in a meeting, despite the enormity of the issues being discussed. We simply weren't home long enough to get a decent night's sleep. Nobody complained, and while this was undoubtedly hard on our families, everyone understood the necessity of the increased workload.

Whether it was adrenaline or something else, I don't know, but I never grew weary. Quite the contrary, I felt energized. I recognized that each of us had an important job to do, regardless how many hours per day or days per week it took. Indeed, most of us in the senior levels of the administration responsible for national security worked seven-day weeks for months after 9/11.

Soon after the attacks, Andy created a group of experts to focus on individual, domestic areas of our nation's response to 9/11. This group, chaired by Deputy Chief of Staff Josh Bolten, was called the domestic consequences group and began meeting daily in the Roosevelt Room on the first floor of the White House. I added another meeting to my daily schedule.

There were plenty of domestic matters with which to cope. The president wanted to know how soon we could reopen the nation's airports. What about Wall Street, which had been closed down since the attacks? How soon could we get our stock market and banks up and running on some sort of normal basis? What could we do about the protection of power plants or other parts of the power grid, which we knew were considered relatively easy targets by terrorists? What about other aspects of our nation's vulnerable infrastructure?

During the first meeting of the new committee on September 13, the group discussed what the Treasury Department, the Securities and Exchange Commission, and the Federal Reserve Board could do to freeze and seize financial accounts and records used by the terrorists, as well as those of terrorist-linked organizations. Stopping the flow of money to the people trying to kill us was crucial.

The group also had to consider issues such as how the attacks might affect insurance coverage against loss of life and damage to property in New York, Virginia, and Pennsylvania.

Certainly one of the top priorities on my desk was the matter of drafting the congressional authorization to use military force (AUMF), granting the commander in chief the tools and ability to respond to the terrorist attacks. Frankly, as a simple legal matter, the expert lawyers on our team and I were convinced that the Constitution granted the president the power to protect our country in response to the attacks. A congressional resolution, however, would strengthen his legal authority and, we hoped, avoid politics becoming a factor. In other words, it would be more difficult for Democrats or Republicans to squawk later about President Bush taking action if the full Congress authorized it from the beginning.

Because of the nature of the attacks, the American response was not simply a matter of declaring war on the enemy. Unlike World War II, in which America was attacked by Japan and we declared war in response, there was not a nation-state on which to declare war. Consequently, part of my responsibilities included determining the legal authorities to use military force against terrorists and to covertly collect intelligence information.

I asked Tim Flanigan to shepherd the drafting of the AUMF. An outstanding lawyer, Tim was excellent at posing the right questions and presenting the issues in cogent terms. Always ready with a humorous remark—a trait no doubt necessary for a husband and his wife who had a large family—Tim could also defuse tension better than anybody I knew. Most importantly, I had absolute confidence in Tim. He went to work on the AUMF.

The mountain of legal issues continued to grow, with each group of lawyers assigned to an issue broaching new, unprecedented areas needing clarification. The military lawyers gave extensive briefings on the "law of proportionality" in wartime. Proportionality implies that a nation may respond to an attack using only such firepower as necessary to destroy a target. For instance, if one cruise missile is enough to destroy an enemy facility, it would be disproportional to strike the area with ten missiles. In a more absurd illustration, if an enemy threw an egg and hit our president, we would not blow up their country's airports. A response should be proportional.

But what sort of response is proportional to the flagrant killing of nearly three thousand people and destroying billions of dollars' worth of real estate and resources? The key standard seemed to be "What is reasonable?"—with acceptable levels of collateral damage depending on the circumstances. That sounded good, but it would be a difficult guide for our military commanders, and even more difficult for our troops, since they would be dealing with an enemy that did not wear uniforms and fought and hid among the civilian population, often using them as human shields.

The lawyers and I also had long discussions over the issues of our country's self-defense and our ability to preempt potential attacks. How imminent did a threat have to be before we could take action in self-defense? Was it enough for a gun to be loaded and cocked? Or must an enemy actually have to be pointing it in our direction with a finger on a trigger? And what about potential nuclear or biological terrorism? Was even more required to justify self-defense, or less? What about verbal or written threats? Osama bin Laden had spoken quite clearly about his intentions to harm America long before 9/11. And was it legitimate to argue that the magnitude of the attack and the potential horrendous degree of harm that would result from the use of weapons of mass destruction—nuclear, biological, or chemical—justified a preemptive attack by the United States? These matters were no longer intriguing points to debate in a classroom; these were real concerns we were dealing with every day.

Because we were discussing highly classified activities in a time of tense hostilities, the number of participants in these meetings was kept as small as possible. Nevertheless, the discussions often grew pointed and intense. The lawyers unabashedly challenged one another, but generally the discussions remained civil and respectful. Lawyers tend to disagree on legal issues; that's what lawyers do. Given the nature of the questions that intersected with the president's powers under the Constitution, our international obligations, and Congress's role, I was not surprised that a room full of lawyers did not always arrive at unanimity at the conclusion of the meeting.

As counsel to the president, I was the top White House lawyer. But I wanted and depended upon the wisdom possessed by the great team of lawyers that surrounded me—not only at the White House, but also those at the Departments of Justice, State, Defense, the CIA, and the NSA. My usual manner in most meetings was to ask questions, as a judge normally would, keeping my opinions to myself, while encouraging others in the room to carry the discussion of contending viewpoints. I wanted to hear everyone's ideas, and I especially wanted the DOJ lawyers to hear the sometimes opposite opinions and appreciate the various views. In the end, I deferred to the DOJ opinion, since by law the Justice Department was charged with advising the executive branch and, if challenged, the DOJ would defend executive actions in the courts.

My job was then to report to the president what I considered to be our *best* option. I could not walk into the Oval Office with multiple legal positions for the president to mull over. Instead, I normally took him only one position—the one DOJ felt strongest about after considering all the other options. I had no statutory authority; I was simply an advisor. If there were strongly divergent views, I'd let the president know that virtually, but in all cases I'd say, "I think you should go with the DOJ." In addition to legal advice, I sometimes gave President Bush my views on policy. But he was the president, elected to make decisions, and he often reminded me of that, sometimes with a twinkle in his eyes, sometimes with firmness in his voice.

On Friday, September 14, after several intense national security meetings at the White House, I met Becky and accompanied her to the National Day of Prayer and Remembrance service held in the majestic Washington National Cathedral, the gorgeous stone edifice with soaring one-hundred-foot-high ceilings and magnificent stained glass windows overlooking the city.

The service was sad, yet inspiring at the same time. The cathedral was packed with people, including five US presidents, two US vice presidents, cabinet secretaries, Supreme Court justices, members of Congress, and the general public. Religious leaders of the three monotheistic religions, Christianity, Judaism, and Islam—the ostensible religion of the terrorists who had attacked us—took part in the service. The music was powerfully evocative, with hymns such as "O God, Our Help in Ages Past," and "The Lord's Prayer," sung by soprano Denyce Graves, setting the tone for a strong but comforting sermon by evangelist Billy Graham.

President Bush presented an eloquent message crafted by Mike Gerson, including the scripture, "The LORD is my light and my salvation—whom shall I fear? . . . Though war break out against me, even then I will be confident" (Psalm 27:1, 3 NIV). The service concluded with "The Battle Hymn of the Republic," and the world watched as five American presidents—Gerald Ford, Jimmy Carter, George H. W. Bush, Bill Clinton, and George W. Bush—and other national leaders stood, singing, "Glory, glory hallelujah, His truth is marching on."

Because of our true faith in God, each of us left the cathedral encouraged and more strongly resolved to do what was right. I knew that President Bush would need that extra spiritual strength. He was leaving right after the service on his first trip to New York City and his initial encounter with victims' families and the rescue workers picking their way through the twisted steel and rubble of what only three days earlier had been a symbol of America's economic might.

Meanwhile, I went back to the White House for another meeting of the domestic consequences group, this one focusing on the airline industry. Although the airlines would resume flights the week following the 9/11 attacks, they were reeling financially. The immediate downturn in passenger travel had crippled Northwest, Continental, and America West airlines in particular, and there was a real question whether some of them would survive at all long-term. Industry officials also worried about potential liability for not doing more to prevent their planes being used in the attacks, and had concerns whether their insurance would cover losses. United, Delta, and American, while viable, faced serious challenges.

The president had called an "all hands on deck" meeting at Camp David on Saturday and Sunday to review our readiness posture and plan for the future. Vice President Cheney, Colin Powell, Don Rumsfeld, and Condi Rice were already there on Friday evening; others were on their way. I worked late on Friday evening, digesting briefing papers and developing a better understanding of how the legal issues might intertwine with policy options to be decided that weekend. Early the next morning, I headed to Camp David, about an hour's drive from my home.

Located in Catoctin Mountain Park in Frederick County, Maryland, the presidential retreat is a lushly wooded 125-acre compound with rustic cabins as well as many of the comforts and communications capabilities of the White House. Earlier in the year, the president and First Lady had invited Becky and me to spend a summer weekend with them at Camp David. Pennsylvania governor Tom Ridge and his wife, Michele, joined us, as did Texas Speaker of the House Pete Laney and his wife, Nelda.

We had all enjoyed a fabulous time of fun and relaxation, taking long walks on Camp David's many trails, riding bicycles, bowling, shooting skeet, working out in the gym, and at night we watched a movie together.

When I arrived at Camp David on Saturday, September 15, an entirely different mood pervaded the retreat. Armed navy personnel and marines from the Marine Barracks in Washington were posted at the security gates and checkpoints. There was no friendly banter with the guards, no unnecessary chatter. Everyone was on high alert.

Although the dress code for the weekend was casual, a brisk autumn chill was in the air, so most of the participants, including me, wore slacks and a sports coat. Several added fleece jackets for warmth. The president wore slacks, a polo shirt, and a green Camp David heavy windbreaker. We met in the wood-paneled conference room of Laurel Lodge, the main conference center at Camp David, containing a large, square, wooden table accommodating twenty people, with extra chairs along the back walls on both sides for additional participants. On one side of the room stood a grouping of six flags, including the Stars and Stripes and a flag bearing the presidential seal. On the opposite wall, beneath an old wooden clock, hung a large, historic map of the local area.

The collective wisdom gathered around the large square table that morning to discuss America's immediate course of action was impressive. I allowed my eyes to move from one person to another, noting his or her area of expertise. Starting with the deputy national security advisor, Steve Hadley, my gaze moved to vice chairman of the Joint Chiefs of Staff, General Richard Myers; chairman of the Joint Chiefs of Staff, General Hugh Shelton; the national security advisor, Condi Rice; the White House chief of staff, Andy Card; director of the CIA, George Tenet; the treasury secretary, Paul O'Neill; the FBI director, Bob Mueller; the deputy defense secretary, Paul Wolfowitz; Defense Secretary Don Rumsfeld; Secretary of State Colin Powell; the president; Vice President Dick Cheney; Attorney General John Ashcroft; and the chief of staff to the vice president, Scooter Libby. As the White House counsel, I sat at the far end of the table within earshot of the president.

Once the meeting convened, in no time, briefing papers cluttered the table along with water bottles, coffee thermoses, and mugs. *We are going to be here for a while.*

First up was Director Tenet, who presented a briefing on a plan to send CIA operatives into Afghanistan to begin gathering intelligence on al-Qaeda and Taliban targets. Although both groups were little known to most Americans prior to 9/11, they were well known and feared in Afghanistan. When the Soviet Union invaded Afghanistan in 1979, Islamic fighters from a variety of groups formed a loose alliance known as the *mujahideen*. With the help of American weapons and cash, as well as funding by Saudi Arabia, these "freedom fighters" drove the mighty Soviet Union out of Afghanistan. The country was loaded with armed Islamic militants flush with victory. The Taliban, an Islamic militant group led by Mullah Omar, seized control of Kabul in 1996, about the time al-Qaeda leader Osama bin Laden, whose Saudi citizenship had been revoked, was "encouraged" to leave Sudan. Bin Laden returned to Afghanistan, where he had once fought with the *mujahideen*, and found a welcome with the Taliban, who condoned and often supported bin Laden's efforts to train terrorists at camps in Afghanistan.

Bin Laden's terrorist threats were well known by US intelligence throughout the Clinton administration, as Tenet, who had served in the previous administration, could attest. A presidential daily briefing for President Clinton on December 4, 1998, was titled "Bin Laden Preparing to Hijack US Aircraft and Other Attacks." As Tenet later said, "Unfortunately, even when our warnings were heard, little was done domestically to protect the United States against the threat."[3]

During his Camp David presentation titled "Destroying International Terrorism," Tenet was joined by his deputy, John McLaughlin, and counterterrorism chief Cofer Black. The CIA, Tenet said, had the plan and ability to shut down the terrorist havens in Afghanistan, "go after their leadership, shut off their money, and pursue al-Qaeda in ninety-two countries around the world."[4] Tenet and his colleagues emphasized, "We are ready to carry out all these actions immediately, if given the authorities to act," which implied permission to expand covert operations.[5] Tenet suggested we work closely with the Northern Alliance in Afghanistan, a ragtag but deeply committed group opposed to the Taliban. The leader of the Northern Alliance, Ahmad Shah Massoud, had been assassinated by al-Qaeda a few days before 9/11—most likely, it was now easier to see, as an effort to diminish the Northern Alliance's will and ability to counteract the Taliban prior to the attack on America.

Next up was General Shelton, an imposing military presence at six foot five inches, but his initial presentation produced strong reactions, since his first option, the use of cruise missile strikes in Afghanistan, looked similar to what the United States had done after terrorist attacks in the 1990s. His second option was cruise missiles accompanied by air strikes by bombers.

President Bush wasn't buying that for a moment. He wanted US military forces on the ground as soon as possible. "We need to unleash holy hell," he told the chairman of the Joint Chiefs. "We're not just going to pound sand."[6]

As with all meetings of the National Security Council, we had an agenda prepared and facilitated by Condi Rice, but the discussions during that morning session were freewheeling, lurching in various directions. Treasury Secretary O'Neill reported on the difficulties in getting financial information about known terrorists and terrorist groups, sparking a lively discussion about the ability and legal authority of government agencies to search the Internet and examine ATM cards and bank account activities of foreigners suspected of terrorism. Yet everyone agreed that bin Laden's financial accounts should be found, seized, and the assets used to help offset the enormous damages of 9/11.

The conversation careened into a candid discussion about our failure to anticipate the 9/11 attacks or to collect actionable intelligence about the hijackers in time to prevent their despicable actions. The president wanted answers. He did not point fingers, but he wanted to know how such a thing could happen in order to prevent a similar tragedy from ever happening again. Everyone agreed that we had to find ways to better collect intelligence information and share it within our agencies, as well as with our allies and state and local governments and law enforcement. We agreed it was vital that we reject policies and practices used in the past that "stove piped" and compartmentalized the collection and analysis of intelligence data. We would seek to change the laws and policies that had discouraged the sharing of intelligence data—especially between the CIA and the FBI. John Ashcroft and the Justice Department were assigned the task of leading the effort to develop a comprehensive new counterterrorism bill that we could send to Congress.

There was some good news. Our intelligence agencies reported that due to improvements in technology, our government was now able to collect electronic information in ways never envisioned by the drafters of the Foreign Intelligence Surveillance Act of 1978 (FISA), passed after the Watergate scandal in the 1970s. Technology and electronic communications had changed drastically since then. We could act much faster on intelligence, and we needed to do so.

Since 1978, our intelligence agencies had been working under FISA, which required advance approval from one member of the FISA Court, consisting (at that time) of seven federal judges—all of whom were selected by the chief justice of the United States.

Under FISA, the Department of Justice was required to submit an application and obtain a warrant from a federal judge on the FISA Court before collecting certain types of electronic information. While FISA is a valuable law, it could also be burdensome and—in the new terrorism-plagued world in which we now lived—potentially deadly, causing delays in the collection of information and action on it to prevent an attack. Several people in the room encouraged the president to seek legislation that would fix that problem and streamline the FISA procedures.

The president understood the challenges imposed by FISA, and its unintended consequences of slowing our ability to quickly collect electronic communications between terrorists, especially those communicating on easily transferable or disposable "no monthly contract" cell phones, not to mention stolen phones and computers. These discussions planted the seeds for what would soon grow into some of the most important protections provided by the USA PATRIOT Act, as well as a controversial classified electronic surveillance program authorized by the president.

Discussion then turned to who was responsible for the deaths of nearly three thousand Americans. Which countries had assisted al-Qaeda, either overtly or indirectly? We discussed the obvious suspects such as Iran and North Korea, sworn enemies of our country. And of course we considered Iraq. With Saddam Hussein's history of animus toward America, we would have been remiss to disregard Iraq without careful investigation. Nevertheless, when Deputy Secretary Paul Wolfowitz suggested we broaden our efforts beyond Afghanistan and into Iraq, President Bush balked. He wanted the focus on destroying al-Qaeda first in Afghanistan. He did agree, however, with Paul's contention that wherever we struck, we should make extensive use of our special operations forces, rather than trying to overwhelm the enemy with sheer numbers of soldiers. The leaders around the table nodded in affirmation.

No one in that room was looking for an excuse to invade Iraq—a popular contention in the media in the years to follow. On the contrary, Powell and Rumsfeld both discouraged such talk because there was no apparent evidence linking Iraq to the horrific attacks. Moreover, if we retaliated by invading Iraq, we could jeopardize support of the United Nations and our North Atlantic Treaty Organization allies, which we wanted as we took action against those who had conducted or assisted in the attacks against our country.

Vice President Cheney and Director Tenet concurred that while we should keep a watch on Iraq, now was not the time for action there. The vice president emphasized that taking down the Taliban was our top priority. Tenet predicted that the Hussein regime in Iraq would make a mistake in judgment at some point, likely providing a stronger justification for the regime change that had been approved by the US Congress under the Clinton administration.

On the other hand, our working relationship with Pakistan was critical. It was vital that we persuade the Pakistani government that it was not in their best interests to provide sanctuary to al-Qaeda. In the past, the US government had been able to influence the leaders of Pakistan, as well as some in Afghanistan. That might work again. We had to be careful, however, not to push too hard, because if the Musharraf government in Pakistan toppled, their nuclear arsenal would be up for grabs, and the terrorists who had attacked us were probably within closest reach. Nevertheless, the president was emphatic that Pakistan had to make a decision: Were they with us or against us? There was no more sitting on the fence. Fortunately for us— and for the rest of the world—Pakistan at least leaned in our direction and decided to stop serving as a safe haven to al-Qaeda and the Taliban.

The next question was how we should best initiate military action. All sorts of possibilities were considered. Rumsfeld wondered aloud if we should simply hit Afghanistan; Tenet suggested that we might be able to sway the Taliban to turn against al-Qaeda. Colin Powell suggested that we give the Taliban an ultimatum, a warning, since our country did not go to war without first warning the other side. He also reiterated the warning to Pakistan: Are you with us or against us? General Shelton assured the president the military would be ready, although he stressed the need for cooperation by our "friends'" in the region. The vice president cautioned that whatever we did, we must be aggressive in taking out the enemy and discouraging a counterattack.

The president dismissed the group for a break, and when we reconvened that afternoon, he went around the table asking each principal for his or her best input on the road ahead. By day's end, the initial stages of America's response to 9/11 were decided. Top priority was preventing another attack, and that involved drastically improving our intelligence programs to provide better security to the American people. At the same time, we were going to pursue the enemy that had hit us.

Sitting at the Camp David conference table, I felt a sense of confidence and optimism. More than ever, I was thankful for the willingness of George W. Bush to surround himself with wise counselors. His experienced advisors—Cheney, Powell, Rumsfeld, Shelton, Myers, and others—understood the ramifications of sending young American men and women into battle, and they were only willing to do so cautiously and purposefully.

The discussion had been lively but serious. President Bush saw matters clearly. He knew that regardless of the legal terminology, America was at war. The president had challenged us, questioned us about capabilities, vulnerabilities, and authorities. Even more than his words, his demeanor impressed me. He was absolutely in charge; he was focused, straightforward, and tough. If anyone had any doubt previously, George W. Bush truly became a commander in chief that weekend.

The strategy session at Camp David changed the world forever. As I write these words, it has been fifteen years since 9/11. Although we have had some serious setbacks and failures, during that time we have not had another 9/11-type terrorist strike against our homeland. That has not been accidental or merely good luck. There is a direct historical line back to that room at Camp David. The plans, programs, and the unrelenting pursuit of the evil intent on destroying us that came out of those discussions have been enormously significant in maintaining our safety and way of life.

My mind pondered the many issues as I drove home through the darkness after the meeting at Camp David. I had spent the weekend with the president of the United States and some of the most influential leaders in our country. But when I walked through the front door of my family's home, I was just Daddy and Becky's husband. My wife's and sons' smiling faces put my work in perspective. Protecting your family and mine was our top priority.

———

Back in Washington the following week, I immediately began working with the administration lawyers on the many legal implications arising from the Camp David decisions. A big question was: What are the legal limitations on our ability to collect electronic communications between terrorists, especially if those communications took place between people located in the United States? We also had to sort out jurisdiction issues with the Justice Department. It was clear after Camp David that we were not simply going to treat the terrorist attack as a law enforcement matter and attempt to capture and bring perpetrators back into our courts for trial. We were going to war against the enemies of freedom.

Tuesday morning, September 18, on the one-week anniversary of the attacks, the entire White House staff went outside and stood on the South Lawn along with President Bush, the First Lady, Vice President Cheney, and Mrs. Cheney for a period of silence at 8:46 a.m., the moment the first plane hit the South Tower. As I bowed my head, I recommitted myself to always remembering the real human toll of the attacks. Because of evil, mothers and fathers mourned for the loss of their sons and daughters; boys and girls had lost mommies and daddies. Husbands and wives had gone to bed the previous night without their spouses who had been vibrantly alive at 8:45 a.m. on that awful day. As we walked silently back inside the White House, I thought of my own family. I could not imagine losing my wife and sons as so many had on 9/11, helpless to do anything about it. The people who had suffered such pain, and the millions of Americans who were counting on the president to do something about it, were depending on us to speak and act for them.

That was the president's focus. And that was my motivation.

That same day, September 18, 2001, Congress passed a joint resolution granting President Bush an authorization for use of military force (AUMF), clearly acknowledging the president had the constitutional authority to defend America. Although this was technically not a declaration of war, Congress justified a military response to protect our national security and our citizens both at home and abroad. The law empowered the president "to use all necessary and appropriate force against those nations, organizations, or persons he determines planned, authorized, committed, or aided the terrorist attacks that occurred on September 11, 2001."[7] The AUMF was overwhelmingly approved by both Republicans and Democrats. Our legislators were united in a way they had not been since Pearl Harbor.

The following day, I went to the Capitol to meet with Senate leaders Tom Daschle and Trent Lott, as well as House leaders Dennis Hastert and Richard Gephardt. The topic was counterterrorism. Attorney General John Ashcroft represented the executive branch, along with his deputy, Larry Thompson; Viet Dinh, the assistant attorney general for policy; and the legislative affairs assistant to the president, Nick Calio. Ashcroft's group had been working diligently on what would come to be known as the USA PATRIOT Act, and Congress wanted to be a player in those negotiations. Rightly so, they expressed concerns about doing what we needed to do to thwart terrorists, while guarding the civil liberties of American citizens. Nevertheless, nobody at that meeting showed any reluctance to give the president the authority he needed to protect our country.

On Thursday evening, September 20, 2001, the president addressed the nation in a joint session of Congress. He expressed concern for the families who lost loved ones in the attacks, and he wasted no time in informing the country that we were at war against al-Qaeda: "On September the eleventh, enemies of freedom committed an act of war against our country."[8]

With conviction and compassion, the president said, "Great harm has been done to us. We have suffered great loss. And in our grief and anger we have found our mission and our moment. Freedom and fear are at war. The advance of human freedom—the great achievement of our time, and the great hope of every time—now depends on us . . . We will not tire, we will not falter, and we will not fail."[9]

Throughout the evening, Congress rose to its feet again and again in heartfelt applause, not the politically correct expressions of partisan politicians who know they are on camera. No, these were clear statements that despite our differences, we were united.

In perhaps the most poignant moment of a speech that had many special moments, the president held up a police badge for the world to see as he said, "Some will carry memories of a face and a voice gone forever. And I will carry this: it is the police shield of a man named George Howard, who died at the World Trade Center trying to save others. It was given to me by his mom, Arlene, as a proud memorial to her son. This is my reminder of lives ended, and a task that does not end."[10]

In a sobering yet inspiring statement, the president concluded, "The course of this conflict is not known, yet its outcome is certain. Freedom and fear, justice and cruelty, have always been at war, and we know that God is not neutral between them."[11] There was no question in anyone's mind that when the president ended by saying, "And may God bless America," he meant it.

In a strikingly memorable moment, as President Bush made his way down from the podium and through the House Chamber, shaking hands with attendees as he went, when he met Democrat Senate majority leader Tom Daschle in the aisle, the president stopped and hugged Daschle. That night, in this critically important moment in the history of the United States, we were not Republicans or Democrats; we were all *Americans*.

In my estimation, George Bush's September 20, 2001, speech to the joint session of Congress was one of his best. I was not alone in that opinion. Afterward, Supreme Court justice Clarence Thomas congratulated him and said, "God bless you!"

President Bush replied, "He already has."

A hint of a smile crossed the burly judge's face. In his deep baritone voice, Justice Thomas said, "Ride tall in the saddle, buddy."

Ride tall, indeed. The lawyers on my staff, some of whom had clerked for Justice Thomas, knew exactly what he meant. The road ahead would be treacherous, and there would be many temptations to back down. But President Bush had stated our intention to protect our homeland, while tracking down al-Qaeda and the Taliban in Afghanistan and bringing to justice those responsible for attacking our nation.

Now it was up to us to do it.

CHAPTER 16

BATTLES ON THE HOME FRONT

The sun was setting in Afghanistan on October 7, 2001, when General Tommy Franks appeared on a secure television monitor from Tampa, Florida. In Washington, DC, Secretary of Defense Don Rumsfeld and the new chairman of the Joint Chiefs of Staff, Dick Myers, watched from the Pentagon. The president was at Camp David, but was not on the teleconference.

General Franks conducted a round-robin, last-minute check with his top commanders in Kuwait, Bahrain, Masira Island off Oman, and Saudi Arabia, and each officer who was tasked with leading a major component into the war in Afghanistan was set to report on the readiness of the US forces under his command. General Franks informed his officers that he had received the execute order from the secretary of defense. As the general moved from one commander to the next, the responses were the same: no issues; all indicators are green; our military forces are set to go. Finally, General Franks looked to the director of the CIA, George Tenet, who was on the teleconference from Langley.

"No issues, General," Tenet reported.

Franks faced his camera in the secure conference room of the US Army's central command in Tampa. "All right," he said. "I'm satisfied. Kinetics begin at 1230 hours East Coast time . . . any questions?" He paused momentarily, and when no questions were forthcoming, General Franks gave his officers a final exhortation. "This is the beginning of tomorrow's history," he said. "I want you to focus on two things: accomplish the mission, and protect the force."[1]

And with that, Operation Enduring Freedom began. It was the first step in the response of the United States—with the support of thirty-one other nations—to bring to justice those who had killed our citizens on 9/11.

Following the teleconference, Defense Secretary Rumsfeld and General Richard Myers called General Franks. "General, the president said to extend to you his respect and best wishes. We're going to finish what began on September 11."

"God bless you, Mr. Secretary," General Franks responded. "God bless America."[2]

Don Rumsfeld later recalled, "In the early hours of the Afghan war, I watched video links from aircraft dropping munitions. Among the first targets were the al-Qaeda training camps at Tarnak Farms and Duranta. B-52s dropped two-thousand-pound bombs on the tunneled caves of Tora Bora near the Pakistani border. All known Taliban tanks were targeted. Fuel depots, training camps, radars, runways, and the few dubious aircraft in the Taliban air force were hit. Over the course of five nights, every fixed enemy target that American intelligence had identified in Afghanistan was attacked."[3] Because so many people were suffering under the Taliban, as well as from a recent drought, American aircraft also carried humanitarian aid, dropping more than 210,000 packages of food for the Afghans within the first forty-eight hours of the war.[4]

President Bush addressed the nation shortly after the first bombs exploded. "On my orders," he said, "the United States military has begun strikes against al-Qaeda terrorist training camps and military installations of the Taliban regime in Afghanistan . . . A commander in chief sends America's sons and daughters into battle in a foreign land only after the greatest care and a lot of prayer . . . I'm speaking to you today from the Treaty Room of the White House, a place where American presidents have worked for peace. We're a peaceful nation. Yet, as we have learned so suddenly and so tragically, there can be no peace in a world of sudden terror. In the face of today's new threat, the only way to pursue peace is to pursue those who threaten it."[5]

Bush was putting the world on notice: the war was on.

In the White House the following day, administration lawyers went back to work fighting a different sort of war, confirming that the president had the legal authorities he needed to press the battle against terrorism on the home front as well as overseas. John Ashcroft and his team at the Justice Department, with some input from the counsel's office, put together the USA PATRIOT Act—USA PATRIOT being the acronym for "Uniting and Strengthening America by Providing Appropriate Tools Required to Intercept and Obstruct Terrorism." The PATRIOT Act would tear down the wall of separation between our various intelligence and law enforcement agencies—most notably the FBI and CIA—so they could more freely share information about potential threats. It would give to the intelligence agencies many of the same tools employed by law enforcement to track criminals. The PATRIOT Act passed with overwhelming Democrat and Republican support and was signed into law by President Bush on October 26, 2001. And not a moment too soon.

The rules had changed. We were now dealing with a whole new breed of enemies who could strike in ways we had hardly considered. Eleven days earlier, our country had been shaken again, this time by threats of bioterrorism when a powdery white substance was found in a letter received and opened by a staff member of Senate majority leader Tom Daschle. The hand-printed envelope contained anthrax, a deadly spore-forming bacterium that can enter a body through the skin, by breathing it, or by eating anthrax-tainted food. Inhaling anthrax spores the size of a speck of dust can be fatal, usually within a few days unless treated with antibiotics such as ciprofloxacin (Cipro) or doxycycline, drugs that were not readily stocked in large amounts by most metropolitan pharmacies. Anthrax, after all, was something that occurred around cattle, sheep, goats, or horses. Now it was feared that anthrax had gotten into the ventilation system of the Hart Senate Office Building, and may have been inhaled by people throughout the complex.

When tests confirmed that anthrax contamination had also been detected in the Dirksen Senate Office Building's mailroom, as well as other locations in Hart, all congressional buildings were closed. Many people on Capitol Hill believed the anthrax was the second round of terrorist attacks coming on the heels of 9/11.[6]

At least twenty-eight people in Daschle's office tested positively for anthrax exposure, which sent the anxiety level soaring. Hundreds of people who worked on Capitol Hill lined up for nasal swab tests. Thousands more were tested over the next few days. Meanwhile, we waited, hoped, and prayed. Although several people were extremely sick, none of those exposed in the senator's office had died.

Then a few days after the anthrax letter had been opened, an individual who worked and lived miles away from Capitol Hill was admitted to a community hospital with signs of anthrax exposure. The patient was a postal worker.

When he first learned this, Senator Bill Frist, a heart-transplant surgeon who was providing information to the public, was alarmed. Frist recalls, "The importance of this seemingly innocuous bit of information could not be overstated: A person who had not been anywhere near the Hart Building . . . now had signs of anthrax. It would have been impossible for someone miles away from the location where the letter was actually opened to have inhaled spores from the anthrax-laced envelope. I feared that the news could portend a much larger scenario. Was this an expansion of terrorist activity? Were there other deadly letters going around the country? Would we start seeing cases elsewhere? Were postal workers safe, or would we have to shut down the mail system in Washington, perhaps even nationally?"[7]

The first postal worker who had been exposed died the following day. Cause of death? Anthrax inhalation. A second postal worker passed away as a result of anthrax inhalation a short while later. Postal facilities in the DC area were instructed to pass all mail through radiation machines because gamma rays could kill anthrax. All mail sent to government offices, including the White House, was thoroughly irradiated. Nearly ten thousand people in Washington received Cipro during that time. Five people eventually died because of anthrax—not all of them in the Capital area—and seventeen others were severely sickened.

Besides the human toll and the enormous costs of trying to treat thousands of people who might have been exposed, the anthrax attack reminded all of us in the White House how vulnerable our homeland was to similar attacks. One letter had shut down the entire legislative branch of the government. Following the attack, the Hart Senate Office Building remained closed for three months. Meanwhile, another anthrax-laced letter was intercepted and opened safely in a laboratory. The letter had been addressed to Senator Patrick Leahy, chairman of the judiciary committee.

The FBI interviewed more than five thousand people trying to discover the perpetrators of the anthrax attack, but the case was never solved.

With Washington still reeling from the aftermath of 9/11, the deadly anthrax attacks added another layer of heaviness and wreaked fear and near panic in the capital. Concerns about other attacks—including everything from chemical and biological warfare to nuclear suitcase bombs—were not the stuff of science fiction movies any longer. They intruded in our everyday lives. People were clearly and justifiably worried that our nation was not safe.

We soon learned that not even the White House was totally secure. On October 18, 2001, the air sensors in the White House tested positive for botulinum toxin, one of the most lethal substances on earth. A few grams of the stuff dispersed in the air over a city could kill millions of people. From my vantage point in the White House, I wondered if we might be targeted next. I also worried about attacks that might affect my family.

The White House biodetectors had indicated at least two separate "hits," which meant that anyone in the building at the time might have been exposed or had possibly inhaled the deadly toxin without even knowing it. That included the president and First Lady, Vice President Cheney, Karl Rove, Karen Hughes, Harriet Miers, all of the White House staff, the maintenance crew, anyone who may have been visiting at the time the botulinum was dispersed, and, of course, me.

The president had left for Shanghai the previous day, his first trip out of the country since 9/11. Vice President Cheney called to inform him of the potential bio-attack. Deputy National Security Advisor Steve Hadley explained the seriousness of the threat to the president and told him that the FBI was conducting tests on mice. The next twenty-four hours would be crucial, Steve told him. "If the mice were still scurrying around, feet down, we would be fine. But if the mice were on their backs, feet up, we were goners," the president recalled later.[8]

The night of the eighteenth, I was on the phone with Tom Ridge (recently appointed Homeland Security advisor), John Ashcroft, and Steve Hadley past one o'clock in the morning, along with doctors from the CDC, attempting to deal with the botulinum threat. The doctors focused on data collection and wanted to determine the medical backgrounds for all of us who had possibly been exposed. Most early indications were good, so we hoped we didn't have a problem, but we wouldn't know for sure until additional tests results were analyzed in the morning, after the twenty-four-hour danger period had expired, when symptoms such as paralysis would begin to show in anyone exposed.

When we felt certain the botulinum scare was a false alarm, Steve called Condoleezza Rice, who was traveling with the president's entourage. His message was simple but reassuring: "Feet down, not feet up."[9]

Somewhere in the midst of the crisis, somebody suggested that those of us in the White House receive various inoculations, which we did. There were no such provisions for our family members. That wasn't surprising, since there was no contingency plan for spouses or family even in the event of a nuclear attack or an attack such as 9/11. Plans existed to move key government officials to safe locations, but other than the First Lady and the vice president's wife, nothing similar was in place for spouses or families. In the immediate aftermath of 9/11, some of the White House wives lamented that they were in the dark, so Becky and Kathie Card called Joyce Rumsfeld and Alma Powell and the other "White House widows" together. Alma and Joyce had been through similar circumstances during Desert Storm, when they didn't see their husbands for long periods of time. Alma in essence told the ladies they were like military families when soldiers deployed. She and Joyce helped the spouses form a "chain of concern" telephone tree.

Andy Card's wife, Kathie, a Methodist minister, was a spiritual mentor to Becky during that time. They talked together and prayed together frequently, and Becky found added strength through their friendship.

I'm often asked, "Were you afraid?" No, I really wasn't. It's not that I'm so brave, but like most others working in the White House during that time, I knew I had an important job to do. Americans expected us to protect them. I never thought about my mortality or my place in history, but later I was gratified when I learned that Hispanics in America were especially proud of my role in helping our country during those crucial days.

———

On October 19, 2001, the first of US Special Forces made it into Afghanistan and linked with our allies from the Northern Alliance. A few weeks later, the Northern Alliance forces captured three hundred Taliban and al-Qaeda soldiers and held them in a nineteenth-century mud-and-brick fort near the town of Mazar-e-Sharif. On November 25, when two CIA agents attempted to question a group of the prisoners in an open area outside their cells, a prisoner leaped toward the agents and began clawing them, setting off a prison riot. It took nearly three days to put down the rebellion. In the process, more than two hundred prisoners were killed and one of the CIA agents, Johnny Micheal Spann, was viciously killed—the first American to die in Afghanistan. Don Rumsfeld later wrote that "his body was booby-trapped with a hidden grenade by the al-Qaeda and Taliban prisoners so those recovering his remains would be wounded or killed."[10]

Among the captured who survived the battle was an American who had aligned himself with the Taliban, John Walker Lindh.

The incident brought into stark focus many of the issues on my desk after 9/11. Clearly, the al-Qaeda and Taliban prisoners our forces were sweeping up on the battlefield were not docile, defeated soldiers who intended to live out their remaining days in American prisons. They were vicious, malevolent killers who would take every opportunity to kill again. How were we going to classify and deal with these enemies of America that we captured and detained as prisoners? What, if any, rights did these terrorists have as prisoners of war designated by the Geneva Convention III on the Treatment of Prisoners of War (GPW)? Even more complex, how were we to handle other Americans we might discover working in collusion with the enemy?

One of the key issues I coordinated among administration lawyers was defining how the Geneva Conventions applied in this new type of war. GPW had been developed by countries fighting traditional, conventional wars, in which the combatants wore uniforms into battle, were under the command of established hierarchies, and agreed not to purposely kill innocent people. None of these practices were followed by the terrorists who attacked America.

I was not an expert on the Geneva Conventions, so I conferred with lawyers from the Departments of Justice, State, and Defense, as well as the CIA. Like most Americans, I supported the foundational principles of Geneva, assuring the basic humane treatment for those engaged in or affected by war. But as I explored the rules with the administration lawyers, some of the points of GPW struck me as being outdated and not relevant or reasonably applicable for the new type of war in which we were engaged—a war against non-state terrorists who did not fight according to the laws of war—and in which information was our primary defense against future attacks. In a document clearly marked "DRAFT" that I circulated to people on our staff and to several cabinet secretaries for their input, a memo that was never intended to become public, I included the word *quaint* when referring to certain GPW provisions—such as providing athletic uniforms, commissary privileges, scientific instruments, and a monthly allowance to captured enemy soldiers. In my judgment, these few provisions and others similar were obsolete, antiquated rules put into place after World War II.

I wasn't the only one to make that observation. In a report about our detention facilities at Guantanamo, the British foreign affairs committee later said something similar, that the provisions of the treaty were outdated and needed revision.[11] The protections of the Geneva Conventions were intended to encourage nations at war to play by the rules. It was an inducement saying, "If you fight according to the laws of war, you will receive all of these protections."

This was crucial because in this new type of war, acquisition of fast, accurate information was critical. If Geneva applied to the people we were capturing, captives could be asked only for their name, rank, and serial number. We could not induce the prisoners to talk, a restriction that was not going to help us in thwarting the next attack by al-Qaeda, something we all worried could happen at any time. Many of our lawyers felt it was important that we not hamstring our intelligence gathering, including any information we might gain by lawfully interrogating captured al-Qaeda and Taliban.

On the other hand, Secretary Colin Powell argued that we had always applied Geneva's provisions in previous wars and conflicts, even when the international law did not require that we do so. We were a country intent on taking the high road. Relying no doubt on his experiences as a soldier, Powell was concerned that by not applying the convention rules, we could be undermining our own military's culture that emphasized maintaining the highest standards of conduct, even in combat.

In pulling together the draft, I drew from the wisdom around me, did my best to represent the competing views, and sent it out. The very next morning, my draft memo appeared on the front page of the *Washington Times*. The document had been leaked to the conservative publication by someone apparently wanting to impugn Powell's conservative standing by implying that he was catering to terrorists. That issue disappeared quickly, but my comments were seized upon as outrageous. "Al Gonzales thinks the great Geneva Conventions are *quaint?*" the critics seemed to be saying. "Gonzales doesn't believe in the values of the Geneva Conventions!" That was sheer nonsense, and not what I said or intended, but that didn't matter to many Washington players and critics of the Bush administration.

In hindsight, had I known the draft was going to be broadcast to the entire world, I might have used a different word than *quaint* when referring to the obsolete provisions. The word hurt me professionally, and more importantly, I felt it hurt our war efforts. But I was not intending to make a public statement; I was hoping to elicit insight and suggestions internally regarding what rules applied to terrorists we engaged on the battlefield before I took a recommendation to the president regarding the protections of the Geneva Conventions.

Dealing with the blowback from the leak was a lesson to me: don't write down things not intended for public consumption, and by all means, don't circulate documents that include controversial positions or statements—especially if they are not final—to other agencies. We didn't have to function that way in Texas, but in the White House, I got in the habit of communicating verbally, or scrawling messy, ambiguous notes that only I could interpret.

Considering whether Geneva should apply to members of al-Qaeda, the logical and legal answer was no. Al-Qaeda was not a nation-state; they were not signers of the Geneva Conventions and could not have been, even if they had desired to do so, since only nations could ratify treaties, not individuals or rebel groups with allegiance to no particular country.

Furthermore, according to GPW, for soldiers to be protected as prisoners of war, they must abide by four requirements: they must operate within a responsible command structure; they must wear identifiable uniforms; they must carry their weapons openly; and they must obey the laws of war, which meant they were to avoid killing innocent people not engaged in battle. Al-Qaeda flagrantly violated every one of Geneva's conditions on 9/11 and afterward. Al-Qaeda does not obey the rules of war, does not wear identifiable uniforms, does not limit fighting to combatants, and has no qualms about killing innocents. As a corollary, al-Qaeda does not keep prisoners. It cuts off captured soldiers' heads, as well as those of other nonmilitary types they deem worthy of death, such as *Wall Street Journal* reporter Daniel Pearl. According to the Department of Justice, they were not legally entitled to prisoner of war status, nor to the protections afforded to POWs.

Considering how we were going to deal with captured Taliban was more difficult. Not because they kept the rules, but because it could be argued that the Taliban was the de facto government in Afghanistan prior to the war. Before the Taliban had taken control, the then government of Afghanistan had indeed signed the Geneva Conventions, so some of our lawyers wondered if that was enough. But the Taliban had never really been recognized as Afghanistan's governing body, so they did not represent a nation-state. Attorney General Ashcroft, as well as other officials within our administration, contended that Afghanistan was a "failed state," and the Geneva provisions should not apply. Moreover, they had forfeited the right to prisoner of war protections because they didn't follow the laws of war, as noted earlier. Therefore, according to the DOJ, the Taliban were not legally entitled to Geneva's protections.

The one variable was the fact that the United States military would ostensibly be treated according to Geneva if our soldiers were captured *only if* we were applying Geneva to the people we captured. President Bush was deeply concerned about that. The principals on the National Security Council, as well as the lawyers, debated these issues extensively. The discussions were always respectful, but they were also passionate. The president listened carefully to all sides, determined to make a decision that would give him the flexibility we needed to gather information, including information from the people we had captured, that was absolutely necessary to protect our country. It disturbed him that terrorists had been operating inside the United States, planning the 9/11 attacks for some time, and we hadn't been aware of it.

Based in large part on a letter from the attorney general, I recommended—and the president accepted my recommendation—that the Geneva Convention's normal prisoner of war protections afforded to soldiers who fight according to the accepted laws of war should *not* apply to terrorists who do not. I acknowledged that some of our allies might not agree with us, but that should not influence our decision. I also emphasized that the United States should still provide captured enemy combatants with the highest level of humane treatment, a policy I knew President Bush readily endorsed.

It seemed that everybody in Washington weighed in on the matter, offering as many divergent opinions. Finally, on February 7, 2002, President Bush settled on a policy that the United States would treat those captured humanely, but that Geneva did not apply to al-Qaeda and that the Taliban were "unlawful combatants" who had forfeited their prisoner of war status.[12]

But that raised another sticky problem. Our troops were already capturing enemy soldiers on the battlefields of Afghanistan and elsewhere. Where should we put the bad guys?

The answers that various people came up with were interesting.

CHAPTER 17

THE ULTIMATE CLUB FED

E ven before the first shots were fired in Afghanistan, many of us in the White House with national security responsibilities wondered what we were going to do with prisoners if we went to war. How and where were we going to detain terrorists and other captives of intelligence value or considered dangerous to our country? Immediately after hostilities began in Afghanistan, the US military began capturing enemy combatants. As early as November 13, 2001, after serious discussions, President Bush issued a military order providing for military commissions and the detention of enemy combatants "at an appropriate location designated by the Secretary of Defense outside or within the United States."[1]

These were not new issues. The United States had dealt with detentions during World War II, detaining not only prisoners of war but, regrettably, thousands of innocent people—many of whom were US citizens—living in the United States. Their only "crime"? They looked Japanese or had Japanese relatives.

We did not want to engage in that same sort of mass detention after 9/11. Moreover, unlike al-Qaeda—or ISIS today—we understood our moral and legal obligations not to kill captives. Yet the question remained about what to do with captured prisoners, most of whom were seized on the battlefield, others of whom were scooped up because they had terrorist ties, and were part of al-Qaeda or assisting al-Qaeda. These were not run-of-the-mill street thugs; many of them were cold-blooded killers who had committed horrific acts of savagery and would do so again if not detained, or if they escaped, were released, or otherwise allowed to return to battle.

At first, we briefly explored the notion of returning captured combatants to their home countries where they could be incarcerated. Most of the early captives, however, were from Afghanistan, and there was no legitimate government in place that could be trusted to keep the combatants detained. We considered placing the captured combatants in an existing facility or building one of our own in Afghanistan, and guarding them with American soldiers. General Tommy Franks considered this inconsistent with having a limited footprint in Afghanistan and too dangerous in a war zone—for our guards as well as the detainees—and proved to be deadly at Mazar-e-Sharif.

A senior Defense Department official suggested we use the crumbling facilities that once held Al Capone and other dangerous criminals on Alcatraz, the federal prison that is now a popular sight-seeing spot a mere mile and a half off the shores of San Francisco. We also weighed briefly using the maximum-security facility at Fort Leavenworth, Kansas, or the supermax prison in Colorado, or even housing the terrorists on military bases within the United States such as the brigs at Charleston and Norfolk. Those discussions were short since few of us believed the American people would sleep better knowing that the terrorists who had killed nearly three thousand of our fellow citizens were now residing in our homeland—even if they were in maximum-security prisons.

Furthermore, I worried about the legal ramifications of bringing enemy combatants onto American soil, where some ambitious lawyers might successfully argue that the terrorists are entitled to certain constitutional rights they would not ordinarily receive if they were detained outside the United States.

We considered places in the Alutian Islands, Guam, and even toyed with the idea of a floating prison—using a Navy ship to detain captives somewhere out at sea. That idea, too, was short-lived, in part because of international law.

Eventually, we turned our attention toward Guantanamo Bay, Cuba, where the United States maintained a naval station used to refuel navy ships and US aircraft patrolling the Caribbean. The site was remote and secure, and there was no large civilian population nearby that might be at risk. It even had a small naval hospital. Gitmo, as it was known, was controlled by the United States under an "evergreen" lease with the Cuban government, so long as the United States used it to resupply ships. The Justice Department gave a qualified opinion that the courts should conclude since Gitmo was not technically US property, it was not subject to American legal jurisdiction. The US Supreme Court would see that matter differently a few years later.

During previous administrations, in addition to Gitmo's military functions, the naval station had also been used to detain Cuban and Haitian refugees, including many boat people who had risked their lives in makeshift crafts trying to reach Florida, where they hoped to receive asylum. Most did not reach Florida and even fewer received asylum. Many of them wound up at Guantanamo for months. In a key precedent, the United States did not afford the refugees the same legal rights as Americans because they were not on US soil, nor were they US citizens. So it made sense to administration lawyers that captured terrorists could be kept at Gitmo without concerns that they would have access to US courts where they could exploit our legal protections and use legal proceedings as a platform to promote their terrorist ideology.

After much discussion, the principals committee recommended Guantanamo Bay as the detention site, and their recommendation was accepted by President Bush. I felt it was the best among a short list of imperfect choices—or as Don Rumsfeld famously put it, "the least worst place."[2] He was right. Of all the bad options we had to choose from, this one was the best. Gitmo was certainly not selected so the United States could operate there beyond US law in respect to interrogations, or without limitations under international law. In fact, the decision to house detainees at Gitmo was made by the Pentagon prior to President Bush's February 7, 2002, decision regarding whether the provisions of the Geneva Convention applied to al-Qaeda and the Taliban, as well as prior to any guidance from the Department of Justice, provided in August 2002, regarding enhanced interrogations under strict guidelines.

On January 11, 2002, the first detainees arrived at Guantanamo Bay. Later in that same month, along with lawyers from the Departments of Defense, State, and Justice, I traveled to Guantanamo Bay to view the facility where we planned to keep the most dangerous or those individuals we had captured who might have intelligence value.

Despite being surrounded by warm, tropical breezes and the sparkling turquoise waters of the Caribbean, the conditions at Gitmo were initially rudimentary. Detainees were housed in a facility built during the Clinton administration for illegal immigrants and refugees. Early critics of the conditions often failed to mention that the US forces guarding the dangerous detainees lived in the same conditions as the prisoners. We planned to construct new, modern facilities, which was done within a few months of my first visit. Over time, the facilities became state of the art. Indeed, eventually Gitmo became comparable to some state prisons and local jails in the United States. Contrary to reports in the media, the detainees had clean clothes, warm showers, toiletries, blankets, healthy food consistent with their religious beliefs, access to television, books, newspapers, movies, their choice of numerous sports and exercise opportunities, medical care, and Korans and prayer mats. In contrast, how many prisoners held by al-Qaeda or ISIS have been given Bibles or other religious books? In addition, signs exist at Gitmo that point toward Mecca to help facilitate the terrorists' prayer lives.

Regular inspection visits by members of the International Red Cross began shortly after the first detainees arrived. Nevertheless, civil libertarians complained that we were not treating the detainees properly because they were housed in cells rather than open areas, and they were not permitted to prepare their own meals. During our visit, however, a marine general explained that several of the detainees had been screaming that they wanted to kill the guards and other Americans. Some al-Qaeda detainees not only tried to kill the guards, but they also threatened their peers who they thought might be cooperating with the Americans. Clearly, affording customary prisoner of war rights to the detainees was going to be unlikely.

One of the first law-related questions to pop up was whether detainees at Gitmo would be entitled to habeas corpus rights in our federal courts, rights that would allow the terrorists to challenge in US courts whether they should be detained at all.[3] Historically, we have never recognized the rights of foreign detainees to petition our courts. During the Civil War, for instance, Confederate soldiers held in federal facilities were not afforded such rights. During World War II, the United States brought thousands of captured soldiers from various countries to the United States, but none of them were granted the right to challenge their detention. An important and often-cited Supreme Court case, *Johnson v. Eisentrager*, supported that policy. Based on that precedent, the Office of Legal Counsel informed the Department of Defense that petitions for habeas corpus rights should not be entertained from detainees at Gitmo. By our logic, detainees held outside the United States, for actions outside the United States, and with no direct ties to the United States, would not be entitled to habeas relief.

Surprisingly, the Supreme Court disagreed with that conclusion years later in the case of *Rasul v. Bush*, finding that the United States exercised complete dominion over Gitmo under an evergreen lease with Cuba. Thus, Gitmo was in essence a territory of the United States. I and many other legal experts were disappointed by that decision.

President Bush had no desire for the United States to be the world's jailer. He much preferred, for most detainees, they be brought to justice in their home country, or dealt with in military courts, but that process was repeatedly delayed or otherwise impeded by lawyers representing the detainees. So Gitmo became an increasingly necessary and permanent part of our lives. The key purposes, however, were to get information, to bring people to justice, and to make sure that the people with evil intent did not harm anyone else.

I visited the naval station and detainee facilities at Guantanamo Bay three times during my work in the Bush administration, and what I witnessed left indelible impressions on me. On each subsequent trip, the detainees' conditions improved rather than worsened, contrary to what the American public was often led to believe by certain members of the media, members of Congress, and human rights activists.

Detainees at Gitmo were living in better conditions than American soldiers who had been incarcerated on foreign soil, and better than some

European prisons, according to one member of the European parliament. If the truth were known, many Americans would be surprised not at the in-humane treatment of detainees but that the detainees were actually treated so well. Many American citizens—especially those who lost loved ones on 9/11—would be disgusted that the terrorists and those who had colluded with them in murdering nearly three thousand civilians were afforded so many comforts and unusual considerations in this "ultimate Club Fed."

The maximum detainee population at Guantanamo reached nearly nine hundred terrorists. Today, there are less than one hundred, most of whom are high-value terrorists who either have valuable information we need to thwart future attacks or who pose a dangerous threat—or both. These are not passive prisoners. In 2006, for example, a group of detainees used make-shift weapons to attack Guantanamo military guards who had rushed to save a detainee who had faked a suicide.[4] Even today, the detainees continue to do all they can to injure or insult their captors, often hurling their own feces at guards.

Heated discussions occurred in the Bush White House about how to best bring these terrorists to justice. In general, we wanted to establish pro-tocols that would survive the test of time. We believed the war on terror would outlast our administration, and we worried whether future admin-istrations would have the courage to do the hard and often unpopular work necessary to protect America.

Nevertheless, serious disagreements continued to exist among lawyers within the administration, as well as the top decision makers, regarding the disposition of certain detainees. Each department made its recommendations to the president. I tried to stay dispassionate, listening to all sides and trying to keep us within the law. The pressures were intense. We soon discovered that not everybody incarcerated at Gitmo was equally dangerous. Some had merely been in the wrong place at the wrong time when coalition forces swept up a bunch of terrorists. When combatants don't wear uniforms, mistakes such as that can happen. So when possible, we tried to release detainees who had no intelligence value or were no longer dangerous, or return them to their own countries. Unfortunately, we soon experienced the deadly consequences of detainees who returned to fight against America again after being released from Guantanamo Bay. Several suspected al-Qaeda and Taliban who were captured and detained initially at Guantanamo were released in 2003 and 2004. They were recaptured in Afghanistan where they were conducting raids against coalition forces. I often wondered how difficult it must have been for the president to speak to the parents of a young soldier killed by someone we had released from Gitmo.

As I write these words, despite George W. Bush's desire to close Guantanamo Bay as a detention center, it remains open because of necessity. And despite Barak Obama's repeated campaign promises that he would close Guantanamo, and his various efforts to do so as president, even risking the trade and release of some detainees who probably never should have been released, he has discovered that closing Gitmo is much easier said than done. Nearly eight full years into the Obama presidency, Gitmo is still open. The problem is extremely complex: as long as the war on terrorism continues, we need a maximum-security detention facility. If Guantanamo Bay did not exist, we'd have to create something similar. Consequently, Gitmo remains the least worst place.

CHAPTER 18

BRINGING
TERRORISTS TO JUSTICE

Anticipating the challenges our government might encounter trying to prosecute terrorists in the US criminal justice system, I began working with Bush administration lawyers in October of 2001 to provide the president with another option—trying the terrorists in military commissions. Similar to my limited background on the Geneva Conventions, I had little experience with military commissions. So I read memos and articles and discussed the subject with civilian and military lawyers. I learned that military commissions reflect a compromise in which our government has attempted to protect our nation's secrets—especially during wartime—while providing due process for the accused. There is not a jury, but the defendant is tried before military tribunals, most of whom are officers or senior judges with extensive knowledge of the issues. The defendant can be represented by attorneys present during the trial, but unlike regular courts, military commissions can close portions of the proceedings when, for example, classified material is being discussed or an enemy leader might testify.[1]

Military commissions have the advantage of being more secure, since they can be conducted on military bases or other safe locations.

Historically, military commissions go back to the early days of our nation. During the Revolutionary War, George Washington used a military court of inquiry to put Major John André on trial for spying. Although the trials were not called military commissions, General Andrew Jackson employed military tribunals during the War of 1812 and then again in 1818. Military commissions were used in the Spanish-American War and the Civil War. They were also used to try President Lincoln's assassins, as well as the commander of Andersonville, the notorious Confederate prisoner of war camp.

Military commissions were employed extensively during World War II. One instance involved a 1942 case in which the United States captured eight Nazi agents who had traveled by submarine from France, landed on the beaches of Long Island as well as North Florida, and planned to blow up factories, bridges, railroad lines, and hydroelectric and other utility plants.[2] All eight had lived in the United States prior to the war, and two were even US citizens.[3]

When President Franklin D. Roosevelt learned of the situation, he insisted that the saboteurs be tried in a military court, and Roosevelt was not bashful about letting his biases show. He wanted the death penalty applied, and swiftly. "Offenses such as . . . these are probably more serious than any offense in criminal law," he said. "The death penalty is called for by usage and by the extreme gravity of the war aim and the very existence of our American government."[4]

FDR fired off two executive orders, the first establishing a military commission to try the saboteurs, and the second establishing the procedures for the trial, ordering that the saboteurs be given a full and fair trial. A two-thirds vote was required for conviction and sentence. Despite objections by the Nazis' military lawyers that the military commissions did not have jurisdiction because US courts were open and the defendants had not been directly in a war zone, in Ex parte Quirin, the Supreme Court upheld Roosevelt's decision to try them in a military commission. The saboteurs were tried, convicted, and sentenced to death. Six of them were executed. Roosevelt commuted the sentences of the other two. The saboteurs were captured in June, tried in July, and executed before the Supreme Court issued its written opinions.

Unquestionably, as DOJ lawyer Jack Goldsmith later expressed, Roosevelt operated in a "permissive legal culture that is barely recognizable to us today. It was an era before Vietnam, before the revelations of Hoover's domestic espionage, and before Watergate. This was a time when the press, Congress, and intellectuals had a higher regard for the executive branch and the military. It was also an era before the judicial civil liberties revolutions of the 1960s and 1970s, when America was much less solicitous of political and civil rights."[5] Nevertheless, given the recent horrific attacks by these non-state actors, we were persuaded that Roosevelt's orders provided sufficient precedent for the use of commissions.

Inside the White House, there was intense debate over whether captured terrorists should undergo criminal trials or military commissions. Some believed that military commissions were appropriate; others favored criminal trials. I thought it depended on the circumstances such as the citizenship of the detainees, where they were first captured or detained, and where their unlawful conduct had occurred. I told President Bush, "I want to present you as many disposition options as possible, Mr. President." I gave him a menu of choices: (1) we try the terrorists in criminal court; (2) we detain them indefinitely at Guantanamo; (3) we return the prisoners to their home countries for detention or prosecution; or (4) we try them in military commissions.

The debate about the proper disposition of captured terrorists intensified over the prosecution of Zacarias Moussaoui, a detainee often referred to as "the twentieth hijacker" since he fully intended to be part of the 9/11 attacks. Moussaoui openly admitted that he was a member of al-Qaeda, that he hated Americans, and that he was in the United States to prepare for attacks.

A French citizen, Moussaoui had ostensibly entered the United States in February 2001 to take flying lessons at a flight school in Oklahoma. In August, he moved to Minnesota, where he continued flight training. He had no prior flight experience, nor had he ever been known to express an interest in aviation or in becoming a pilot. He was known to hold jihadist beliefs and had traveled to Pakistan. He had ties to Ramzi bin al-Shibh, an al-Qaeda facilitator, and had $32,000 in his bank account at the time of his apprehension, but could not—or would not—explain where it had come from.

US immigration officials detained him for overstaying his visa prior to 9/11, but because of the wall prohibiting the sharing of information between various law enforcement and intelligence agencies put in place by the Justice Department during the Clinton administration, the FBI turned down a request for a warrant to search Moussaoui's computer and belongings, which contained information that might have led to the discovery of the 9/11 plot.

During the initial detention of Moussaoui, the administration was working to establish military commissions. Attorney General John Ashcroft felt strongly that Moussaoui should be tried in civilian courts rather than military. To the surprise and disappointment of some in the administration who believed military commissions were necessary to bring people like Moussaoui to justice, the DOJ indicted him in December 2001 for conspiracy to commit terrorist attacks. He would stand trial in Alexandria, Virginia, only a few minutes drive from the scarred face of the Pentagon.

The attorney general believed that Moussaoui had committed crimes and the DOJ could successfully prosecute him. He also felt it was important to show the American public that our criminal justice system could successfully bring a high-level terrorist to justice during an ongoing conflict. Although there were contrary views in the White House, I was reluctant to interfere with an indictment, and I agreed with the attorney general that we needed to answer the question whether courts were a realistic option. This case provided the opportunity. I reluctantly went along with the attorney general's recommendation that DOJ try Moussaoui in US criminal court rather than a military tribunal. It was risky; while we had a strong case against Moussaoui, there was always the chance that a judge would disallow key evidence or a jury would find exception and set him free. The National Security Council engaged in serious discussions about what we would do if that occurred, but there was no clear answer.

President Bush accepted the DOJ recommendation but warned me, "If this goes south, I am going to yank Moussaoui out and put him in our military justice system."

My fears were realized months later when the district court ruled that we make Gitmo detainees available for Moussaoui's defense. I could already hear

"I told you so!" ringing throughout the White House. Fortunately, on appeal by the government, the Fourth Circuit Court of Appeals overruled the lower court, holding that the government had offered sufficient substitutions for the defense.

Moussaoui was less than cooperative with counsel. He initially pled guilty to conspiring with al-Qaeda to carry out the 9/11 attacks and then changed his mind a week later. It was clear from the outset that he was going to play the US criminal justice system for all that he could get out of it, frequently grandstanding in court with vitriolic comments about the United States. He fired his public defenders and chose instead to be his own attorney. His erratic behavior worked to our advantage. Throughout Moussaoui's incarceration and trial, US forces continued to capture other al-Qaeda terrorists. Sharp lawyers could have dragged things out for years by demanding access to al-Qaeda leaders, or even that they appear in court, possibly disclosing all sorts of intelligence information and sources and disrupting operations. We dodged a bullet when Moussaoui cooperated by pleading guilty again on April 22, 2005. I tried to follow the proceedings the best I could given my other commitments. Periodically, the DOJ lawyers gave me status reports regarding the case.

Five years after his arrest, rather giving him a death sentence, the jury frustrated Moussaoui's martyrdom wishes and sentenced him to life in prison. It was a victory of sorts for us, but the Moussaoui case was a classic example why, in certain circumstances, military commissions were a preferable alternative to trying terrorists in our criminal justice system. The Moussaoui case partially answered some of the questions regarding our ability to try a high-level terrorist in an ongoing conflict, but it left many unanswered questions as well. And even though the government did not face a high-powered defense team, the case was hard fought and took years, costing American taxpayers millions of dollars. The next time the United States might not be so fortunate.

During the Moussaoui saga, work on military commissions continued. I spoke repeatedly with William J. Haynes II, general counsel for the Department of Defense, about using commissions as an option to bring enemy combatants to justice. Jim was a fellow Harvard Law graduate who served in the army before being appointed as general counsel to the army during the administration of George H. W. Bush. He was a friend and an experienced lawyer with stints as a partner at Jenner & Block and as deputy general counsel at General Dynamics. Like me, he was a morning person, and we often had serious early-morning telephone discussions. We both agreed that with the right safeguards, commissions would be preferable to an international tribunal or a criminal trial in the Southern District of New York. Jim anticipated strong reservations, however, by the Judge Advocates General (JAGs), who would likely be concerned about any policy that might tarnish the image of the military justice system. Nevertheless, used correctly, commissions would protect our nation's national security interests and bring terrorists to justice.

After studying the historical use of commissions and consulting with John Yoo, a bright young lawyer at OLC, in the fall of 2001 I concluded the president should at least be given the opportunity to consider that option to deal with captured terrorists. An immigrant from South Korea, John was a likable lawyer with degrees from Harvard and Yale. He had come to the administration from academia, where he had been a law professor at the University of California–Berkeley. He had previously been a law clerk on the DC Federal Appeals Court and for Supreme Court justice Clarence Thomas, as well as serving as general counsel for the Senate Judiciary Committee under Utah senator Orrin Hatch. Although he was relatively young and did not hold a Senate-confirmed position, he was a significant influence at the DOJ because of his previous work on national security and terrorist-related issues. John was viewed as an expert within the Justice Department on many of the legal issues regarding terrorism, so it fell primarily to him to provide legal advice on presidential powers.

John felt strongly that military commissions were a good option for President Bush. I envisioned using military commissions for special cases such as bin Laden and other top al-Qaeda leaders; others who were less high profile or less dangerous, we could detain indefinitely at Gitmo, return them to their home country, or bring them to justice in our criminal courts.

On the morning of October 24, 2001, I first discussed the topic of military commissions with President Bush in the Oval Office. I explained the Roosevelt precedent and told him of the Nazi saboteurs and the Supreme Court decision in *Ex parte Quirin*, upholding President Roosevelt's military commission.

The president was intrigued and concluded that having military commissions was a strong move. He told me that he wanted military commissions as a tool, but even though two of the saboteurs in the Nazi case had been American citizens, the president was reluctant to try American citizens in a military commission.

Because military commissions operate under the authority of the Defense Department, I discussed details about this subject with Jim Haynes. Since the government was debating prosecutions, the Justice Department was understandably interested as well. Attorney General Ashcroft had serious concerns, which he raised directly with the president and vice president. From my observation, the attorney general well understood the United States had to utilize the assets of law enforcement, the military, and the intelligence community to defeat al-Qaeda.

General Ashcroft was a staunch defender of the Department of Justice as an institution. He argued rightfully for the Justice Department to have an important role in bringing terrorists to justice in our criminal courts and, if we were to establish military commissions, in helping to develop them and in decisions regarding their use. As far as I could tell, John understood the commissions were a military proceeding under the authority of the Department of Defense, but he strongly emphasized that the courts and the public would be reassured knowing that the Justice Department had a role too. He was right. And in any event, the Justice Department would have to defend the military commissions from legal challenges that were sure to come in our courts.

Toward the end of October into early November, the lawyers began work on an executive order, to be followed by separate regulations issued by the Defense Department as to how the military commissions should operate.

I assigned Tim Flanigan the task of drafting the order, with assistance from David Addington and John Yoo, and input from Jim Haynes. Our goal was to model the order as closely as possible to the one used by President Roosevelt to create military commissions during World War II, since the Supreme Court had upheld Roosevelt's authority to do so in the Nazi saboteurs' case.

The Roosevelt military commission that tried the Nazi saboteurs was actually held in a room on the fifth floor of the Justice Department. When I mentioned that fact to President Bush, he replied that he was reluctant to hold commissions inside the United States. John Ashcroft also expressed reservations about holding the commissions on American soil. President Bush did not want to rule out the possibility, but he wanted the flexibility to conduct the commissions inside or outside the United States, in places such as Guantanamo or possibly even other foreign countries. I agreed that it was wise not to limit the president's options.

On November 13, 2001, President Bush signed a military order governing the detention, treatment, and trial of certain noncitizens in the war on terrorism.[6]

Opposition from civil liberties groups erupted immediately. Critics claimed that the commissions would be unfair, that they would deny detainees basic due process, and that the procedures all but guaranteed a conviction. Some argued that the whole idea of military commissions was inconsistent with America's rule of law, that the FDR approach had been superseded by new rules such as the protections in the Geneva Conventions and the Uniform Code of Military Justice. Some of our own military lawyers were critical of military commissions. Even Condoleezza Rice was upset, not that she was opposed to military commissions per se, but because we had created the order for the president to sign without vetting it with the various agencies. Colin Powell, for example, claimed he first heard about the order through CNN.[7]

I was irritated by the negative reactions. Yes, the order was developed outside the NSC process precisely because an existing NSC subcommittee had failed to make progress on recommending disposition options. We had not even committed to conduct a military commission, but it seemed that critics were unwilling to give the administration the benefit of the doubt and await the DOD regulations. Critics assumed the worst and pounced on President Bush's order as evidence that he did not believe in the rule of law and wanted to grab power for the presidency normally reserved for Congress.

That was utter nonsense.

In fact, by rolling out the order now—before we actually were ready to proceed to trial—Jim Haynes could openly enlist other experts and get feedback regarding the procedures. Jim had established an outside consulting group, including Lloyd Cutler, Bill Coleman, Griffin Bell, and others who provided advice regarding the legality of the regulations. I had hoped that by moving the process to the DOD, the president would be more insulated from its criticisms. That did not turn out to be the case.

Critics howled that using military commissions would endanger Americans abroad, since there would be nothing to stop other countries from bringing US citizens before similarly secret tribunals to convict them without evidence and without the right to counsel. That, too, was ridiculous, but the media and others went with it.

We responded that the president's order clearly provided for a "full and fair trial" and the admission of all relevant evidence. That meant the military commissions could not convict individuals unless the government presented evidence demonstrating that the defendants were guilty of war crimes. Moreover, the order did, in fact, provide terrorists the right to counsel. As such, the commissions would stand in stark contrast to the unfair and inhumane procedures sometimes used by other countries. In truth, the regulations compared favorably to the procedures used in Nuremberg and multiple other international tribunals.

Other critics squawked that military commissions cannot be established without congressional authorization. History counteracted that false claim. We pointed out that the president's power to establish commissions stems from his constitutional authority as commander in chief. An act of Congress is not necessary. Various presidents from both parties have used this authority, and the Supreme Court has upheld it.

Despite our efforts to explain why military commissions mattered, especially in the post-9/11 world, challenges to the procedures soon showed up in the courts and from members of Congress. I knew it would be only a matter of time before the issue would land at the Supreme Court.

I guess we could have expected criticism from the media, but I was disappointed when opposition flared by one of our closest allies.

CHAPTER 19

THE BRITISH REBELLION

Many countries claimed to be with the United States in our efforts to combat terrorism, but our strongest allies in the war on terror were Great Britain and Australia. Together, our three countries understood the stakes, and government officials were prepared to go to extraordinary lengths under the law to track down terrorists, to thwart future attacks, and to protect each nation's national security. John Ashcroft worked closely with his counterparts in London and Melbourne—Lord Peter Goldsmith and Daryl Williams, respectively—and occasionally I joined these discussions.

Shortly after hostilities commenced in Afghanistan, coalition forces captured enemy combatants on the battlefield, including seven British citizens and two Australian citizens. The captives were processed in the same manner as those from other nations. Following our usual review of their files, these nine detainees were transferred to Guantanamo in anticipation of bringing them to justice in our military commissions.

Ironically, both the British and the Australian governments wanted to have their subjects tried first in military commissions—that is, until the lawyers got involved. Lord Goldsmith was concerned that military commissions did not meet standards of international law. Consequently, he worried that British citizens—enemy combatants or not—would not be afforded due process under international law.

The Australians, on the other hand, were comfortable with the procedures, but as a matter of appearance, they felt they had to demand the same level of process that we provided British detainees. "The Australian people," Daryl Williams contended, "will not look kindly upon their citizens being treated differently than British citizens."

In the summer of 2003, DOD officials, along with DOJ lawyers, provided the White House with documents that included a list of detainees at Gitmo whom they believed should be designated enemy combatants by the president and placed in line to receive justice through military commissions. These documents, contemplated in the president's military order, were referred to as RTBs—for Reason to Believe—because the United States had reason to believe these detainees satisfied the legal definition of enemy combatants, had violated the laws of war, and should be tried in military commissions.

On July 2, 2003, I met with the president to discuss the RTBs and to discuss where we were on military commissions generally. The group initially identified by DOD included several Brits, and the president was worried about the reaction from our friends in London. I agreed that the response might not be favorable, but suggested that we move forward with the package despite the probable outcry across the pond, then see whether we could work through our differences.

The following day was a federal holiday, but most of the White House was working. When I received the package of RTBs for the president's signature, I headed straight to the basement of the president's residence. The secretary of commerce, Don Evans, and the deputy secretary of HUD, Alphonso Jackson, longtime Texas friends, were there waiting to see the president.

When the president arrived, he and I went into the Diplomatic Reception Room in the residence where he signed the RTBs. "This is historic," I told him. "No president since World War II has done this."

He looked at me and quipped, "No *lawyer* has recommended it since World War II."

The reaction from the British was swift and predictable. A few days later, Colin Powell reported that the British foreign secretary had conveyed his serious concern. "The British fought side by side with the United States," Powell said, repeating the foreign secretary's comments. "The United States should treat British citizens as they treat their own. Otherwise, the United States should return the British detainees to the United Kingdom." But they gave us no assurances that if we returned their citizens that they would ever be tried.

Nevertheless, Secretary Powell said the British insisted on five conditions for British detainees who might stand trial: (1) no death penalty, (2) access to lawyers, (3) open trials, (4) promise of release after serving sentences, and (5) unfettered communication between their government and the British detainees.

By July 10, the British were demanding the return of the British detainees, but they continued to refuse to promise that they would be brought to trial in the United Kingdom. As an alternative, they insisted on procedural changes in our military commissions. I worried that such changes would result in a commission different from the Roosevelt order, and thus different from the precedent of the Supreme Court. I also was concerned that changing our procedures might cause the commissions to look more like a criminal proceeding. That would defeat the whole purpose for the creation of the commissions in the first place. Federal judges who saw a trial that looked like a traditional criminal matter might be less inclined to defer to the president's wartime decisions.

I felt the pressure to get the military process up and running. Although it was a DOD process, the president questioned me repeatedly, "Why have there not been any military commissions?" He was clearly frustrated by the legal machinations and wanted to see some action.

I called Jim Haynes at DOD and said, "Jim, it would be helpful to our relationship with the international press and community to have the British government embrace the commissions." I asked Jim to look at additional assurances such as independent judicial reviews, use of civilian lawyers, open hearings, and access to all witnesses—basically looking for some way to satisfy the British demands. I knew we were stuck. "Jim, this is what the Brits want. See what you can do."

Meanwhile, the Australian government remained cooperative. The attorney general and foreign minister had both made supportive statements about the commissions, but they acknowledged Great Britain's concerns. They asked that we put the process on hold regarding the Australian detainees until we worked things out. More delay. I knew my boss would not be happy.

Indeed, after an NSC meeting on July 14, Condi confided to me that the president was seriously considering returning the British detainees. Prime Minister Tony Blair, who had previously supported military commissions for the British detainees, was now getting clobbered in the British press and had apparently asked Bush personally.

I wondered how the return of the Brits would affect other countries and their detainees. Should we insist that in exchange for a transfer of a detainee we would receive a guarantee that the home country would agree to bring the detainee to trial? I had learned later that even in Great Britain the decision was not unanimous. In fact, the home secretary had fought hard to comply with the US standards, but ultimately he was rolled by the British attorney general, Lord Goldsmith.

Over the next week, my office continued our work on developing a process to return detainees to their home countries. I suspected the president wanted to clear out as many detainees as possible from Guantanamo so we could begin military commissions, yet no one seemed in a hurry to deal with the British detainees.

Despite Condi's earlier comment to me, the president continued to urge us to talk to the British and reach an accommodation on our procedures. Jim Haynes traveled to London twice for day-long meetings to help facilitate that process, and I conducted several phone calls with Lord Goldsmith and met with him during his visits to DC; we did make some accommodations to what he wanted.

On July 30, I met with the president and Andy Card in the residence. I explained that while we had made progress, we had reached an impasse on Goldsmith's demand that there be an independent review panel that would examine the decisions of military commissions.[1] "What Goldsmith wants," I speculated, "is for our courts to hear appeals of the decisions made by military commissions, and we are stuck there." I mentioned that Tony Blair might call President Bush about the matter.

I reminded the president that we had modeled our commissions on the Roosevelt precedent to create two independent sources of justice—both constitutional but independent of each other. To accommodate Lord Goldsmith's request would require a fundamental change in the structure of our military commissions. That would be dangerous for the United States, according to what OLC had advised me. Goldsmith's request would essentially merge the two legal frameworks that we wanted to keep separate. It would invite more legal challenges and encourage judges to view commissions as merely an adjunct to our criminal courts. Everyone at OLC with whom I had discussed this matter insisted this was a serious danger.

The president understood. "Work something out," he said. "Find a bridge for now." That seemed to be his favorite advice to me these days: find a bridge, by which he meant find something that would work for the time being so we could buy some time.

"Well, sir, we probably won't be able to reach an accommodation," I said. "I recommend the Brits take their people, rather than making the structure changes Goldsmith wants."

The president asked me several more questions about possible alternatives and pressed me on the importance to the United States of maintaining the structures.

A couple of days later, the president mentioned to me that he had told the British the review panel was a problem for us. He had spoken to Tony Blair and told him that unless their terrorists were taken back to the United Kingdom, Blair would need to talk with his attorney general and, presumably, "straighten him out." Bush was pitching the ball back to Blair.

I continued working on this matter while the commissions remained on hold. The delay was fine with the British. We continued to hold their people in Guantanamo, so they were in no rush, but I pushed to get the matter settled one way or the other.

On September 5, I had another of many 6:30 a.m. telephone conversations with Jim Haynes about the Brits. Jim told me that he had sent them large amounts of material about the British detainees and these were being reviewed. "The Brits are coming to Gitmo," Jim said, "so they can talk to the British detainees." They also planned to meet with DOD officials in Washington. This would be another in-person meeting with Lord Goldsmith. Jim reported progress on various fronts, but he did not see it going much further. Although he'd heard that Lord Goldsmith remained interested in resolving our differences, Jim was pessimistic. Eventually, Lord Goldsmith might back down, Jim suggested, since the home secretary and others thought it crazy to ask that the British detainees be returned. Officials at DOD felt that Goldsmith would somehow conclude that the commission's procedures were fair, although he would probably not recommend them.

I wasn't so sure. Peter was an extremely confident man and a good lawyer. His courtly manner provided the perfect disguise for the ambitious and savvy street fighter he was. I felt sure we still had a problem with him.

A month later, we were still negotiating. Goldsmith asked that the president be bound by a decision of a review panel. I saw that as another problem. Even review panels are not infallible and sometimes make mistakes. We might get a runaway panel that decided to reach beyond the merits of a case and focus on the war on terrorism itself; or a panel might choose to ignore findings or conclusions of a commission. A president needs flexibility; he might have more information about the detainee or the overall threat situation than the review panel.

Perhaps we could assure the British that, absent extraordinary circumstances, the president would respect the will of the review panel, or at least represent to the British it would be unlikely the president would not follow the recommendation of the review panel. But to accommodate Goldsmith, we'd have to amend the president's November 13, 2001, military order, and I preferred not to do that.

In early November, I discussed our concerns with Lord Goldsmith. Later, I met with the president, Andy, and Condi on the matter. I explained that we were prepared to give some assurances regarding (1) the fairness of the appeals process; (2) written submissions could be accepted; (3) it would be possible to get an extension from the review panel to consider appeals; and (4) we were willing to agree that all interlocutory appeals would go the review panel and not to the appointing authority.

I recommended to the president that we *not* agree to Goldsmith's requests that (1) the president unconditionally honor and accept the review panel recommendations; (2) no part of the proceeding would be closed to the detainees or their civilian lawyers; and (3) the accused would have access to all material witnesses and materials. These concessions could easily compromise our national security.

Our discussions with the British continued, but I sensed that President Bush's patience with them was approaching an end. The Brits were solid allies and we did not want to offend them, but the president was done. John Bellinger, our national security legal advisor, told me that on a secure video-conference between the president and Prime Minister Blair, the president repeated his offer for the Brits to take back the British detainees if they wanted them. Clearly, they didn't want them. What were they going to do with the detainees? Incarcerate them? Try them? Let them walk? For the Brits, the detainees were a problem they didn't need. After all, the terrorists were already in custody. It was an ironic standoff between allies.

On November 9, I had another frustrating conversation with Lord Goldsmith. He was as courteous as ever . . . and just as stubborn. I liked Peter and admired his character, even if I didn't agree with his view of the law.

Peter informed me that the issue of the review panel was a red line for Great Britain. He recognized this was a difficult process, but if the review panel decisions were not binding on the president, it simply did not accord with his view of a fair trial. He acknowledged that our concerns were based on national security. To him, however, these would be criminal trials.

I was perplexed at Peter's insistence that it was unfair for the chief executive to have the final say. As Jim Haynes had told him, we had inherited our military justice system from the English. How could they now complain that the English model was unfair?

Not to allow detainees or their civilian lawyers complete access to all evidence was also a red line to him—as it was to us. We wanted to be able to deny access when necessary to protect our national security. Goldsmith disagreed and said the deciding factor should be the issue of justice. Easy for him to say; he didn't have three thousand recently murdered victims thanks to al-Qaeda. As far as I was concerned, our attempts at finding a resolution with the British were done, regardless of the fallout in our relationship. There was nothing else we could offer. The lawyers at OLC had warned me repeatedly that if we made the changes Goldsmith demanded, we would encourage US courts to view military commissions as nothing more than an extension of the criminal justice system. We refused to do that.

It was clear to me now that the British did not really want these enemy combatants returned. But at the same time, the status quo was unacceptable to them. So be it.

In January 2004, others in the administration floated the idea of trying only the British detainees in our criminal courts. Blair wanted something done.

The timing could not have been worse. We were arguing a case in the Supreme Court that enemy combatants should be tried in military proceedings and that the Supreme Court should not take jurisdiction of these claims by foreigners captured overseas on the battlefield. Our arguments would be undercut if we voluntarily afforded access to terrorists by bringing them into our criminal courts.

I hoped to push the decision regarding the Brits to the summer, simply because we had other issues that hopefully would be resolved favorably within a few months. I also believed that trying the Brits now in our criminal courts would be interpreted as our giving up on military commissions. Certainly, the Australians would insist on similar treatment. No doubt, every European country would want their nationals tried in Article III courts, and we couldn't do this for the Europeans only and have the terrorists from Arab nations tried in military commissions.

I worried, too, that criminal trials would present serious challenges to our national security. Furthermore, we would be increasing the risks of having our intelligence sources and methods compromised during the legal discovery process. We now knew that this was no longer merely a hypothetical possibility to be debated by law school students. During the trial of Omar Abdel Rahman, the blind sheikh who led the attempt to blow up the World Trade Center in 1993, the prosecutors complied with standard criminal justice discovery procedures and handed over to the defense a list of two hundred possible unindicted coconspirators. The list was basically our best information on al-Qaeda at the time. Within days of the list's introduction in court, it was in the hands of Osama bin Laden, who simply by looking at it could tell who among his ranks had been compromised, and worse yet, how US intelligence had learned the information.[2]

Thanks to the documents disclosed in public court, when bin Laden realized that the United States could intercept his cell phone calls and track his GPS location, he simply stopped using mobile devices.[3]

So the possibility of revealing more information during the trials of detainees was extremely dangerous. Even if security measures were stringent, we would still most likely be confronted with the same challenges over procedures and evidence that bedeviled us during the Moussaoui trial.

On February 7, 2004, I had another call with Lord Goldsmith. The British attorney general was accustomed to getting his way with the law. But so was I.

He wanted his citizens charged now (rather than simply leaving them in detention while decisions were being made), but doing so would undercut our argument in the Supreme Court case, while put into play discovery risks of our sources and methods, and jeopardize the entire military commission process. So we declined to charge them.

Now facing growing pressure from its media as well as the British public, the Brits asked us to return its detained citizens. I was disappointed by their decision, but relieved that President Bush had chosen to institutionalize policies that hopefully would long outlive his tenure in office. I also sensed that the president, Andy, and Condi were simply happy to get this problem off our plate. We did ask the Brits to keep the terrorists incarcerated, but of course, we received no guarantees they would. Consequently, we emphasized to them that if any of the returned terrorists reentered the fight against the coalition, that would be the Brits' problem, not ours.

The Australian government had remained resolute throughout the long negotiating ordeal. They had been comfortable with our plans for military commissions to deal with detained terrorists, including ones who were Australian citizens. After Great Britain requested that its citizens not be subjected to military commissions, however, Australia insisted on similar treatment for its citizens.

The entire matter took an enormous amount of time and energy and resources for an extremely frustrating result with one of our strongest allies.[4] Looking back, it was one of the more disappointing experiences I'd had since being in government.

It would not be the last.

CHAPTER 20

INTERROGATIONS
FOR INTELLIGENCE

Twelve al-Qaeda operatives were sleeping in a two-story apartment building in Faisalabad, the third-largest industrial town in northern Pakistan, the night of March 28, 2002, when they were awakened by Pakistani forces raiding the safe house. Four young al-Qaeda fighters fled by leaping to the roof of a nearby building. In the firefight that followed, the leader of the group was severely wounded, shot three times in the thigh and groin.

When coalition troops searched the apartment complex, they found sparse living accommodations and an entire section of the apartment filled with computer equipment, an al-Qaeda treasure trove for our intelligence agencies. But the troops soon realized that they had captured something even more important than weapons and hard-drives: the wounded operative was none other than Abu Zubaydah, al-Qaeda's number three leader, a name that had been all over our daily threat reports, ranking in importance only behind Osama bin Laden and Ayman al-Zawahiri. Zubaydah was the most important member of al-Qaeda that we had yet captured.

Our troops had the ironic task of trying to save a terrorist's life to discover what he knew about plans for future plots and attacks. Because of his insider status with al-Qaeda, we were convinced that Zubaydah had information that could possibly save thousands of lives. The CIA officers who had been aiding the raid arranged for a special, chartered flight to whisk a world-class doctor from John Hopkins Medical Center to Pakistan, where he helped keep the killer from dying.[1]

Although we had Zubaydah, there was no consensus in the Bush administration about what we should do with him. Spirited discussions took place about how to mine the mother lode of information Zubaydah likely possessed. He was a tough guy, an al-Qaeda all-star. He was not likely to willingly give up information, squeal on his friends, or reveal future plots simply because we asked him. He was young and strong—physically and intellectually—with fierce inner fortitude. He was irrevocably committed to his cause. He had been responsible for training al-Qaeda recruits and was an expert at resisting usual interrogation methods. Simply asking him to be forthcoming would be a waste of time. Verbal threats weren't going to affect him either. And using mind games and good-cop/bad-cop traditional law enforcement methods of convincing him to tell us what he knew would be useless. Similarly, the experts believed using interrogation under the US Army Field Manuals would be ineffective.

If we were going to get Zubaydah to talk, the CIA experts believed they needed something stronger. They needed enhanced types of interrogations if they were ever going to make any headway with him at all—and every day that went by in which we did not gain the information he knew allowed al-Qaeda another opportunity to hit us.

So what do you do when you catch a bad guy like this? You follow George Tenet's wry observation: "Despite what Hollywood might have you believe, in situations like this you don't call in the tough guys; you call in the lawyers."[2]

Contrary to what Americans see on television or in the movies, before any CIA operative will do anything not permitted in the United States Army Field Manuals—which detail the interrogation guidelines for military personnel—they want a written legal opinion from the Justice Department advising them that whatever they intend to do is legal. Otherwise, the CIA agents and their leaders could be prosecuted under the existing US anti-torture statute.

In 1988, the United States signed an international treaty, the United Nations Convention Against Torture and Other Cruel, Inhumane, or Degrading Treatment or Punishment (known as the CAT). Under Article 2 of the CAT, the United States committed to passing a law outlawing torture. Furthermore, under Article 16, the United States agreed to prohibit acts of cruel, inhumane, or degrading treatment or punishment that do not rise to the level of torture.[3] The US State Department summary and analysis of the CAT stated that "torture is at the extreme end of cruel, inhumane, and degrading treatment or punishment," and that to constitute torture an act must be "of an extremely cruel and inhumane nature, specifically intended to inflict excruciating and agonizing physical or mental suffering."[4]

Because of concerns regarding the ambiguity of the terms "cruel, inhumane, or degrading" in Article 16, the State Department recommended that the United States express an understanding that the terms of Article 16 mean cruel, unusual, and inhumane treatment or punishment that is prohibited by the Fifth, Eighth, and/or the Fourteenth Amendments to the US Constitution.[5]

Human rights groups immediately pushed back, claiming the bar for an act to constitute torture was too high, causing the United States to reassure the world that we were not raising the threshold of pain required for an act to be torture. This was reflected in a statement from the legal advisor to the State Department in 1990, explaining that to constitute torture, an act must be a deliberate and calculated act of cruel and inhumane nature, specifically intended to inflict *excruciating* and *agonizing* physical or mental pain or suffering. In that same letter, the legal advisor recommended that the United States take a "reservation" instead of the weaker "understanding" to Article 16, because of the ambiguous nature of its terms, particularly "degrading treatment."[6]

The head of the criminal division of the Justice Department, the office that would prosecute acts constituting torture, confirmed the extremely high threshold commonly understood in international law when he wrote:

As applied to physical torture, there appears to be some degree of consensus that the concept involves conduct the mere mention of which sends chills down one's spine; the needle under the fingernail, the application of electric shock to the genital area, the piercing of eyeballs, etc. Techniques which inflict such excruciating and agonizing physical pain are recognized as the essence of torture. Hence, the Convention chose the [word] "severe" to indicate the high level of the pain required to support a finding of torture.[7]

Anticipating the question of why the United States even had to define torture, the head of the criminal division wrote that the definition of torture is imprecise, making it doubtful the United States government could enforce the law consistent with constitutional due process constraints. Further, the imprecise definition would have the effect of generating "unwanted litigation in areas of law enforcement." Against this backdrop, the United States ratified the CAT, but took a reservation to Article 16, reflecting that the United States concepts of "cruel, inhumane, and degrading" differ somewhat from international law as understood by other nations.

At our April 1, 2002, NSC meeting, Zubaydah was a major topic of discussion. Everyone in the room knew he was a senior level operative in al-Qaeda, and we also knew there was a lot of chatter on the terrorist hotlines.

The president was concerned about increased threat reporting and our intelligence agencies' inability to obtain actionable intelligence—information that would help prevent attacks on America, as well as information that would actually lead to capturing or killing other terrorists who were threatening our nation. "We need to hustle to come up with a strategy to deal with this person," President Bush said regarding Zubaydah.

In answer to the president's unstated reasons for his sense of urgency, the CIA developed a series of procedures that came to be known as "enhanced interrogation techniques," procedures beyond those allowed in the US Army Field Manuals. With the Justice Department in the lead, the lawyers were immediately asked to look carefully at these procedures because of prohibitions under domestic and international laws against using torture.

Contrary to reports in the media and in blogs, from the earliest days following 9/11, President Bush emphatically declared that the United States would *not* torture captured terrorists under any circumstances, not in secret CIA sites, not at Guantanamo Bay, not anywhere. Unlike our enemies, President Bush had emphatically stated that America would treat our enemy captives humanely, so we wanted to make sure that the enhanced interrogation methods our CIA was hoping to use did not violate domestic or international laws as they applied to the United States.

Since the Church Committee investigations of the mid-1970s, most spies and intelligence agents worked warily under the specter of the committee's report. The Church Committee—which took its name from its chair, Senator Frank Church of Idaho—ordered investigators to the CIA, FBI, and NSA to look for wrongdoing. The committee found what it was looking for, including the NSA's original Operation Minaret, a surveillance program put in place by President Lyndon B. Johnson in 1967 that resulted in spying, wiretapping, and eavesdropping electronically on opponents of the Vietnam war, civil rights activists, and others critical of US policies. In addition to tracking bona fide criminals and potential terrorists, the committee discovered that US intelligence agents had been watching people ranging from Martin Luther King Jr. to *Washington Post* satirist Art Buchwald to Muhammad Ali.

The investigators also discovered CIA and FBI domestic spying that infiltrated and sought to disrupt black activist groups in hopes of pitting them against one another, as well as foreign spying that encouraged assassination plots against Fidel Castro. Concerns over the government looking into American citizens' private lives as well as questionable conduct in our foreign intelligence activities led to a number of reforms, including the enactment of the FISA law and the creation of the FISA Court. The conclusions and recommendations of Senator Church's committee provided a constant backdrop and sounding board for everything the CIA, FBI, and NSA did from that time to today.

So when we began talking about interrogation techniques that would help agents get information out of someone like Zubaydah, many agents were wary of aggressive, potentially controversial actions. They wanted assurances they would not be prosecuted for torture. Although this was an issue that primarily concerned the CIA and DOJ, because of the sensitivity of torture issues and President Bush's clear directive that the United States would not engage in torture, I became involved in many of the discussions of the legal analysis of certain techniques. I, too, worried that no matter what we did, or how carefully we proceeded, we were likely to be second-guessed and criticized.

I wrestled with how much detail I—or anybody else—should tell the president about specific interrogation techniques. On one hand, if we didn't do this right, it could severely hurt his presidency. Some people might say, "Are you kidding? This is exactly the kind of issue and decision that *only* the president of the United States should make." On the other hand, part of my job was to protect the *presidency*, as well as President Bush himself. Moreover, Andy Card expected me to keep controversial issues out of the White House unless necessity demanded that the president know of certain facts or where information was necessary to make a decision. Layered on top of these considerations was the president's directive: do whatever is necessary and consistent with our laws to protect America.

On April 18, 2002, I talked to the president about Zubaydah. He assured me he had instructed CIA director George Tenet *not* to torture Zubaydah. Although I had been present at all NSC and principals committee meetings, I had not heard these specific directions to George Tenet. I assumed that Tenet had discussed Zubaydah with President Bush during one of his many briefings in the Oval Office. George met with the president almost daily to review threats that had come in over the past twenty-four hours and what we were doing to prevent attacks. The threat matrix put together by the FBI and the CIA and given to the president every day in his Presidential Daily Briefing (PDB) was ominous. But that made getting information from Zubaydah about impending attacks even more important.

I told the president that to protect him and his presidency, we would not inform him in specific terms about various interrogation techniques, but we would reassure him that the techniques were effective, that the lawyers were continually examining CIA activities to confirm that they were lawful, and that we would not engage in any conduct that would be in violation of our domestic anti-torture statute or the CAT. The president wanted to agree with that approach, but he seemed to be torn. He was not the sort of person who wanted to be oblivious to the facts or kept in the dark about what was going on, but he understood the precarious nature of the interrogation program.

During the next few weeks, administration lawyers poured themselves into figuring out what we could and couldn't do. John Yoo, who had the lead at Justice and was working on providing the legal guidelines, came to my office from time to time to share his most current thinking about the issues with John Rizzo, a senior lawyer with the CIA, Tim Flanigan, David Addington, and me. My charge to John was direct: "I want you to provide guidance to the CIA as to the scope of the anti-torture statute. The analysis should guide the administration away from conduct that constitutes torture." John understood the assignment and what was at stake.

On July 17, I had a conversation with John about his draft opinion on the interrogation methods that included a discussion of the president's commander in chief authority. I expressed my concern about possible interpretations and suggested that he discuss the application of the anti-torture statues to specific techniques desired by the CIA. I also was concerned about tying the president to the discussions about torture. I really didn't want the president making a commander in chief determination that the techniques were necessary. I told John that while the opinion should certainly discuss presidential constitutional authority, I wanted the opinion addressed to the CIA. They were the agents who needed the immediate guidance, and they were the ones who would be dealing with other terrorists like Zubaydah that we hoped we would be apprehending soon. They were also most at risk of future prosecutions.

The following day, I talked by phone with Attorney General Ashcroft regarding the legal issues. I was reassured by a comment Ashcroft made that he wanted to talk to his folks about the issues under the anti-torture statute. That showed me that the advice I was receiving from John Yoo was not simply Yoo's alone, but actually reflected the views of the Department of

Justice leadership. Ashcroft also expressed concern about describing specific techniques and providing safe harbors in advance of the conduct.

"I understand that the CIA really wants approval of specific techniques," I told the AG. "I will defer to you, but time is of the essence."

The following afternoon, I spoke again with Ashcroft, and he informed me that the DOJ could give a fact-specific opinion. "Who was involved in the discussions at Justice?" I asked him.

"Larry Thompson, Michael Chertoff, John Yoo, Pat Philbin, and Adam Ciongoli," John replied. That was encouraging. These individuals whom Ashcroft mentioned—the deputy attorney general, the head of the criminal division, the other DOJ lawyers—were fine attorneys, some of the brightest in government, and deeply committed to protecting our country. I was satisfied that the opinion had received the appropriate level of review and supervision.

On July 23, I met with the president and gave him an update on the legal analysis. I told him DOJ was nearing the completion of its work on the matter. He responded that he was comfortable with the administration going forward with the enhanced techniques.

I continued to resist explaining the techniques, and the president agreed that he did not need to know specifics; he just wanted to know that the techniques were effective and lawful. "If not," he said, "we won't do it." He appeared pleased we would be able to use enhanced techniques to get information from Zubaydah in a manner consistent with US domestic and international obligations.

The following morning, John Yoo told me the attorney general had signed off on the opinion. DOJ's approval would be communicated to the CIA. John anticipated that the agency would begin the approved techniques on the basis of oral advice from DOJ, with the written opinion to follow shortly.

On July 26, I spoke to John again around 4:30 in the afternoon. "The procedures are lawful," John said. Ashcroft, Larry Thompson, and Michael Chertoff had all signed off on the opinion, he reported.

The CIA would only apply enhanced techniques to high-value detainees approved by a senior CIA official, after a determination that the detainee likely possessed knowledge of an impending attack. An interrogation profile developed by a medical doctor and a psychologist would be developed for each detainee.

As we had anticipated, Zubaydah was resistant to efforts to get information under the usual methods prescribed in the Army Field Manuals. So our CIA interrogators had asked for permission to use enhanced interrogation techniques to get information out of him. A medical team would be on-site to ensure that Zubaydah suffered no severe physical or mental pain or suffering.

Nevertheless, despite these precautions and all the work of the lawyers, John and I knew that these techniques would invite criticism and scrutiny. The International Criminal Court (ICC) was originally proposed in the 1990s as a court for crimes against humanity, genocide, and war crimes. The United States withdrew from the jurisdiction of the court early in the Bush administration because the court could prosecute Americans without regard to their constitutional rights. The ICC would likely launch an investigation. While I trusted the legal judgment of the senior leadership at Justice, I remained worried about the political and legal fallout. To reassure myself about the advice from Justice, I studied the history of the ratification of the CAT and the US anti-torture statute. While some in the European Union and human rights groups wanted a lower threshold of pain, it was clear to me that the legitimate international standard was higher, consistent with what we had adopted, requiring pain that was "excruciating" and "agonizing." I knew there would be public pushback and I was concerned about that, but my job was to ensure the president received the correct legal advice, unshaded by fear of criticism or personal bias. He could decide to ignore it if he was uncomfortable with the legal standard.

We anticipated that there would be so-called legal experts, university professors, civil liberties groups, and foreign countries—both enemies and allies—who would view the use of these techniques as a violation of international law, based on their own applicable legal standards. The discussion of torture would undoubtedly become muddled with conduct regarded as "cruel, inhumane, and degrading." But even if we were to judge our techniques by this lower standard, they would arguably still be lawful. We had not criminalized cruel, inhumane, and degrading treatment, but the United States had clearly announced that the lower standard of cruel, inhumane, and degrading would be only "those acts that shock the conscience"[8] in the context of surrounding circumstances.

John Yoo was fearless and I appreciated his intestinal fortitude; I also admired the attorney general and the lawyers at Justice for their courage. They could have shaded their opinion to protect themselves, but they were more concerned about lawfully protecting American lives than their own reputations. We were about to head down a dark, lonely road, one riddled with landmines and other hidden dangers.

At 5:30 that day, I met with Andy Card and George Tenet about Zubaydah. George was ready to go forward with the interrogation. He believed it was important that we get the information the al-Qaeda operative possessed. I reminded him that what we were doing would invite scrutiny that would surely escalate when our actions became public one day. It was an eventuality that he no doubt had considered over and over in his mind.

George had been the director of the CIA and the deputy director before that, long before many of us in the Bush administration had come to town. As much as anybody, Tenet understood what was at stake, both the dangers to us of being persecuted, if not prosecuted, and the dangers to our country if we did not take the actions we were contemplating.

At 7:00 p.m., I walked over to the residence to tell the president about the interrogations talks. "With the DOJ opinion, there should be relatively little risk from a domestic law context if the techniques are administered according to the guidelines," I told him, "but I can give you no assurance that there will not be a prosecution or attempted prosecution of the agents, or even of you, yourself, by a foreign country." I also told him about my conversation with George Tenet. "He will probably call you in the morning," I said, "and tell you how important it is to get this information." Tenet was serious about the need to do this now that the Justice Department had concluded that the interrogations were legal.

I emphasized to the president that Tenet also believed that the techniques approved by Justice were effective. It was during this conversation that I first raised the subject of waterboarding. But President Bush had already talked to Tenet about it. He seemed to be reassured about moving forward by the fact that thousands of our own military troops had been subjected to this procedure as part of their survival training.

I informed the president that Tenet had asked me why we were so worried from an international law standpoint. "I told him the truth," I said to the president. "Because some ICC prosecutor might try to pick us all up someday!'"

After my conversation with the president, I spoke again with George Tenet. He was now nervous about moving forward with the enhanced interrogations. He wanted something in writing, declaring they were legal and that the CIA could proceed. "You'll have it shortly," I promised. The lawyers in my office and I had been reading a draft of the opinion from DOJ that very afternoon. I encouraged him that if he felt the country was at risk, based on the verbal go-ahead from Justice, he could proceed. He responded that he was having trouble with his group. He needed to get them back on board. He also expressed concern about being brought to The Hague for prosecution.

I had mixed emotions about the CIA interrogations after our conversation. The agents lived to gather information to protect our country, but they would be placing their careers in jeopardy by doing these interrogations. It was hard to view this as strictly a legal judgment. Even with a DOJ opinion, in the future, agents could be subject to second-guessing and criticism by a hostile Congress, and most certainly by the international community. Although Congress was quite cooperative with the president following the devastating attacks on 9/11, the atmosphere could change quickly. There was no guarantee that our own senators or congressmen would not decide at some future date to come back and demand—on the basis of legal guidance from the Justice Department—that the agents be prosecuted for doing their jobs.[9]

While having an opinion from the DOJ made it unlikely that agents would actually go to jail—unless they acted beyond the scope of the opinion—the enormous expenses and prolonged inconveniences incurred by an agent having to hire lawyers to defend himself or herself would decimate most, if not all. It was a ludicrous situation: if the agents did their jobs well, getting the information we needed to protect our nation from attack, the agents themselves might be attacked in court. And worse yet, our DOJ could not protect our interrogators from potential lawsuits and prosecutions in foreign courts, where they might lose. They were at risk, not because they had violated a legal standard applicable to Americans but rather one that had been rejected by the United States and adopted by other countries.

I was glad that Tenet was thinking about these possibilities. It was a time of courage, regardless of the consequences.

On July 30, I received a call from Senior Attorney John Rizzo at the CIA. He reported that Tenet was ready to go forward with the enhanced interrogation of Zubaydah. *These past four days must have been interesting at the CIA*, I thought, *as Tenet worked to reassure his team.*

The OLC legal opinion—stating that it was lawful to proceed in questioning detainees such as Zubaydah by using enhanced interrogations—was signed by Jay Bybee, the assistant attorney general for the Office of Legal Counsel. It came out August 1, 2002, and was addressed to John Rizzo. Because we might have to rely on it someday, the OLC issued a second important opinion addressed to me that examined the United States anti-torture statute in relation to the president's commander in chief authority.

Think about that: we captured Zubaydah on March 28, 2002, and it took four months to weigh out the issues surrounding his interrogation. Some of the most brilliant lawyers in our government grappled with the questions of how, why, in what manner, and the ramifications of interrogating the terrorists who had perpetrated the 9/11 act of terrorism. These were not knee-jerk reactions, casual conclusions drawn in haste or in the heat of emotion. These techniques were analyzed from every angle and deemed necessary to gather information that would protect our citizens. And the decisions were made by people who love our country and who were willing to risk their careers and reputations to protect it in accordance with the law.

The OLC opinion regarding the CIA-designed techniques, including waterboarding, was the first attempt by the executive branch of our government to interpret the scope of the domestic anti-torture statute.

Until recently, most Americans had little idea what the enhanced interrogations entailed. When the media and others decried the Bush administration for authorizing "torture," understandably many people imagined the worst—needles under the fingernails, piercing of eyeballs, electrodes to genitals, and broken limbs—all of which were prohibited by the administration guidelines. Yet in a day when ISIS is decapitating Christians with swords, CIA efforts to extract vital information regarding future al-Qaeda plans might seem embarrassingly benign to many people, especially those American families who have lost loved ones to terrorism. From the OLC order originally classified as top secret but recently declassified, this is the description of the ten enhanced techniques that the CIA was initially authorized to perform:

(1) Attention grasp. The attention grasp consists of grasping the individual with both hands, one hand on each side of the collar opening, in a controlled and quick motion. In the same motion, the individual is drawn toward the interrogator.

(2) Walling. A flexible false wall is constructed and the individual is placed with his heels touching the wall. The interrogator pulls the individual forward and then quickly and firmly pushes the individual into the wall, so his shoulder blades hit the wall. The head and neck are supported to prevent whiplash.

(3) Facial hold. The facial hold is used to hold the head immobile.

(4) Facial slap. The interrogator slaps the individual's face with fingers slightly spread. The purpose of the facial slap is not to inflict pain but to induce shock, surprise, and/or humiliation.

(5) Cramped confinement. This restricts the individual's movement in a dark, confined space.

(6) Wall standing. Standing with arms stretched out, fingers against the wall to produce muscle fatigue.

(7) Stress positions. These are not bodily contortions, but positions such as sitting on the floor with the legs stretched out or arms above the head.

(8) Sleep deprivation.

(9) Insects placed in a confinement box. The individual is placed in a box along with a "stinging insect," that is actually a harmless insect such as a caterpillar.

(10) Waterboarding. The individual is bound securely to an inclined bench, feet are generally elevated. A cloth is placed over the forehead and eyes. Water is then applied to the cloth in a controlled manner. As this is done, the cloth is lowered until it covers both the nose and mouth. Once the cloth is saturated and completely covers the mouth and nose, air flow is slightly restricted for 20 to 40 seconds due to the presence of the cloth. This produces the perception of "suffocation and incipient panic," i.e., the perception of drowning. The individual does not breathe any water into his lungs. During those 20 to 40 seconds, water is continuously applied from a height of twelve to twenty-four inches. After this period, the cloth is lifted, and the individual is allowed to breathe unimpeded for three or four full breaths. The sensation of drowning is immediately relieved by the removal of the cloth. The procedure may then be repeated.[10]

Legal support for four additional techniques was provided and the "insect" technique removed in a May 10, 2005, memo to Rizzo from OLC's Steven Bradbury. The added techniques were diet manipulation, nudity, abdominal slapping, and water dousing.

These were the techniques that OLC advised could be done. Certainly most people would consider some or all of these techniques unpleasant, perhaps even cruel, inhumane, and degrading. I surely would consider it awful if they were applied to me. Some people might even regard them as "torture," but according to the Justice Department, these techniques, when administered in a controlled environment with the appropriate safeguards, fell within the guidelines of our domestic and international legal obligations.[11]

The following week, the CIA briefed key members of the congressional Intelligence Committee regarding the enhanced techniques they planned to use. I worried that by informing Congress, we ran the risk of leaks that might alert our enemies of our plans, but the CIA understood it was only a matter of time before their actions would become public. They wanted the White House and the Congress alongside when the critics started howling and everything hit the fan. Over time, congressional leaders, both Democrat and Republican, would receive more than thirty briefings about the interrogations. For our so-called leaders to say later on that they were never informed about these matters or did not understand is not only a lie, it is unconscionable and cowardly.

Nevertheless, concerned about another attack and our inability to collect helpful intelligence, the CIA—*not* the military, which ran Gitmo—sought and received approval to use enhanced techniques when questioning senior-level detainees who might have knowledge of impending attacks. The two key questions President Bush repeatedly asked me regarding the enhanced interrogation techniques were: "Is it lawful?" and "Is it effective?" In both cases, I replied, "Yes." To my knowledge, during my time in the Bush administration, enhanced techniques were approved and applied to only three senior-level detainees.

Of course, as a Christian, I grappled with the morality of any actions that hinted at treating another human being—even a known terrorist—inhumanely. Every step of the way, however, these techniques were deemed lawful by the Department of Justice and accepted by key members of the National Security Council, unlike the abuse of Iraqi detainees by a few miscreants that took place at Abu Ghraib prison.

Indeed, over time, OLC rendered several legal opinions, signed by three separate top-tier lawyers and approved by three separate attorneys general, regarding enhanced interrogation techniques. President Obama's FBI director, in his former capacity as deputy attorney general, also agreed the techniques were lawful, when applied individually, so it wasn't Bush's war on terror or Cheney's advocacy of interrogation that carried the day.[12] These techniques were declared legal and necessary because they were.

These were not arbitrary decisions made in a moral vacuum. Even after receiving Department of Justice approval, CIA director George Tenet was concerned about going forward with enhanced interrogations for fear of future political witch-hunts. But as Condi Rice reminded us in the Situation Room, this was a group decision and we all had to "hold hands" and assume responsibility as we took a leap of faith together, believing that our course was not only effective, but lawful and just.

According to Tenet, NSA director Mike Hayden, and others testifying under oath, the valuable information obtained through the interrogation methods helped save many lives.

Using the enhanced methods, CIA interrogators helped Zubaydah loosen his tongue. He provided key information that led to the capture of Ramzi bin al-Shibh, a Yemeni student who had studied with three of the 9/11 hijackers and possibly would have been one of them, but he could not obtain a US visa. Instead, he served as the communications link between the hijackers and the planners of the 9/11 attacks. Following 9/11, bin al-Shibh was in Pakistan plotting to use commercial airliners to strike London when he was captured by Pakistani authorities on the first anniversary of 9/11.

It was bin al-Shibh who then led to the capture of Khalid Sheikh Mohammed, KSM as we came to refer to him, the so-called mastermind of the 9/11 attacks and the preeminent source on al-Qaeda. Similar enhanced interrogations helped KSM to provide information on future al-Qaeda attack plans and probable targets. It was KSM who disclosed a terrorist cell in Karachi, Pakistan, where al-Qaeda terrorists were thought to be plotting to fly a hijacked plane into the tallest building on the West Coast.[13]

The guidance from the DOJ was for interrogations done by agents of the CIA, not the military. Historically, our soldiers have long abided by the interrogation methods outlined in the US Army Field Manuals. Consequently, at the beginning of Operation Enduring Freedom, our military interrogated enemy combatants according to those standards. The al-Qaeda training manual, however, taught their recruits how to defeat or resist the well-known US interrogation techniques. Not surprisingly, our soldiers were frustratingly unsuccessful at getting valuable information from the combatants they questioned. Clearly, there was a national security need for the Department of Defense to develop alternatives.

That became even more obvious when a captured al-Qaeda member, Mohammed al-Qahtani, was detained at Guantanamo Bay. A skilled liar, al-Qahtani flicked away FBI questions and those of the military officers at Gitmo. But interrogators were convinced that he knew about the inner workings of al-Qaeda, and the information he held could be important. The intercepted terrorist chatter throughout the late summer and early fall increased, causing us concern that al-Qaeda was planning something big—soon.

Meanwhile, a detainee with potentially valuable information sat comfortably in Guantanamo Bay. Military intelligence believed that al-Qahtani knew information related to ongoing al-Qaeda activities or another attack. But they weren't getting anywhere questioning him according to the US Army Field Manuals techniques.

Consequently, on October 11, 2002, officials at Guantanamo asked for permission to use additional methods. During the next two months, Jim Haynes worked with John Yoo to develop a set of interrogation techniques that would be effective and would also satisfy domestic and international anti-torture standards. These would be presented to Defense Secretary Rumsfeld.

Jim kept me generally informed about the legal issues affecting DOD, but I did not get involved in these discussions to the depth that I had initially concerning the CIA interrogations standards. We discussed the DOD progress, but whenever Jim raised an issue regarding the techniques with me, I told him he needed to work it out with DOJ. I anticipated that the methods the military would be comfortable adopting would not be as aggressive as those of the CIA. But I trusted Jim and John Yoo to work through these matters. For the same reasons previously noted, I did not have conversations with the president regarding specific details of the DOD plans, except to let him know that DOD was working on it and would review their plans with DOJ for effectiveness and legality.

Following the receipt of legal advice from OLC, on December 2, Jim Haynes presented three categories of interrogation techniques for Don Rumsfeld's approval. Understand, we're not talking about pulling off a detainee's fingernails or applying electric shocks to his genitals—as had been done to some American POWs. No, in category one, interrogators could yell at a captive; in category two, they could deprive the detainee of light and sound or do other things that might cause him or her to feel isolated or dis-oriented, such as making him stand in the same place or standing with his face to a wall for hours; they might even deprive the detainee of hot meals and make him eat military-style packaged meals. In category three, the techniques included subjecting the detainee to cold temperatures, removal of his clothing, making the detainee believe that he or his family member might suffer pain or death if he did not cooperate, poking a detainee in the chest with a finger, pushing, grabbing, and other mild physical contact, water dousing, up to the use of waterboarding.[14]

Although all three categories of interrogation techniques were approved by the DOJ, the military JAGs responded with strong criticism and pressure. Within a month, the secretary of defense withdrew permission for categories two and three and sent a written directive approving only the techniques in the Army Field Manuals. He also directed the formulation of a group chaired by Mary Walker, air force general counsel, to examine military interrogation techniques.

All the while, al-Qahtani remained in a cell in Guantanamo.

And US officials worried about another possible plot. But again, contrary to the public's perception fostered by movies, the military culture is strongly averse to using questioning techniques beyond those in the Army Field Manuals. US military personnel know that one of the fastest ways they can find themselves in a court-martial situation is to act contrary to the field manuals.

It was my understanding that the field manual pertaining to interrogation was designed with the assumption that the United States would be dealing with prisoners of war, a status to which we granted the highest protections—including protections from torture. I do not believe the manual was ever intended to deal with unlawful enemy combatants—terrorists—who violate the laws of war. The military, however, made no such distinction between those it detained.

Don Rumsfeld expected the results from Walker's working group within a couple of weeks. That didn't happen. Their work stretched from two weeks to two months. When Khalid Sheik Mohammed was captured in early March 2002, the urgency to complete the DOD rules of interrogation heightened.

Exacerbating matters, by the end of March, the CIA inspector general launched an investigation into possible wrongdoing by CIA agents in connection with the death of a detainee. I also heard rumors of an interrogator waving a gun at a detainee—something that an American interrogator was not permitted to do. That went beyond the legal guidance DOJ had provided to the CIA.

Additionally, the Senate Select Committee on Intelligence requested a copy of the DOJ opinion to the CIA. Keep in mind, from the outset of the program, the senators had received periodic briefings on the CIA's enhanced interrogations. But now they had also been briefed about the death of a detainee and the possible gun-waving incident. They wanted to know what was going on.

Normally, the DOJ would not turn over a highly classified legal opinion such as the one regarding the CIA interrogations. When I was consulted, I suggested that we should first propose giving an oral briefing to the members of the Senate committee.

As the DOD finalized its rules on interrogation techniques, it planned to implement up to thirty-five techniques, twenty-five of which essentially mimicked the Army Field Manuals. It appeared that DOJ would be willing to sign off on the remaining eleven techniques if there were proper precautions. If, however, Rumsfeld decided to authorize these eleven, John Ashcroft wanted him to brief the appropriate members of Congress.

On top of everything else swirling around the interrogation issues, the inspector general for the Department of Justice had begun an investigation of the treatment of people in custody under DOJ following 9/11. I was informed of a draft IG report finding that Larry Thompson, the deputy attorney general, made mistakes regarding certain detention actions he authorized—nothing criminal—that led to certain people's rights being violated in the wake of the 9/11 attacks.

I was irritated by this news. Larry Thompson was the quintessential professional. In the immediate aftermath of the September 11 attacks, he responded as anyone in his position would have, doing all that he could to collect information and identify threats to America. I didn't like the inspector general's twenty-twenty hindsight as he second-guessed the professional judgment of DOJ leadership on a national security issue in a time of war. It would not be the last time I'd encounter it.

The next day, Jim Haynes called me at about 6:30 a.m., as he often did. Jim informed me that Rumsfeld planned to approve only twenty-four of the thirty-five techniques suggested by Mary Walker's group, which he did on April 16, 2003. Ultimately, the JAGs' opposition carried the day.

In no case was I ever specifically aware when or if the CIA or DOD intended to use enhanced interrogation techniques on a particular detainee. There was no reason for me to know. Justice had provided the legal guidelines, so it was now up to the intelligence and military professionals to follow that advice. Contrary to highly partisan reports issued in 2015, for the most part both the CIA and DOD interrogators maintained the highest integrity during the questioning of detainees. In the few cases when they did not, disciplinary actions were taken immediately.

Nor was I regularly informed about what information was ascertained as a result of the enhanced techniques, only that they were effective.

During the latter part of July 2003, our intelligence community reported major threat concerns. On July 29, the NCS met in the Situation Room at the White House to evaluate the reports. I learned that al-Qaeda was intent on conducting another 9/11-style attack in the summer of 2003. Despite hardening our assets, our intelligence officials believed al-Qaeda still planned to use airplanes as weapons.

We had no specific target, but we also had great concerns about biological attacks using anthrax. The president decided that if we had imminent threats, we needed to set priority names on the watch list. He asked multiple questions of his team that morning, such as: Will the nationality of the enemy change?

Most certainly, was the answer.

Is there anything more that we can do to protect domestic flights?

With the greater threat from international flights, have we assessed vulnerabilities of foreign airlines and asked them to change procedures?

Of course, we were already looking at foreign cockpit crews and foreign air marshals. Would raising the threat level change al-Qaeda's behavior?

Does it make sense to play with their minds and plant false leads about what we know?

The questions kept on coming.

In early 2004, news broke about a scandal at Abu Ghraib prison—complete with photographs of US soldiers taunting naked Iraqi prisoners. The photos documented sadistic abuse of the prisoners in disturbing and humiliating sexual acts, devoid of human dignity.

I first learned of the despicable acts from Jim Haynes. I knew immediately that this would do major damage to our interrogation efforts. Sadly, the actions of a few acting on their own initiative would tarnish the reputations of so many people taking extraordinary steps to legally gather information and to protect our country.

Critics immediately blamed the president's decision on the application of the Geneva Conventions as a contributing factor to the lessening of our values, asserting that this in turn resulted in the atrocities at Abu Ghraib.

Nothing could be further from the truth. What happened at Abu Ghraib had nothing to do with interrogations or gathering of information from detainees. The soldiers abusing those prisoners were not acting according to orders; they had no authority to conduct interrogations; they were not in charge of getting information out of the prisoners. And frankly, the particular prisoners themselves were not of great interest to our military or CIA intelligence, nor were they being held at Abu Ghraib so they could be interrogated.

No, unfortunately, the abusive guards were acting on their own, totally contrary to military conduct and all sense of human dignity. No senior officials in the Department of Defense or in the entire Bush administration encouraged or condoned such actions.

What those soldiers did was cruel, sadistic behavior that I condemned immediately, as did many others in the administration. Blaming the atrocities at Abu Ghraib on Bush policies also ignored the fact that only a handful of guards on one cellblock involving one night shift engaged in this conduct. All other American personnel at Abu Ghraib prison understood clearly their legal obligations to treat prisoners humanely. No one else was confused about the legal requirement. The abusive soldiers knew right from wrong. To absolve the few offenders of their responsibility for their actions and blame President Bush robs credit and honor from the hundreds of thousands of American soldiers who followed the rules. Indeed, between 2001 and 2006, more than eighty thousand captured personnel passed through DOD custody. When an allegation of wrongdoing was asserted, it was promptly investigated and prosecuted when appropriate.[15] In all that time, and with the large number of detainees handled, only a few known instances of abuse took place and the abusers were punished; some went to prison.

Unfortunately, the Abu Ghraib disclosures placed a spotlight on the interrogation efforts of the Bush administration and ignited a firestorm of debate on torture, despite President Bush's adamant orders to the contrary from the outset.

Although I had not authored the guidance memos, because of my role in ensuring the issue received appropriate legal review and my involvement in the legal analysis during the process, my name became associated with "the torture memos." Still today, critics attribute the DOJ legal opinions solely to me and hold me responsible for the interrogation policy. In truth, I never wielded that much power.

Interestingly, some people argued that circumstances might necessitate torture if it meant saving lives. At a June 2004 Senate Judiciary Committee hearing, New York's Democratic senator Charles Schumer bluntly stated:

There are times when we all get in high dudgeon. We ought to be reasonable about this. I think there are probably very few people in this room or in America who would say that torture should never, ever be used, particularly if thousands of lives are at stake. Take the hypothetical: If we knew that there was a nuclear bomb hidden in an American city, and we believed that some kind of torture, fairly severe maybe, would give us a better chance of finding that bomb before it went off, my guess is most Americans and most senators, maybe all, would say, "Do what you have to do." So it is easy to sit back in the armchair and say that torture can never be used. But when you are in the foxhole, it is a very different deal. And I respect—I think we all respect—the fact that the president is in the foxhole every day.[16]

Ironically, there was no equivocation on the part of President Bush. He was firm; he reiterated that under no circumstances would he authorize or encourage our intelligence agencies or military personnel to engage in torture. Personally, I supported his position based on my understanding of the law and history, not simply because that was what the president wanted.

No question about it, our post-9/11 world requires us to make tough choices about coercive actions that might prevent future attacks. Not everyone has the stomach for it. But we should never lose sight of the advantages to our citizens when our government makes tough but lawful choices. It has not been accidental that our nation, thanks to our intelligence agencies and law enforcement personnel, has thwarted other similar attacks.

A good bit of credit should be attributed to the fact that we are also very good listeners.

CHAPTER 21

RACE TO THE COURTHOUSE

George W. Bush's tenure in the White House is irrevocably linked with what happened on September 11, 2001, but there was much more that required our attention. Certainly, after 9/11, threats of further attacks pervaded every aspect of life and work in the White House. Nevertheless, while grappling with the daily briefings on potential terrorist threats, we were also dealing with a myriad of other major issues—everything from tax cuts to a new national energy policy to evaluating and planning for potential Supreme Court nominations to "no child left behind" improvements in education to stem cell research and a host of other efforts to move our country forward. In addition, we had concerns over a resurgent Russia, a less-than-cooperative China, a nuclear-threatening North Korea, as well as serious emerging issues in Syria, Iran, Iraq, and Israel.

Meanwhile, I was still attempting to maintain a "normal" family life, no easy task since I was working so much. Consequently, Becky shouldered more of our parenting responsibilities. We were one of the few couples in the upper echelons of the Bush administration who had young children. Karen and Jerry Hughes had a son, Robert, in his early teens; others had older teens, and a few had young adults out on their own. But our younger boys were Cub Scout and Boy Scout ages. Everyone in the administration, of course, was concerned about balancing time as parents with their many responsibilities. To me, Becky stood especially tall and strong through this time in our marriage and family. In many ways she served as both mom and dad during those early years in the lives of our boys. She is one of the most remarkable women I have ever known.

———

Prior to 9/11, President Bush had wanted to sign into law a comprehensive immigration reform bill. Unfortunately, after 9/11, talk of immigration reform disappeared, except for the need of increased security on our borders. A few years later, during my first meeting in Mexico as attorney general, my counterparts there admitted to me that their worst nightmare was a 9/11-type attack beginning with an illegal crossing of our border from Mexico. *If they are worried about such an attack, how can we ignore immigration issues?* I wondered—and still do.

———

Speculation continued in the media in 2002 about my becoming the first Hispanic on the Supreme Court. Washington's legal elite and social conservatives, however, expressed strong reservations and quite negative opinions about me. I was not a Washington insider, nor was I part of the legal elite; I was not reliably "conservative enough" for them. Some of my Hispanic friends wondered whether the opposition was because of my race.

I was intrigued by all the attention and by now slightly amused by the criticism, but I focused on my job. I hoped the hostility was not racial. As a Hispanic and as a Christian, I understand well the need for better racial relations in America. Certainly "black lives matter," but the truth is, every life matters. Racially charged responses to incidents such as those experienced in Ferguson, Staten Island, and Baltimore often can be prevented when we remind one another that we are all made in the image of God, that as the Sunday school song concludes, "red and yellow, black and white;

they are [all] precious in God's sight." The answer today is not more laws, as important as they have been in the past; the answer is the transformation of our hearts.

Consequently, when a race-related issue popped up early in the Bush administration, I knew we could not ignore it. But I failed to anticipate how it would damage my relationship with leading members of the Justice Department and further impair my reputation among conservative movers and thinkers.

Among the less publicized but highly important domestic matters with which I was concerned were the competing views of "affirmative action," spawned by a pair of controversial cases involving the admissions programs in the college and at the law school of the University of Michigan. The university and law school were using a deliberate admissions model to decide which students were allowed entrance.

For supporters of affirmative action programs in education, the legal justification for considering race in admission decisions was Justice Louis F. Powell Jr.'s opinion in the landmark 1978 case of *Regents of the University of California v. Bakke*. In this case, Justice Powell stated that "the attainment of a diverse student body . . . clearly is a constitutionally permissible goal for an institution of higher education." Although no other Supreme Court justice joined Powell's opinion, it has been relied upon by universities as justification to consider race, among other factors, in making admissions decisions. Unfortunately, over time, faced with growing pressure to attract a more diverse student body, many schools began giving greater weight to race when deciding which students to accept.

The University of Michigan was an example of this. In 2003, the university's undergraduate admission process admitted students based on their scores on a 150-point scale. A student received twenty points for being a racial minority, compared to only twelve points for SAT/ACT test scores; ten points for in-state residency; four points for alumni relationships; three points for an outstanding essay; and five points for achievement in leadership on a national level. Obviously, skin color played a major role in deciding who got into the University of Michigan and who did not.

At the same time, the University of Michigan law school's admission program evaluated a composite of a student's law school admission test scores (the LSAT) and undergraduate grade point average. Factored in were "soft" variables, which included a potential student's race. According to the law school, it did not set aside or reserve spots exclusively for minority students. It did, however, consider the total number of "underrepresented students," and it sought to enroll a significant number of such underrepresented minority students.

In 2002, a group of white students who had been denied admission to the University of Michigan's undergraduate program and to the law school sued the university and the law school, alleging violations of equal protection under the law. Prior to this, under equal protection decisions, an academic institution could consider race in its policies only if it served a "compelling government interest" and the admissions program was "narrowly tailored" to meet that interest. The US Supreme Court had ruled that to satisfy the requirement of narrow tailoring in the field of education, a state institution would first have to exhaust race-neutral alternatives to address the compelling government interest. Consider, for example, Texas's top 10 percent law: if you graduate in the top 10 percent of your public high school class, you are automatically admitted to a state school. So for high schools in South Texas where there are large Hispanic populations, more Hispanics have a chance to go to college regardless of their SAT or ACT scores and without consideration of race in the admissions process.

Except for Justice Powell's lone opinion on the matter, the Supreme Court had never weighed in on whether racial diversity in university admissions policies is a compelling government interest. So conservative groups viewed the Michigan cases as the best opportunity in several years to eliminate affirmative action once and for all, to strike down Powell's opinion in *Bakke*, and to prohibit any future consideration of race in university admissions decisions.

I was advised by the leadership at the Justice Department that the Supreme Court had always solicited the views of the sitting administration with respect to race cases, so that placed pressure on the Bush administration to take a position on the Michigan litigation. As White House counsel I had an important role to play, working with the Department of Justice, to develop a recommendation for the president. Because my name was increasingly bandied about as a potential Supreme Court nomination, some conservatives viewed my advice on the Michigan cases as a test of my fidelity to the Constitution, and to conservative values. I had never endorsed racial quotas or publicly expressed an opinion about race preferences. That alone caused great consternation and suspicion in some conservative ranks.

I approached the Michigan cases with an open mind, but my own life experiences heightened my sensitivity to the importance of every American, regardless of his or her skin color, having the same opportunity to pursue higher education. I readily acknowledged in some of my speeches to various groups that I had probably experienced both extremes—I had received benefits by being Hispanic, and I had been denied opportunities because of my race. For example, when Governor George W. Bush appointed me to the Texas Supreme Court in 1999, he acknowledged publicly that my ethnicity had been a factor in his decision, but he quickly added that I was appointed primarily because of my qualifications.

On the other hand, I had endured discrimination at times throughout my life, albeit not as overtly as my parents and previous generations of Hispanics. Nevertheless, I choose to believe that the pluses and minuses of my experiences cancel each other out over my lifetime. I believe it is more important to focus on what a person does when given an opportunity, rather than why that person was given that opportunity.

In November 2002, I asked Noel Francisco, one of the associate counsels on my staff, to prepare a memorandum for me outlining the issues in the Michigan cases. The Supreme Court would decide in January whether to take the cases and hear oral arguments. Before doing so, the court would likely ask whether the administration believed they should determine the constitutionality of the Michigan admission programs.

Noel was extremely bright, a former clerk for Supreme Court justice Clarence Thomas, and a member of the Federalist Society. He had a reputation for being one of the most conservative lawyers on our staff. While I knew Noel would give me an excellent assessment of the cases' merits, I also knew the Washington grapevine would soon buzz with news that Noel, a bona fide conservative, was advising me on this case. I hoped that Noel's involvement would calm the concerns of conservatives who fretted that a Hispanic counsel—namely me—was incapable of evaluating affirmative action programs consistent with the Constitution.

Noel leaned toward the notion that the Supreme Court would invalidate the Michigan programs. Because the cases involved an issue of race, the programs would be subject to the strict scrutiny standard—that racial considerations are constitutional only if they are narrowly tailored to further a compelling government interest. Noel believed that the court would hold that educational diversity is not a compelling government interest and that the Michigan programs were not narrowly tailored.

I scheduled a meeting for December 6, 2002, in my White House office with Attorney General Ashcroft and Solicitor General Ted Olson to get their thoughts on the cases. Just days prior to our meeting, in one of our early-morning conversations, I spoke with President Bush about affirmative action. He told me, "I don't need another mess over race." Republicans were still dealing with fallout from comments made by Senate majority leader Trent Lott regarding Strom Thurmond's 1948 presidential campaign, in which Thurmond had supported segregation between the races. Consequently, Lott would eventually be toppled as leader and replaced by Senator Bill Frist.

In our meeting, President Bush expressed concern about taking a position on the issue. "I'd rather steer clear of the cases," he said. I didn't argue, but I knew it would be unlikely that the administration could avoid taking a position on such a high-profile issue, particularly one involving racial matters.

I knew well President Bush's long-standing concerns for disadvantaged people, especially children. I recalled that shortly after I had joined then governor Bush's staff in Texas, I attended a budget meeting about funding for more prisons in our state. While he was definitely a law-and-order governor, I was struck by his compassion. Rather than pouring more money into prisons, he suggested, the money could be better spent on improving schools for poor Hispanic kids living along the Texas-Mexico border. So I was not surprised by his initial reluctance to weigh in on the Michigan cases if it signaled that he was opposed to hope and opportunity for minority students.

I hoped my meeting with Ashcroft and Olson would clarify whether we should encourage the Supreme Court to consider the Michigan cases. I valued their opinions. Moreover, the attorney general is charged by statute to give advice to the president and the executive branch on questions of law. The solicitor general is charged with developing and arguing legal cases on behalf of the executive branch before the Supreme Court and lower federal courts. John Ashcroft had been a US senator from Missouri, a state rife with racial tensions, and Ted Olson was one of the finest constitutional lawyers in America, so I knew their insights would be invaluable.

They presented a strong briefing about the cases, and expressed serious concerns about the Michigan admissions program in relationship to the Constitution. They did not, however, recommend whether or not the administration should ask the Supreme Court to accept the cases; nor did they suggest what the president's position should be.

The following day, I met with Andy Card and reported my impressions of the meeting with John and Ted. Andy reiterated that the president did not want to get involved in this matter.

I understood, but I also knew that his neutral position was probably not sustainable. So I continued to discuss with various administration lawyers what the president should do. Virtually all advised me that the Michigan programs' objective to achieve diversity did not represent a compelling government interest, nor were they narrowly tailored. Furthermore, Michigan had not even tried race-neutral alternatives that could achieve diversity, as universities in many other states had successfully done.

The consensus within the counsel's office was that the president had four options. First, he could choose to file a brief in support of the Michigan admission programs, contending that racial diversity in our law schools and universities is a compelling government interest and that the Michigan programs were sufficiently tailored.

I sincerely doubted that would be the direction he would want to go. I could not recall a single conversation in which the president ever considered supporting the Michigan admissions programs. And contrary to press reports, nor had I ever advocated for or supported the idea of filing a brief in favor of the Michigan programs. I believed that the programs—particularly at the undergraduate level—placed too much emphasis on race.

The president's second option was to file a brief opposing the Michigan admissions programs because racial diversity in our universities—although desirable—is not a compelling government interest. Indeed, this was what most conservative groups hoped he would do—urge the court to sweep aside the Powell opinion and end all considerations of a person's race in the admissions process.

The third option was to file a brief taking no position on the question of whether racial diversity is a compelling government interest, but to oppose the Michigan admissions programs on the grounds that they were not narrowly tailored. This approach could contend that the Michigan programs were unconstitutional because the schools had failed to consider race-neutral alternatives. The president was well familiar with the 10 percent rule in Texas; the policy had significantly increased the enrollments of minority students in Texas universities.

While they were willing to live with this option, conservatives worried that this option might allow the court to resolve these two Michigan cases, while leaving the question of whether racial considerations in academic admissions decisions were constitutional for another day.

The fourth possible option for the president was to not file a brief at all. Some conservatives who were eager to strike down the *Bakke* decision preferred this option over the third.

In mid-December, a group of advisors including Andy Card, Karl Rove, and I met with the president to help him develop a position on affirmative action. I sensed that he was torn between his desire to promote opportunities for minorities and his commitment to his conservative values. He said he believed that race should be a valid consideration, and that it was a factor he considered when making his appointments. He sincerely wanted to be known as a Republican who endorsed genuine diversity. He asked us to look at university programs around the country that were successful in promoting racial diversity. As with most policies, the president encouraged us to articulate what we as an administration were *for*, rather than talking about what we were *against*.

Karl and I advised the president that opposing racial diversity because it was not a compelling interest of government would alienate some groups and please others. We further advised him that he did not have to take a position opposing racial diversity but could still oppose the Michigan programs because the university had failed to achieve diversity through race-neutral methods. We presented the four options, and he chose the third, deciding that he wanted the solicitor general to prepare a brief opposing the Michigan admissions programs because they looked too much like quotas and placed too much emphasis on race. This would leave it to the court, if it elected to do so, to answer the question of whether racial diversity in our universities is a compelling interest. I was not surprised by the president's decision.

I recognized that he wanted to see a brief written that would not kill the hopes and dreams of disadvantaged minorities, but would reaffirm his stated opposition to quotas. This was what I believed every judge and court should do—namely, to decide each case on the narrowest grounds possible.

"I think it is important for Michigan to try race-neutral means first," the president told me. "Then, if that fails to produce diversity, I'm more comfortable considering race as one of many factors." He directed me to inform the Justice Department of his position, and that he wanted a brief soon. He also emphasized that he did not want his position leaked to the press prematurely.

I met with Ted Olson in his office and delivered the president's instructions. Ted seemed slightly surprised by the decision, and perhaps a bit disappointed. Although he disagreed with the approach, he was the quintessential professional and promised that he would write the brief.

I believed doing away with quotas was the right decision. For a university to reserve a certain number of admissions for students based solely on race was a bad idea, and our courts have never accepted racial quotas as constitutional. Consequently, the president and I both felt quotas should be opposed, even if that hurt Republican outreach to minorities.

Yet this remained a conundrum for me, and driving home from the White House one evening, the father in me wondered if I was advocating a position that would work against my younger sons in the future. Would Graham and Gabriel one day be denied an opportunity of admission into a highly select university because a school could not consider the color of their skin as one factor among others? As a father, I had questions, but as a lawyer, the answer seemed straightforward.

The president favored a moderate, middle-ground position. He could support an affirmative action program that considered race as only one of many other factors, not as the preeminent basis on which an admission decision is made. But if the court wanted to end affirmative action, that would be the court's decision.

Unfortunately, despite the president's admonitions about leaks, on December 18 the *Washington Post* reported that the president's aides— including me—opposed the stance against affirmative action advocated by the Justice Department because it could impair the president's efforts to woo Hispanics and other minorities to the Republican ranks. Ironically, even with my Hispanic heritage, I had not encouraged the president to support quota-like affirmative action programs.

The next day, December 19, I talked with Ted Olson by phone. Ted pushed back on the approach chosen by the president. He felt it was unrealistic and wrong to assume that racial diversity was constitutional, or to pretend that this issue didn't matter. He felt strongly the court deserved to have our position on both issues.

I had no problem with the court deciding the fundamental questions surrounding affirmative action, but I also knew the president neither wanted to invite the court to decide the question, nor tell the court how he thought it should be decided.

Meanwhile, the *New York Times* editorialized that the solicitor general was eager to weigh in against the Michigan admission programs, but I was opposing such a stand, arguing that it would hurt Republican efforts to attract minority voters. That was utter nonsense. The truth is, I never argued in favor of the Michigan admission programs. Furthermore, the debate between the White House and the Justice Department centered on how best to *oppose* the Michigan programs, not whether or not to *support* them. The *Times* got the story wrong.

Although the president seemed to have made up his mind, the White House legal team continued to discuss the pros and cons of various options as we awaited a memo being prepared by Justice. We had recently brought in a new deputy counsel, David Leitch, another outstanding lawyer who had clerked for Chief Justice Rehnquist and was highly regarded by the conservative community. David and Noel made a good team and, I hoped, would help solidify our position among conservative groups.

The memo from the solicitor general's office arrived at my office a few days before Christmas. The memo included a discussion of the president's stated position, as well as a discussion of the department's preferred position, and they were not the same. In fact, if there had been any question about the department's unhappiness with the president's position, the memo made clear their preferred position. Ashcroft and Olson believed the president should unequivocally oppose racial diversity as a compelling state interest. They suggested the president should ask the court to sweep aside the Powell opinion. They did, however, agree that the Michigan programs were not narrowly tailored because the university had failed to consider race-neutral alternatives.

On January 2, 2003, I received a call from Ted Olson. He continued to be unhappy with the president's preferred position. Four days later, I had another difficult conversation with the solicitor general. He informed me that he was having serious problems writing the brief.

I met with President Bush, Vice President Cheney, Andy Card, Condi Rice, policy advisor Jay Lefkowitz, and speechwriter Mike Gerson to again discuss the options. The vice president seemed sympathetic to Justice's suggestion, but the president decided to stay the course. He wanted the solicitor general to file a brief opposing the Michigan admission policies based on the narrow tailoring grounds, but not take a position on whether racial diversity is a compelling interest. Perhaps because he knew that Ted and I were already at odds over this matter, the president asked Vice President Cheney to call Ted with his instructions. I wasn't privy to the call, but apparently Ted asked permission to present both arguments and the president agreed so we could compare both options.

The *Wall Street Journal* wrote that day, "We're told that White House counsel Alberto Gonzales is afraid if the administration comes down against racial quotas, he won't get the smooth Senate passage he wants if he is nominated to the Supreme Court to fill any opening later this year."[1] I didn't know where the newspaper got their information, but the *Journal*, too, was wrong. I had always opposed quotas. Additionally, I had never advocated for supporting the Michigan programs. Nor was my advice ever affected by any concerns about my being a potential nominee to the Supreme Court. The allegation was ridiculous. Besides, it was the president's position being debated in-house, not mine. I began to wonder if opponents to my going on the court were leaking false stories to intensify opposition to me.

The following day, January 7, I had a quiet conversation alone with the president in the Oval Office. He told me he wanted to go on record as being for the rights of minorities. "I don't want to be known as the president who did away with affirmative action," he said.

I reminded him that Ted would have to make some persuasive arguments before the Supreme Court, and that the views of the Department of Justice were important. He nodded, but I could tell, based on our conversations and what I knew of him, he had not been persuaded to change his mind. I sensed that he did not feel that doing away with affirmative action, other than quotas, was in the best interests of the country—at least not at that time.

A steady stream of stories and editorials in the press reflected the strong interest in the president's decision. Commentators drew lines in the sand, for and against affirmative action. The Knight Ridder/Tribune News Service reported that Hispanic leaders planned to ask the president to support the race-based policy at the University of Michigan. "White House officials reportedly are lobbying Bush on both sides of the issue," the *Washington*

Post printed. "Solicitor Ted Olson is said to be eager to file a brief opposing the University's policies while White House Counsel Alberto R. Gonzales is urging Bush to support the policies."[2]

Around noon on the ninth, the first full draft of the brief arrived at the White House from the Department of Justice. Our circle of advisors met briefly with the president to discuss it. We also informed Press Secretary Ari Fleischer for the first time about the case.

I spent a long evening reviewing the brief with my lawyers. At 6:00 a.m., I was back in my West Wing office preparing for an early meeting with the president. Once again that morning, Andy Card, Karl Rove, Condi Rice, Jay Lefkowitz, Dick Cheney, Mike Gerson, and I discussed with the president in the Oval Office what might be his best approach. No one disagreed that the University of Michigan programs at the undergraduate level and the law school should be opposed because neither the university or law school had attempted to find race-neutral alternatives. The tactical question—and the one implicating social policies, not to mention politics—was whether racial diversity as a societal matter or educational diversity in our universities was a compelling government interest. At the conclusion of the discussion, President Bush said that he still preferred not to take a position on those issues, and that he would oppose the Michigan programs based on the fact that they were not narrowly tailored.

The attorney general and the solicitor general were not included in that meeting. In retrospect, I wish I had encouraged the president to invite them. Of course, their opinions were reflected in their brief and were advocated in that meeting by the vice president. But it may have been helpful for the president to have heard from them directly in the presence of his other advisors.

I doubt it would have made a difference. Ashcroft and Olson wanted the president to take a position opposing racial and educational diversity as a compelling interest. They wanted him to declare that race could never be considered in making admissions decisions, unless to rectify past discrimination, and only after exhausting race-neutral means. Essentially, they wanted the president to say that admissions programs that considered race in any way at institutions anywhere in the country—including our military service academies—would have to be redefined. President Bush simply was not going to move that far right.

Nevertheless, I should have encouraged more direct communication between the president, John, and Ted. If I had been the attorney general at that time, I would have insisted to the chief of staff and to the counsel that I be present, and I would have been angry if excluded from the White House discussions. I would have wanted to speak directly to the president. On the other hand, nothing prevented the president from reaching out to the attorney general, of course, and the president has the final say on who is in an Oval Office meeting.

No doubt, some people at Justice may have wondered if the department's positions were being fairly presented to the president. They were, and we also had the written brief in front of us in all of our deliberations. I understand how the media stories may have generated resentment and jealousy, and this entire episode further damaged my relationships with conservatives within the Department of Justice. In turn, that fed the anger and suspicion toward me among conservatives outside the government. Certainly I would have preferred they not be mad at me, but I had a job to do.

That anger manifested itself in my next phone conversation with Ted Olson. When I informed Ted the president did not want to take a position on whether racial or educational diversity was a compelling interest to the government, he responded, "If the president believes race can be a factor, then we have a problem."

On January 13, I gave the president an update on the development of the brief, and he reaffirmed his position. He felt that the vice president could help sway Ted in that direction.

David Leitch and Noel Francisco had done tremendous work in analyzing the cases, but as we moved toward the final brief, I also asked associate counsel Brett Kavanaugh to work with the deputy solicitor general, Paul Clement. Brett had clerked on the Supreme Court with Paul and they were friends, so I hoped his involvement would facilitate the editing process on the brief.

Their relationship was quickly tested. That same evening, in a phone conversation, Paul reported to Brett that Ted Olson did not believe the White House position made any sense. It was inconsistent, Ted said, to oppose racial diversity as a compelling government interest, but at the same time, support educational diversity through our silence. Paul suggested that Ted was dug in and unlikely to change his opinion.

Ted was more comfortable not filing a brief than filing a brief suggesting a distinction between racial diversity and educational diversity. He wanted to reject the Powell construct that recognized a difference between the two and that had permitted race to be considered in admissions decisions. Ted believed it was only appropriate for an institution to consider race where there had been clear instances of past discrimination by that institution.

Exacerbating matters further, the following day, I received word from Paul Clement that neither Ted nor he would sign a legal brief to the Supreme Court that distinguished between racial and educational diversity.

Fortunately, the news was not all bad. Ted had developed a new argument that he wanted us to consider. He contended that government should try to address societal discrimination, but it had an obligation to do so through race-neutral means. We know such measures work, but if they fail, then we can presume that ongoing discrimination exists, and then it would be permissible to consider race.

When we presented this new idea to the president, he seemed to like it and indicated that such an approach might work. He didn't mind answering the question of whether race can ever be considered if the answer was yes. He reminded us that we should promote diversity and allow people who have suffered from discrimination to have an equal shot in our society.

Later that afternoon, we had another meeting in the Oval Office with the president, Dan Bartlett, Mike Gerson, Jay Lefkowitz, and Karl Rove. The president seemed to like the proposition that if a school exhausted race-neutral means and still failed to achieve diversity, then the school could consider race as a factor in its admissions process. He viewed this as consistent with his views. Our lawyers worked late into the night, trying to incorporate this caveat into the government's brief.

The next day, January 15, I was in my office by 6:00 a.m. and already assessing where the affirmative action arguments stood. To me, it appeared the president was still struggling over how best to promote diversity in our universities. Two competing interests were working against each other: on one hand, he had a desire to remedy past discrimination, and on the other hand, he had a strong belief that government should not make distinctions among people based on race.

Liberals and many minority organizations focused on the first goal. They saw affirmative action programs that took race into account as not only permissible but necessary at times, especially when trying to correct the mistakes caused by past discrimination.

At the opposite end of the spectrum, conservatives usually focused on the second goal, and insisted that government should never consider race when making decisions. Because of this, many minority groups—Hispanics included—felt that conservatives paid only lip service to the notion that affirmative action is necessary to remedy past causes and effects of discrimination.

The president was trying to find the right balance between these two competing goals, and at times, he pushed us to find a way to meet both. The working group met with the president from approximately 7:00 a.m. to 8:00 a.m. in the Oval Office. The discussions were spirited regarding the new section of the brief, but for reasons only he knew, the president decided to stay with his initial instinct and say nothing about whether race could be considered as a factor. He was back to opposing the Michigan program, solely on the basis that the university and law school had failed to exhaust race-neutral alternatives. He felt the Michigan programs were more like quotas.

Indeed, in a written dissent, Sixth Circuit Court of Appeals judge Danny Julian Boggs described the Michigan Law School admissions program in blunt terms:

An examination of the admissions data shows that even the most qualified majority students (those with an LSAT over 170 and a GPA over 3.75) do not achieve the perfect admissions percentages for under-represented minority students with a GPA nearly a point less and an LSAT score in the 164–166 range. More roughly speaking, under-represented minorities with a high C to low B undergraduate average are admitted at the same rate as majority applicants with an A average with roughly the same LSAT scores. Along a different axis, minority applicants with an A average and an LSAT score down to 156 (the 70th percentile nationally) are admitted at roughly the same rate as majority applicants with an A average and an LSAT score over a 167 (the 96th percentile nationally).

More shocking is the comparison of the chances of admission for applicants with the same academic credentials (at least numerically). Taking a mid-range applicant with an LSAT score 164–166 and a GPA of 3.25–3.49, the chances of admission for a White or Asian applicant are around 22 percent. For an under-represented minority applicant, the chances of admission (100 %) would be better called a guarantee of admission.[3]

Once again, the president asked Vice President Cheney to inform Ted Olson of the new instructions. When Cheney did so, Ted responded that if it were left up to him, he would not file that brief; however, he knew for whom he worked. If the president ordered him to sign the brief, he would, but he'd have to consider whether to continue working in the department.

The president called me around 2:00 p.m., but I had no new information for him so I had Brett Kavanaugh call Paul Clement to inform him that the White House wanted a revised brief that evening, one that reflected the president's original decision. Shortly afterward, John Ashcroft called me to find out what was happening with the brief. "The vice president has already called Ted," I told him, "with instructions to prepare a narrow tailoring brief." The AG seemed unaware of these recent events, so I assured him that I would have Brett call Clement to discuss the president's instructions.

Within fifteen minutes, the two young legal stars had spoken. Following my instructions, Brett had given unambiguous directions regarding the brief. Though normally calm and unflappable, Paul responded, "Should I just rip out the first section of the brief arguing that educational diversity is not a compelling government interest?"

Brett responded, "You should do whatever makes the brief good."

Exasperated, Paul replied, "I've been working for three weeks to make the brief good!"

Tensions mounted and tempers flared. Around four o'clock that afternoon, the vice president called me down to his office on the first floor of the West Wing. It was one of the few times the vice president summoned me. His voice was stern as he asked, "Do you have a Brett Kavanaugh working for you?"

"Yes, sir," I replied, uncertain where the VP was going.

"Well, Ted Olson complained to me that Kavanaugh had informed the department that the counsel's office was taking control of the brief. According to Ted, Kavanaugh said that the department should send everything over to the counsel's office and we would finalize the brief." The vice president questioned why anyone in the White House was interfering with the work of the solicitor general.

I told him respectfully that the attorney general had called me and had appeared uninformed and confused about the president's decision. Therefore, I had asked Brett to call Paul with clear directions. I also told the vice president that although I would check with Brett, I was quite confident he would not have told the Department of Justice that the White House was taking over the brief.

The vice president said that he had persuaded Ted to prepare a narrow tailoring brief, but Ted would not sign it. Clearly frustrated and angry, Cheney said, "I'm done with this."

As soon as I left the vice president's office, I spoke with Brett, who confirmed that he had *not* informed the Justice Department that the White House counsel's office was taking control of the brief. But apparently the lawyers at DOJ were unhappy with the direction we were going, and the fact that I seemed to be steering the process away from the position advocated by the department leadership.

Afterward, I walked down to the Oval Office to talk with the president. Vice President Cheney was there as well. The president said that he liked where things stood, and he reiterated that he did not want to be the one to end affirmative action. "Let the courts do that if they want to," he said.

I reassured the vice president that we had not asked the department to take over writing the brief. The president expressed admiration for Ted and his work, but said they simply had a difference of opinion. He told me not to worry about Ted and the others at Justice. He felt this was an opportunity to show America that he was not as far to the right as some thought.

"Okay, thank you, sir," I said as I started to leave the office. Just outside the Oval Office doorway, I overheard President Bush say to the deputy communications director, Dan Bartlett, "Be sure to protect Al in the media."

His words, though meant in kindness and concern, hit me like a punch to the gut. Obviously, the president believed that the department lawyers and outside conservative groups had me in their sights, and they weren't above firing whatever volleys necessary to minimize my input on White House policy and to keep me off the Supreme Court.

The White House staff finalized the president's remarks about the decision, and he announced his position from the Roosevelt Room. As he informed the world of his support for opportunities for minorities and his concomitant opposition to the Michigan programs, I stood nearby. I let out a sigh of relief that this moment had finally arrived.

The next morning, I walked down from my office to the president's office to see how he was feeling about the most recent events. He told me that he had dinner the previous night with the associate attorney general, Robert McCollum, a college buddy of his. He had directed McCollum to tell the Justice Department that *he* had made this decision, so the department should not attack the counsel's office; he'd said we needed to work well together going forward. He also assured me that he would talk to the attorney general about what had happened during the past month regarding this affirmative action matter and the way we all had handled it.

The media was quick to pick up on the tension in our ranks. Ron Fournier, with the Associated Press, reported, "[T]he decision to come out against the Michigan plan was vigorously debated by the president and his top advisors. Sources familiar with those discussions said Bush's chief political advisors, Karl Rove and White House counsel Alberto Gonzales urged the administration not to oppose the Michigan program."[4]

This reporter, like so many others, continued to miss the mark. Neither Karl nor I ever urged the administration to support the Michigan admission programs. To the contrary, Karl and I recommended opposing the programs.

I gave an interview to CNN that afternoon explaining the president's position. On the way back to the White House, I learned that Ted Olson had agreed to sign the brief after all. I called the president from the car and informed him of the news. He was pleased. Once again, he expressed his appreciation for the work of the lawyers at Justice and in the counsel's office. He also reiterated that I should not worry about the fallout. He'd deal with that. I appreciated his willingness to go to bat for me, but his repeated assurances only reminded me that the affirmative action case had further damaged my standing within the conservative community. I would not come to realize just how severely this incident had hurt me until a few years later when I desperately needed the support of conservatives in Washington, and the community remained painfully silent.

A week later, I spoke with Senator Orrin Hatch, who told me that the brief was a good approach. He also told me that if I were to be nominated to the Supreme Court, as chairman of the Judiciary Committee, he would fight to get me through the confirmation process. I listened quietly and thanked the senator for his support. Orrin Hatch was one of the most decent men I had met since arriving in Washington.

The following day, I spoke with Ted. He was his usual professional self. "Disagreements happen in Washington," he said. He allowed that the president had a right to stake out his territory, and as solicitor general, he would do his best to defend it. I admired Ted even more following that conversation.

Consequently, because we had settled on a compromise position, conservatives on the right attacked me, saying that the Bush policy—condemning the Michigan programs as unlawful quotas, but remaining neutral and not calling for the end to affirmative action—reflected the first indication of my positions as a potential Supreme Court nominee. One wag proffered, "Gonzales is Spanish for Souter," recalling the liberal tendencies of the justice nominated by President George H. W. Bush.

Those feelings were reinforced five months later, on June 23, 2003, when the Supreme Court announced its decision regarding the Michigan cases. The court upheld the use of race under certain circumstances. It upheld the admissions program for the law school, but it struck down the admissions program for the university.

It was a bittersweet victory. In one sense, the president had gotten what he wanted. But as conservatives had feared, Justice Sandra Day O'Connor, considered by many a moderate conservative, wrote the majority opinion, which held that diversity in education is a compelling government interest. Therefore, race could be used as a factor in admissions decisions, although this must be individualized determinations—no quotas or formulas, separate tracks, or reserved spots for minorities. The decision emphasized that race-based programs should be limited in scope, and that institutions, when possible, should pursue race-neutral alternatives. While some regaled that as a victory, the Powell construct from the *Bakke* case was now the law of the land.

Not surprisingly, conservatives were disgusted—and especially at me. Even the *New York Times* picked up on it in their June 24 edition: "Conservatives will want to make sure that anyone appointed to the court in this administration is a strong and sure opponent of racial preferences . . . many do not believe that Mr. Gonzales fits that description."[5]

The *Wall Street Journal* concurred: "In one sense, it is the first Supreme Court decision issued by White House Counsel Alberto Gonzales, who is widely believed to be President Bush's choice for the High Court when the next justice retires. Mr. Gonzales helped to override those at the Justice Department who understood how Mrs. O'Connor would interpret their brief's legal ambivalence."

I never seriously dwelled on whether I might go on the court. Good thing. Any chances I had of being the first Hispanic ever to serve on the US Supreme Court were disappearing, propelled ironically, not by liberal opposition, but by my conservative "friends."

The battles over race continue today. We hear the same debates over consideration of race in college admissions decisions; we find similar discussions playing out in regard to immigration; we see increasing concerns about attitudes toward the police in many communities around America. How we accommodate people of different skin colors or different viewpoints remains a bitterly divisive and often antagonistic issue.

Several months later, Washington would buzz with rumors that I had overruled the Justice Department again. The issue then would be the collection of intelligence information. In the meantime, one of the most defining challenges of the Bush administration was looming ahead of us. We were going to war in the "Cradle of Civilization," to topple the evil regime of Saddam Hussein in Iraq.

CHAPTER 22

"CASUS BELLI"—THE
TWISTED ROAD TO IRAQ

During the weekend strategy session convened by the president at Camp David immediately following the 9/11 attacks on America, the possibility of Iraq's involvement was raised. We were aware that Saddam Hussein had earned his reputation as the "Butcher of Baghdad" by his record of brutal human rights abuses and his use of chemical weapons against his own people. In 1988, he had attacked the Kurdish town of Halabja with mustard and nerve gases, killing thousands of innocent people including mothers and children. We also knew from information seized after Operation Desert Storm in 1991 that Saddam's nuclear weapons program was much more advanced than we had thought. The International Atomic Energy Agency reported that had it not been for the war, Hussein likely would have produced a nuclear device by the end of 1992.

In 1995, when Saddam's son-in-law and the son-in-law's brother defected to Jordan, revealing portions of Iraq's weapons program—in particular Saddam's efforts to develop nuclear and biological weapons—Saddam had the defectors and both of their families murdered.[1]

During those post-9/11 Camp David discussions, there was little doubt that given the opportunity, Saddam would not hesitate to inflict maximum harm on America. Yet no one claimed in those discussions to have evidence linking Saddam to 9/11.

Moreover, there was absolutely no talk of trying to grab Iraq's oil for the United States, or any discussions about Bush the younger finishing the job begun by his father during Desert Storm. Nor did the president express any revenge, wanting to get even for Saddam's attempt to assassinate his father. Quite the contrary—from the beginning, the focus was on al-Qaeda and clearing out the camps in Afghanistan, the safe harbors where the terrorists had trained under the leadership of Osama bin Laden.

Then came the CIA report of potential weapons of mass destruction in Iraq, and the reconstituting of al-Qaeda, driven out of Afghanistan by our troops, but now present in remote parts of Iraq. This exponentially heightened our concerns that Saddam would provide weapons of mass destruction to terrorists who had already proven their willingness to use them.

During 2002, the National Security team engaged in intense meetings about thwarting the Iraqi threat to our nation's safety. The history of Iraqi defiance was clear. In 1998, Hussein demanded that international weapons inspectors cease their work and leave his country, and the inspectors had complied. The US Congress responded by passing the Iraq Liberation Act that President Clinton signed into law. It established a regime change in Iraq as official US policy and provided $100 million to fund groups who worked for Hussein's ouster.

Saddam continued to flout the UN resolutions to send inspectors into his country to certify he did not have weapons of mass destruction, whether chemical, biological, or nuclear. His Iraqi jets repeatedly violated the UN-mandated no-fly zone prohibiting Iraqi planes from flying in certain parts of the country—safeguards put in place after Desert Storm partially to protect the Kurds in northern Iraq and the Shiite Muslims in a large portion of southern Iraq. The NFZ was enforced primarily by British and US fighter jets, and Saddam made a point of challenging the enforcers, firing on US and coalition forces more than a thousand times.[2]

I believe I attended virtually every meeting of the National Security

Council and every meeting of the principals committee[3] focused on Iraq and the dangers Saddam Hussein posed. It was obvious the president and the principals believed Saddam was a threat to his people, to the countries in the region, and, ultimately, to us.

The president did not respect Hussein and regarded him as a dangerous bully. Bush was clearly frustrated that the UN wouldn't do more to force Saddam to comply with his international obligations. Consequently, during the summer of 2001, the National Security team engaged in intense discussions about an effective strategy against this tyrant.

The September 11 attacks heightened our concerns over Iraq. Although the intelligence community quickly concluded that the attack was the work of al-Qaeda, we initially questioned whether that group was capable of pulling off such a horrendous event without help. Because Hussein's hatred for America was well known, Saddam was suspect number one. But Secretary of Defense Donald Rumsfeld, Vice President Dick Cheney, and Secretary of State Colin Powell all concurred: Iraq was not connected and had no responsibility for the attacks on America. Powell even warned that if we took action against Iraq right now, Saddam would prove he was not complicit in the attacks, which would actually impede our international support for the war on terror.

By May 2002, coalition troops had made good progress in Operation Enduring Freedom, destroying al-Qaeda's camps and toppling the Taliban in Afghanistan. Consequently, the National Security team turned their attention to other trouble spots around the world, including Iraq. The congressional resolution in 1998 stated that a regime change in Iraq was the policy of our nation. In other words, Congress wanted to see Saddam deposed and went on record saying so. That did not authorize military action, or covert action necessarily, nor did it encourage the assassination of Saddam, which would violate our stated values against the assassination of civilian officials. But essentially it said: because of Hussein's ongoing despotic actions, we'd like to see new leadership in Iraq.

We had quietly been discussing this possibility with our Arab friends. They agreed that Saddam needed to go, Powell reported, but that we must be swift and successful. The European Union would be looking for moral and legal justification, and the Iraqi people were looking for assurances that regime change was really going to happen this time. Their hopes had been dashed when Desert Storm stopped short of replacing Hussein, and some of them had paid a high price for their public opposition to Saddam in 1991. They were not about to make that mistake again based on vacuous promises from the United States or anybody else.

Secretary Rumsfeld warned that we needed to vastly improve our intelligence, especially intelligence inside Iraq, where we feared WMD (weapons of mass destruction) and missile sites existed. I sensed an uneasiness among all of the NSC members about "not knowing what we did not know," but the group shared concerns about another terrorist attack, and a genuine worry that Saddam's WMD might fall into the hands of al-Qaeda.

We also discussed possible contingencies that might force our hand. What would America do, for example, if Saddam complied with UN resolutions and allowed inspections? What if he shot down one of our aircraft? What if there was another terrorist attack? What would we do if Saddam attacked the Kurds in the northern part of Iraq? How would we respond to an attack on Israel?

We had lots of tough questions and few easy answers. Although nobody had yet suggested going to war, I made a note to myself to explore and confirm our legal authorities to take those actions; I also concluded we needed to examine our presidential findings authorizing covert actions. Something told me we might need both.

Ten days later, on May 10, I attended another Iraq briefing in the Situation Room. We discussed budgeting for a possible future conflict with Iraq. I didn't know whether we had received some new intelligence showing increased threats, nor was I told why, all of a sudden, we were so worried about how to pay for another war. We were already shelling out millions of dollars to pay for the war in Afghanistan. Nevertheless, I made arrangements to visit with John Bellinger, the National Security Council lawyer, to examine all the legal work to justify use of force in Iraq.

The war in Afghanistan was still the main subject of continual congressional curiosity and scrutiny, but inside the White House, there were quiet conversations about Iraq as well. On May 13, I attended another meeting in the Situation Room with the president, and again, the subject was Iraq.

Colin Powell spoke about the need for a strategy in dealing with Iraq at the UN and the EU. I admired Secretary Powell for his wisdom and experience. He knew firsthand the challenges ahead if we ever went to war with Iraq, having served on the battlefront during Desert Storm. "This will be a long-term proposition," he said, speaking of another potential war in Iraq. "It will require a lot of money, and we need to understand this is probably a long-term commitment of our troops."

In years to come, Vice President Cheney would receive a great deal of criticism for his support of the war in Iraq, but in this early-morning May 2002 meeting, he was the first to challenge the justification for military action. "What is the case?" he asked. "Is the case strong enough to justify our military actions? Is the case strong enough for our allies to join us?" The vice president used the words *casus belli*, a Latin phrase meaning an act or event that justifies war. He was warning that we must have a legal justification for war, both for the American people and for our allies.

In a June 3 NSC meeting, the president and the members discussed the possibility that Iraq was developing unmanned aerial vehicles, including unmanned drone-like helicopters. The statements from the military and from intelligence sources painted a picture of Iraq as sophisticated and defiant.

Every day, new legal questions arose in connection with a possible conflict in Iraq if the president decided the United States needed to take action. The lawyers explored the legal authority for the use of military force as well as covert actions. We were also asked to look at practices and rules governing the spoils of war. For example, who would have legal rights to Iraq's oil fields? The president challenged his advisors in these meetings, asking questions and posing hypothetical situations with which we might have to deal if we liberated Iraq. I watched and listened in admiration as Powell and Rumsfeld detailed opposing views on a variety of issues. They were like two heavyweight boxers, experienced and savvy. Powell was conservative and careful when it came to talk of war. He was a career soldier, a patriot as well as a diplomat. Rumsfeld was a street fighter, wise in the use of the bureaucracy of war. He was also an innovator, always looking for the best ways to streamline so we could fight more effectively. Some people said he was a difficult boss at the Department of Defense, but his subordinates all seemed to respect and admire him. I know that Jim Haynes, his top legal counsel with whom I had many dealings, had the utmost regard for Donald Rumsfeld, and I did too.

The president wanted a coalition of friends if he decided it was necessary to take action, and the military considered the nation of Turkey critical for quick access to Iraq from the north. Saudi Arabia would also be important for overflight rights. Like the vice president, President Bush vocalized his concerns about casus belli. "Do we have casus belli?" he asked. "What does that look like?" I sensed his caution about using military force to oust Hussein. Still, although the president didn't have a future leader of Iraq in mind, he did say, "Whoever replaces Saddam Hussein will be better for the Iraqi people and for the world."

On July 11, the NSC meeting once again focused on Iraq. Most of us had come to appreciate how crucial Turkey would be to any quick and successful regime change in Iraq. We didn't expect them to do much militarily, but it was important that Turkey permit coalition invasion troops to transit across their country—to create a noose around the country and to keep terrorists and Saddam's troops from fleeing. But the Turks were playing hardball. The Turkish government wanted money, billions of dollars, before they'd even present our request to their parliament, and even then, there was no guarantee of approval. Although we needed Turkey's support, Secretary Powell questioned whether now was the right time to present a plan to them, since their own government was shaky.

We also discussed CIA involvement in Iraq, whether and how they could provide money to opponents of the regime and engage in covert, nonlethal disruptive activities.

We wondered aloud whether we should issue an ultimatum to Saddam regarding weapons inspections. He had already defied sixteen UN resolutions since 1991 demanding complete, open inspections, and an end to Iraq's support for terrorists; so there was little hope that he might regard another UN resolution as meaningful. An ultimatum from the United States might be effective. Some members of the NSC suggested that defiance of the UN resolutions and Saddam's refusal to allow future weapons inspections provided casus belli already.

At a 7:00 a.m. principals committee meeting in the Situation Room on July 24, 2002, I witnessed a remarkable discussion of the merits of US military action in Iraq. Sitting next to Colin Powell, Don Rumsfeld suggested that if the president gave the order to liberate Iraq based on casus belli, the military commanders preferred to go in the winter, rather than the summer. The president had already talked about a possible window between the November elections and Thanksgiving.

Sitting across the table from Powell, Dick Cheney countered that the longer we waited, the more likely Hussein could hurt us.

Rumsfeld responded that the driver in this situation was the coalition of countries we hoped to help us. How long would it take to get others on board? And what demands on Saddam would other countries want to make before participating?

Vice President Cheney reminded everyone that making demands on Saddam would not solve the problem. He expressed concern about relying on Hussein to make our task easier. "This is wrong," he stated bluntly. "We need to be honest with the American people. This is the most important obligation for the president."

Secretary Powell added, "We're not there yet internationally."

"What would make the case good enough for them?" Cheney challenged with a rhetorical question, knowing that countries such as Germany and France were making enormous amounts of money from contracts with Iraq.

"Some feel that Saddam has been contained somewhat," replied Powell.

"Things are different now," Cheney said. "Saddam has seen how al-Qaeda hurt us. He has smallpox weapons. He has worked hard to develop WMD. He has a lot of the world's oil reserves. He has enormous wealth. He has become a tougher target over time." The vice president concluded, "We have to do it; the sooner, the better. Yes, we need allies, but we do not let them set the pace or tell us what to do."

The secretary of state stood his ground. "Our allies and friends do not agree with that assessment," he said. "They do not view this as a real danger or a crisis. Our allies know this devil; they do *not* know the devil that may come. It is not clear that Saddam's ambition is to go beyond the region." Powell went on to warn, "If we attack, it will take 250,000 troops to take down the regime. You have to have a strong case before taking action. Can we make the case? Yes, but it will be expensive in terms of international opinion. Some allies will join us, but perhaps tepidly. Also, this will take up our whole agenda for the next four months."

As he always did, Vice President Cheney responded calmly but firmly. "We have already started the selling process. People think we are going after Iraq anyway. We have today a different scale of threat. And our doctrine of preemption is new and different."

Secretary Rumsfeld interjected, "We must not forget that the case is most certainly worse than we know. Second, a change will affect Syria, Turkey, Lebanon, and perhaps Saudi Arabia, and others, causing them to behave in a different way. Third, the president is way ahead out there. He is cocked and he needs to fire. Fourth, Congress and the EU have to realize we are now in a new environment. Do we have to wait for another Pearl Harbor–type of attack or is the situation different, that we now have the right and obligation to guard against those types of attacks? If we force the EU to answer this question, they will agree with us on a conceptual basis."

Andy Card spoke less frequently than the others at these meetings, and I often observed Andy doodling on the agenda page as he listened intently to the discussion. But on this day, he spoke up. "There is no doubt that Saddam is a clear and present danger to the United States. The president has said that we will have the courage to preempt, to prevent future attacks. The case has been made for us. I believe the world will come with us once we act, but will not be with us if we do not act."

I glanced at Condi. I knew that her relationship with the president was similar to mine, having the freedom to speak candidly with him in private on all national security matters. Although her role in these meetings was that of a facilitator, she spoke forcefully. "The president is ready to go. It is not a matter of provoking Saddam or making demands, but a matter of making the case."

From her comments, I concluded the president believed in the case to take action, but was concerned whether we could make the case to the American people and our allies. If we could not present a credible case to the world, the president would be faced with an even more difficult decision.

Anticipating casus belli and the removal of Hussein, the discussion moved to a post-Saddam Iraq. What type of government should the United States expect in Iraq after shedding American blood to deliver freedom to the Iraqi people? It seemed unrealistic to think in terms of a Jeffersonian democracy. Our forefathers had forged the greatest democracy in the history of the world after living under a monarchy. But the people of Iraq had never known such a government, and for years had experienced only dictators and tyrants.

While the opinions might not have been unanimous, the vice president summed up the feelings of most people in the room. He said, "We may create problems for ourselves if we do not create a higher bar. We would be viewed as hypocrites, particularly since we just told the Palestinian people they need to make changes toward democracy. That is our goal here and our regional objective as well."

The tenor of these meetings took a dramatic turn on August 2, 2002, when, at an afternoon principals committee meeting, the discussion focused on a chemical factory in Khurmal, a small Kurdish town in northeastern Iraq. The CIA asserted that an underground facility was located there, used for testing chemical weapons such as ricin and cyanide.[4] Some worried that al-Qaeda might be producing anthrax in Iraq. The CIA also reported that a number of al-Qaeda terrorists, including Abu Musab al-Zarqawi, a high-level al-Qaeda leader, had fled from Afghanistan and had relocated to Khurmal. The presence of chemical weapons and al-Qaeda were serious, and the CIA contended that it would be almost impossible for them to be there without Saddam Hussein's knowledge and approval. The CIA reported that this was the clearest evidence yet that al-Qaeda was in Iraq, making poison and planning on killing people.

I had not seen the intelligence, but I realized the significance of this report. The vice president announced, "This is a violation of the Bush Doctrine. If you are involved with terrorists, then you have a problem with Bush." I admired Vice President Cheney's directness. We did not always agree, but I never doubted his patriotism. The report placed the facility in a remote location, raising the possibility that other factories might be hidden away inside Iraq.

The principals agreed that the United States needed an approach to get in, but not destroy the evidence of the WMD factory. The US government set about strategizing the optimal method to destroy the plant. I focused my attention, along with other administration lawyers, on the legal justification for the use of force in Iraq. One of the theories we discussed was a humanitarian justification, since Saddam was known to have sponsored genocide against his own people. The notion of using force in response to a humanitarian catastrophe appealed to people at the State Department who believed it may encourage other nations to join us.

Administration lawyers also examined the leading cases in anticipatory self-defense. Generally, a country is permitted to defend itself in response to an attack or in the face of an imminent attack. Some of the lawyers argued, however, that international law required certain conditions to be present. The gun had to be loaded, cocked, and pointed, and the attacker had to have declared an intention to use force and demonstrated the capability to attack.

Others argued that the doctrine of anticipatory self-defense should be expanded in the twenty-first century, given the degree of harm resulting from weapons of mass destruction. How did these factors apply to Iraq?

Iraq had declared itself an enemy of the United States and had repeatedly demonstrated its intentions, going so far as an attempted assassination of President George H. W. Bush. They had continually fired on our aircrafts in the no-fly zone. They had chemical weapons and had already used them against the Iraqi people. We had little doubt Saddam would use chemical or biological weapons against the United States if given the opportunity, or share them with organizations such as al-Qaeda, who would use them against us. Given the massive scale of harm that would result, some of the lawyers argued that the threat to our country need not be as imminent or immediate as in the past.

The well-accepted *Caroline* test of self-defense stems from a nineteenth-century incident that affirmed the concept of preemptive self-defense in international law. This test says the necessity for preemptive self-defense must be instant, overwhelming, and leave no choice of means, or moments of deliberation. Many of the administration lawyers now concluded that the *Caroline* test was outdated and anticipatory self-defense should take into account the degree of harm. I asked John Bellinger to put together a memo summarizing the arguments the lawyers presented.

The principals also asked for legal guidance on the authority to use force in the no-fly zone in Iraq. The destruction of targets not posing a direct threat to our planes was a tricky question. The test was one of making a symmetrical response to an offense. In other words, if an Iraqi soldier shot an antiaircraft gun, we would not respond by dropping a nuclear bomb, but we might hit his site with a cruise missile.

A few days later, the principals received a threat assessment on the chemical plant in Iraq. The report said there was no hard evidence of a sophisticated lab. We had, however, various samples and other evidence to review, but they were delayed at the Turkish border for some reason. We did have some "signals" intelligence and information gleaned from detainees who hinted at the production of poisons, but we had no tangible evidence of biological or chemical weapons. Fortunately, the US government believed if the plant were struck, there was no high danger that any poisons there would be released into the air. A strike, however, would destroy any existing evidence.

The US government also believed that the plant had multiple layers of defense. The plant was defended by a dedicated group of fighters on-site and a second group stationed at a nearby town.

Vice President Cheney suggested the possibility of a B-2 airstrike, but he worried about the likely destruction of evidence, and how strong a case the United States could make afterward that we had destroyed an al-Qaeda chemical facility inside Iraq. Nevertheless, he felt we should take out the plant within days.

Secretary Rumsfeld wanted to wait until we received the samples of evidence, even though we could not have complete confidence in the chain of control confirming where the chemicals came from or how we obtained them. The samples could easily be compromised or provide false positives if tested. Yet Rumsfeld, too, felt we needed to act soon.

Even Colin Powell, who normally urged caution, conceded that if there was a facility up to no good, we should put together a target package. Unquestionably, the principals were concerned that the facility presented a medium-to-high danger. More sobering was the CIA's assessment that Iraq was the alternative site for al-Qaeda, which had scattered after we invaded Afghanistan.

Twenty-four hours later, the principals were back in the Situation Room debating whether we should give Iraq an ultimatum before taking military action. Secretary of State Powell suggested that it would be better if many countries, not just the United States, issued the ultimatum. If not, many might question our authority to lay down an ultimatum. We would claim to be doing it as an agent of the UN Security Council, but without their approval.

Powell was right, of course, but I suspected others in the room held different opinions. In particular, I watched Rumsfeld. After a few seconds, he said, "The problem with a joint ultimatum is that you have multiple decision makers deciding whether the conditions of the ultimatum have been met." For Rumsfeld, the ultimatum must require regime change.

Vice President Cheney agreed with Secretary Rumsfeld. He said, "We went to the UN last time because we felt we could get them on board and we believed this would put pressure on Congress. The number of coalition members isn't as important as the quality. Hopefully, we will have others, but the UK, Australia, and Turkey are about all we need."

This was not the first time Powell disagreed with Cheney and Rumsfeld. He responded, "Regime change is not UN policy. That is our unilateral policy. If this is our policy, I'm not sure you want to issue an ultimatum. We probably could not get the UN to agree to a regime change."

Rumsfeld suggested that we issue an ultimatum but leave it on the table for three or four days before acting on it.

Vice President Cheney said that the president was interested in giving an ultimatum, however he cautioned again that we should attempt to replace Hussein's regime with something more democratic. "This will affect the whole region," he said, "so we really need to try to get a new representative government."

Powell expressed skepticism about pushing for a democratic government. He suggested that we study further what Iraq might look like after Saddam and discuss our expectations.

As we moved into mid-August, the NSC continued to discuss the best option for dealing with the chemical plant—everything from air strikes to boots on the ground. The president continued to probe his advisors and seemed skeptical about the evidence. As usual, Cheney and Rumsfeld were aligned on their positions that we needed to act, while Powell and Rice took a more cautious approach.

On August 13, the principals received an updated report from the CIA. This time there was no equivocation; the report expressed no doubt the facility in Khurmal was producing toxins, and the CIA expressed a high level of certainty that the facility was linked to al-Qaeda. We still did not have "eyes on" tangible proof, but this was another serious confirmation.

Powell again suggested a cautious response. He believed that an air strike was one thing, but a large strike might present some problems with the Turks. "Is this target of sufficient value and are we confident of the intelligence?" he asked.

The vice president reiterated his earlier position on taking out the plant. "If we do not do it, there will be serious questions about our commitment to the war on terror," he warned. He was convinced the Bush Doctrine demanded a response, if even a limited one.

It now appeared that the administration was on a course to effect change in Iraq. We were meeting every day at this point, either as the National Security Council or the principals committee, to discuss one aspect or another of dealing with Saddam. I took some comfort in knowing that the president wasn't making this decision based on emotion or a whim, but he was taking his time, encouraging his advisors to study and discuss every issue, weighing carefully each aspect and all contingencies.

Moreover, the president wanted to have international support for military action, but he was not about to compromise our national security for the sake of any international body. Our challenge was to present an argument that would generate the broadest range of support. Powell believed that we should make the case that Iraq was ignoring the UN resolutions—which they were, flagrantly. Cheney agreed that the offended party is the international community and the only way to protect the integrity of the UN for future cases was to deal with this problem now.

On August 16, Powell reiterated his oft-stated concern, "The UN will not agree there is legal justification for war." Secretary Powell was right. For the UN, there were only two scenarios where use of force was lawful. The first, when acting in self-defense. The second, when acting pursuant to a UN Security Council resolution. All other military action was not supported under international law, according to the UN secretary general.

The president listened carefully to his advisors, then said, "We need to be careful not to condition our efforts on a UN resolution, but we do not want to look like we are designing future governments around the world. All we should be determining is that the world is more secure and more peaceful."

I appreciated the president's motives, but his goals seemed like a tough balancing act to me.

Then he continued his remarks about Hussein. "We need to make the case that this guy is a threat, and this is part of the war on terrorism. This is a dangerous guy," he said. "If we don't believe that, we should stay with the old containment policy."

On September 4, 2002, the president and his advisors met with congressional leaders in the Cabinet Room to discuss Iraq. I sat in my usual spot, just behind the president, as he outlined the case against Iraq and his concerns about Saddam.

Senator Tom Daschle asked several questions: What was the evidence of nuclear weapons or WMD? Who would be in the new regime after Saddam? How do we as a country do this?

The president and other members of the National Security team provided patient and thorough answers. The president concluded the responses to Daschle by saying, "We are the powerful person—we will use might to protect people."

Representative Dick Gephardt voiced concerns about Saddam, emphasizing that we needed to relay to the American people the danger to them from weapons of mass destruction, but he also expressed worry about what might happen after Hussein was gone.

Senator Joe Biden said he was glad we were saying that this was a "world problem," rather than simply an American concern. "It's important to check all the boxes," he said. "It will cost a lot of money and we will be there for a while. We need to tell the American people."

Representative Henry Hyde said, "Everyone has a stake in this." He urged that we try to get inspectors in, and when Iraq balked, we would have the high moral ground.

Representative Nancy Pelosi said it should be a pillar of foreign policy that a country not contribute to the development of weapons of mass destruction.

I listened carefully, and not a single person in the room suggested, "Do not use force against Iraq." Not one. Senator John Warner commented, "This meeting is one of the most important meetings ever to be held in the Cabinet Room."

Senator Carl Levin said that there was no question Hussein would use all his weapons if we attacked. The question was, therefore, would he use the weapons if we did not attack? Levin believed that Saddam wanted to stay in power. "Is he deterrable? Can he be contained?" he asked, and then reminded us Bush 41 had told Hussein if he used nuclear weapons he was done.

During the meeting, the president promised full cooperation with Congress, keeping them informed of events and providing information, but the words *congressional approval* were never uttered. Nevertheless, as Senator Warner had noted, this was an important milestone. Congressional leadership was now informed that the Bush administration was weighing military options consistent with the regime change authorized by Congress during the Clinton administration in 1998.

Afterward, I spoke to the president briefly, congratulating him on a good meeting. Although I believe that our country is better off when both elected branches agree on the use of force, I also cautioned him not to use the term *approval* when talking about congressional support. Certainly, the president understood that given the right circumstances, he had a certain degree of authority under the US Constitution to take military action as commander in chief, with or without approval by Congress. I understood it was important for the president to have Congress's support, but I also understood it was my job to help protect the institution of the presidency, even if that complicated the president's efforts.

The weekend of September 6, the National Security team met with the president at Camp David. Attending the meeting were General Tommy Franks, Dick Cheney, Andy Card, Colin Powell, Don Rumsfeld, Condi Rice, Steve Hadley, George Tenet, General Myers, and me. Although we spoke at length about the president's upcoming speech to open the United Nations session, much of the weekend was spent discussing what to do about Saddam Hussein.

It was a thorny issue, because it seemed the president was convinced the United States needed to do something to protect our national security, but he genuinely hoped to garner international support, and the chances of doing that did not look good. The question, of course, was what would we do if we could not rally international support? Would we go to war in Iraq alone?

The president said, "The idea of attacking Iraq is not an easy one. Sending troops into harm's way is not my first choice. Before we do, I want to make sure the cause is just, that we have the support we need, and that we will win." I nodded in agreement. One of the requirements of a lawful war is that the reason for war is legitimate—that there is just cause.

Colin Powell suggested taking the case to the UN in hopes that at least some of the nations would agree and get on board. All nations expected the inspectors to be allowed into Iraq, so if we could get a UN resolution for a firm date and time for inspections, with no conditions, Powell thought he could get the votes of the Security Council.

The president added that the inspectors had to be able to go anyplace in Iraq, anytime.

Tenet predicted that Saddam would try to find ways to negotiate out. He would attempt to buy as much time as possible.

Powell dismissed this, saying that we should not enter into any negotiations on inspections.

The president listened carefully, then said, "I'm leaning toward going to the UN for an ultimatum." He acknowledged we were in a cloudy period, in part because our own weak policy had created ambiguity in the international community. The president said, "First, I'm concerned that a go-it-alone policy will affect our relations in the Middle East. Second, post-Saddam will require an international effort, so our current policy ought to be something that works with the rules of the past. But any abrogation will lead to war." Bush nodded as he noted that he shared Vice President Cheney's concern that we not get stalled by the international community.

In an odd moment that became almost funny, we discussed what it would take to find Saddam. Everyone agreed that it would be difficult, since Saddam often used doubles for himself. The president was surprised to learn that Saddam employed impersonators, and he laughed at the idea.

Someone said, "You have a double too. You just don't know it."

President Bush laughed again. "Yeah, I do. Dana Carvey!" The president's quick response evoked a chuckle from everyone in the room who had heard the comedian's impersonations of Bush's father.

It was a much needed, albeit brief moment of levity in another tense round of discussions, and the president quickly got serious again. "If it expedites the mission, I'm willing to let Saddam leave Iraq." It was an idea worth considering. Other despots such as Uganda's Idi Amin, Haiti's Claude "Baby Doc" Duvalier, and even the Shah of Iran had escaped turmoil in their homeland, been granted asylum in friendly countries, and lived comfortably in exile. While the thought of Saddam absconding with his billions of dollars and living in luxury for the remainder of his life was not a pleasant one, it might be worth it if it prevented the loss of lives—especially American lives—in Iraq.

Don Rumsfeld questioned whether our efforts in Iraq would take away from our war on terror.

"This is *part* of the war on terror," Bush responded. "We cannot let al-Qaeda get the upper hand. That would be a disaster." After more discussion, the president concluded the meeting. "The key," he said, "is to get this done as quickly as possible. We have to be prepared to deal with any contingencies. The hardest part is the run-up; the second hardest is the post-Saddam Iraq, and the third part is the military piece."

I returned to Washington from Camp David with a much clearer understanding of what the president wanted. We were going to walk a tightrope, pushing the international community but preparing to take action alone if our national security warranted it.

The September 9 NSC discussion centered around a recent meeting between President Bush and British prime minister Tony Blair. Interestingly, though Blair was a liberal and Bush a conservative, they both viewed the threat from Hussein through similar lenses—Saddam was dangerous not only to his own people but to people in our nations as well. It was reassuring to know that our closest ally saw the situation similarly.

Bush and Blair had discussed seeking two possible UN resolutions, the first of which would find Iraq in material breach of previous resolutions, and explain what Saddam must do to come into immediate compliance. A second resolution could be passed later, we hoped, if Saddam failed to comply, and would authorize member nations to use all necessary force to secure Saddam's compliance, including the use of military force.

Blair believed the United States should push for the first resolution, but remain silent about the second until we were sure it was needed. Everyone in the NSC meeting agreed that one resolution was the neatest package. Further, we did not want to give the UN a veto over the president if he felt we needed to act unilaterally to protect our nation.

Rumsfeld and Cheney expressed concerns about relying upon the UN inspections. A resolution calling for inspections would allow the inspectors to greatly influence the timetable of US actions, and perhaps drive the military decision. They asked questions such as, "How firm will United Nations weapons inspector, Hans Blix, be with Saddam?"

After the NSC meeting, I studied previous UN resolutions about Iraq; many seemed ambiguous and open-ended, reflecting the UN's inclination to avoid conflict if possible. At 4:30 that afternoon, the principals met again. With all the talk of war in the room, it was almost refreshing to hear Condi remind everyone, "The president is not anxious to go to war. War is the last resort. He is not ready to go to war without demonstrating reasonableness." She emphasized that it was important to President Bush that whatever proposal we settled on must look different from the status quo. It must be something new, compared to the old ways of dealing with Saddam, which clearly were not working.

The following day, September 10, the NSC met at 7:30 a.m. in the Situation Room. I sat in my usual spot, along the wall a few feet directly to the president's right. With the first anniversary of 9/11 only a day away, not surprisingly, the president began by asking CIA director George Tenet about the overnight threat reports. George replied, "We're in a tough place right now; there is a lot of intelligence chatter." Against that backdrop, the potential danger of a marriage between Saddam and al-Qaeda seemed particularly ominous.

While discussing the need to seek international support, in a rather somber tone, Vice President Cheney remarked, "Saddam is a threat to the United States. We have to eliminate the threat, and if we adopt a strategy to put the decision out of our hands, that is a mistake."

Secretary Powell commented, "There is no support internationally for giving cover to the United States for regime change in Iraq. Our allies have said they will support any type of inspection regime. Most of our allies, however, want one last ultimatum to Iraq. If we go alone, we may have trouble getting access from other countries."

The president replied, "There is no question that if it looks like the same old stuff, we will look weak." He continued thoughtfully, "Before we commit troops to war, people have to believe that we were reasonable . . . We cannot look as though we are looking for an excuse. We do not want to go alone. It would be a mistake. We need to find a way to make it easier for countries to join us."

I studied the president as he spoke. He seemed uneasy about the way forward, but he was strong at the same time, believing that we had to put the burden—would there be war or not—on Saddam Hussein. The president looked at Secretary Powell. "Be tough," he said. "The world wants to avoid war. They will be weak and want to compromise and negotiate with Saddam. But be tough." He urged Powell to push for a UN resolution that included a finding of material breach on Iraq's part, and an authorization to pursue all necessary means. "Unfortunately, the best way to clean up Iraq is through war," President Bush said. "It is expensive, but it is the best way to achieve disarmament. But it is not my first choice."

I wondered, *What choice does the president really have?* If he does nothing and something horrific happens, and it is later discovered that we suspected Saddam might be dangerous but ignored the threat, the American people would never forgive us. The president's intelligence team has been telling him that Hussein was a dangerous threat to the United States. No one in the room honestly expected Saddam to willingly disarm, and few—if any—held on to hopes that he would allow inspections. Beyond that, I didn't believe that anybody in the room had confidence that the UN would be tough and refuse to negotiate with Saddam.

The president concluded the meeting by acknowledging that critics would use the war in Afghanistan against us. "We need to make sure there is a clear focus there, no distractions," he said.

Another related issue that concerned President Bush was the Middle East. He told Powell, "It's important that we start dialogue, because we need to show some progress there." He instructed Secretary Powell to show the world that we were still engaged on this issue.

Throughout this time period, we were still dealing with Yasser Arafat, the duplicitous leader of the Palestine Liberation Organization (PLO), trying to reach a lasting peace between the Israelis and Palestinians, and we had little progress to show for it. In an NSC meeting, Colin Powell had wryly commented about the PLO leader, "Arafat never misses an opportunity to miss an opportunity." Arafat was well known for speaking incessantly about peace, yet inciting violence against the Israelis. Nevertheless, during Secretary Powell's trip to the Middle East only a few months previously (April 2002), Powell had suggested the possibility of an international conference on the

Israeli-Palestinian issues. That was not an option the president endorsed, and Powell had to backtrack. Now the president was expressing hopes that Secretary Powell could still influence the Middle East toward peace.

There were many complicated pieces to the entire Middle East puzzle, and all were interrelated. How we resolved one issue impacted our options on another.

The president addressed the UN General Assembly on September 12, 2002. In his speech, he laid out the case against Saddam Hussein, outlining the UN resolutions and the breaches by Saddam. President Bush challenged the UN to be relevant, to do its job and demand Saddam's compliance with the UN resolutions—or else. He ended in stirring fashion:

> But the purposes of the United States should not be doubted. The Security Council resolutions will be enforced, the just demands of peace and security will be met or action will be unavoidable and a regime that has lost its legitimacy will also lose its power.[5]

The response to President Bush's speech among UN delegates was unenthusiastic. A few applauded politely, while many delegates exhibited no outward response at all. Too bad; he was the one world leader who was still saying, "The resolutions of this body need to be respected."

A few days later, on September 18, the principals met again in the Situation Room to discuss the congressional and UN resolutions regarding Iraq. Powell reported that the president's speech was "electrifying," possibly even changing the dynamics of the UN. Really? You'd never guess that by the outward responses of the delegates. Nevertheless, that was hopeful news.

The president joined us about a half hour into the meeting. He said, "It is important for us to continue clarifying that Saddam is trying to create doubt. There has to be clarity of thought. We need to remind people that Saddam Hussein is the bad guy." He emphasized, "It is important the UN understands that if there is no tough resolution, we will take matters into our own hands."

If we got a strong UN resolution and Saddam continued to resist inspections, we could join a coalition of countries under the resolution to use force. If, however, the UN resolution was weak or ambiguous with respect to weapons inspections, or did not include an "all necessary means" provision for enforcement, the United States might have to rely on some other legal doctrine to use force.

On September 19, the president called together key congressional leaders for a briefing in the White House Cabinet Room on our Iraq strategy and to discuss a congressional resolution regarding the use of military force in Iraq, if necessary. The president opened the meeting by stating, "This is a historic moment for our great country to deal with this threat." He clearly told the leaders that he wanted to see the military option in their resolution. He also emphasized to them that we would win. "Once the people of Iraq see that the war is being lost, that Saddam is the problem, the people will rise up."

Not surprisingly, the congressional leaders raised concerns, especially about putting US ground troops in Iraq, as well as the post-Saddam Iraq, and, of course, the cost. They also wondered how to best share this information with the public. The president assured them that the military option was the *last*, not the first, option, and that congressional hearings could educate the public.

President Bush did not back off. "Yes, military action would be expensive," he said. "We are already spending a lot in Afghanistan, and we need to modernize our military assets." Nevertheless, as I listened to the congressional leaders, I felt sure that if they felt they were responding to a national security threat, they'd find a way to come up with the money. Nobody wanted a repeat of 9/11.

My work on the congressional resolution took top priority for me over the next few weeks. We asked for a provision recognizing the president's constitutional authority to defend the United States against acts of terrorism. Congress insisted on receiving reports, and we agreed to provide a presidential determination letter, warranting certain conditions had been met before using force. One of the conditions was, in the president's judgment, that the use of force against Iraq would not negatively impact the war on terrorism. The president balked at including this in the certification. We compromised and included a "whereas" provision that recognized the use of force in Iraq was a furtherance of the war on terrorism.

One "whereas" provision we included was extremely helpful in our self-defense argument. The provision stated, "Whereas Iraq has demonstrated capability and willingness to use weapons of mass destruction, the risks that the current Iraqi regime will either employ those weapons to launch a surprise attack against the United States or its Armed Forces, or provide them to international terrorists who would do so, and the extreme magnitude of harm that would result to the United States and its citizens from such an attack, combine to justify action by the United States to defend itself."

On September 30, a large group of advisors met with the president regarding new homeland security legislation. During that meeting, President Bush initiated a discussion about the congressional resolution on Iraq. Karl Rove was in this meeting and indicated that we needed more time to sell our Iraq plan to the public. That was the first time I had ever heard Karl speak about any national security matter. Indeed, he was never present at the National Security Council or principals committee meetings, so I considered his commenting on a national security matter noteworthy.

The president, however, told Karl that he had already been selling the Iraq plan to the public for three months.

Karl wasn't convinced. He repeated that he thought we needed more time because the polls showed that support was soft.

President Bush responded, "I don't care if the polls showed 20 percent for the plan and 80 percent against, I would still do this because it is the right thing to do." Courage. It is one of the characteristics of every successful president—the courage to do what is right no matter how unpopular.

As we worked toward finalizing a congressional resolution, we encountered new challenges regarding a UN resolution. Apparently, not only were we *not* going to get a resolution that included a finding of material breach on the part of Iraq and the authority to use all necessary means, it now appeared that some countries were backing away from saying that Iraq had committed a material breach of their responsibilities under previous resolutions.

At an NSC meeting on October 2, the president expressed frustration with the UN and cautioned the National Security Council team to "be strong." Speaking of the UN, he said, "We need to put them on the defense.

It has to be clear that it is their responsibility to force Iraq into compliance. The status quo is unacceptable. Whatever resolution we arrive at, it must provide for unfettered, unrestricted access for inspections.

"We have a problem," the president said. "We know Iraq is arming, but our intelligence agencies cannot find the arms. This is a dynamic process, always changing. We have to be able to adjust. Saddam will game the system, so we have to be aggressive about getting an aggressive resolution in place."

He shook his head as though frustrated. "The UN does not want force to be used; they want the problem to go away. This is not about inspections; this is about disarming Iraq. If Blix is serious about disarming, he will come here with serious plans."

The president was clearly concerned. The French were uneasy about saying out front that there was a material breach, since arguably this would allow the United States to use force under previous resolutions. The Germans were equally tepid in their response to Iraq's breaches. Both of these countries, it would later be suggested, had ulterior motives for their reticence.[6] Some members of the UN wanted the Security Council to determine whether there was a breach before authorizing action. It was this potential second vote that most troubled the president. The delays such a vote represented could be interminable, and potentially deadly if Saddam and his cohorts got wind of it, as they surely would.

"The burden of proof is on him," the president said of Saddam. "If he is not serious about disarming, we will go disarm him, and others need to come along. The key is not to agree to something that two months from now we regret. If he doesn't disarm, we are moving against him."

The president then turned his attention to the chief UN inspector, Hans Blix. "Will Blix allow himself to be manipulated? Does Blix understand how dangerous Saddam Hussein is? If Blix does not believe Saddam is a threat, he has no incentive to find something that may lead to war."

It was a good assessment of the challenges we faced. The president's final question summed up our dilemma: "How do we negotiate a UN resolution that achieves our objectives?"

How indeed?

CHAPTER 23

DANCING WITH A DEVIL

The political pot was already stirring. On September 9, 2002, Democratic senator Richard Durbin contacted George Tenet, urging him to produce a National Intelligence Estimate (NIE), a written assessment of Iraq's WMD threat potential and programs. The following day, Tenet received a letter from Bob Graham, chairman of the Senate Select Committee on Intelligence, officially asking for an NIE "on the status of Iraq's programs to develop weapons of mass destruction and delivery systems, the status of the Iraqi military forces, including their readiness and willingness to fight, the effects a US led attack on Iraq would have on its neighbors, and Saddam Hussein's likely response to a US military campaign designed to effect regime change in Iraq."[1] The Democrats were apparently seeking more information before an anticipated October vote on the use of military force in Iraq.

But an NIE report of this sort would normally draw information from at least six different sections of the intelligence community, and would involve a process requiring six to ten months. The Senate Intelligence Committee wanted it produced within weeks. The CIA delivered a ninety-page NIE around 10:30 at night on October 1, 2002.[2] While refusing to excuse the CIA's responsibility to deliver accurate intelligence information,

Tenet would later look to that truncated time frame as one of the major reasons some of the included information was flawed or uncertain, and some was just wrong.[3] Making matters worse, this same flawed report would provide some of the material on which Colin Powell based his much-publicized speech to the UN about Iraq's WMD on February 5, 2003. But of course we didn't know then the report was flawed.

Complicating matters further, the NIE included information gleaned from British intelligence about a purported attempt by Saddam to acquire milled uranium oxide, a substance known as yellowcake, an element that can be enriched to produce nuclear weapons–grade uranium. Ostensibly, Saddam had hoped to purchase these materials from Niger, a large, heavily populated, impoverished country located on the southern rim of the Sahara Desert in Africa. Niger's main export is uranium ore.

The NIE reported that Saddam might have tried to obtain yellowcake from Niger, but even that inclusion was a relatively minor point. More importantly, the NIE noted Saddam already possessed a whopping 550 metric tons of yellowcake in Iraq—enough to produce at least one hundred nuclear weapons. This fact was known to the international UN inspectors who were supposedly keeping tabs on Saddam's yellowcake. Saddam's attempted purchase was never proven, but the fact that it was noted in the NIE came back to haunt us a year or so later.

Although it seemed obvious that Saddam wanted a nuclear bomb, even if he had received yellowcake from Niger, the NIE remained nebulous about his ability to produce a nuclear weapon within a year. Perhaps he could succeed in several years, almost certainly by the end of the decade.

As Tenet later pointed out, the phrase *we do not know* appears some thirty times in the ninety-page report, and the words *we know* appear only three times. Instead, the CIA used language such as *we judge* or *we assess* as analytical statements, not as facts.[4] The document also included dissenting and alternative views, even highlighting them in colored boxes within the report.

The CIA included a five-page summary (presented as "Key Judgments") at the front of the document. Tenet later commented these were written in terms that were too assertive, especially concerning chemical and biological weapons, and "convey[ed] an air of certainty that does not exist in the rest of the paper."[5]

Even noting Tenet's disclaimers, the NIE report was damning against Saddam. The now declassified document included the following statements in the summary:

> We judge that Iraq has continued its weapons of mass destruction (WMD) programs in defiance of UN resolutions and restrictions. Baghdad has chemical and biological weapons as well as missiles with ranges in excess of UN restrictions; if left unchecked, it probably will have a nuclear weapon during this decade.
>
> Although we assess that Saddam does not yet have nuclear weapons or sufficient material to make any, he remains intent on acquiring them. Most agencies assess that Baghdad started reconstituting its nuclear program about the time that inspectors departed—December 1998.
>
> Saddam, if sufficiently desperate, might decide that only an organization such as al-Qaeda—with worldwide reach and extensive terrorist infrastructure, and already engaged in a life-or-death struggle against the United States—could perpetuate the type of terrorist attack that he would hope to conduct.
>
> In such circumstances, he might decide that the extreme step of assisting the Islamist terrorists in conducting a CBW [chemical or biological weapon] attack against the United States would be his last chance to exact vengeance by taking a large number of victims with him.[6]

With caveats like "if left unchecked" and "Saddam . . . might," the document was far from definitive in tone. The problem is that although the statement about Iraq's missiles was accurate, the judgments about biological and chemical weapons should not have been characterized as *facts*, as Tenet himself acknowledged.[7] In his 2007 book, *At the Center of the Storm*, he writes that the report *should* have read as follows:

> We judge that Saddam continues his efforts to rebuild weapons programs, that, once sanctions are lifted, he probably will confront the Unites States

with chemical, biological, and nuclear weapons within a matter of months and years. Today, while we have little direct evidence of weapons stockpiles, Saddam has the ability to quickly surge to produce chemical and biological weapons and he has the means to deliver them.[8]

Several Democratic senators pushed to declassify and release to the public portions of the hearing on the NIE report by the Senate Select Committee on Intelligence, which they did, prompting even more confusion.

It's important to note, however, that the CIA was not alone in assuming Saddam had become a dangerous threat. Intelligence services from Britain, Australia, Spain, Poland, and Italy shared that opinion, and France and Germany expressed similar concerns.

In October 2002, Congress passed a strong resolution authorizing the use of military force in Iraq. The resolution reflected a broad view by both Democrats and Republicans that Saddam Hussein's rule in Iraq needed to end, by force if necessary, to protect the United States and international peace and security. This was a big deal, and even some of George W. Bush's staunchest political opponents agreed that Saddam Hussein must go.

Senator John Kerry, who later ran for president against President Bush before serving as secretary of state in the Obama administration, said at the time, "When I vote to give the president of the United States the authority to use force, if necessary, to disarm Saddam Hussein, it is because I believe that a deadly arsenal of weapons of mass destruction in his hands is a threat, and a grave threat, to our security and that of our allies in the Persian Gulf Region."[9]

Democratic senator and future vice president Joe Biden had made up his mind back in August. "We have no choice but to eliminate the threat," Biden said. "This is a guy who is an extreme danger to the world."[10]

Senator Hillary Clinton weighed in as well. "In the four years since the inspectors, intelligence reports show that Saddam Hussein has worked to rebuild his chemical and biological weapons stock, his missile delivery capability, and his nuclear program." Senator Clinton spoke confidently of information most of those attending the early-morning White House meetings were still reticent to mention because of the lack of reliability of our intelligence sources. Clinton said Saddam "has also given aid, comfort, and sanctuary to terrorists, including al-Qaeda members."[11]

With the congressional resolution in hand, we were now able to focus on securing a strong UN resolution and hopefully strong support from a coalition of allies. One of our former friends, however, continued to be a thorn. Once a West-leaning Muslim democracy and member of NATO, the country of Turkey had been a longtime friend of ours. We had maintained military facilities at Incirlik Air Base inside Turkey, which helped greatly during Desert Storm, and from which we had conducted humanitarian aid to Kurdish refugees in northern Iraq. But by 2002, new leaders representing the Islamist AKP party won a majority in the Turkish Parliament and were now encouraging the nation to move further away from the United States. The new Turk leaders opposed any additional US actions against Iraq.

As we moved into late October, President Bush seemed to have less confidence in the UN inspections. "A weak inspections regime is not satisfactory," he said during an NSC meeting. "There has to be something in place as an option to strengthen our hand. We want to be able to follow through if the UN fails to act with a strong inspections regime." He surprised me by saying, "It's my fault that we are at the UN and subject to UN trigger mechanisms." He didn't mean, of course, that it was his fault that we were members of the UN, but rather that we had attempted to evoke their involvement in making Saddam comply. The statement reflected his frustration.

He quickly pivoted and reminded us, "We need to be patient; we need to stay on top of things and not avoid this moment to make the world more peaceful. This is a huge part of our responsibility. It is a hard issue, and we need to make sure that Blix understands there is another alternative. Blix needs to know that if there is a war, it is Bush's responsibility and not Blix's. But we are not the guilty party—we are the saviors."

I shook my head in appreciation of what we had just witnessed. One moment the president was frustrated at the UN's sluggish participation, and the next he was the leader of the free world with shoulders big enough to handle the world's problems.

At the beginning of November, I worked with other lawyers to refine what we hoped would become an acceptable UN resolution, conferring with OLC and the NSC to resolve language issues that could create obstacles. Specifically, I worked on the matter of lethal force against certain individuals, members of al-Qaeda, and anyone who was a threat to the United States. Condi Rice and John Bellinger were particularly helpful in this regard.

On November 6, the day after the midterm elections, I discussed the resolution with President Bush in his office. He was on the phone a lot, making congratulatory calls to the election winners, but we still had a good conversation. He pressed me about whether this resolution would take away his presidential authority.

President Bush and Prime Minister Blair, along with Secretary of State Powell and his British counterpart, Foreign Secretary Jack Straw, finally won the day with the UN Security Council. Despite Russia and China's frequent opposition to US proposals, and France's and Germany's coziness with Saddam—which may have caused him to think he could escape unscathed with merely another limp slap on the wrists—on November 8, 2002, the UN Security Council voted 15–0 to support Resolution 1441, condemning Iraq's weapons programs and demanding that Iraq open suspected facilities for inspection. The resolution threatened "serious consequences" if Iraq failed to provide the UN with a comprehensive list of the WMD it had retained. Like a parent demanding a child obey before the count of three, and then counting, "One, two, two and half, two and three-quarters . . ." the UN warned Iraq that this was its final opportunity to come clean and comply with the requirements of the international community.

And then we waited for Iraq's response.

Meanwhile, the National Security Council discussions coalesced around three main topics regarding Iraq: (1) The implementation of the UN resolution and getting international support for a possible war; (2) the actual military campaign; and (3) the post-Saddam Iraq. For more than a year, rarely was I in the Situation Room with the National Security team when at least one of those components was not discussed.

General Tommy Franks joined us for our December 4 meeting of the

NSC, so not surprisingly, the discussion focused on actual war planning. Again, the president expressed his concern about Turkey's lack of cooperation in providing access to Iraq from the north. "We need to know what they are willing to do and plan around them if they will not help," he said. "Can we win if Turkey will not help?" The president addressed his question to General Franks.

"We will win," Franks answered.

"The key is flexibility," President Bush said. "We have to be able to change our plans quickly, without any doubt of victory. If Tommy Franks has no doubt, then I have no doubt of victory." General Franks's astonishing success in Afghanistan gave everyone great confidence that his efforts in Iraq would also be successful, but everyone understood that Iraq was a much more sophisticated enemy than the Taliban.

President Bush continued probing the general's confidence level. "If I told you to attack within five days, what would it look like?"

Franks said, "It could be done within four hours' notice, but there are more risks. It will take a number of days to set up Patriot missiles, deal with Scud missile defenses, and move forces from the north, hopefully through Turkey. Additional time will be needed to move southern ground forces into position. The size of our force would be substantially smaller than one ordered to fight within thirty days' notice."

The president nodded. Yes, we could go sooner, but more time for preparation was safer. Still, he pressed Franks to reduce the number of days necessary to initiate military activities.

Franks reiterated, "You can go even sooner, but there are more risks involved."

President Bush directed General Franks to take all necessary defensive measures, but to develop a plan to bring down the risks early. As I listened to this discussion, I sensed the president had crossed a line in his deliberations on the subject. "If we have to do this alone," he said, "we will do it alone." Then he continued firmly, "This may be the most important decision I ever make. Once we go, there is no turning back. We must tell our coalition partners that there is no turning back."

Franks nodded. "We will be in Baghdad very quickly," he said. "The initial blast will take out much of the Republican Guard, although inside Baghdad we may encounter pockets of resistance, especially around mosques and schools. The enemy will seek to use human shields."

Don Rumsfeld suggested the formation of some type of advisory committee to help control the country after the fall of Saddam, facilitate the destruction of WMD, and round up any remaining bad guys. This was serious.

I knew we had to be prepared for any contingency, but I left the meeting slightly discouraged that we would not be able to avoid conflict. We were no longer talking about the possibility of war. Now we were deciding how the war would be waged.

On the UN front, the next big event was Saddam's submission of a declaration of weapons. The president was skeptical. At the December 6 NSC meeting, he asked George Tenet whether we would be able to tell if Saddam's weapons declaration was false. Tenet said, "Yes."

The president remained suspicious. "Saddam is moving stuff to Syria," he said. "He will not disarm." Nevertheless, he was resolved to wait on the Hussein declaration.

Saddam's report was received from the UN on December 10, and the principals met that afternoon to discuss it. The first impression by the CIA was that the declaration fell far short of being truthful, even more so than the 1998 report. There was no admission of an ongoing nuclear weapons program. Sections of the report appeared copied from previous unreliable declarations. The new declaration did not include specific information, and there was nothing to support Saddam's claim that they had destroyed weapons stockpiles. Iraq acknowledged unmanned aerial vehicles, but did not connect them to their weapons programs. Their report on ballistic missiles we knew was inaccurate and incomplete.

The CIA would complete its review in the next few days—probably before Blix completed his—so we agreed on the importance of going to the UN and the P5 nations (the United Kingdom, France, Russia, China, and the United States) to condition the environment. Blix and the P5 needed to have their eyes opened to the list of omissions and inaccuracies in Saddam's declaration. These constituted a material breach and demanded a response.

When the CIA completed its analysis of Saddam's declaration, the NSC met in the Situation Room on December 18. We knew by now that Blix would report that there were gaping holes in the weapons report. The president spoke calmly but firmly: "If there are gaps, it is clear he is not willing to disarm. This is significant."

Colin Powell concurred. "Saddam has put the rope around his own neck," he said. "It is up to us how quickly to tighten it." Powell knew that Saddam was a bad guy, but he also wanted us to make sure our actions were based on truth, not rumor. He had been in Iraq during Desert Storm; he knew firsthand Saddam's evil, and when he was convinced the Iraqis had purposely submitted an incomplete and incorrect weapons report, he knew what had to be done.

Vice President Cheney asked whether we should trash Saddam's declarations now. "Instinct is to go hard and heavy on material breach," he said, "laying the groundwork to explain why we may have to use force. No one else will describe the declaration as clearly as the United States. Blix will offer a squishy assessment of the declaration."

Secretary Rumsfeld reported that deployment orders for a major force were nearly ready to go. He noted with concern that we might declare Saddam had committed a material breach and then not do anything about it. He cautioned that our words and actions must match.

The president then asked the question I had been asking myself for months, especially after receiving Saddam's bogus weapons declarations: "Is war inevitable?"

Powell answered quickly, "No."

President Bush was not so sure. "I think war is inevitable. Saddam is not going to disarm. The quicker we determine, the better off we are." In discussing what sort of statement the administration should make, the president stated emphatically, "We need to ratchet up the level of concern. We need language that is tougher than Blix, but short of a declaration of war. People want us to exhaust all options before we go to war. I believe in plain speaking. Tell the American people what we think."

As the nation prepared for Christmas, we prepared to deal with Iraq. On December 19, the NSC met to discuss threats from al-Qaeda and to assess preparations for Iraq. The president asked whether our priorities were too broad—in other words, could we deal with both al-Qaeda and Iraq? "We have told the country that we can do both," Bush said, "so by God, we have to do both. The first priority is to go after the terrorists that come after the United States; the second priority is terrorists who take action in other countries."

After the al-Qaeda discussion, we received a briefing by Tommy Franks. He reported that the ratio of man to man would be different in this war. Historically, it is three to one, offensive versus defensive. "Here it is one to six," Franks said, "the first time in history that manpower is combined with technology so completely." He also said, "We are cocked and ready to go in February; our force will be 250,000 strong."

The president asked, "When you get to Baghdad, tell us again why the operation doesn't bog down? Do we hit the wall?"

Rumsfeld added, "We have to precondition what victory is."

Tommy Franks replied bluntly, "There will be dancing in the streets."

The president looked at Tommy and said wryly, "If not, then we will be doing some dancing to explain what we have done."

Discussions with General Franks continued the following day. The president seemed to have great confidence in the general, a fellow Texan. "I don't expect everything to go perfectly as planned," he said. "I just want to win."

We moved to a discussion of targets and the anticipated casualties. The president emphasized that we wanted to bomb facilities, not the people of Iraq. He was particularly interested in hitting Saddam's "hardened" facilities, including tunnels. "Saddam either doesn't believe us, or does not know that we are about to hit him."

"On the first day of the attack," Tommy Franks said, "Saddam will believe us."

President Bush nodded. "That is sad," he said.

Complicating matters further, right before Thanksgiving the UN sent inspectors to Iraq for another round of inspections. While we hoped this might work to our advantage with the international community, especially if Saddam was uncooperative, the process was painfully slow, and I could tell that President Bush was growing weary of it all. He had shown great patience to this point, but the inspections once again placed our timetable in the hands of equivocators. We had lived with issues surrounding Iraq now for nearly a year. At the same time, I was immersed in the Michigan affirmative action cases, while attending every meeting of the National Security team. It was a busy time.

In our January 17 discussions, the president was emphatic that the United States would not go into Iraq for oil. The oil belonged to the Iraqi people, he stated repeatedly. I nodded as the president said, "I want the first message to the Iraqi people to be that I am not just bringing guns; I am bringing butter."

As Rumsfeld and Franks continued to monitor the movement of more American troops into a position where they could attack Iraq, we received some disappointing news. On January 22, 2003, French president Jacques Chirac and German chancellor Gerhard Schroeder announced they would not support the US ouster of Saddam Hussein if the use of force proved necessary. At a time when our coalition of countries was building, this was a setback. No doubt, Saddam smiled in his palace as he imagined his business partners protecting him. Ironically, the decisions of France and Germany would make war more likely rather than less, since Saddam would have a reduced incentive to cooperate and comply with the UN resolutions.

Despite France's and Germany's decisions, nearly fifty nations eventually joined the coalition led by the United States and Great Britain. Thirty of those countries contributed visibly, while others, particularly Arab states, participated in important but more discreet manners. The Arab countries, especially, wanted the United States to deal with Saddam quickly and decisively, to get in, take him down, deal with the WMD, and get out as fast as possible.

As Cheney had predicted, the United Nations weapons inspector, Hans Blix, indeed provided a squishy analysis of Saddam's contemptuously incomplete weapons declarations. Blix told the UN Security Council, "Iraq appears not to have come to a genuine acceptance, not even today, of the disarmament which was demanded of it and which it needs to carry out to win the confidence of the world and live in peace." Blix also acknowledged that one thousand tons of toxic nerve gas, a lethal chemical weapon that Saddam had actually used previously, remained "unaccounted for."[12] A logical assumption might be that Saddam still possessed the nerve gas or had access to it.

On January 28, the president hosted a cabinet meeting in which reports about ongoing events in Afghanistan and Iraq were presented. He was calm and determined as he spoke about the United States doing the right thing, no matter how difficult. "We are the light," he said, "in a very complex world. We will have allies with us when we attack. We are a compassionate nation, and we must help others to pursue opportunities."

I was struck by the resolve in the president's tone. I'd known him for quite a while, and I could tell that he seemed resigned to a course of action in Iraq. It was the first time that I truly believed that war was inevitable. But I definitely believed.

CHAPTER 24

FOR THE SAKE OF
PEACE AND SECURITY

The NSC met with the president at the White House at 9:00 a.m. on January 31, 2003. By the conclusion of this meeting, the president was committed, at least as far as he could be—he had chosen to initiate military action on February 22. Subject to a dramatic turn of events, the air war would begin on March 10, and the ground troops would move into Iraq on March 15. Certainly the plan could change, but we now had a roadmap to follow.

Vice President Cheney reminded everyone that we needed to prepare for all contingencies. Saddam could do anything. There were still off-ramps on the road to war. On February 5, Colin Powell was scheduled to present the case for action in Iraq to the UN, to let them know that time was running out. The president would speak to the nation about Iraq the following day. A second resolution might be presented to the UN on February 7, but that was still very much up in the air.

The president contended, "The military plan should not be geared for diplomacy; it will be geared to win militarily."

General Franks noted we needed to figure out how we wanted to give advance notice to civilians in Iraq, warning them about the ensuing war. Tommy Franks was a realist. "Ten percent of our munitions might be off," he said. "There will be civilian casualties."

On February 3, the principals met to discuss the content of Powell's upcoming speech to the UN. Colin Powell was a man of great pride in his reputation, and he would never say anything to a government body that he did not believe to be absolutely true. He had only one caveat: "There will be no smoking gun."

Otherwise, he intended to say straightforwardly that Iraq's most recent weapons declarations were false and inaccurate. Saddam had not cooperated or complied with the UN requests.

Second, he intended to present a thorough review of Iraq's weapons programs, including biological, chemical, and nuclear.

Third, he intended to discuss Saddam's ties to terrorism.

And fourth, he intended to cover Hussein's human rights violations imposed upon his own people.

I sensed that Secretary Powell was comfortable making the case; he had been screening the intelligence reports and removing any questionable assertions from his presentation. He had even gone out to CIA headquarters at Langley, along with several speechwriters and senior aides, checking and double-checking his facts against the most up-to-date information. The CIA assigned a number of senior intelligence professionals to help check the accuracy of what Powell and his writers were including, but as CIA director George Tenet later acknowledged, "Despite our efforts, a lot of flawed information still made its way into the speech."[1]

As planned, on the morning of February 5, 2003, Secretary of State Colin Powell made the case for war to the United Nations. Sitting behind him on the platform were John Negroponte, the US ambassador to the UN, and George Tenet, director of the Central Intelligence Agency. In a dramatic address before the UN Security Council, Secretary Powell did an exemplary job of laying out the case against Saddam. He presented recordings, satellite photographs, and documents that proved Iraq was engaged in WMD activities and defying the UN. Everyone in the room understood the seriousness of the subject and the quiet intensity of the man who presented the US intelligence information. The speech purported to prove that Saddam Hussein had, or could soon have, weapons of mass destruction and a history showing his willingness to use them.

"My colleagues, every statement I make today is backed up by sources, solid sources," Colin Powell told the UN. "These are not assertions. What we are giving you are facts and conclusions based on solid intelligence."[2]

Powell left little room for his listeners to doubt his message or Saddam's ultimate goals. "We have more than a decade of proof that he remains determined to acquire nuclear weapons," Powell said. "Saddam Hussein is determined to get his hands on a nuclear bomb."[3]

Then Secretary Powell drilled down on the chemical plant in Khurmal, highlighting the WMD and revealing our knowledge of al-Qaeda's presence in Iraq. "The Zarqawi network helped establish another poison and explosive training center camp . . . and this camp is located in northeastern Iraq."[4] It's easy to imagine the terrorists in Khurmal starting to pack the moment Powell's words left his mouth. Their secret was exposed.

Everything I heard Secretary Powell say in his speech was absolutely consistent with the information I had been hearing in NSC meetings and principals meetings for more than a year. Like the rest of us, Powell based his judgment on the intelligence information provided by the CIA. He obviously believed it to be true; the president of the United States believed it to be true; the director of the CIA believed it to be true; everyone on the National Security team believed it was true; and I certainly believed it was true.

Unfortunately, by the time our troops reached Khurmal in March 2003, much of the chemical facility had been destroyed—either dismantled by the operators or demolished by cruise missiles or ground fighting. Clear signs of chemical weapons production were found, however, including chemical hazardous materials (HAZMAT) suits, manuals written in Arabic describing how to make chemical weapons, and traces of deadly toxins, including cyanide, ricin, and potassium chloride.[5]

No huge stashes of WMD, however, were ever found, which led to the oft-repeated mantra in the media, "Bush lied, people died."

Bush did not lie; nor did he intentionally mislead. Nor did Tenet or Rumsfeld or members of Congress—both Democrat and Republican—or our allies who came to the same conclusions. And the truth is, we may never know how many innocent people might have died had we not taken action in Iraq.

When the NSC met on February 12, Powell reported that despite his speech, Hans Blix was set to present another nuanced performance to the UN. While Blix would be honest, saying there had been little cooperation by Iraq, he would probably lobby for more time.

The president was done waiting on Blix. "Is February 22 still a good day to initiate military action?" he asked Don Rumsfeld.

"Yes," the secretary of defense replied bluntly. He reported that reconnaissance flights were already occurring over Baghdad.

Bush questioned how we should respond if Hussein attempted to flee the country.

Cheney responded that we needed to be careful about letting Saddam out of Baghdad to reestablish himself someplace else, where he could use his billions of dollars to assist terrorism. Then, in a moment of almost stunning candor, the always-direct vice president said, "We need to study carefully whether we should let him leave or whether we should kill him."

I assumed Cheney was not suggesting political assassination, but was reminding us that Saddam was the commander in chief of an opposing force and therefore a lawful military target.

On Valentine's Day, Hans Blix delivered another report to the UN Security Council, advocating more time for Saddam. Blix's report questioned the accuracy of some of Colin Powell's assertions before the Security Council. It also cited increased cooperation by Iraq, although it did not conclude that Saddam would allow access to inspectors, or that he was in compliance with the UN resolutions. But the Blix report provided enough cover for countries who wanted to sit on the sidelines.

People in the White House, not surprisingly, were not in a conciliatory mood. More importantly, we were hearing that some of our Middle Eastern partners were growing impatient and nervous, and though they had privately pledged to be with us when we liberated Iraq, they were expressing increased skepticism and questioning our resolve, due to the delays. In the NSC meeting that day, President Bush seemed concerned about Great Britain's resolve more than ours. He asked Tommy Franks, "If Great Britain doesn't go, can we go?"

"We do have a contingency plan," Franks replied.

Bush responded, "Contingency may happen."

I was not sure the president would seriously entertain an attack scenario without Great Britain; I thought he was simply expressing frustration over the UN's fickleness. Nonetheless, the president had information that I did not.

He seemed greatly concerned about Iraq's oil fields being booby-trapped and set on fire by Saddam supporters. The oil fields were a valuable asset for a post-Saddam Iraq, and the president wanted to make sure they were as safe as possible. He posed a hypothetical question to Tommy Franks: "If Saddam attempts to blow up the oil fields, how long would it take to get equipment there to put out the fires?"

"A month," Franks estimated.

The president frowned at Franks' comment, but nodded that he understood.

Turkey was a concern. While Tommy Franks had hoped to gain some tactical and strategic advantage by moving troops and supplies through Turkey, the country's new leaders were cautious, but also anxious for assistance to help modernize their economy.

At the NSC meeting on February 8, we discussed options on how best to support our military aims and Turkey's interest in modernization.

The following day, Condi, Andy, and I met with the president to discuss targeting issues. I expressed concern that in a push to win a decisive and quick victory, we must not forget our legal obligations as a nation under the laws of war and applicable international treaties. We suggested to the president the importance of reminding our military that while we want to win quickly, if opportunities existed to minimize civilian casualties, we should attempt to do so.

President Bush scowled at us and said that we were stating the obvious. The president eyed Condi, Andy, and me standing around his desk. "This is a cover-our-ass discussion," he said. "I've decided to move forward in Iraq regardless of the political consequences."

"We understand that," I said, "and we support it. I'm just saying that we need to follow certain rules." I reiterated that civilian casualties should be proportional to the value of the military target. "We should try to warn civilians before the attack, and we should do what is feasible and consistent with military necessity to minimize casualties among civilians."

The president agreed.

At an NSC meeting shortly after that, President Bush turned to Tommy Franks and said, "It should be clear to our military that I expect everything to be done to minimize the loss of innocent life and still win the war."

"I understand," Franks replied.

The president glanced at me as if to say, "There, is that what you wanted to hear?"

I nodded discreetly and forced myself not to smile.

We then discussed efforts to minimize loss of life, beginning by dropping leaflets over Iraq and doing radio broadcasts two to five days in advance of an attack without naming the site of the attack. At forty-eight hours, we would alert media to vacate. At twenty-four hours, we would broadcast more radio warnings, as well as television, warning civilians to stay away from military targets. At one hour before the attack, we would broadcast again, advising people to flee selected, specific targets.

This was a fine line to walk between warning civilians and alerting the enemy, which might put our own troops at risk. The president expressed his concern about tipping our hand. "It's important to give warnings, but not to jeopardize our initial strikes."

Two targets we discussed—a downtown hotel and a communications center—were particularly troublesome. The president asked if we needed to hit the hotel. "Yes," came the answer, because of certain equipment Saddam had placed inside it. Earlier that day, I had conferred with Jim Haynes about potential targets near a "protected site," such as a hospital or mosque, or a "sensitive site," where civilian casualties might exceed thirty. Haynes reported that our military had to get permission before hitting these sites.

Regarding a Baghdad mass communications site, the president asked, "What happens if we do not destroy it?"

Franks responded, "This is an important target. We need to hit it to destroy command and control."

The vice president agreed. "If we leave them in place, it makes the battle harder and we might suffer more casualties."

I watched the president's face as he considered each protected or sensitive target. "We need to use accurate weapons," he said. "If we want to minimize loss of life and win the war, we need to use the most accurate weapons we have."

The president then raised a good question relating to the costs of rebuilding a post-Saddam Iraq. "If we destroy the telephone system, I presume we get to pay to rebuild the system," he said. This was certainly a difficult consideration in waging war in a relatively modern, developed country such as Iraq. We had to destroy some of the infrastructure to defeat the enemy, but we would then spend American money to rebuild that same infrastructure after the war.

When we discussed hitting the Al Rashid Hotel, the president again voiced concern for civilians nearby or in the hotel. "We need to make sure our warnings are effective," he said. He cautioned also about the Baghdad main exchange at Khag and the Baghdad television studios. "Don't you want to strike these targets at night?" The president recognized that while our military possessed the technology to be as accurate as possible, civilian casualties would be unavoidable.

"How many military targets have you decided not to hit?" he asked General Franks.

"None," Franks replied. "Every target we want to hit is on the list."

"Can you achieve success without bombing downtown Baghdad?" he asked.

Rumsfeld replied, "We need to hit Baghdad to weaken Hussein."

Franks said, "We will not destroy power grids and bridges because we will need them. But as the war progresses, we will continue to analyze and decide if we help or hurt ourselves by taking out a target."

By now, the National Security team was meeting daily on the subject of Iraq, but the meeting on the afternoon of February 20 was highly unusual. An Iraqi military general had indicated that he wanted to attempt the assassination of Saddam Hussein. The principals committee discussed the proper response to such an offer, then decided that because of bans on assassination, we could not overtly encourage the general's plan, but would simply say that Saddam's death could possibly prevent a war. We also discussed whether the United States should promise immunity to an assassin, and again the answer was no.

At the February 26 NSC meeting, Powell remarked that although Japan was with us, the prime minister was facing public pressure. It would be helpful to tone down any rhetoric about Japan's involvement. "Our largest challenge is Mexico," Powell said. "As Mexico goes, so goes Chile."

Despite President Bush's friendship with Mexican president Vicente Fox, Bush speculated, "If Mexico goes with France, America will treat them the same. Mexico needs to understand that our reaction to the French is real, and they do not want that same reaction."

On February 28, the president said, "We are through speculating; we are moving forward." He peppered the National Security team with questions about post-Saddam Iraq. "Have we thought through what we want to see in Iraq?" he asked. "How do we hold people accountable?" After a briefing on how Iraq might function following the war, the president asked again, "How do we keep things going within the country? How do we provide services to the Iraqi people?"

These were simple yet profound questions, signifying Bush's intentions. They also set the tone, prior to the war, for how the United States hoped to help Iraq after Saddam was removed.

Preparations moved into March. During all that time, I never saw one report or piece of new information to discredit our assumption that al-Qaeda was operating freely in Iraq, or that Iraq did not have weapons of mass destruction. We did note some conflicting reports regarding the amount of WMD Saddam had, but without full inspections, there was no way to be sure.

After months of negotiations and cajoling, Turkey continued its non-committal attitude, Powell reported. While overflights might not require the Turks' parliamentary approval, moving ground troops and supplies through their country would. Tommy Franks wanted to bring the Fourth Infantry Division into northern Iraq through Turkey, but with the Turks stonewalling, we were in limbo. The principals suggested that we needed to reassess our monetary assistance to Turkey, given the timeliness and scope of their cooperation. Rumsfeld put it bluntly, "Our clear message to the Turks should be that we are going to be in the north, even if we have to come in from the south."

Tommy Franks reported some good news: the oil platforms in Iraq had not been dynamited and should be easy targets to capture. He explained that he planned to do hundreds of sorties (defensive attacks) over Iraq to do reconnaissance but also to condition the Iraqi people to hearing large numbers of aircraft overhead. Franks used the term *shock* to describe the Iraqis' anticipated response to the initial attack.

"Yeah," Bush deadpanned. "I read about the shock in the *New York Times*." He was referring to an article published by the newspaper over DOD objections that the article might risk American lives. The reporter revealed detailed information based on classified war plans, declaring the United States planned to move forces into Iraq from the north and the west by racing through Turkey. Ironically, the paper's attempt at a scoop may have assisted our troops, since Saddam's generals prepared for an attack through Turkey, despite the fact that after all our efforts, Turkey's Islamist-dominated parliament did not approve the US transit request.[6]

President Bush raised another interesting question to his top advisors: "Are we telling the Iraqi Republican Guard that they will be war criminals if they use WMD against their own people or others or destroy the oil fields? We need to be sure our declaration to them is clear. I would say it every day if I had to."

On March 9, I met with John Yoo about confirming our legal authorities for war. The president was ready to go, and I asked John to make sure we had all domestic and international legal authorities in place to use force in Iraq without a new UN resolution authorizing military intervention. The congressional authorization to use force provided domestic cover, but I worried that our authority under international law would be challenged without a UN resolution to use force, unless we were acting in self-defense.

At the March 10 NSC meeting, the president was concerned about the United States' message to the Iraqi people. "The Iraqi people must understand we trust them. The people can run their own country. We will let them know that soon there will be an interim body, but it is only a temporary institution. The Iraqi people have suffered greatly under Saddam, and they deserve to have the power once he is gone. We have to be careful, though, about empowering any specific group."

The following morning, I met with the president, Condi, and Andy in the Oval Office. In these small-group discussions, I sensed that President Bush was more open about his thoughts and feelings about going to war. Even in the secretive atmosphere of the Situation Room, it seemed to me the president sometimes kept his personal views in check. But that morning, with just a close circle of friends, he was more open, and visibly irritated about waiting for the UN to take a stand against Hussein. Nevertheless, he was incredibly candid and left me with a solemn warning, "We have to win quickly or that will be the end of this administration."

I agreed, adding, "My only fear is Saddam using WMD."

"Or a dirty bomb," replied the president. He sighed slightly, then looked at me and asked, "What about my legal authorities? Are they airtight?"

"The lawyers at Justice believe they are," I said, "although you are likely to be challenged."

The president sat back in his chair and seemed to roll his eyes. He said nothing for a few moments. Finally, turning to Condi, he said, "Tell Powell to be tough today. We have to end the debate today about this new UN resolution." The UN debate continued throughout the day.

The next morning, the NSC met at 8:55 in the Situation Room. The president was clear about what he wanted. "It is time to get out," he said, referring to the UN debate. "Today is the day."

The previous evening, President Vicente Fox had checked into a Mexican hospital without informing the United States or talking to President Bush about his plans. "He didn't want to decide," Bush said. "The Mexicans are afraid."

Powell confirmed the president's suspicions. "Mexico is not going to be a party to this," he said. Nor was Chile moving our way. "The French will veto anything," Powell said, "because they see any resolution as a license to war."

The president shook his head. "We are through with the Latins," he said. "Such a sad testimony to friendship." Bush expressed great disappointment that Mexico and other Latin American countries did not step up. He didn't expect them to offer troops or material, but he did expect their support.

The president looked at his team. "We have to end this. The cleanest way is to go with no vote." He suggested that we give the UN notice on Thursday afternoon. "On Saturday, we start operations and on Monday, the air war starts."

We pulled down our request for a resolution from the UN. We had little choice since one "no" vote from the Security Council would have stymied our plans again. Powell reported that Russia and other countries were apparently pleased they would not have to vote on a resolution concerning Iraq.

On March 17, the NSC met at 9:00 a.m. The president said he was going to give a televised speech about the situation. "This is an ultimatum speech, not a go-to-war speech," he said. "It will be up to Saddam to avoid military conflict by allowing peaceful entry. We have not declared war, and this can still be done peacefully, but there's only one way."

President Bush gave General Tommy Franks a seventy-two-hour notice. "This is not an execute order. This order allows everyone to be ready so when the execute order is issued, we can move immediately. We will provide briefings to Congress about the speech between 5:45 p.m. and 6:15 p.m., and the speech is scheduled for 8:00 p.m."

That evening, President Bush offered a gracious overture, giving Saddam Hussein one last chance to avoid an invasion. "Saddam Hussein and his sons must leave Iraq within forty-eight hours," the president said in

lberto R. Gonzales, the only lawyer in history to serve as counsel to the president and attorney neral of the United States.

Although my parents were poor seasonal migrant workers, they went all out for their wedding. To my Catholic parents, marriage was a sacrament they did not take lightly, 1952.
Gonzales Family Photograph

My father, Pablo Gonzales, worked constructi but on Easter and the Fourth of July he dresse up for a family barbecue in Houston's Herma Park. This shot of me—almost three years old is a rare photo of my dad wearing a hat and ti 1958. Gonzales Family Photograph

Mom and Dad raised eight children in a two-bedroom house with no hot running water. (Top row, L to R) Alberto, Antonio, Rene. (Bottom row, L to R) Angelica, Christina, Paul, Theresa, and Timothy, 1973. Gonzales Family Photograph

For my first deployment in the air force, I chose to serve in subzero temperatures at Fort Yukon, Alaska, defending the country as part of the United States early warning system, 1974. Gonzales Family Photograph

With aspirations to serve my country as an air force pilot, I was proud to be a cadet at the US Air Force Academy. Less than perfect eyesight changed my plans and the course of my life, 1977. Gonzales Family Photograph (USAFA)

I played intramural football at Rice University; the same school where, as a boy, I sold soft drinks at football games. My dream came true of one day attending Rice, 1978. Gonzales Family Photograph

One of the greatest influences in my life has been my mom, Maria Gonzales, 1987. Gonzales Family Photograph

I asked Rebecca Turner to marry me on Tuesday, and by Saturday we were standing in front of a minister in a picturesque country church in Kingwood, Texas. The guest list included family, friends, and many children, including Becky's bright young son, Jared Freeze, 1991.
Rick Staudt

Governor Bush's first senior staff was a group of idealists who planned to accomplish great things. Many of the staff, including Karl Rove, Karen Hughes, Clay Johnson, Margaret Spellings, Joe Allbaugh, Israel Hernandez, Albert Hawkins, Andi Ball, Tony Garza, and I became known as "Bushies," Texans who accompanied President-elect Bush to Washington, DC, Christmas 1995.
Bill Records Photo

Becky and I celebrated Governor Bush's fiftieth birthday at the Texas governor's mansion, where lieutenant governor Bob Bullock, a Democrat, surprised everyone by declaring that George W. Bush would be the next president of the United States, 1996.
Bill Records Photo

I took the oath of office as Texas secretary of state from Governor Bush using Sam Houston's Bible. Our son Gabriel also wanted to have a hand in the ceremony. As secretary of state, I was the governor's lead liaison on Mexico and border issues, 1997.
Gonzales Family Photograph

Chief justice Tom Phillips swore me in as a Texas supreme court justice. I thought this would be a long-term position—but Washington called, 1999. Gonzales Family Photograph

As White House Counsel, I would often meet privately with the president to discuss policy issues and Supreme Court appointments, 2002.

Photo by Paul Morse, Courtesy of the George W. Bush Library and Museum/NARA

Vice President Dick Cheney and his wife, Lynne, attended President Bush's first state dinner, hostir Mexican president Vicente Fox, just days before the 9/11 attacks, 2001.

Photo by David Bohrer, Courtesy of the George W. Bush Library and Museum/NARA

On the evening of 9/11, Karen Hughes and I waited on the White House portico as *Marine One* landed on the South Lawn. Karen carried a draft of a speech and I brought research on the constitutional authorities of the president to respond to the attacks on our country, 2001.
Photo by Paul Morse, Courtesy of the George W. Bush Library and Museum/NARA

When the president returned to the White House on 9/11, Karen Hughes, Condi Rice, Ari Fleischer, Andy Card, and I met with him in his private dining room to discuss the message he would deliver the nation that night, 2001.
Photo by Paul Morse, Courtesy of the George W. Bush Library and Museum/NARA

Meetings were often held in the president's office on *Air Force One*, including one with homeland security advisor Fran Townsend and the Ohio congressional delegation.
Presidential Materials Division, National Archives and Records Administration

Condi Rice, Karen Hughes, and I regularly reviewed drafts of the president's remarks on national security issues. Photo by Eric Draper, Courtesy of the George W. Bush Library and Museum/NARA

Former president George H. W. Bush always supported and encouraged his son. Everyone enjoyed the moments he dropped by, including Andy Card, Dan Bartlett, and, of course, the president, December 2002. Presidential Materials Division, National Archives and Records Administration

he Old Executive Office Building next to the White House has a bowling alley, where my team of hite House lawyers and staff relaxed. We may have been, as we were described, "super-lawyers," it we were not necessarily "super-bowlers," 2003. Carrie Nelson Spurlock

At my confirmation hearing as attorney general before the Senate Judiciary Committee, I was introduced by senator Ken Salazar of Colorado and senator John Cornyn of Texas, January 2005.
Presidential Materials Division, National Archives and Records Administration

As the first Hispanic to serve as US attorney general, I was honored that justice Sandra Day O'Connor, the first woman on the US Supreme Court, administered the oath of office, February 2005. Photo by Paul Morse, Courtesy of the George W. Bush Library and Museum/NARA

Joint meetings of the National Security Council and Homeland Security Council usually took place in the Situation Room. The president always sought wise counsel, but the final responsibility to make decisions was his alone.

Photo by Eric Draper, Courtesy of the George W. Bush Library and Museum/NARA

ne of my signature issues as attorney general was bringing child predators to justice. I strongly vocated for the Adam Walsh Childhood Protection and Safety Act, which the president signed to law in the presence of Adam's parents, John and Revé Walsh, July 27, 2006.

Photo by Eric Draper, Courtesy of the George W. Bush Library and Museum/NARA

President Bush began each cabinet meeting with one of the members leading in prayer, 2006.
Photo by Eric Draper, Courtesy of the George W. Bush Library and Museum/NARA

Becky, Graham, Jared, Gabriel, and my mom joined me at my ceremonial swearing-in as attorney general, February 2005.
Photo by Paul Morse, Courtesy of the George W. Bush Library and Museum/NARA

e President Cheney's commitment to
blic service spans decades, and it was a
vilege to serve with him, 2005.
e Presidential Records of the Photography
ice (George W. Bush Administration)

FBI director Bob Mueller and I often spoke with
the press together. We began every morning with
a terrorism briefing from the CIA, and we made a
good team in the War on Terror.
United States Department of Justice

I was in hundreds of photos with President Bush, but the departure shot with
my family was bittersweet. I was glad to be with my family, but despite my smile
I was sad to leave before my work was done, September 2007.
Photo by Eric Draper, Courtesy of the George W. Bush Library and Museum/NARA

President Bush connected well with Hispanics, who responded to him enthusiastically. I was honored to join him when he met with Hispanic groups.
Photo by Eric Draper, Courtesy of the George W. Bush Library and Museum/NARA

Laura Bush was a remarkable First Lady, maintaining an air of dignity and class, quietly commanding respect. Photo by Eric Draper, Courte of the George W. Bush Library and Museum/NARA

As the US attorney general I always found it meaningful to attend the National Peace Officers Memorial Day events every May 15 to honor our nation's fallen law enforcement heroes. United States Department of Justice

NSA director Mike Hayden, CIA director Georg Tenet, Vice President Cheney's counsel David Addington, and I paused for a discussion outsid the Oval Office before briefing the president on national security matter.
Vice Presidential Records of the Photography Office (George W. Bush Administration)

As political pressures mounted, President Bush spoke candidly with me at Prairie Chapel Ranch in Crawford, Texas, about my resignation as attorney general. In an emotional time, I appreciated the president's encouragement about the future, August 2007.
Photo by Chris Greenberg, Courtesy of the George W. Bush Library and Museum/NARA

President Bush and I admired his and the First Lady's official portraits in the East Room of the White House. I believe history will prove that decisions made by the president helped protect America, May 31, 2012.
Freddy Ford

It was an honor to serve with President George W. Bush on behalf of the American people.

Photo by Paul Morse, Courtesy of the George W. Bush Library and Museum/NARA

a nationally televised address from the White House. "Their refusal to do so will result in military conflict commenced at a time of our choosing."[7]

The following day, Saddam appeared on television, dressed in full military regalia, along with some of his top generals. The message was clear. He had no intentions of disarming . . . but the clock was ticking.

I was at my desk early the morning of March 18, 2003, preparing to monitor the federal execution of Louis Jones Jr., a decorated soldier who came home from the Gulf War in 1991 a changed man—and not changed for the better. According to court testimony and psychiatric reports, he drank heavily, divorced his wife, and left the army after serving twenty-two years.

In February 1995, Jones kidnapped a nineteen-year-old woman on a military base near Lubbock, Texas, raped her, and then bludgeoned her to death with a tire iron. He was caught and convicted in federal court, despite his defense's contention he'd suffered head trauma as a result of chemical agents encountered on the battlefield. Jones exhausted all of his appeals and was scheduled to die on March 18, 2003. This would be only the third federal execution since we'd come to Washington, the first being Oklahoma bomber Timothy McVeigh and the second being drug lord and murderer Juan Garza, both of whom were executed in June 2001.

The case weighed heavily on President Bush as he contemplated sending our troops into battle again in Iraq. As we had always done with every execution, the president and I reviewed the details. Jones was a convicted killer, but he was also a decorated veteran, a man who fought against Saddam Hussein for America and the world. His lawyers contended that he had been exposed to small amounts of Saddam's lethal nerve gas when a weapons depot had been destroyed. Maybe so. But he had willfully committed a heinous crime, and there was no new evidence on which the president could in good conscience commute his sentence.

At 6:00 a.m., I spoke with Peggy Griffey at the Department of Justice. There were no appeals on Jones's behalf pending in the courts; there was no new evidence; the execution moved forward. When asked if he wanted to make a last statement before his execution, Jones recited a verse of Scripture and then began singing an old hymn, "Near the Cross." At 7:08 a.m., he was pronounced dead by lethal injection at the US penitentiary near Terre Haute, Indiana. When I conveyed the news to the president, he said nothing, but I sensed he was torn.

The following morning, March 19, 2003, I stepped into the Oval Office at about 7:15 a.m. to have a conversation with the president about judicial candidates. As I concluded my analysis of a potential federal judge, President Bush seemed distracted. Without even commenting on the judgeship, he got up from his chair and spoke to me matter-of-factly. "I'm prepared to give the authority today to the commanders to go on Operation Iraqi Freedom."

Realizing the import of his words, I nodded and simply said, "Okay, let's go."

I walked across the hall to the Roosevelt Room for a senior staff meeting at 7:30 a.m. and then met with my lawyers at 8:00 a.m. Afterward I walked down to the Situation Room and sat in my chair on the back row, along with Steve Hadley and Scooter Libby.

This was going to be a historic day. I looked around the room and wondered who else knew what the president was about to do. The vice president, Condi, and Andy no doubt knew. Other members of the National Security team, including Colin Powell, Don Rumsfeld, Hugh Shelton, and Richard Myers, as well as George Tenet, arrived soon after. As usual, everyone knew to be early.

The multiple video monitors were up in the small, wood-paneled Situation Room, and General Tommy Franks appeared on the largest screen, with several of his commanders on other monitors. When the president arrived, he sat down at one end of the long conference table, his chair right beneath the presidential seal, placed so he could look directly at the video monitors. As always in National Security Council meetings, Vice President Cheney sat directly to the president's right, and Colin Powell sat to Bush's left.

President Bush began by hearing briefly from each of the generals.

Then he asked Tommy Franks for the name of the operation. "Operation Iraqi Freedom," Franks replied confidently.

Bush spoke to Franks, but clearly the question was to all the military leaders. "Do you have everything you need to win? Are you pleased with the strategy?"

None of the military commanders expressed any reservations. The president asked one more time, "Does everyone have everything you need?"

General Franks replied, "Mr. President, this force is ready. D-Day, H-Hour is 2100 hours tonight Iraqi time, 1800 hours Greenwich Mean, 1300 hours East Coast time."[8] President Bush nodded to the members of the National Security team, then turned back toward Tommy Franks.

Anticipating his next words, I turned away from the video screens and stared at my friend, the president of the United States. "Tommy," he said, "I've been briefed by the secretary of defense and have now received these briefings. For the sake of peace in the world and security for our country and the rest of the free world"—he paused and everyone listened intently—"and for the freedom of the Iraqi people, I will give Secretary Rumsfeld the order . . . I hereby give the order to execute Operation Iraqi Freedom."

Pausing momentarily, and then speaking with great emotion, the president said, "Tommy, may God bless the troops."

General Franks stood and responded, "Mr. President, may God bless America." The general saluted the commander in chief, who returned the salute.

Then, in a rather surreal moment, the president stood and simply walked out of the Situation Room without saying another word to anyone. The room remained silent for several seconds with nobody moving. Ordinarily, when the president stands at the conclusion of a meeting, everyone in the room stands. But on this day of days, when the president saluted General Franks and left the room, nobody budged, reflecting, I believe, the historical significance of the moment. The liberation of Iraq was now in the hands of the military generals, who would act swiftly and effectively.

I walked quietly up to my office, thinking about the many months of work and preparation in which we had engaged. I recalled Don Rumsfeld once saying that the best military plans often went out the window once the first shot was fired in a war. The first shot was soon to be fired.

I entered my office, sat down in my chair, and looked at the neatly stacked piles of memos and paperwork on my desk. A book of US international agreements given to me by John Yoo sat on one corner above a draft of the Iraqi use of force congressional resolution. It was no longer a mere resolution; it was now a harsh reality.

For more than a year, I had watched the intense interactions between incredibly bright, thoughtful leaders—who did not always agree on every point—as they considered any and every alternative to war in Iraq. In the years to follow, the media often portrayed the president as the Texas cowboy cavalierly stomping off to war with his naïve cabinet members following docilely behind him. Nothing could be further from the truth. The run-up to Iraq was a long, tedious process that could have turned at any point if Iraq's dictator had ever done the right thing. But he didn't.

Especially after 9/11, the president was not about to risk underestimating Saddam's WMD capabilities, as the world had done prior to Operation Desert Fox, the limited four-day bombing attack on Iraq during the Clinton administration. If he had nothing to hide, Saddam could have allowed the UN inspectors open access to his country, and a major rationale for the US invasion might have evaporated. But as has often been observed since, when it came to Saddam's WMD and our willingness to disarm him, the Bush administration never dreamed that Saddam was bluffing and Saddam never dreamed that the United States was not.

Was it a mistake to invade Iraq based on the information we had at the time? If so, the mistake was in the intelligence, not the decision to defend America, to disarm Hussein and punish him for disobeying multiple UN resolutions. I question the fitness of anyone to serve as commander in chief who—when confronted with the same information after the attacks of 9/11—would have made a different decision.

The Bush administration, members of Congress on both sides of the aisle, our allies around the world, and even some Arab nations all concurred that Saddam Hussein either had or was developing weapons of mass destruction. In hindsight, of course, the obvious question is how could so many have been so wrong? But at the time, the overwhelming consensus view was that Saddam posed an imminent threat through his WMD program. Subsequent accusations that "Bush lied" about WMD and our reasons for going into Iraq—which undermined our credibility and efforts in the region—are simply false, and Bush's political opponents, who incessantly and effectively pounded that idea into the national psyche, knew it.

The president was deeply frustrated over Saddam's failure to comply with repeated United Nations resolutions, UN weapons inspections, and Iraq's frequent misrepresentations of its weaponry. For more than a year, the president and his cabinet debated the options.

In laying the groundwork for attacking Saddam and liberating the Iraqi people, President Bush struggled with the need to build an international coalition. He believed that if we hoped to succeed in Iraq and in the war on terror, we needed the cooperation of our allies, but he refused to allow the safety and fate of the United States to lie in the hands of an international organization such as the United Nations or any other international body. He understood that he was the president, that his top priority was to do what was right and in the best interests of the United States. He was more than willing to work with our friends and allies, but not at the expense of our nation's security.

Iraq was an almost daily topic of discussion for many months. President Bush certainly did not go to war hastily or unadvisedly. My activities during this time were focused primarily in two areas: affirming the legality of the United States going into Iraq on the basis of self-defense; and preparing to help the Iraqi leadership develop their own constitution and rule of law framework, once the allied coalition toppled Hussein from power.

As the president made final preparations to speak to the nation that night, I walked down to the Oval Office, where, as they did for every speech from that location, workmen moved furniture to make room for the television cameras and microphones. The technicians moved respectfully as I stepped into the waiting area just outside the Oval Office. Then at 10:00 p.m., I walked inside the Oval Office and the doors closed behind me.

At 10:10 p.m., the president came out of his study. He looked to be in a confident mood. I glanced around and saw Karen Hughes, Condi, Andy, Ari Fleischer, Dan Bartlett, and Mike Gerson, who had no doubt been helping the president refine his speech.

We watched quietly as the president began his remarks at 10:16 p.m. He spoke slowly but deliberately, giving a short speech, straight to the point, that lasted less than five minutes. It was vintage Bush.

Immediately afterward, photographers came in and took pictures of the president sitting resolutely at his desk. He then grabbed some moisturized cloths to wipe the television makeup from his face. As he left for the residence, he looked at those of us standing in the Oval Office. "Go home and get some sleep," he said kindly.

Most of us didn't.

I worked for several more hours, talking with other administration lawyers, reexamining the legal memos and related issues. Just prior to going home, I thought of my sons. Soon sons and daughters would be moving into harm's way because of what happened earlier. I prayed they would be all right.

The president had done what he thought was right, based on the information given to him by the best intelligence sources in the world. The United States had patiently waited since 1991 before taking action to disarm Saddam Hussein. Now Hussein's fate was in our hands, and the legacy of the Bush presidency would be determined in part by the outcome.

CHAPTER 25

LISTENING TO THE ENEMY

While rescue workers continued combing through the rubble at the World Trade Center and the Pentagon, and investigators still searched through the forest in Shanksville, Pennsylvania, hoping to find fragments of United flight 93, on October 4, 2001, the president authorized an enhanced form of electronic spying to help track down terrorists and prevent future attacks. The code name for this top secret surveillance program was Stellar Wind. One of the most secretive activities in which the Bush administration ever became involved, the surveillance program was operated under the direction of the National Security Agency (NSA). It was designed to engage in multiple intelligence activities, including the secret monitoring of international communications between suspected terrorists associated with al-Qaeda—especially communications between terrorists and someone *already* within the United States. This program was in addition to what other US intelligence agencies—we had several—were already doing at the State Department, the FBI, the CIA, and in lesser known groups, and expanded the NSA's authorization to collect information electronically by collecting and examining data secured from phone calls and e-mails.

In 2005 and 2006, the *New York Times* published unauthorized articles revealing information about classified surveillance activities—revelations for which numerous people within the administration believed the newspaper, its editors, and the reporters involved should have been prosecuted under Section 798 of Title 18 of the US Code, which prohibits the publishing of classified information. Added to that were the revelations of "domestic surveillance" in classified documents disclosed by Edward Snowden,[1] a contractor for NSA, published in the British newspaper *The Guardian*, on June 5, 2013. Consequently, questions, controversies, and allegations have swirled about the surveillance program authorized by the president. Many Americans have assumed that the NSA is listening in on every phone call they make and that somebody from the government is reading every e-mail they send or receive. I have no reason to believe that is happening today, and it was definitely *not* the case or the intent of the programs authorized by President Bush in 2001. Indeed, the programs were not designed or intended as domestic spying in the least, unless someone inside the United States had links to al-Qaeda and was a party to an international communication.

In the aftermath of 9/11, critics often commented that the United States had been unable to "connect the dots." The truth is, at that time in our history, not only could we not *connect* the dots, we were not even able to *collect* the dots. Worse yet, we didn't know what dots existed to collect.

Nevertheless, from that first strategy session at Camp David the weekend after the 9/11 attacks, everyone in the room understood that this new kind of war demanded a new kind of response. In an age where electronic communications are instantaneous, delays can be deadly. We recognized early on that the greatest need we had was for more precise intelligence information. If we hoped to uncover terrorists' threats and thwart them before they could be launched, we had to improve our ability to see and hear electronically. Information about our enemies was our first line of defense in stopping terrorist attacks, as well as our best hope of bringing terrorists to justice.

But that created a whole new set of problems when it came to balancing the protection of our citizens' civil liberties and the vigorous pursuit of terrorists. In a lively discussion at Camp David, CIA director George Tenet told the president that we had a number of *capabilities* to gather information, but because of legal interpretations regarding the laws existing at the time, there were some limits and questions about whether or not we had the statutory legal *authorities* to use these capabilities—especially when it came to collecting clues about possible terrorist activities inside the United States.

As noted earlier, our intelligence agencies were working under the Foreign Intelligence Surveillance Act (FISA), which focused primarily on legal permissions for the government's acquisition and collection of certain electronic communications, obtained for a foreign intelligence purpose. While FISA was a valuable tool in collecting information and a valuable safeguard against intelligence agencies overstepping their boundaries, it was outdated for some types of intelligence investigations. Furthermore, it was designed more to look backward at crimes to conduct prosecutions, rather than looking forward to prevent attacks on the American people.[2]

Vice President Cheney asked George Tenet if the NSA had the authorities they needed to protect America. Tenet said he would check with the NSA director, Mike Hayden.[3] General Mike Hayden was one of the most highly regarded officials in the Bush administration. An articulate, soft-spoken man, and an air force four-star general, Mike looked more like a university math professor than a rough-and-tumble military general, but he was a smart leader and a straight shooter whom I respected and liked. He was passionate about doing everything possible to protect our country, yet he recognized the need to protect our citizens' privacy as well. As did most people in the Bush administration, I had the highest regard for General Hayden's honesty and integrity.

The morning our nation was attacked, General Hayden immediately moved to enhance NSA's collection of information. He later recalled, "On September 11, there were authorities within the range of abilities of the director of the National Security Agency to adjust how America collects intelligence, how aggressive America might want to be. Fully within my authorities, I made some decisions about being more aggressive. I mean, we're held to the reasonableness standard of the Fourth Amendment, [of] no unreasonable search and seizure. Well, what constitutes the reasonableness that afternoon was different than the reasonableness that morning, and I made some changes."[4]

Following the Camp David session, George Tenet contacted Hayden about what else could be done. Hayden recalls the conversation:

> George calls me and says: "Mike, any more you can do?"
>
> I said, "George, no, not within my authorities, not within my current authorities."
>
> And he paused and said: "That's not actually the question I asked you. Is there anything more you could do?"
>
> I said, "I'll get back to you."
>
> So I sat down with my leadership team, both operations and legal, and put together several things that we could do, that we felt might have specifically addressed the problems that were laid bare by 9/11, if we had the authority to do it.[5]

My job was to work with lawyers in the administration, particularly at the Department of Justice and NSA, to provide the legal guidance to support the NSA in gathering information. The goal was to help NSA do whatever was necessary, yet lawful, to gather information useful to prevent another attack and to make our country more secure in the future. No easy task.

Moreover, Attorney General John Ashcroft and his team were already working on proposed legislation known as the USA PATRIOT Act that would tear down the wall of separation between our various intelligence and law enforcement agencies so they could more freely share information about potential threats. The PATRIOT Act would allow our law enforcement officers to now track terrorists with tools that had been readily available and often employed to investigate organized crime in the United States. The PATRIOT Act was passed by overwhelming bipartisan majorities in both houses of Congress and signed into law by President Bush in October 2001.

The Fourth Amendment prohibits *unreasonable* searches or seizures of a person or property. A search with a warrant based on probable cause and issued by a federal judge is considered reasonable. There are, however, long recognized exceptions to the warrant requirement. For instance, exceptions have been recognized by the courts with respect to security checkpoints at airports, locker searches at schools, sobriety checkpoints, searches inci-dent to arrest or to prevent the destruction of evidence, or to protect a life. Another recognized exception to the warrant requirement allowed searches based on national security needs. But there was still a statutory hurdle of FISA we had to overcome.

Once the NSA reported that they could do more when it came to col-lecting information about terrorists' phone calls and e-mails, the Justice Department was asked to examine whether using those capabilities was lawful. The governing statute was FISA, which set out the general rules for the government's collection of certain forms of electronic surveillance. The task of analyzing the statute fell primarily to John Yoo, OLC's resi-dent expert lawyer regarding presidential war powers and who was also regarded as OLC's best on the legal issues regarding our response to terror-ism. Because such a thing had never been done before, over a period of time, General Hayden had three of his most experienced lawyers in the field of electronic collections as they related to privacy rights examine the program. Hayden's lawyers at NSA concluded the activities were legal based solely on the commander in chief's authority.[6] More important, Yoo and other law-yers at Justice agreed that the president had authority to defend the nation in response to an attack by the enemy. It has always been a fundamental aspect of war to collect information about the enemy. John Yoo concluded that the president's commander in chief authority under the Constitution to do everything necessary to protect our nation gave the president limited authority to collect and analyze electronic data beyond the rules of FISA.

Consequently, on October 4, 2001, bolstered by the legal guidance of the Justice Department, the president executed a presidential memoran-dum that authorized for a specific period of time a number of electronic intelligence collection activities, code named Stellar Wind. During World War I and World War II, Presidents Wilson and Roosevelt respectively had authorized massive collection of all sorts of information about private citizens. The lawyers examining the current situation and the precedents concluded we were on safe legal ground. Of course, unlike in previous wars, before moving forward with Stellar Wind, we had to analyze whether the

FISA law did not preempt, diminish, or extinguish the president's authority under the Constitution.

The presidential authorizations were generally only for a period of forty-five days and then they were required to be reauthorized by the president, based on the recommendations of a number of high-level administration officials.

The DOJ lawyers concluded that the president's legal ability to authorize Stellar Wind was based in part on the threat to America. Consequently, the president's written authorizations to the NSA to conduct Stellar Wind were based on the intelligence threat at the time of each respective reauthorization. The most current CIA intelligence threats were reflected in a written document and attached to the authorization each time it was renewed by the president.

Only a handful of individuals in the White House were even aware of Stellar Wind or the authorization process. David Addington, the vice president's chief counsel, and I were the only White House lawyers involved. Not even the White House staff secretary—charged with overseeing every document presented to the president—touched the Stellar Wind authorization.

The total program contained what we referred to as three large "baskets," one of which, Basket I, came to be known as the Terrorist Surveillance Program (TSP). It involved content collection by telephone—actual intercepted international calls when an experienced intelligence officer at NSA had probable cause to think that at least one of the parties on the call was a member of al-Qaeda or an affiliate of al-Qaeda. This was Basket I, and it was the only content collection authorized by the president under this program.

Basket II involved the acquisition and analysis of bulk telephone *metadata*—information about the participants, time, date, and the duration of telephone calls, but not the content. We did not initiate the gathering of this information. The telecom companies collected it for their own purposes.

Basket III concerned bulk e-mail metadata. It is important to understand that Basket III consisted of two distinct activities. The first related to the *collection* of bulk e-mail metadata; the second involved the *analysis* of the collected bulk e-mail metadata. These three baskets included *everything* President Bush authorized under Stellar Wind.

How did it work?

Some aspects of the Stellar Wind program remain classified, including the mechanics of intercepting international calls under Basket I, so many of the details cannot be disclosed. We were, however, able to collect certain information about international calls—and *only* those international calls on which an experienced intelligence officer at NSA suspected that one or more members of al-Qaeda or an affiliate group were involved on the call.

The telephone records collected under Basket II consisted of dialing-type information (the originating and terminating telephone numbers, and the date, time, and duration of the call), but not the content of the call. The Supreme Court has long held that there is no reasonable expectation of privacy in such records; therefore, the Fourth Amendment is not implicated with respect to government searches of such records.

Building a database of billions of domestic phone records was deemed necessary and lawful. After the database was created, then the information was targeted specifically to al-Qaeda or other terrorism.

When a suspicious number comes across NSA's "radar," that specific phone number can be a search target or "seed" for a query of the massive metadata reposity only if one of NSA's seasoned, designated officials (they never numbered more than a few dozen) first determines there exists reasonable, articulable suspicion that the phone number is associated with terrorism. Once the number is approved as a seed, the NSA analysts can run inquiries that will show the call records, and permit "contact chaining," to retrieve not only the numbers directly in contact with the seed number—referred to as the first "hop"—but also numbers in contact with all first hop numbers—known as the second hop—and numbers in contact with those numbers, referred to as the third hop.

With respect to Basket III, the government's bulk e-mail metadata collection, the NSA could conduct chaining, similar to the chaining of telephone metadata, as part of its analysis targeted to al-Qaeda and terrorism.

Keep in mind, permission for the NSA to engage perpetually in this specific electronic surveillance was not a given; nor was it a blanket approval authorized once by the president. As noted, every forty-five days Stellar Wind was carefully reviewed; the permission by the president to proceed was contingent upon the recommendation and signature of the CIA director that the surveillance was necessary due to the dire nature of the threats. The secretary of defense also had to sign the recommendation, since NSA operated under the Defense Department; and finally the attorney general examined the program—*again, every forty-five days*—to make sure what our intelligence people were doing was lawful. Even after the attorney general's determination and signing off on the legality of the program, continuation of the program remained contingent upon the approval of the president.

The review deadlines were taken seriously. This procedure of checks and balances was considered vital to the program. On one occasion, because of rapidly shifting intelligence, we could not get all the signatures in time before the presidential authorization was set to expire and the president left for a trip to Asia. David Addington and I literally flew overnight to California and back to catch the president and secure his signature so Stellar Wind could continue while he was away. Without the president's signature, the program would have come to a halt.

Because of the sensitive nature of the intelligence sources and methods involved, beginning in late 2002, almost from the program's inception, certain congressional leaders were regularly briefed on Stellar Wind. The information in these briefings was highly classified, so we did not do open sessions with the entire Congress, or even the full intelligence committees; only the chairmen and ranking members and key leaders were included. The chief judge of the FISA Court was also briefed in early 2002. With limited exceptions, usually with respect to operational necessity, the president had to personally approve anyone before he or she could be read in to Stellar Wind.[7]

It was purported afterward that then House minority whip Nancy Pelosi had some problems with Stellar Wind and raised some concerns. Other congressional leaders said they weren't briefed on the e-mail metadata program.

Michael Hayden later adamantly exposed that lie. "That's just not true," he said. "They were briefed on everything we were doing. I had no restrictions from the White House. Look, the White House did not approve my briefing. These were almost always given in the vice president's office. The vice president was getting it for the first time when I was briefing Congress. We had total control over what we were to tell them. There were no filters, all right? There is no upside in us not being totally candid with members of Congress."[8]

The program worked. A tremendous amount of data was collected, and thanks to Stellar Wind, numerous potential or attempted terrorist actions were interrupted. Bluntly stated, terrorists were captured and terrorists' plans to kill Americans were thwarted in part because of leads or information learned through such surveillance.

Years later, reports came out that the surveillance was ineffective, and that it could not be certain it had ever stopped an imminent terrorist attack. That's ludicrous logic. Have airport security and the billions of dollars spent on the Transportation Security Administration (TSA) ever stopped an imminent terrorist attack? It's hard to say, since no attack has happened in our airports since 9/11. But that doesn't at all mean it's not worthwhile. Moreover, we can be certain of what happened when we did not have Stellar Wind. Hayden pointed out a poignant example:

Two guys, Nawaf al-Hazmi and Khalid al-Mihdhar, living in San Diego . . . meeting in Kuala Lumpur, come to the United States, call home, call Yemen, call a safe house in Yemen seven times. We intercepted every one of the calls, right?

Nothing in the physics of the intercept, nothing in the content of the call told us they were in San Diego. If we'd have had the metadata program, okay, if we'd have had that basket of stuff and that phone number of that safe house in Yemen, which we knew, and we would have walked up to that metadata and said, "Hey, any of you guys talked to this number in Yemen?" those numbers in San Diego would have popped up.[9]

Hayden's point is clear: if we had Stellar Wind in place prior to September 11, 2001, we might have been able to intercept two of the 9/11 hijackers. Mike Hayden, George Tenet, Bob Mueller, and John McLaughlin have all testified *under oath* that the program was useful and effective, that the collection of this intelligence saved lives.[10]

For more than two and a half years following 9/11, the monitoring of telecommunications and cyberspace continued without interruption or interference in the lives of most American citizens. Every reauthorization was reviewed and approved by Attorney General John Ashcroft and the other senior officals during this period of time—on more than twenty occasions.

When John Yoo left OLC in 2003 to return to teaching at UC–Berkeley School of Law, the review of Stellar Wind was turned over to Pat Philbin, then deputy assistant attorney general at OLC, a good, conscientious lawyer with degrees from Yale, Harvard, and Cambridge universities, who had clerked for Supreme Court justice Clarence Thomas. Pat had expertise in telecommunications, and was familiar with the program and Attorney General Ashcroft's support. Subsequently, Jack Goldsmith, another bright, thoughtful academic, was confirmed as the new head of OLC in October 2003. Jack had earned degrees from Washington and Lee University, the University of Oxford, and Yale, and had taught law at the University of Chicago as well as the University of Virginia before serving in the Department of Defense from September 2002 to June 2003. Prior to that, he had clerked for Supreme Court justice Anthony Kennedy, as well as Court of Appeals judge J. Harvie Wilkinson. Pat and Jack were very bright; I liked them and had confidence in both.

When these men were brought in at the Department of Justice, I reiterated the White House's position—to look carefully at Stellar Wind to make sure we continued operating within the law. With my knowledge and blessing, Jack and Pat plunged into a major review of Stellar Wind, to make sure it remained on as strong a legal footing as possible. To better understand what NSA was doing, they visited the operators and analysts at the agency's Fort Meade headquarters. They had total access to everything about Stellar Wind, as well as NSA's legal and operational staffs. I fully supported and encouraged the efforts by Jack and Pat to understand the technical aspects of Stellar Wind.

Pat, especially, became a regular visitor to NSA. Pat asked pointed questions and peeled back the surveillance program one layer at a time, never voicing anything specifically but giving the impression that he was not totally comfortable with what the NSA was doing, but not stating why. He was liked by Mike Hayden and others at the agency, but he showed up at NSA so often, his presence piqued Hayden's curiosity. Early in 2004, General Hayden crossed paths with Pat right outside the NSA director's office. Hayden recalls, "I went up to Patrick one on one, nose to nose, and said, 'Patrick, do I have to stop doing anything?' He said, 'No, no, you don't.'"[11] But Philbin continued to probe.

In early 2004, Jack Goldsmith informed me that he had concerns about some of the previous OLC reviews, but we could continue to rely on prior OLC legal opinions until his review of Stellar Wind was complete. He had questions about John Yoo's broad view of the authorities granted to the president.

I said, "Fine, get comfortable. We want to make sure that what we're doing is lawful." So Jack went back and looked at the program and the law some more, and we had several subsequent conversations. I welcomed that kind of review, because it was important for the president to be assured that Stellar Wind was lawful. We had already tweaked the surveillance program from time to time, and in certain cases, we had narrowed it when necessary. It wouldn't have been the first time lawyers in the Department of Justice were telling us to change the program in certain ways. That had had happened before, so I wasn't overly concerned. In fact, I was happy Jack was looking at it and was making sure we were doing the right thing.

During the first two months of 2004, Stellar Wind operated as usual in its entirety, including the Terrorist Surveillance Program (Basket I). Attorney General Ashcroft signed off on it, as did the CIA, the DOD, and, of course, the president. The attorney general's signature was particularly important to telecom companies who were relying on the Justice Department to say that their assistance with the government was legal and did not violate the rights of US citizens. Moreover, the AG had met with representatives of some of these companies, assuring them that their cooperation was legal.

Unfortunately, on Thursday, March 4, 2004, just days before the Stellar Wind program was required to be renewed again or else be discontinued,

John Ashcroft developed severe abdominal pain and was hospitalized at George Washington University Hospital. He was diagnosed with acute gallstone pancreatitis, an extremely uncomfortable and potentially life-threating illness in which a gallstone blocks a duct of the pancreas, a gland that produces enzymes that aid in digestion. The doctors stabilized Ashcroft's condition but kept him in the hospital, where he underwent surgery on March 9.

Meanwhile, on Friday afternoon, March 5, Jack Goldsmith and Pat Philbin came to my West Wing office to meet with David Addington and me regarding their concerns about the collection of certain metadata in the Stellar Wind program. As the head of OLC, Jack understood what his mission and charge was from the White House. His job was to tell us where we can draw the box in terms of what is lawful. The president would decide how close to the lines of the box we would move for the sake of national security. For months, Jack had expressed concerns, but had never presented those concerns as a final position. My response was always the same. "Well, fine. Keep looking. Make sure we're doing the right thing."

During our previous meetings in the early months of 2004, Jack had hinted that perhaps we needed to narrow the activities and tie them more closely to the 2001 authorization to use military force. Jack had a different, more narrow perception of the scope of the president's constitutional authority than John Yoo had presented. John held a rather expansive view that FISA could not limit the president's commander in chief powers under the Constitution regarding electronic surveillance. Jack's view was far more limited. Consequently, Jack seemed more comfortable if the activities under Stellar Wind fit neatly within the authorities granted in the AUMF.

Jack would later write, "For months, Patrick Philbin and I had been trying to find a way to put an important counterterrorism initiative on a proper legal footing. We had come up empty, however, and were now meeting with Alberto Gonzales and David Addington to explain that the Justice Department could not support the initiative's legality."[12]

It wasn't until this meeting—the one Jack is referring to that took place on March 5, 2004—that Jack first provided his specific opinion that certain collection of metadata could not be supported by the president's constitutional authority, nor by the 2001 AUMF; thus, we had a problem under FISA. Now, neither Jack nor Pat said that any aspects of Stellar Wind were unlawful and should be discontinued; instead, they both expressed the idea that to keep everything legal, the collection of certain information should be modified and certain aspects of the program narrowed in scope to minimize the collection of US person data (data about a US citizen, a lawful permanent resident, or a US corporation).

David Addington was clearly irritated at this news, and not bashful about expressing his disgust. After all, the Justice Department had blessed these activities for more than two years. Jack recalls David responding, "If you rule that way, the blood of the hundred thousand people who die in the next attack will be on *your* hands."[13]

He was not being bombastic or overly dramatic. We lived with the daily threat of extraordinary evils, from conventional attacks to catastrophic destruction. Much of our intelligence was drawn from billions of communications, a portion of which Jack was now saying were off limits for NSA surveillance. Granted, many of the daily threats never materialized; other potential threats were thwarted before they grew into something more serious. But as we were often reminded, the terrorists could be wrong a thousand times; we could not be wrong even once.

Moreover, attempting to prevent attacks from such an obscure, nebulous, nationless enemy made matters even more complicated. Jim Baker, the former head of the Office of Intelligence Policy and Review, compared our task to that of a goalie in a soccer game who must stop every shot because the enemy wins if it scores a single goal. The problem, Baker says, "is that the goalie cannot see the ball—it is invisible. So are the players—he doesn't know how many there are, or where they are, or what they look like. He also doesn't know where the sidelines are—they are blurry and constantly shifting, as are the rules of the game itself." The invisible players might shoot from the front of the goal, or from the back, or from some other direction— the goalie just doesn't know.[14] Baker was not the first or the last to use this sort of metaphor, and it alarmed me every time I heard it.

I knew that Jack and Pat had worked hard to make sure the advice from

OLC was solid and could be upheld in the courts. To their credit, legal opinions often change based on new information or circumstances or even court decisions. I could accept their different opinions if that was the motivation behind their reticence to continue Stellar Wind as it was. But I wanted them to be sure of their position.

I never once questioned the integrity of these two men, their commitment to the law, or their love for our country. Jack was relatively new to the Justice Department, so it made sense for him to question some of the things that had been done from his office in the past. Pat had been there since 2001, and knew the terrorism playing field well. He also understood the positions of the telecommunications companies well, and had extensive experience challenging federal agency decisions in the courts of appeals. Pat had served as one of Verizon Communication's primary outside counsel challenging multiple FCC rulemakings implementing the Telecommunications Act of 1996. He knew both sides of the coin.

So I had no qualms about *what* Jack and Pat were doing. Nevertheless, I worried that they might be retreating from previous OLC opinions simply because the Stellar Wind program was sure to be controversial if it were ever discovered—as it most certainly would be one day. Jack was also an expert on "lawfare," the attempts by foreign countries to claim "universal jurisdiction" whereby they could indict and prosecute US officials as far ranging as Henry Kissinger, Donald Rumsfeld, or General Tommy Franks and others for war crimes, based on the actions of our country. The United States did not agree to this policy, but I wondered about Jack's concerns regarding possible future international prosecutions.

"Certainly, the president is free to overrule me, if he wants," Jack told David and me. We knew that, of course, but we also knew—and I'm guessing that Jack did as well—that the president would not likely want to overrule the OLC when his entire administration had been relying heavily upon the OLC for approval of Stellar Wind for more than two and half years. I would have advised against overruling OLC as well, since acting in contravention of DOJ guidance in normal circumstances placed the president in legal jeopardy and serious political danger.

Jack implied that there were precedents for a president to do whatever he felt was necessary to protect the country during times of crisis going all the way back to Thomas Jefferson, Abraham Lincoln, and Franklin D. Roosevelt. That, too, was known to us, but helped little in solving our problem. During dangerous times, I believed the president was willing to go to the edge of the box in doing what was lawful, but I did not believe he would allow us to engage in illegal surveillance activities, on anything outside the box.

As Jack and Pat were preparing to leave my office, Jack reiterated that he felt that OLC should advise the president to narrow the scope of the collection activities NSA was conducting, making it fit neatly under the AUMF.

"Do whatever you need to do," I told them, "but only what you need to do." I knew that Stellar Wind was an important program for our nation's security and President Bush would not want to change it unless something about the surveillance activities was considered unlawful. Jack and Pat understood and went back to work on the opinion.

Later that afternoon, I called Jack and told him that if OLC was going to require a change in the scope of the surveillance activities, I wanted to make sure the OLC legal opinions covered the new parameters of what the NSA could do. "Whatever you do," I said, "make sure that whatever our intelligence people need to do is covered by the OLC opinion."

It was an innocuous request, but my exhortation to Jack set in motion a series of events that changed the security of our country, and nearly destroyed my reputation and career.

CHAPTER 26

STUNTING STELLAR WIND

I t had been quite awhile since I'd enjoyed a simple, fun weekend in Washington with my family. This weekend would be no different in that respect, but pivotal in many others.

On Saturday afternoon, March 6, Jack called me and urgently demanded a meeting with David Addington and me. Along with Pat, we met in my office at about 3:30 p.m. and discussed their concerns about various aspects of Stellar Wind for several hours. Jack explained that following my call to him the previous day, he and Pat had gone back to review President Bush's authorization of Stellar Wind, and the various existing legal opinions that had been rendered about it. After thinking about it overnight, Jack essentially said, "I don't think all of the Stellar Wind collection is covered by the opinions that we've been giving you."

It was as though he had experienced an "Oh, my God!" moment and now he could see that one element of Stellar Wind was problematic.

Jack had two main concerns about the Stellar Wind program: one, the language of the authorizations that President Bush had signed did not specifically authorize the full scope of the collection, nor was it covered by the language of the previous OLC opinions. And two, in Jack's legal opinion, the president's constitutional commander in chief authority was not broad enough to authorize all aspects of the collection program currently being implemented by the NSA. Specifically, certain aspects of the program involved the collection of too much US person information. Further, Jack felt the AUMF would not provide the necessary legal authority.

Lawyers frequently disagree about the scope of the president's constitutional authorities, particularly during a time of war; that was not new. The original author of the OLC opinion, John Yoo, and the previous head of OLC, Jay Bybee, both believed that the president's constitutional authority was, indeed, broad enough. The lawyers at NSA believed the same. Jack, however, did not. And Jack was now the head of the OLC.

I was surprised at Jack's unwavering reliance on the AUMF because a previous OLC opinion considered FISA as a safe harbor that could not impinge on the constitutional powers of the commander in chief during a time of war. Jack, however, continued to hold firm.

As we discussed the situation, Jack felt confident that we could fix his first concern relatively easily, simply by having David Addington write a new authorization with President Bush expressly authorizing the collection of all three baskets and ratifying the collections under previous authorizations. David, Pat, and I agreed that Jack's proposed solution made sense to us.

The second concern was much more complicated. Jack and Pat could not find legal authority to support one particular aspect of Stellar Wind collection, which was an indispensable step in the targeted search and analysis—the very activity that Jack believed was lawful. Ironically, the OLC had no qualms about finding lawful the remainder of Stellar Wind.

As I mentioned earlier, because the detailed mechanics—how things are actually done—and the steps followed are still classified, the US government places limits on what can be said about it. To better understand what the concerns were in 2004, recall the old saying, "Trying to find a needle in a haystack."

At times, attempting to identify a threat to our country or gather intelligence to prevent another attack *was* like trying to find a needle in a haystack. Now imagine that you do not even have the haystack!

That gives you some idea of the situation in which we found ourselves when the Department of Justice lawyers shifted their position. We no longer even had the haystack in which we wanted to search for the needle. We could do targeted searches for the al-Qaeda "needle," but the department lawyers now contended that we had no legal grounds on which to gather hay or even to add hay to an existing stack.

Jack told me he and Pat had already consulted with James Comey, Ashcroft's new deputy attorney general who had joined the Justice Department in December 2003 after serving as the US attorney in the Southern District of New York, a district painfully aware of the consequences of our inability to connect the dots prior to 9/11. Comey's Manhattan office had been just a few blocks from Ground Zero.

Standing six foot eight inches, Jim would have been extremely intimidating had it not been for his quick smile. But his ready smile did not diminish his serious, black-and-white approach to the law as a prosecutor. Shortly after he had been confirmed by the US Senate and had moved his wife and five children to the Washington area, Comey was read in to the Stellar Wind program by Mike Hayden on February 19, 2004, just a few weeks before Jack Goldsmith first reported to me that he had concerns. When Jack revealed his concerns to Jim, the new DAG concurred: the president's constitutional authority as commander in chief at a time when there was no direct threat of danger to the United States was insufficient to overcome the congressional prohibition under FISA to order the collection of metadata records that unavoidably included the records of millions of innocent Americans.

It was during that Saturday-afternoon meeting with David Addington and me that Jack fully articulated the specific concerns he had related to one particular aspect of Stellar Wind and suggested to us that he could not, as head of OLC, recommend going forward with that part of Stellar Wind. Jack emphasized that there was no finding of past illegality, but he also felt that we could not continue certain other aspects of the collection, based on the existing, previous legal guidance from OLC.

This was serious. Here we were only five days before the expiration of the president's previous authorization, and Jack was telling us we had a problem with a key component of it—with no apparent solution.

Exacerbating matters still further, the 9/11 Commission had been exploring the reasons for 9/11, including all the efforts that should have been made to prevent the attacks. They had already teed up nationally televised hearings and wanted everyone from Condoleezza Rice and John Ashcroft, to Bob Mueller and George Tenet—and even the president and vice president—to testify or be interviewed about what went wrong. The commission's not-so-subtle implication was that we would be held accountable by the American people should we fail to stop another major terrorist attack. Even Congress agreed with the commission that we needed to be forward-leaning in our efforts against terrorism, certainly more aggressive, and more creative as well. Clearly, this was not a time to be cutting back or impeding one of our key intelligence programs.

Jack understood this well, and perhaps that was why I sensed that he struggled with the message he presented to us. He might even have been embarrassed to tell the White House that we had to stop doing something that the Department of Justice had been approving for more than two years. Regardless of the bad news, I never questioned Jack's commitment or his willingness to work toward a solution. Pat's agreement with Jack buttressed his boss's position, and made the situation even more untenable, since Pat was considered one of OLC's best communications law experts.

Now that we had been fighting in Afghanistan for three years and Iraq for a year, I worried that some people in the White House would think these new lawyers at Justice—with nothing vested from the beginning of the war on terror—were backing away from controversial stands. I also worried that the DOJ lawyers were now—even if unintended—hanging out to dry the agents and operators who had relied on the guidance.

After Jack and Pat left my office, David and I remained behind for quite a while, earnestly discussing what we could do. Stellar Wind was important to our country's safety. The disputed aspects of the program depended on the telecom carriers, and absent DOJ approval, they were unlikely to cooperate. Without that collection, at least one aspect of the program would become virtually useless over time, and the entire Stellar Wind program would be far less effective.

Worse yet, the threat level during this time was high, especially the overseas threat reports. We feared that another terrorist attack was coming somewhere in the world—soon. And now we had to go to the president of the United States, whose primary concern was the protection of the American people, and tell him that NSA must discontinue one of our primary means of intelligence gathering—all amidst an ominous gathering storm of terrorist chatter and other intelligence warnings.

This was not good—stomach-wrenching, in fact. I was irritated and disappointed, but most of all, concerned that the actions Jack and Pat were recommending could jeopardize our nation's security. I wondered how Attorney General Ashcroft felt about all this, and whether he even knew. Moreover, this put me in a difficult position. After all, I was the person charged with ensuring the legal advice provided to the White House by our various agencies was solid and consistent. And now I was going to have to tell the president he had been receiving wrong legal advice for more than two and half years. Certainly, I could explain to him that Jack was the new guy on our team, and he saw things differently than others, and he was in a key position. Maybe he was smarter than everyone else around us; maybe he would perceive the problems differently after more experience on the job; or maybe he was right.

I suspected the president would not be happy with the news. He was not a lawyer, and although he did not enjoy running a war from the legal department, he was always respectful of the legal process and the courts. Even when court decisions went against us, his attitude was always, "Well, that's what the courts are for, to make sure we are doing things right."

Nevertheless, I worried that when we presented this new legal opinion to him on an activity we had been doing for more than thirty months, his response might also be, "You lawyers don't know what in the world you are doing!"

But this matter went well beyond professional pride or reputation. This was a matter of national security. Although OLC and the Justice Department would agree that the other aspects of the president's surveillance program could continue, one key element that led to our ability to obtain information important to preventing possible attacks would be curtailed.

Before talking with the president, I called Andy Card. Andy was in

Florida on a personal trip, but as soon as I explained the problem, he agreed to return to Washington early the next day. I also spoke with George Tenet and Mike Hayden. We arranged for a meeting in Andy's office on Sunday afternoon at 3:30 p.m. The vice president was attending a function Saturday evening, but David Addington left a message for him to call.

I called Jack and asked him to meet with David and me at 1:30 p.m., prior to the larger group meeting. I wanted to make sure that I fully understood his concerns, and I also wanted to test how strongly he and Pat felt about their position after another day of reflection on the larger issues. I intended to urge Jack to consider maintaining the status quo, at least until we had additional time to conduct a more thorough legal analysis now that we were aware of the specific problem.

I was also hoping to buy a little time to allow Attorney General John Ashcroft to sufficiently recover from his illness to engage in the discussion. The thought of stopping a part of the program while John was in the hospital did not seem right to me, especially since he had signed off on the program more than twenty times. As a cabinet official who had blessed these activities, Ashcroft's views and voice were valuable, and he had a vested interest in the decision. I felt it was important to hear from him personally about the legality of the surveillance program, and I felt sure the president would want to hear from his attorney general on this matter as well. It seemed wise to maintain the program at least until then—assuming we could find a way to do so.

As Jack and Pat sat down with David and me in my office that Sunday afternoon, I still had high hopes that the concerns about the program could be resolved in a way that would allow our country to be as protected as possible, yet in a manner consistent with the Constitution and with the support of the Justice Department. My hopes were soon dashed.

We met for an hour, but saw no solution. We were at an impasse. Jack and Pat seemed more entrenched in their positions and unwilling to compromise. In their opinions, a needed aspect of collection, necessary to make Stellar Wind effective, was not specifically included in the president's authorizations; therefore, while the previous OLC opinions supported all analytic aspects of Stellar Wind, they did not cover all particular aspects of collection.

Jack suggested again that the omission from previous presidential authorizations could be fixed easily, simply by having the president sign a new document that specifically authorized the operational step of collection, and that ratified such collection from the beginning of the program. That problem was solvable, but Jack could not find a legal basis for all of the ongoing collection. In fact, Jack and Pat both said that prior to probing into the program more deeply, they had been unaware of certain operational details of the program. That surprised me, and raised a number of red flags. *How could they possibly have been unaware? The AUMF scope concerns identified by Jack and Pat created downstream operational concerns.*

We all knew that collection was essential to all three baskets of Stellar Wind. For example, how can you analyze information if you do not have it and cannot first collect it? How can you search for the needle if there is no haystack? I was perplexed—given Philbin's knowledge of technology and communications—that he had not previously appreciated that the value of the program hinged on the collection of certain metadata. *Could they have been so careless?* I wondered.

I viewed the collection as an indespensible part of analysis; indeed, a part of the same activity. That is why I was not troubled by the language in the presidential authorizations.

In this meeting, Jack went one step further than he had in previous conversations. He said definitively that he could not give the president and NSA an opinion from OLC to support all aspects of collection, even if it were explicitly authorized by the president.

David and I listened intently; we asked questions and probed the OLC lawyers' positions. The conversation was cordial, but futile.

After Pat and Jack left the office, David and I discussed what we had heard. David was skeptical. Granted, this sort of surveillance program had never been done before, but the technology and its potential for good or evil had not existed. Now it did. The legal team and the operators at NSA believed that the president's authorizations by necessity included all aspects of the collection. It had to; otherwise, the targeted searches that the Justice Department had said were lawful could not have been accomplished. Mike

Hayden's team of lawyers were experts in the fields of privacy, intelligence, and surveillance matters; nobody knew that business better than they did, and they believed NSA was on solid legal ground.[1]

While the views of the NSA lawyers were significant, I deferred to the Justice Department on all major legal positions because Congress has charged the attorney general to provide legal advice to the executive branch and because when one of our policies is challenged in the courts, the Justice Department is responsible to defend us. Nevertheless, I was troubled. This was not an obvious call. Reasonable minds could differ, and when the national security of our country hung in the balance, I could not help but wonder whether maintaining the status quo until Ashcroft's return wasn't the most prudent course.

At 3:30 p.m., David and I walked from my second-floor office down to Andy Card's office on the first floor of the West Wing of the White House. We joined him at his conference table along with Dick Cheney, George Tenet, and Mike Hayden. I explained the situation to the group and described David's and my most recent conversation with Jack and Pat.

Everyone in the room understood what was at stake. I think we all felt that the ambiguous legality could be resolved in such a way that the program could continue, as long as the Justice Department supported it. And Jack had told me that if there were a real threat to the national security of our country, then the president's constitutional authority would be at its apex, and arguably would allow the disputed aspects of the program. Especially with the increased threat level, and the attorney general in the hospital, and another authorization approaching, we decided it would be wise for our assembled group to set up a conversation with the deputy attorney general to better explain why the collection was so important to the security of our nation.

At that point, I did not know if John Ashcroft had been told about the dispute and whether he agreed. I was also unaware of the seriousness of his medical condition. Additionally, as far as I knew, nobody had yet informed the president about the problem. That wasn't unusual. I knew the president well enough to realize that he did not micromanage his subordinates; you did not bring him a problem unless you had a solution or had exhausted all efforts to find one.

Besides, on that Sunday evening, I think we all believed this legal problem with the surveillance program could be resolved without the president's direct involvement. Even if we had informed the president, I was quite confident he would have advised us to keep trying to find a solution—the very course of action we were pursuing.

The following day, we set up a meeting with the deputy attorney general, James Comey. I wondered, however, if these efforts might be in vain. After all, it was John Ashcroft's insight we needed. As a former governor and senator from Missouri, Ashcroft had great political instincts and good judgment to do what was practical. I knew his deputy was an experienced attorney, but he had been in that position for only a short time, and he had not signed his name to the presidential authorization every forty-five days as Ashcroft had done. Nevertheless, we set up the meeting with the DAG.

On Tuesday, March 9, at about 7:15 a.m., Andy and I spoke to the president in the Oval Office about the concerns over Stellar Wind. Whether Andy or the vice president had mentioned it previously, I didn't know, but that was my first time to broach the subject with him. We explained that we would be meeting later in the day with the deputy attorney general, and hopefully we'd find a solution.

President Bush did not seem overly concerned at that point, even though we told him that an important intelligence tool was in jeopardy. This matter needed to be resolved by Thursday. Nevertheless, the president did not pick up the telephone to call the attorney general, who was still in the hospital; nor did he call the DAG. As he often did when we encountered obstacles, and as I had anticipated, he simply told us, "Find a bridge"—which meant find a temporary solution until Ashcroft gets out of the hospital. I think we all recognized that even after Ashcroft was well, we'd have to address the issues Jack had raised, but hopefully we could do so without the added pressures of an approaching reauthorization deadline in the midst of increased terrorist threat reports.

Later that day, our group reassembled in Andy's office, led by Dick

Cheney, and included George Tenet, Mike Hayden, David, Andy, and me. Also at the meeting were James Comey, Jack Goldsmith, and his deputy, Pat Philbin. Earlier that day, the vice president had met with Bob Mueller, Andy, and Mike, as well as Tenet's deputy, John McLaughlin, about these same matters.

In that late-afternoon meeting, we discussed all the major issues surrounding Stellar Wind, aided by Mike Hayden's charts, emphasizing how critical the surveillance program was to our national security—especially with increased threats looming. The deputy attorney general seemed to understand the importance of our intelligence efforts and did not express a problem with most of Stellar Wind; it was simply that one sticky issue that Jack, Pat, David, and I had been discussing for several days that seemed to cause his consternation. He said straightforwardly he couldn't find a legal basis for the collection of certain metadata, so he believed it should be discontinued. Undoubtedly, he—and everyone else at that table—realized this would render at least one aspect of the program virtually useless.

The conversation with the DAG confirmed my concerns. For some prosecutors, there is no gray area, only black and white. While I appreciated his standing on principle—I had done so myself on several contentious issues over my career—I wondered what it would take, what kind of threat to the United States would be necessary, to persuade the DAG to approve the full spectrum of collection. His refusal to defer to Ashcroft's previous judgments puzzled me. He said he supported most aspects of Stellar Wind, including content collection, but there was one aspect of collection that acquired too much US person information for him to support. He also supported enhanced interrogation techniques in trying to get vital intelligence information from the enemy. So the DAG understood the importance of gathering information and taking bold steps to do so. Why oppose giving the US government another forty-five days to calmly think through the issues and find a substitute for the disputed operational activity or develop a legal strategy to maintain it? Why not defer to the attorney general who had repeatedly supported all of the Stellar Wind collection activities? Why put the entire nation at risk when the NSA had been tracking leads to terrorists in the exact same manner for more than two years, and their best privacy experts had expressly stated that these efforts were within the president's constitutional powers to authorize them? I had repeatedly assured DOJ lawyers that we would abide by their judgment. But in the face of these circumstances, I wondered then, and still wonder to this day, *Why?*

Regardless of the reason, the DAG had staked out his position, and it seemed unlikely that he might change his mind over the next thirty-six hours.

Around 6:30 p.m., Andy and I called the president from Andy's office. We informed him that we had been unsuccessful at persuading the DAG to extend the program until General Ashcroft returned to work, or to give the lawyers more time to find a solution.[2] I knew the danger of going forward without DOJ support. "There are serious risks in moving forward," I told the president, "and I would find it hard to recommend you do so without the Department of Justice. But, of course, it is your decision. You'll have to decide if it is worth it to go forward."

"It doesn't sound like it is," he responded in a curt tone.

I could tell the president was uncomfortable continuing the disputed collection activities. Worse yet, I think we all knew that if we pushed this further, disagreements such as the one we had encountered don't stay secret for long. Despite the number of people who had been read into the Stellar Wind program, it had remained undercover for more than two years. As far as we knew, al-Qaeda was unaware of our surveillance ability to track them or circumvent their efforts because of the collection of information.

But disputes such as this produced stories that inevitably leaked, and that would lead to more intense media scrutiny, and most likely calls for congressional investigations, and all or portions of the president's surveillance program would be compromised. Our avowed enemies would know precisely how we had been locating them and they would change their tactics, making it harder for US intelligence agencies to find them, and making all of us less safe every moment of every day.

I suspected the president realized, as did Andy and I, that without the support of the Justice Department, the telecom companies who had assisted our country's efforts to prevent another attack would discontinue their cooperation. It wasn't as though they enjoyed the government's nose in their records every day anyhow, but they had been good corporate citizens and had cooperated well up till now. But without the attorney general's signature, some of the telecom companies probably would not be willing to risk the enormously costly and time-consuming lawsuits that would likely follow if their cooperation were to become known.

The president directed Andy to notify the vice president that we needed to meet early the next morning. As I left the Oval Office that evening, I believed the president was leaning toward discontinuing the collection of certain metadata under Stellar Wind, although he probably guessed the vice president would strongly object to doing so, simply because some lawyers had changed their minds. I shook my head and thought, *Tomorrow's meeting will certainly be a lively one.*

CHAPTER 27

JOINING FORCES
WITH CONGRESS

By 7:30 a.m. on March 10, 2004, the vice president, Andy Card, and I were in the president's office, talking with him about the Stellar Wind predicament. Cheney reminded the president the program would expire the next day.

"How can it possibly end?" President Bush asked. "It's vital to protecting the country."[1] Andy briefly updated the president on the situation.

"What are my options?" The president addressed this question to me.

"There are three," I replied. "First, you could discontinue the entire program. Second, you could reauthorize all of it. Finally, you could reauthorize those portions, including the Terrorist Surveillance Program, that we know the deputy attorney general will support, but omit the part in question."

Later, when Andy informed the president that John Ashcroft was still in the hospital, the president seemed surprised.[2] After a period of discussion, the president told Cheney that it would be difficult to go forward without Ashcroft. He would have no OLC cover, no Justice Department cover, and the telecom companies would likely balk without the DOJ's involvement.

I was concerned the president would decide to suspend the disputed aspects of the NSA's surveillance. I worried about disarming ourselves. But I was simply an advisor to the president; he was the leader of the free world upon whose shoulders this heavy decision rode.

President Bush directed Vice President Cheney to summon the congressional leaders to the White House as soon as possible to inform them of our plans. Clearly, if the president was going to suspend the collection of vital intelligence, he wanted to make sure Congress was in agreement with him, but he also hoped the congressional leaders might be able to help us find a legislative solution.

I left the Oval Office believing that OLC and the Justice Department had carried the day. It seemed inevitable; certain aspects of the program would be shut down or altered. Perhaps, with the passage of time, and once Ashcroft was healthy, we could find a way to reconstitute the full collection capability of Stellar Wind so we would be less vulnerable to attacks. I certainly hoped so.

That afternoon, before the congressional leaders arrived at the White House, I reexamined the legal advice given to us by Justice over the past two years. I understood Jack's and Pat's concerns, but to me, the previous OLC advice appeared broad enough to cover the entire program, including the disputed operational collection activity. The earlier legal opinions had indeed interpreted FISA to be a "safe harbor" only to avoid difficult constitutional questions related to the president's power to protect our country. That legal analysis undergirded the entire surveillance program.

Just before 4:30 p.m., I walked from my office down to the Situation Room, where I was soon joined by Mike Hayden, George Tenet, John McLaughlin, and David Addington. The president came to welcome the members of Congress and then left. The meeting was chaired by the vice president, and the congressional leaders in attendance were Senate majority leader Bill Frist, Senate minority leader Tom Daschle, Speaker of the House Denny Hastert, House minority leader Nancy Pelosi, chairman of the House Select Committee on Intelligence Porter Goss, and ranking member Jane Harman, as well as chairman of the Senate Select Committee on Intelligence Pat Roberts, and ranking member Jay Rockefeller. House majority leader Tom DeLay was not present, but was briefed later.

Several of these leaders were already well aware of Stellar Wind and had been periodically briefed about its ongoing operations by Cheney and Hayden. For only a few members was the information brand new.

The vice president opened the meeting by describing Stellar Wind in general terms and disclosing that we had encountered a problem that jeopardized the continuation of one key aspect of the surveillance activities. He also noted the president wanted the congressional leaders' advice about the way forward, including possible new legislation to support the NSA's clandestine activities, and especially the disputed operational step necessary to make the program work. Basically he said, "We've been doing this. We think it's very useful. We think it's lawful. We're having a problem with one aspect of the program with the deputy attorney general. I want Mike here to explain to you what we're doing." And he turned the meeting over to Mike Hayden.

General Hayden and one of his NSA technical experts presented the surveillance program in detail to these top government officials. Mike was very thorough and explained how the activities in Stellar Wind worked, and acknowledged the value of the program to the security of our country. His expert analysis provided detailed descriptions of actual classified operations in which these intelligence activities were currently being used effectively. Mike patiently answered any questions the leaders posed about the program. At no point did I hear Mike Hayden say, "Sorry, I can't answer that." He concluded the technical discussion and then took a seat in the back row.

"Well, ladies and gentlemen, that's where we are," Vice President Cheney said. "And we're having some problems with the lawyers."

"You ought to get some new lawyers," one of the leaders quipped. And that began the discussion.

Cheney laid out two specific questions to the group. "First," he said, "we would like to know whether you believe the program should be continued. Second, should we come to Congress for an amendment to the FISA statute so we have additional congressional authority to do what is necessary?"[3] Those were the two primary issues discussed that afternoon.

At one point, I was asked specifically by one member, "What is the problem?"

I answered straightforwardly, point-blank, "The deputy attorney general does not believe the president has constitutional authority to do this activity." I was very clear about that. "Nor does he believe the president's constitutional power can override the provisions of FISA."

Months later, a Department of Justice inspector general report examining this meeting questioned why the DOJ had not been included. Although there may have been other reasons, I can easily think of two primary ones: first, the president decides who in the administration he wants to attend high-level national security meetings at the White House, particularly those with congressional leaders. I believe it was arrogant for the DOJ inspector general within the executive branch to second-guess this. Second, there was no purpose in having the DOJ attend. The White House had already accepted their opinion and accurately presented the department's position. Moreover, the reason for the meeting was not to present both sides of the legal argument and ask the congressional leaders to decide who was right. No, accepting the OLC opinion was a foregone conclusion for President Bush. He wanted to know how Congress could best help us protect our country—given the new legal position—without giving away our spy trade secrets to the enemy.

So we next moved into a discussion about a possible legislative fix to the problem. Before the conversation got very far, Andy Card offered a sober but accurate insight. He said, "If an attack happens, and we could have stopped it if the president had not suspended the disputed technical portion of the surveillance program, it may be hard to explain to the American people why we didn't use this authority."

Everyone in the room seemed to agree. Several members said they even felt an obligation to continue the program, including the disputed operational step. That seemed to be the prevailing opinion among the leaders, that we must go forward with the surveillance program, even without the Justice Department, for a period of time while we pursued a legislative fix. One member stated that if the DAG would not sign the authorization, he should be fired. Before continuing, Andy asked, "Does anyone have any reservations?" No one voiced an objection. As such, it is fair to say that there was unanimity about going forward.

We turned our attention to what could be done legislatively. The challenge was twofold: first, to actually develop and pass legislation that allowed the NSA to have the authority necessary for collection purposes, to include building the haystack; and second, to pass that legislation "secretly" in the open Senate and House of Representative chambers without providing key information to the enemy.

We talked about whether it was possible to get legislation passed. The prevailing view, which soon became the unanimous view, was that there was no way to do that without compromising our intelligence efforts. Even a secret session of Congress was mentioned but considered too risky.

The meeting lasted until about 6:00 p.m. Before we left the Situation Room, the vice president summed up the discussion: "What I'm hearing is that we should all move forward, that we'll continue this activity, and we'll continue to work to try to find a legislative fix."

That was key. "We need to find the legislative fix for this. But for right now, let's just move forward."

Some of the leaders cautioned that Congress should remain involved in the solution, as well as the oversight of the program going forward. None of the congressional leaders, however, could honestly say they were unaware of, or had expressed misgivings about, continuing the program—although several of them later did. West Virginia senator Jay Rockefeller later said that he did not even recall attending such a meeting. There were plenty of witnesses in the room—not to mention White House logs—that could help refresh his memory.

I was surprised by the outcome of the meeting. I had fully expected the congressional leaders to accept the Department of Justice's position without question, and to tell the president he must find other ways to protect our country. Instead, they had all stepped up and agreed to do what was necessary to ensure our nation's safety and security. It was a remarkable display of courage, and . . . dare I say it? *Leadership.* We left the meeting with the full concurrence of the congressional leaders to continue even the disputed surveillance activities. I had not expected that sort of reaction, and it encouraged me greatly.

Mike Hayden also felt inspired by the reaction of the congressional leaders. He later said, "I left the meeting and I actually went back and had dinner with my wife that night. During our dinner conversation, I said, 'I had a big meeting in the White House today. It was really kind of interesting. And you know what? I was proud to be an American, because no one took a political stance in that meeting, and people were trying to do the patriotic, right thing. They opted for patriotism and defense and support of the program rather than political advantage.'"[4]

Sometime afterward, when rumors of the surveillance program were leaked to the press, Tom Daschle and Nancy Pelosi attempted to distance themselves from the president, claiming they were unaware of certain aspects of the program or there was not unanimity about moving forward. That is simply disingenuous posturing. We gave them a full briefing about the surveillance programs and every opportunity to ask questions and voice their opinions.

In terms of the legality, I could not have been clearer in saying, "The Department of Justice does *not* believe the president has constitutional authority to do this."

And the congressional leaders said, "Go forward."

CHAPTER 28

THE INFAMOUS HOSPITAL VISIT

Following the meeting with the congressional leadership, the vice president, Andy Card, and I walked from the Situation Room over to the president's residence in the White House to debrief him. The president was working out, so we waited for a few minutes in the hallway by the elevator while he completed his exercise regimen. We were in a good mood. The meeting could not have gone better. We met President Bush in his private study on the second floor of the residence, where he was sitting at his desk and appeared relaxed as he munched on some nuts while chewing a cigar. We informed him of the meeting, and he seemed pleasantly surprised and quite happy about the outcome.[1]

We talked for a while, and either the president or the vice president reminded us it would still be helpful to have John Ashcroft's signature on the authorization since the telecom companies knew him and were accustomed to Ashcroft signing off. They would likely have reservations about cooperating without assurances from the Justice Department—even with congressional concurrence.

I agreed. Ashcroft had been a mighty warrior in the fight against terrorism and had ardently advocated taking measures to prevent another strike against our homeland. He was a patriot who had already endured numerous heavy blows from critics about the Justice Department's more aggressive efforts. Ashcroft well understood what was at stake. I also believed that as a former US senator, John Ashcroft would appreciate the significance of the meeting we had just concluded with the congressional leaders and would be reassured by their bipartisan support for the president to continue the program necessary to protect our country during a time of heightened danger.

We knew that Ashcroft had undergone major surgery for pancreatitis only the day before, but we had heard that he had been up and walking earlier in the day. While we were still at the residence, the president picked up the phone and directed the White House operator, "Get John Ashcroft on the phone."

The call was connected to John's hospital room. Although I could not hear the person on the other end of the line, I assumed it was General Ashcroft. Only later did I learn that, in fact, it was Janet Ashcroft, who was at her husband's bedside in the hospital. Nevertheless, the president briefly mentioned the meeting with the congressional leaders and his need for help regarding the program. He did not say anything specific about the program, but asked if it would be okay for Andy and me to come to the hospital to discuss something.

When the president hung up the phone, he looked at Andy and me and directed us to go to Ashcroft's room at the hospital to see if he was willing to sign off on the authorization, despite the flap with some of the others at the Justice Department.

We left the residence immediately. As Andy and I walked along the White House colonnade past the Rose Garden, heading back to our offices, we talked about the possibility that if Ashcroft's condition was not stable or if he was still on postoperative pain medications, he might not be in any shape to understand and evaluate the legal issues in question, nor the significance of the congressional meeting. The last thing we wanted was to be accused of trying to take advantage of the AG if he was legally incompetent or not aware—even if he had ascribed his signature to the authorizations on numerous previous occasions. Andy and I agreed that we knew John well enough that we would be able to tell whether or not there was an issue. If

John did not sound or appear competent, we would not ask him to sign the authorization.

Once back in my office, I talked with David Addington and asked him to prepare a new authorization. No doubt, David had already been working on the revised authorization with the language corrections Jack Goldsmith had suggested, stating that among other things, the president was authorizing the collection, acquisition, and retention of telephony and e-mail metadata, and it ratified what had been done previously; in other words, that his previous authorizations had covered these same types of collection activities as well. The changes were intended simply to preserve the president's position that the prior program was lawful and to protect those who had acted while relying on those authorizations. By 7:15 p.m., David had the authorization ready to go.

Granted, everything about these events was unusual, but this was an unusual situation; the current authorization for Stellar Wind would expire in a matter of hours. If we once flew to California to get the president's signature to keep the program intact, surely we could travel a few city blocks from the White House to George Washington University Hospital to get Ashcroft's signature affirming the legality of the program.

Andy, David, and I piled into Andy's Suburban and headed for the hospital. On the way, we again discussed our concern about Ashcroft's competence and having a signal if one of us felt Ashcroft was unable to fully comprehend the purpose for our visit. We agreed that if either of us was uncomfortable, we would simply say, "We have to go."

When we arrived at the hospital, we were met by the attorney general's security detail. I suggested to David that he should not come to John's room with us. I thought it best to minimize the number of visitors, but more importantly, I knew that Addington and Ashcroft had clashed in the past over legal interpretations. Now was not the time for further friction. David handed the classified document pouch to me, and Ashcroft's security officers escorted Andy and me to the attorney general's room.

The hospital room was large, with the lighting turned down low. As I walked through the door and my eyes adjusted, I immediately focused my complete attention on John Ashcroft, who was lying in the hospital bed with his wife, Janet, to his right side, near the head of the bed. A lovely, charming woman with a keen intellect, Janet Ashcroft was a lawyer who had taught law at Washington's Howard University. She had weathered many firestorms with her husband during his tenure as governor of Missouri, and later as the state's US senator, and especially during his confirmation hearings for the job of US attorney general. She was a strong woman. Although she must have felt fatigued, and was probably not happy about all the commotion, she well understood the pressures under which we were all operating. No doubt, though, her primary concern was for her husband's well-being.

Standing with Andy at the foot of John's bed, I sensed that other people were in the room, perhaps a nurse, an aide, or part of John's security detail, but I kept my gaze on the attorney general. Most of us who spent a great deal of time in the White House were accustomed to having security officers around us. The officers purposely did their best to blend into the background, and after a while, even the most sensitive person grew comfortable with their presence.

I was concerned immediately because Ashcroft did not look well. Indeed, he looked pale and weak, and was unshaven. Andy greeted him first, as Janet stroked her husband's arm. Then I said hello and asked him how he was doing.

"Not well," John replied.

"We're here to discuss the matter the president called about," I said discreetly. That's all it took; it was as though I had pressed the On button and Ashcroft took over from there. He began by saying, "I was told this morning that I'm no longer the attorney general."

What? That was news to us.

Later, I became aware of a fax that my office apparently received from the DOJ informing us that the attorney general was temporarily relinquishing his authority to his deputy, so I accept full responsibility that my office had constructive notice of the transfer of power (I later testified to that effect). But standing there in that hospital room, I had no previous knowledge of the transfer of power. To this day, it remains a mystery to me that with respect to the health of the chief law enforcement officer in the country, why, in a time of war, our office would receive a faxed notification and not a phone call. Moreover, why was notification not supplied to the president's chief of staff or to cabinet affairs?

Neither President Bush nor Vice President Cheney knew that Attorney General Ashcroft had turned over the reigns to his deputy. Indeed, in 2010, in his book *Decision Points*, in discussing when Andy Card informed the president of the change, President Bush states the matter straightforwardly: "I was stunned. Nobody had told me that [Jim] Comey, John Ashcroft's deputy, had taken over Ashcroft's responsibilities when he went in for surgery. If I had known that, I never would have sent Andy and Al to John's hospital room."[2]

Certainly, had the vice president, Andy, or I known about the matter, we would have informed the president, and he could have simply summoned the deputy attorney general. But none of us knew until John Ashcroft announced the news to us in his hospital room.

John raised up slightly in his bed and then began laying out the legal issues in a coherent and logical synopsis, using language quite similar to that of Jack Goldsmith and Pat Philbin, as well as the DAG. It sounded as though Ashcroft had been well briefed.

Andy and I stood silently listening to John. As he spoke, I became more and more comfortable that he was fully competent. He seemed as coherent and as competent as any time I had ever heard him during White House briefings.

Ashcroft spoke for a few minutes uninterrupted and then concluded his soliloquy by saying, "I've been told it would be improvident for me to sign the presidential authorization, but it doesn't matter, because I am no longer the attorney general."

When I heard Ashcroft use the word *improvident*, I smiled inside. I knew he was okay. Nobody else I knew used such a word in ordinary conversation; only John Ashcroft, the son of a minister.

The attorney general shifted gears slightly, complaining that so few of his people had been read in to the surveillance program. "You've got all these

FBI agents and all those NSA operators that are read in to the program, but I can't even get my chief of staff read in."

Now I felt more comfortable that John was competent. If Ashcroft was complaining about such matters, he must be feeling better. I knew that John's chief of staff, David Ayres, was his longtime and trusted associate, but David was not a lawyer. "The president decides who gets read in," I gently reminded him. I looked at him with admiration. He was tough, even following serious surgery.

Ashcroft mentioned some meetings at the White House and questioned why the DOJ had not been invited. I appreciated his concern for defending the institutional prerogatives of the Justice Department, even though was not feeling well. He then repeated that he was no longer the AG, and he was done talking.

I still held the authorization in my hand. "Thank you," I said. "We'll raise this with the deputy attorney general. I hope you get better soon."

Andy echoed my get-well wishes, and with that, he and I left the room.

I had really hoped that we could describe to John the meeting with the congressional leaders and their encouragement for the president to continue the full surveillance program. As a former US senator, Ashcroft would appreciate their responses, I felt sure. But we never got that far. As soon as he emphasized that he was no longer the attorney general, we left without asking him to sign anything. According to the logs of the FBI security detail guarding Ashcroft, the length of our visit in the hospital room was less than ten minutes.

In recent years, press accounts have described this scene as a tense confrontation. That is simply not true. No one spoke on behalf of the Justice Department except Attorney General John Ashcroft, and his tone was civil and respectful. As I said, Andy and I barely spoke, and there were no demands or threats by us. I later testified before the Senate Judiciary Committee, under the threat of perjury, on July 24, 2007, about the events related to this hospital visit. Nobody in Congress had challenged my recollection of those events, and the DOJ inspector general, in a subsequent investigation, found nothing untruthful about my description of these events.

The details later presented by Jim Comey, and facilitated by Senator

Schumer's staffer, Preet Bahara, describing flashing lights, sirens, and dashing up the hospital staircases may or may not be technically true, but they certainly do not accurately depict what happened later in that hospital room. Contrary to Hollywood-style myth, there simply was no confrontation.

Andy and I did not speak until we were back in the Suburban, where we found David waiting. Even in the dimly lit vehicle, the look on David's face asked, "How did it go?"

"It didn't go well," I said. I handed the unsigned authorization back to David.

Andy and I looked at each other. "Yeah, he was competent," Andy whispered. I nodded. We both agreed that Ashcroft had been competent and understood the intricacies of the disputed surveillance matter. He seemed to have been well briefed by the DAG, Goldsmith, and Philbin. In an ironic twist, it is possible some or all of those briefings occurred while the attorney general was hospitalized and in a weakened condition, thus raising the question of whether his subordinates had taken advantage of him.

I muttered softly, "I did not know Ashcroft was no longer AG." Andy shook his head. We said little more during the short ride back to the White House.

We went to Andy's office, from which he called the president and told him what had happened. I could hear only Andy's side of the conversation, but it was obvious that the president was displeased. He was unhappy that he had not been informed about the change in Ashcroft's status. He told Andy, "Well, you've got to call Comey and tell him about the congressional leaders' meeting." At that point, no one at Justice knew about the afternoon meeting with the congressional leaders, and we felt it was important to communicate that information to them.

While I was still in his office, Andy called the deputy attorney general and asked him to come to the White House that night. It was then I first learned it had not been a nurse or a security detail in the hospital room with us. It had been Jim Comey, Jack Goldsmith, and Pat Philbin.

Apparently, as soon as the president had called the hospital room, Janet Ashcroft had contacted the AG's chief of staff, David Ayres. David had called the DAG, who had been on his way home, but redirected his path toward the hospital. On the way, he called FBI director Bob Mueller, who in turn contacted the security detail guarding the attorney general to allow Comey, Jack, and Pat to enter the hospital room. Comey arrived at the hospital and, according to his account, he literally raced up the stairs to John Ashcroft's room, just minutes before Andy and I arrived.

Why they didn't speak up or at least attempt to talk to Andy or me after we left the room is a mystery to me. But they didn't. And I have to admit, I never allowed my eyes to leave Ashcroft and his wife, so I had no idea they were in the room or I might have said something to them, especially about the congressional leaders' meeting.

As I listened to Andy on the phone, it sounded as though the DAG wanted to bring someone with him to the White House.

"I really prefer to speak to you alone," Andy said.

Apparently the DAG insisted on having a witness present.

"You are overreacting, Jim," Andy said calmly.

Although I could not hear his statement, apparently the DAG told Andy that what he had witnessed at the hospital was the most outrageous thing he had ever seen.

Andy responded, "We barely spoke."

The call continued, and Andy refused to argue. "Please get here as soon as you can."

When the call concluded, Andy immediately called the president and gave him the bad news. A series of calls ensued between the president, the vice president, and Andy regarding what to do. More calls between Andy and the DAG ensued. Meanwhile, the clock was ticking on our most valuable intelligence program.

I sat silently in Andy's office, listening to Andy's end of the conversations. The more I heard, the sadder and angrier I grew. The very thing that Andy and I had feared—accusations that we had tried to take advantage of the attorney general's ill health to get what we wanted—were being cast in our direction. Andy and I knew that had not been the case, but we also knew that stories like that took on a life of their own in Washington.

When we finally met with Comey in Andy's office much later that evening, the mood was cordial but serious. We talked for about fifteen minutes, and it quickly became obvious that we were not going to reach a solution. Given the late hour and the fact that we had been trying in vain to find a way that Jack, Pat, and Jim could support the continuation of the full surveillance program, I suggested that we get some rest and talk in the morning. The others concurred.

It was close to midnight by the time I arrived at home. I was tired but could not sleep. I stepped outside onto our back porch. The cool air revived me as I thought back through the events of a most tumultuous day. Although I understood the DAG's objection, I could not understand his apparent unwillingness to give us time to find a solution. He had been in office only a few months. Perhaps he was not used to having his legal judgment questioned. Perhaps he was trying to protect the Department of Justice as an institution and ensure its role as chief legal advisor to the White House. Lawyers disagree often. In this case, maybe I was wrong, but perhaps he was wrong. I wondered if he had considered that possibility. Regardless, I worried that our collective failure, whatever the true reasons, threatened our nation's security. I stepped back inside our home.

Tomorrow was certain to be another eventful day.

CHAPTER 29

RESIGNATION THREATS

People in the United States awakened the next morning, March 11, 2004, to another tragic reminder of the importance of the president's surveillance programs. Ten bombs packed with dynamite and nails exploded on trains in Madrid, Spain, killing 191 people, wounding nearly 1,800 others. The explosives were strategically placed on four trains in three busy Madrid train stations during rush hour. The devices were carried on board trains in backpacks and detonated simultaneously by using mobile phones. Three other bombs had failed to detonate or the death toll might have been even higher.

When I arrived in my office at 6:00 a.m., the first crisis I encountered was the news of the Madrid train bombings. As soon as I heard that, I knew immediately what the president would do regarding our surveillance. He would go forward. The congressional leaders' positive response that prior evening had encouraged him to stay the course. Now, with nearly 200 dead bodies and nearly 1,800 wounded, he was not about to leave our nation vulnerable to attack. There would be no compromise.

Jack Goldsmith called me shortly after six. He wanted to bring over the deputy attorney general's final offer.

Final offer? Are you kidding? I thought, but didn't say. Instead, I benignly responded, "Sure, Jack. Come on over."

Jack soon arrived with what was not really an offer at all, but sort of a more conciliatory, compassionate order of surrender. The DAG would allow the full surveillance program to continue under certain conditions for ten days as part of a wind-down order for the disputed collection activities.

I was irritated at the offer. I discussed Jack's message with Vice President Cheney, who did not receive it well. Then around 7:00 a.m., I went to the Oval Office to explain the offer to the president and Andy. The president expressed irritation at having to negotiate with a subordinate, and then despite our shared concerns about the telecom companies likely backing away, he said he was ready to sign the authorization.

Meanwhile, David Addington had contacted Mike Hayden at NSA and said, "I couldn't get the signature. Are you willing to do this without the signature of the attorney general, but with the signature of Al Gonzales and authorization from the president?"

Hayden thought for a few moments and said, "Yes."

Despite his relatively quick response, Mike later said he had at least five strong reasons behind his answer: "Number one, I had a safe-drawer full of orders signed off by the attorney general saying what we had been doing was lawful. I don't know what had happened to change that. Again, I wasn't privy to some of these other discussions. That was one thing. Number two, my lawyers said it was lawful. Number three, we had gotten what I thought was broad political support from the members of Congress that preceding afternoon in the Situation Room. Number four, this looks like it was being done in haste. And I felt that another forty-five-day cycle, while we sorted this out, was probably the right thing to do, given the balancing act, legal, political, operational security we were trying to do. So let's take the next forty-five days to get to the final answer.

"The fifth reason was pretty straightforward: 200 dead Spaniards that were killed overnight between the afternoon meeting in the Situation Room and David Addington's phone call to me that morning, right . . . given that starkness of the al-Qaeda threat, and given the ambiguity of the situation, I thought the correct operational, legal, and ethical decision was: 'All right, we'll do this one more time on a somewhat different framework. We've got to sort this out.'"[1]

Because the presidential authorization relies on legal determinations, and the president was not a lawyer, I signed the authorization, certifying it as to form and legality. I sighed as I signed the document, knowing that this would further alienate the conservatives at the Justice Department. My signature would be Exhibit A to support their accusations that I wanted to be attorney general so badly that I would try to take advantage of a sick man. I knew my signature would not likely be sufficient to ease the concerns of the telecom carriers regarding the program's continued legality. From my perspective, at best, this was an interim authorization. More importantly, I signed the document because I believed, at that moment, with the spilled blood in Spain and growing chatter about another attack, the president had constitutional authority to protect America. Although the bombings were not within the United States, they were against one of our closest allies in the war on terror. If Madrid could be targeted, could New York or Washington be hit again?

I certainly wasn't trying to usurp the authority of the Justice Department or supplant the attorney general by signing. I knew, and the president knew as well, that this authorization was only a bridge, a temporary thing, because of the necessity of having the cooperation of the telecom carriers. We would have to work out something with the Department of Justice as soon as John Ashcroft was well enough to be back on the job.

The president showed no hesitation as he picked up his pen and signed his name to the authorization with a flourish, as though making a point. As head of the executive branch of government, the president could accept the previous OLC determinations or he could decide the appropriate legal standard. With the president signing the authorization, we now had another forty-five days to figure things out, and meanwhile, our intelligence agencies would not be impaired in their efforts to protect Americans.

Later that morning, I stopped by Andy's office. He was calling the congressional members who had been involved in the meeting the previous evening in the Situation Room. Andy informed the members that because of the Madrid train bombings, the president had decided to continue Stellar Wind, including the collection of certain metadata. Andy asked if anyone had any reservations about this course of action or second thoughts about continuing the program. No one expressed an objection. Indeed, some felt that in light of the bombings, they were obligated to go forward.

I talked to Jack Goldsmith by phone to inform him that because of the circumstances in Spain, the president had determined he had the power to authorize all aspects of Stellar Wind. I reminded Jack that the president's determination was binding on the executive branch, and for now, there was no need to continue searching for a solution to our disagreement. Goldsmith agreed without equivocation. He sent a memo to the interested parties within the Justice Department to reinforce the point.

Later Jack called to tell me he had a document he wanted to deliver. I was fatigued and asked that he wait until the following day.

That night, I received another phone call from Jack Goldsmith. He said he needed to see me immediately.

"Jack, it's been a long couple of days. Won't this wait till morning?"

"No, I must bring you a package right now."

"No, don't come here," I said. "I don't want you coming to my home." I tried again to wave him off, but Jack insisted. I acquiesced, and around 10:00 p.m., Jack Goldsmith and Pat Philbin showed up at my front door.

My wife, Becky, had heard me talking with Jack on the phone. She had no idea what this was all about, but she was worried that whomever I had been talking with and warning away from our home wanted to hurt me. Although I didn't know it, when Jack and Pat came to the door, Becky sat at the top of the stairs, listening, just in case of trouble, and worrying about whom to call. Our boys were already in bed.

I let Jack and Pat inside and we sat down in our dimly lit living room. Jack handed a letter to me. I opened it and read Jack's confirmation of my instructions to him and the Department of Justice that I had given earlier, after the president had made his decision and signed the authorization. I'd said the continuation of the program was lawful, and basically told him he could stop working on the OLC opinion until we wrangled out the direction we were going to go concerning the technical point in dispute. It was basically a cover-your-butt letter, and I had no clue why it could not have waited until morning. Jack had already given that same guidance to the DOJ leaders, indicating that the president's determination was binding upon the entire executive branch.

Jack and Pat seemed tense and unsure about what might happen next. I told them, "I don't know either. I just want to get through the weekend and let emotions cool down and heads clear before we go back to work on Monday."

"There's talk of resignations at the department over all this," Pat said soberly. Jack agreed.

What? I thought. I thought momentarily about the infamous 1973 "Saturday Night Massacre" when the attorney general and deputy attorney general both resigned rather than fire the independent counsel investigating Richard Nixon for wrongdoing. But this was nothing like that. President Bush had not taken action for personal or political gain. He had acted in what he thought were the best interests of the country based on previous advice from his attorney general. And he hadn't acted in secret to hide wrongdoing. He had informed the congressional leadership of his actions. This was nothing like that sordid chapter in American history. *This is ridiculous*, I thought.

I had no way of verifying threats of resignation, or knowing whether Pat's and Jack's comments were simply an angry response to the president's actions. "Let's just get through the weekend and see where things stand on Monday," I repeated. I looked at them and shook my head. "You know," I said, "what is amazing is that less than forty-eight hours ago, the president had accepted your positions. He had decided that he was going to go along with Justice regarding the disputed portion of Stellar Wind. You guys had won. But then the congressional leaders met and voiced their support for maintaining the status quo, and then the Madrid train bombings changed the dynamic for the president."

Jack and Pat looked at me as though they had not even heard about the congressional leaders' meeting.

"Isn't that ironic?" I said. "You guys thought it was Andy or me who had changed the president's mind, but actually it was the congressional leaders that swayed him."

Jack and Pat didn't respond.

"Good night, gentlemen," I said, getting up and walking toward the door. Jack and Pat followed and I closed the door behind them. I turned out the lights and went upstairs to find Becky, still concerned, but relieved that I had not been hurt.

As I lay in bed, I wondered how the lawyers at Justice were feeling. Did they feel disrespected? Did they feel irrelevant now that the president had ignored their advice at the urging of the congressional leadership? Comey and Goldsmith were relatively new in the department. They were not with us during 9/11. I wondered how effective they would be in their jobs after all this died down. How long would it take for people in the White House to trust them? These were important questions, because we needed the Justice Department's support to continue Stellar Wind and fight the war on terror in allegiance with the Constitution.

I viewed the March 11 authorization as an interim authorization. As far as I was concerned, it was intended to serve two purposes: one, to preserve the president's position that Stellar Wind, including the activities involving the collection and retention of metadata, were lawful; and two, to protect those who had acted in reliance on the previous authorizations. As I drifted off to sleep, I knew we had a lot of work ahead.

The president called for me the next morning as soon as his morning national security briefings were completed. The deputy attorney general, temporarily holding the position of attorney general, had attended the meeting in place of John Ashcroft.

In his book *Decision Points*, the president recounts meeting alone with Comey that morning following the larger group session, and after listening to Jim's concerns about Stellar Wind, saying, "I just don't understand why you are raising this at the last minute."[2]

Comey responded, "Mr. President, your staff has known about this for weeks."[3]

The DAG was both right and wrong. He was right that I had known for months that DOJ was conducting a scrub of the program. I had encouraged it. I certainly had known for weeks of concerns and the possible necessity of change to the program. But the DAG was wrong to say we had known about the specific problems that long. It was not until Jack Goldsmith's "Oh, my God!" moment on March 6, 2004, a mere five days before the authorization's expiration date, that he admitted their failure to understand the program, and articulated that, for a specific aspect of Stellar Wind, he could not find legal grounds to continue.

Over the years, various commentators and politicians have picked up on Comey's remark to the president and expanded it to say that President Bush's staff knew of the specific surveillance problem *for months* before broaching it with the president. That is absolutely false, and the implication that the president was ill served by individuals attempting to keep information from him about a highly sensitive matter is also disingenuous.

I am confident that had I gone to the president with general concerns, he most likely would have said for me to stay on top of it and keep him informed if a specific problem arose. Once knowing the specific problem, he would have said the same thing that he did: "Find a solution, or at least find a bridge." Find some way to make things work until we have time to do whatever is necessary to fix the problem.

According to President Bush, Comey had told him that he was not the only one contemplating resignation, but the head of the FBI was too.[4] Bob Mueller had been waiting for Comey in the White House lobby. The president called Mueller back to his office, and the FBI director confirmed that if the president continued the Stellar Wind program over the Justice Department's objection without resolving the collection activity that he had been convinced was without legal grounds, he would no longer serve in the Bush administration.[5] That news changed everything.

As soon as I entered the Oval Office, the president told me that Bob Mueller was talking about resigning because of the NSA surveillance flap. Indeed, it was later revealed that both the DAG and the head of the FBI had anticipated resigning that very morning—but hadn't.

"Yes," I said. "I just learned about talk of resignations at Justice last night." I mentioned my two late-night visitors. Apparently, Mueller had hinted that others within the Justice Department might resign too.

President Bush did not wish resignations to raise red flags that might call more attention to the NSA surveillance program. Some resignations are more problematic for a White House than others. The resignation of Bob Mueller, the director of the FBI since September 11, would definitely raise eyebrows. For one thing, Bob was well respected in the White House. Everyone regarded Bob as the square-jawed marine who could be counted on to do his duty, no matter how difficult. He was known as a man of integrity, and I greatly appreciated Bob's calm, wise manner in running the FBI. For the FBI director to resign over a matter of principle, and especially a concern about the lawfulness of something our own intelligence people were doing, would be big news, and in Washington, it would ignite a firestorm.

His resignation would raise questions about the reasons for the departure, which would inevitably lead to the existence of Stellar Wind, revealing it to terrorists, and thus jeopardizing the national security of our country. The intelligence activities would likely be compromised, the tools would be less effective, and Americans would be less safe. Undoubtedly, this would lead to congressional hearings and political grandstanding—all further compromising the program. At the very least, a resignation brouhaha would cause the telecom companies to be reticent about providing assistance to the government. The president and I talked about the likelihood that the carriers would discontinue their cooperation without the DOJ assurances that their revelations were lawful. Without their help, we would have to curtail the surveillance activities, regardless.

The president shook his head and spoke slowly. "Okay, I said this was a bridge. It may be a shorter bridge than we anticipated. Talk with Mueller. Work with him to come up with a solution to this."

"Yes, sir." I left the president's office and immediately contacted Bob. He agreed to lead an effort at Justice to help find a solution.

I found it remarkable that the president would bestow this responsibility on the FBI director, the head of an investigative agency, to find a solution to a legal issue—a constitutional question—rather than with the acting attorney general, the person charged by statute to provide legal advice to the executive branch. It was an indication of the faith and confidence the president had in the maturity and judgment of Bob Mueller.

Throughout that weekend and into the following week, I communicated directly with Mueller, and along with the lawyers at the Justice Department, we tried to develop the legal theory that would allow us to bring the collection of US person information to a level acceptable to the DOJ. By midweek, relying on their existing legal interpretations of what the law required and their assessment of the scope of presidential power, DOJ concluded that there was simply no way to do it under our current laws. We also concluded that if Congress attempted to pass a law that might somehow grant permission for the activity, the enemy would learn they could no longer operate as freely in that realm, and the program would be much less effective.

Ultimately, to accommodate the concerns of the Justice Department, the president authorized modifications to the program in an order signed on March 19.

———

Within weeks after the tumultuous events surrounding the March 11 authorization, I was glad to hear that John Ashcroft had recovered and returned to work. The first time he came to the White House, we had a meeting in my office, and afterward, I asked, "General, may I talk to you privately for a second?"

I ushered out the other folks in the room, and I said to him, "Listen, in terms of the hospital visit, I can't apologize for having gone there, because I was directed to go there by the president, but I wish it had never happened."

Ashcroft seemed to understand my predicament; I hoped he understood the unusual, extraordinary circumstances surrounding Andy's and my visit to his hospital room, given everything that was happening at that time.

Neither John nor I have spoken publicly a great deal about that incident. We came close once, after we were no longer serving in the Bush administration, when we were both on stage together at an event in California and the moderator asked about the "infamous" hospital visit. John declined to comment, so I did too.

Nevertheless, over the years, descriptions in the media and other books about that private visit have been voluminous, and virtually all have been inaccurate or skewed. I know it is something that both John Ashcroft and I wish had never occurred. He may have his own reasons for that. Perhaps he was embarrassed that DOJ lawyers had missed or misunderstood the collection activities that NSA was carrying out pursuant to Stellar Wind. Perhaps he was embarrassed that the White House and congressional leaders had ignored the Department of Justice.

For my part, after Andy and I got back to the White House from the hospital and everything blew up, I knew that eventually he and I would be accused of having tried—on our own and without direction from anyone—to take advantage of a sick man. I knew it would hurt us, and it did.

I was particularly saddened and offended for Andy. I was already a pariah to many of the Washington elite, especially in some of the most conservative circles. But Andy's reputation as a dedicated public servant was impeccable. Nobody spoke ill of Andy Card, and a kinder and more caring person would be difficult to find. But if one believes the scuttlebutt, the impression might be that Andy was a mean-spirited manipulator, trying to force the will of his boss on a sick man. Nothing could be further from the truth.

As for John Ashcroft, the incident did nothing to lessen my opinion of him. He's a great patriot, and I admire his service to our country. He took numerous arrows for the Bush administration, but even more for his efforts to do what he believed was right.

———

Later that fall, I was made aware of an unlawful leak in October 2004 to the *New York Times*, providing information regarding Basket I of Stellar Wind—the interception and content collection of international calls. Reporters James Risen and Eric Lichtblau were preparing to publish a story that would alert our enemies that they were at risk within the US telephone systems. Condi Rice and Mike Hayden convinced the reporters and the *Times* to hold the story.

In a rare face-to-face meeting, President Bush also met personally in the Oval Office with the *New York Times* publisher, Arthur Sulzberger Jr., and editor Bill Keller. The president had Mike Hayden explain the importance of the classified information for our country's safety, as well as the safeguards in place to guard against abuse of the surveillance, and provided some illustrations of the program's effectiveness. The president strongly urged the newspaper to hold the story for national security reasons.

Later that year, the paper threatened to run the story again.[6] I met with the editors as well as the reporters in two separate meetings, hoping to persuade them to hold the story because of the classified information it exposed. Our second meeting occurred close to the 2004 presidential election. At the conclusion of the second meeting, along with Deputy Attorney General Jim Comey and his chief of staff, Chuck Rosenberg, the newsmen asked me two telling questions. One: "What do you plan to do when you leave here?" subtly implying that I would not be employable as a result of this incident becoming public. The second question was even more ironic, considering the reason for our meeting in the first place. The newsman asked me, "Do you have any problems sleeping at night?" implying that our actions were morally wrong.

My answer was simple. "Our morals are reflected in our laws, and as long we are complying with the law, I can sleep perfectly well."

In December 2005, with one of the reporters set to publish a book about the surveillance, the *New York Times* chose to ignore the president's request and disclosed the classified information about Basket I, alerting terrorists to our surveillance and potentially putting millions of American lives at risk. The disclosure of the classified information seemed suspiciously timed to affect the reauthorization of the PATRIOT Act. It did not prevent the PATRIOT Act's renewal, but it did ruffle the sails (and probably the sales) of the tell-all book describing only a portion of Stellar Wind.

Despite his disappointment in the *Times* and his anger at whoever had betrayed our country by leaking the information, the president decided to diffuse the situation by addressing it head-on in his radio address that weekend.[7] To his great credit, he did not want Americans to think their government was acting unlawfully, and he certainly did not want to lend credence to people suggesting the NSA was a rogue agency, operating on its own, or that agents within the NSA were acting on their own, spying on American citizens—or even, for that matter, unilaterally spying on al-Qaeda. The president acknowledged the existence of the Basket I surveillance; he discreetly said nothing about Basket II or Basket III.

The Justice Department launched a criminal investigation to discover who had disclosed the highly classified information. According to widespread reporting, Thomas M. Tamm, a DOJ employee, leaked some of the information. In 2011, according to subsequent media reports, an investigation into Tamm was dropped by the Obama DOJ.

When I had been confirmed as attorney general and had to defend the president's surveillance program, I discussed the 2004 dispute with the DOJ in hearings before Congress. I was repeatedly asked questions that related to classified information regarding top secret activities of our nation's intelligence agencies. They grilled me again and again about the same issues, but they were not privy to the information that other people in the intelligence community knew, and that I knew as well. Not a single person on the Senate Judiciary Committee before whom I testified had been read in to the Stellar Wind program, so trying to explain it to them without compromising classified information was difficult and frustrating, both for the inquisitors and for me. I refused to give away our nation's vital, classified information in a public hearing simply to placate a senator or congressman. In truth, I could not have revealed the classified information to legislators even in a secure, private session if they had not been read in to the program, and that permission could only come from the president himself. Consequently, I was excoriated by various members of Congress and whispers of perjury ensued.

———

Although the president's surveillance program had taken a hit, it was not dead. And because the program was valuable, administration lawyers began considering whether the more problematic portions of the program could be moved to a more permanent status under supervision of the FISA Court.

Beginning shortly after the president's modified order on March 19, we took our case to the chief judge of the FISA Court, Judge Colleen Kollar-Kotelly, and asked her to look at the program, including the disputed portions. The FISA Court was briefed on all aspects of Stellar Wind, to include the disputed ones. DOJ focused on changes to decrease the collection of US person information. Sometime thereafter, DOJ filed an application with the FISA Court seeking authority to collect bulk e-mail metadata.

In the summer of 2004, Judge Kollar-Kotelly reviewed one basket of collection activities conducted under Stellar Wind and concluded that the collection of bulk e-mail metadata was indispensible to the lawful targeted searches.

Moreover, the FISA Amendment Act of 2008 in essence codified the surveillance activities authorized by the president and greatly expanded them. When Stellar Wind was first designed and implemented, it was not directed broadly at worldwide terrorism. It was initially authorized to combat al-Qaeda and its affiliates. As such, other terrorist groups were not intended to be monitored by this program. Now the FISA Amendment Act of 2008 allows some of the things we were doing against al-Qaeda under the president's authority, and it allows them to be used against all legitimate foreign intelligence targets. So in a sense, the FISA amendments not only validate Stellar Wind, they expand it.

Ironically, President Barak Obama, who, as a US senator and during his campaigns to be elected president, gave the impression that if he were in the Oval Office, he would discontinue or greatly restructure the surveillance program, has continued the programs and even expanded them. I understand that. It is one thing to talk about stifling our intelligence programs when you either don't know or don't have the full picture of the terrorist efforts aligned against us. It is quite another when you see the reality.

If ever a president might have said, "That program is over; I'm not George Bush, and I won't have it," Barack Obama would have been inclined to do that. But he didn't. That may actually be one of the strongest arguments with regard to both the lawfulness and the effectiveness of the Bush-authorized Stellar Wind program. If our forty-fourth president believed that he needed, in good conscience, to end the program, he could have done so. He did not.

The president swears to preserve, protect, and defend the Constitution, and implicit in that is the mandate to protect the health, safety, and welfare of every American citizen. So when he (or she) looks at these surveillance programs and discovers they're effective, and the best lawyers in our government are saying, "Yes, we do have the authority to engage in these kinds of activities," the choice is obvious.

Do we need safeguards against domestic spying and abuse of our intelligence programs? Absolutely. But the collection of information is vital if we want to keep our country safe.

Now, because the government is so good and so efficient at gathering intelligence information, and the technology is improving every day, it is even more necessary to ensure that Congress fulfills its responsibility of oversight. It is equally important to ensure that the inspector general, the general counsel of the NSA, and our other intelligence agencies are doing their jobs. And when discrepancies or mistakes happen, there must be accountability.

Despite the dangers and concerns, I don't think our surveillance efforts should be discontinued. Congress has gone a long way to minimize the potential harm that could arise from abuse of our intelligence programs, so the notion that we should discontinue monitoring information from phone calls, e-mails, and other activities that are vitally important to the national security of our country is shortsighted and dangerous.

CHAPTER 30

GET YOUR UNIFORM ON

O ften the branches of the US government engage in what I call an intense "dance," resulting from the separation of powers envisioned by our Founding Fathers. Like two passionate flamenco dancers facing off with each other, at one moment flirting, at another moment flitting away, tantalizing and tempting as they interact, sometimes embracing each other, at other moments each violently stomping his or her feet, as though saying, "We will do this my way." Ironically, the dancers in the branches of government are supposedly working together. Usually they do, but when Congress established the National Commission on Terrorist Attacks Upon the United States, or more simply, the 9/11 Commission to investigate the 9/11 attacks, including the US intelligence failures, I knew the dance would eventually get heated—and it did, including threats of subpoenas.

As White House counsel, I spent an inordinate amount of time with the 9/11 Commission over a two-year period. While the president wanted the White House to be helpful, and most importantly, to learn how we could better prevent future attacks by examining where we were vulnerable on September 10, 2001, my job—one that I exercised to the fullest—was to protect the institution of the presidency. These were uncharted waters relating to an unprecedented national tragedy, and I understood all too well that the way we provided access to personnel and information would set a precedent for future officials in the White House.

I had numerous official conversations with the members of the commission, especially Chairman Thomas Kean and Vice Chairman Lee Hamilton, resulting in some concessions and many disagreements over access to classified and privileged documents, as well as public testimony of executive branch officials. I also had many back-door conversations with certain commission members that helped pave the way to various compromises.

One of the more difficult debates revolved around whether National Security Advisor Condoleezza Rice would present public testimony before the commission. Condi had already given hours of testimony in private interview sessions, so I resisted because I felt the commission simply wanted to make a spectacle of her public testimony. No sitting national security advisor had ever testified before Congress on a matter not related to possible wrongdoing. Neither Andy Card nor I wanted Condi to testify. It would establish a harmful precedent. Historically, members of the president's senior staff do not testify before Congress about events, policies, or conversations relating to or involving the president or the White House. This privilege was intended to encourage candid communications between the president and his advisors. The president also did not want Condi to testify in public. But for reasons that only Condi could explain, she wanted to testify, and she advocated strongly for that position. I suspected that she felt the need to publicly defend her integrity, partly to counteract accusations by former counterterrorism director Richard Clarke in which he indicated that we had prior information that Condi and others could have used to help prevent the attacks. Condi was offended—with good reason—and kept pushing the president for permission to publicly testify.

I was at my son Graham's high school track meet on a Saturday afternoon when I received a call from the president. I casually slipped away from the bleachers where Becky and I had been watching the events. I walked down toward the end of the track to take the call.

President Bush expressed his concern about whether Condi should testify. "I just want to confirm that you think the right thing to do is to hold the line."

I could sense that his opinion was not as strong as it was previously. I guessed that he was trying to gauge whether my position was still firm.

"Yes, sir, I do. The notion that she has to testify publicly under oath is silly. Condi has already testified privately, testimony that must be lawful under penalty of law. They have already asked her all their questions, they already have her answers; anything more is just theater."

"I understand and agree."

When I got off the phone, I breathed a sigh of relief. *Okay . . . we're okay. We're going to hold the line.*

Somewhere between that afternoon and the next morning, the president changed his mind. Andy and I were disappointed, but this was the president's decision to make. My job was simply to make him aware of the possible repercussions on the institution of the presidency. Perhaps President Bush was responding to the wishes of the families of the 9/11 victims. No doubt he also hoped the attacks were a once-in-a-generation crisis, and future presidents would not be burdened by this precedent.

To help reinforce that point, I wrote a letter to the Speaker of the House and to the Senate majority leader stating that Dr. Rice's testimony was highly unusual, but given the circumstances of 9/11, the president was going to permit it. From the White House's perspective, however, her testimony would not be considered a precedent in future requests for testimony by high-level executive branch officials. It was the best I could do to protect the institutional prerogatives of the presidency.

An even more significant issue arose over the commission's desire to interview the president and vice president. For months, the president refused the commission's repeated requests, but after acquiescing to Condi's requests, he later agreed to a private interview in the Oval Office, with all ten of the commission members. Their unprecedented interview, conducted with both the president and vice president at the same time, was historic. I was the only senior White House staff person in that three-hour-long, unrecorded interview, and Bush spoke bluntly about the events on 9/11 and his assessment of the war on terror. The president said it was his responsibility to protect America. "If previous administrations could have stopped al-Qaeda, they would have. If we could have stopped al-Qaeda, we would have." He paused and then with firmness in his voice said, "The best strategy is to kill them. They are cold-blooded killers." Referring to the Madrid train bombings, the president said bluntly, "When bin Laden sees Spanish troops pulling out of our conflict because of the train bombings, he will kill more." Regarding the safety of America, the president reiterated strongly, "I am responsible."

It was Bush at his best.

While I was working in the White House, my mother visited my wife, boys, and me in Washington. We toured the majestic historic monuments in the capital city and visited many of the museums, just as other tourists. But I also took my mom to the Oval Office to see the president. It was important for me to show this shy, seventy-year-old woman, who stood five foot nothing and had picked crops as a young girl, what I had accomplished, thanks to her sacrifices and those of my father.

Thanks to my parents, my siblings enjoyed lifestyles unimaginable to our grandparents, and I was living the American dream. At the time, my sister Angie lived with our mom and cared for her; my brother Tony had become an officer with the Houston Police Department, and for more than twenty-five years would serve as a key member of the force's SWAT team. Our brother Timmy went through some difficult times, getting involved with drugs and alcohol and temporarily losing his way. But he would eventually return to his faith in God and became a minister of the gospel. Theresa and Christine were thriving, and our youngest brother, Paul, was an overachiever who one day would travel the world for his business.

As I took a few minutes to show my mom around the White House and then to the Oval Office, I thought, *This is the American story; it is my story; it is all of our stories—that we live in a free country where dreams still can come true—and it remains a story worth fighting for, dying for, and living for.*

On the last day of her visit, she was up before dawn to make breakfast for me. Reminiscent of the daily ritual I had enjoyed as a child, Mom filled the table with eggs and tortillas, just as she had done every morning for my father before he left for work. But I wasn't dressed in coveralls and a hard hat, ready to go work at a construction site. I was wearing a business suit, and I was reporting to work at the White House to advise the president of the United States. I imagined the wonder that filled my mother's heart. What a miracle, that her son could take her from the cotton fields of Texas to the Oval Office in the White House.

———

While President Bush's initial agenda had been redirected by the 9/11 attacks, transforming him into a wartime president, perhaps nothing defines a president's legacy any more than the men and women he selects to serve on the US Supreme Court. Similarly, no position in government has as much potential to impact and shape the long-term course of the nation as does a Supreme Court justice. The court's influence on American society is enormous. Consider, for example, the court's decisions about prayer in public schools, or the *Roe v. Wade* decision regarding abortion, or the more recent June 2015 *Obergefell v. Hodges* decision in which the court declared the Constitution guarantees a right to same-sex marriage, thus redefining the meaning of marriage.

The president recognized the powerful influence wielded by justices, and long before any openings occurred on the court, he and I engaged in a number of informal conversations about various aspects of the Supreme Court, including how a potential Supreme Court nominee should interpret the Constitution and the laws passed by Congress, and what role judges should play in our system of government. President Bush readily acknowledged that he was not a lawyer, so he and I discussed my view of the limited role of a judge, as well as my views of specific potential nominees.

About each potential nominee I asked myself several questions to help me properly advise the president. For instance: Is the person qualified by virtue of education and achievement? Is the nominee confirmable? Who controls the Judiciary Committee before whom the nominee must appear and be recommended for confirmation? Is the person a member of a minority group? Most important, what is the person's judicial philosophy about the role of the court in our constitutional framework? And finally, I asked about intangibles such as character and courage. Is this person's character strong enough to withstand the intense scrutiny that goes with the nomination and the job? And does the person have the courage to apply a consistent set of conservative principles, not merely today, but ten or twenty years from now?

I gave the president straightforward answers about the pros and cons of various possible selections. I emphasized that the best way to guess how a potential nominee might rule from the bench is to look at how he or she judged other cases (assuming the person under consideration had previous judicial experience).

Of course, my own possible nomination to the Supreme Court created an unspoken awkwardness. The president and I conducted our conversations against the backdrop of numerous stories in the media suggesting that he might make a historic choice by nominating the first Hispanic to the highest court in our nation—namely, me. That raised the hopes of Hispanics and raised the ire of ultraconservative types, as well as liberals.

From our conversations, I understood that while the president intended to nominate only someone with a conservative track record and stellar credentials, he had no desire to take on a difficult confirmation battle because of a person's prior record, rulings, or remarks on controversial issues such as race, religion, or abortion. While I knew this would disappoint hardcore right supporters, my sense was that the president was comfortable moving the court to the right in incremental steps.

The president had campaigned on the promise of appointing justices in the conservative vein of Justices Antonin Scalia and Clarence Thomas, but privately he also emphasized diversity. There is no doubt in my mind that he would have been delighted and proud to have appointed a woman or a Hispanic to the court. When discussing our wish list, the president often reminded me, "Bring me diversity." He looked to me to recommend only people qualified by virtue of their education, training, and experience, but I also understood his habit of going with his gut. I knew that in the final analysis, he would base his decision on subjective factors, intangibles such as how he felt about the candidate as a person. For that reason, it was all the more important that I meet with the serious contenders and get to know them on a personal level. Well before any Supreme Court vacancies occurred during the Bush administration, I met privately with Samuel Alito and Emilio Garza in my West Wing office. I met with Michael Luttig at his home in northern Virginia. I spent an hour with John Roberts in April 2005 at my office at the Department of Justice.

Beginning as far back as the presidential transition, lawyers in the counsel's office and the Department of Justice developed a list of potential nominees. We compiled thick notebooks filled with information about each of the potential nominees. The notebooks included the nominee's biography, court opinions, speeches, books, articles, or other writings, and any other pertinent information. Knowing the importance of a president's Supreme Court nominees, we kept a running list of potential justices. Our search was not limited to current or former judges; we also looked at university and law school professors and scholars, current and past members of Congress, sitting or former government officials, and community and legal leaders from around the country. We initially considered more than three hundred individuals, and then narrowed our list to one hundred, then to fifty, and then did extensive research and write-ups on approximately twenty potential nominees that we had ready for consideration by the president at any given moment. The president had made it clear to all of us that he wanted to be well informed and ready when openings on the court occurred. He was adamant that he did not wish to make the same mistake his father had made in nominating someone like Justice David Souter, who was assumed to be conservative, yet often leaned more liberal in his decisions once on the court.

During the last year of President Bush's first term, as chances of a court vacancy increased, the president agreed that a small group of individuals would make final recommendations to him in the event of a vacancy. This unofficial, unnamed committee began meeting to discuss potential nominees. The group included Dick Cheney, John Ashcroft, Karl Rove, Andy Card, and me.

Cheney was not bashful about letting his opinions be known regarding the possible selections. He wanted the bluest of blue conservatives possible. He recognized that might engender a fight with liberals. "I'm telling you right now," he said, "we'll come up with a list of conservatives, and if the first one gets knocked down, we'll move on to the next." I suspected Ashcroft was in the same camp. Andy, Karl, and I all favored conservative jurists, but were realistic in terms of how far the president could move the court to the right.

Prior to the end of President Bush's first term, he and I engaged in candid conversations about my future. While I was honored that my name had ever been mentioned as a possible Supreme Court justice, I expressed my concerns that due to my roles in the detainee interrogations, the terrorist surveillance programs, and other controversial decisions, I would be too heavy a lift when it came to confirmation. Moreover, I worried about how conservative groups might view my positions on affirmative action based on the Michigan cases, and abortion based on my votes while serving on the Texas Supreme Court regarding the parental notification cases. No doubt, Karl Rove and others expressed those same concerns to the president. As White House counsel, I would have done the same about a candidate with my history.

———

It was obvious that President Bush was going to run for a second term, so my wife suggested I resign and that we leave Washington at the completion of his first term. That would be a natural transition for the president and for us. That would also give me a chance to earn a little more money, before—if or when—the president might want me to go on the court.

Becky and our children and I would have been perfectly comfortable returning to Texas after serving out the first term, but the president requested that I stay aboard. "I have plans for you in the second term," he told me.

When John Ashcroft resigned as attorney general the day after the 2004 election, the president, who often used sports metaphors, said to me, "Get your uniform on; you're going in."

I mentioned the president's comment to Becky. My wife still had reservations about my staying on in the Bush administration. Becky was anxious for us to get back to Texas and for me to continue my law practice. She realized that our boys were growing up fast, approaching college age, and we needed to earn some money. Contrary to popular opinion, most people serving in high-profile positions in government do not get rich while in office. Although government service pays well compared to many other jobs, the cost of living in Washington evens the playing field. We had been living frugally since serving in Texas, and Becky had done a great job of pinching pennies. But with college for our boys on the horizon, she knew our budget was stretched beyond our means.

Becky was also sensitive to the fact that because of my intense work schedule, our boys were growing up with an absentee dad who was living in the same house. We simply were unable to do many of the enjoyable father-son activities because I was away from home so much, and even though I tried desperately to be a good dad, it's tough when you see your kids only a few minutes every day or a few hours on the weekends.

Yet Becky had mixed feelings because of her deep affection and respect for the president—and he had personally asked me to stay. So instead of my declining to serve, Becky resigned herself to four more years in Washington.

We could not have imagined the firestorm we were about to encounter. Nominated November 10, 2004, as the attorney general, the confirmation hearings in January 2005 were intense, with numerous sensitive questions. I had spent weeks in preparation, including several mock hearings, and it had been time well spent. Senator Orrin Hatch, with whom I had worked closely on a number of judicial nominations, was particularly helpful during my confirmation process before the Judiciary Committee, as was the committee chairman, Senator Arlen Specter. Although the grilling was tough, I did not receive a single unanticipated question. Nevertheless, I was exhausted and relieved when the process was completed and I was confirmed.

I began serving as the eightieth attorney general of the United States on February 3, 2005, guiding a department composed of about 105,000 smart, dedicated employees. I was determined not only to continue waging the war on terror but to address other important issues that touched our nation, including organized crime, narcotics, human trafficking, border enforcement, mass-marketing scams and corporate fraud, political corruption, and one of the most pernicious plagues ever perpetrated: the abuse of children through child pornography. My heart ripped apart when I discovered the horrendous abuses imposed on innocent, defenseless children, and I vowed to do everything within my power to work with state and local officials to stem the tide of perversion and prosecute the vicious and vile perpetrators of these crimes.

Becky and I knew we had entered a sobering new realm when the FBI approached us and offered to fit our boys with large, bulky watches containing GPS wristbands in case they were abducted. The GPS could not be removed by anyone but us or the FBI and would help agents locate our boys in an emergency. While that sounded like a good idea, we turned down the watches because Becky feared if our boys were kidnapped, the bad guys would not think twice about severing their arms to remove the tracking devices.

My new normal involved tracking down terrorists through the FBI, meetings with world leaders, and helping with their concerns in preventing future terrorist attacks. But I also sought to establish important priorities at the Justice Department for the protection of children from sexual predators, the extradition and prosecution of drug kingpins, and the prosecution of corrupt public officials.

From the beginning of my term as attorney general, criticisms surfaced that I could not be objective as the nation's top law officer because of my close relationship with President Bush. The fact that I felt like a friend to the president was a double-edged sword. I had access to the president, and my relationship with him gave me clout with other cabinet members. On the other hand, our friendship raised questions about whether I would ever challenge the president if I thought he, or someone in his administration, was doing something unlawful.

This was another illustration of the ridiculous double standard that exists in Washington political circles. For instance, these same critics conveniently ignored the fact that President John F. Kennedy chose his own brother, Robert F. Kennedy, as attorney general. Moreover, in recent years,

President Obama tapped his good friend Eric Holder to lead the Justice Department. One of New York's senators, Democrat Chuck Schumer, pushed for and succeeded in getting his own staffer, Preet Bharara, confirmed as the US attorney in New York—the same office that would direct any investigation of wrongdoing in Manhattan by Senator Schumer or his staff. This was the same Chuck Schumer who called to tell me that he would not vote for me in the Judiciary Committee because he viewed me as too close to the president. In my opinion, having an attorney general who understood and shared the concerns of the president was a plus, rather than a negative.

Although we had made many controversial decisions during President Bush's first term, including a few that were overturned by the Supreme Court,[1] the only major investigation involving the White House during my tenure was over the phantom leak that precipitated the outing of CIA undercover agent Valerie Plame. Her husband, Joe Wilson, had traveled to Niger, ostensibly to confirm information that Iraq had tried to acquire uranium from Niger. Wilson had claimed that he was sent to Africa at the request of Vice President Cheney's office, and later vociferously criticized President Bush's discredited assertion that Iraq had attempted to procure weapons-grade uranium. When Wilson's wife's identity as an undercover CIA operative was disclosed—in violation of federal law—and then noted in a newspaper column by Bob Novak, Wilson claimed the disclosure was because of his opposition to Bush. That was ridiculous and proved to be false.

Nevertheless, Plame's identity had been compromised, instigating an enormously expensive and time-consuming investigation of the White House led by special counsel Patrick Fitzgerald. This ultimately led to the indictment of Scooter Libby, the vice president's chief of staff, not on charges of outing a CIA agent, but on charges of false statements and obstruction of justice.

For a short time early in the probe, the president, Andy Card, and I had serious concerns that Karl Rove was accidentally responsible for the leak because of conversations he'd had with Novak contemporaneous with Novak's article. As it turned out, he was not, but I urged certain members of the administration to hire attorneys to help them negotiate the investigation by Fitzgerald. Because this investigation involved potential criminal wrong-doing, as a government lawyer, I could not counsel or represent White House employees. For the same reason, neither could I represent the president. Although the president had done nothing wrong, I helped him identify and hire a personal lawyer. Before the engagement, I had clandestine meetings with the lawyer, in hopes of concealing from the media the fact that the president had hired outside legal representation. Because of my job in the White House, I was eventually called to testify as a witness in the grand jury proceedings as well.

Scooter Libby was convicted of the charges against him—but not of outing Plame. Indeed, it turned out that Colin Powell's deputy secretary of state, Rich Armitage, had unwittingly slipped the information about Valerie Plame to reporter Bob Novak, as well as to reporter Bob Woodward. What was puzzling and frustrating to Libby allies is that it was likely that Fitzgerald learned early in the investigation that Armitage was the culprit, yet he spent more than two years and a lot of taxpayer money in what even the *Washington Post* decried as "a lengthy and wasteful investigation."

By the time Scooter Libby's case went to trial, I had moved on to the attorney general's office, so I recused myself from the case, as John Ashcroft had done before me. I agreed with President Bush's decision to commute Scooter Libby's sentence so he wouldn't have to serve prison time. Nevertheless, it pained me to watch as a friend's career was destroyed. It was a lesson to which I should have paid more attention.

I wasn't at Justice long before a delicate matter set me at odds with the White House staff. John Yoo's legal opinions had guided many of the Bush administration's terrorism-related decisions immediately following 9/11. By the time I moved over to the Department of Justice, John had returned to teaching law at UC–Berkeley.

By 2005, in our constant effort to provide clarity on how we conduct the war on terror, the Office of Professional Responsibility (OPR) within the Justice Department—charged with evaluating whether DOJ lawyers satisfied professional and ethical standards—wanted to examine John's work on the early legal opinions. They were especially interested in Yoo's opinions regarding the interrogations of detainees and the Stellar Wind program, which had been initiated within a month of 9/11. I had no qualms, believing that John's opinions were thorough and could stand or fall on their own.

To study Stellar Wind, however, the OPR officials needed clearances to be read in to the program, and only the president could grant that permission. Shortly after I became attorney general, my chief of staff, Kyle Sampson, came to me and said, "OPR had to stop their investigation of John Yoo's opinions because they can't get read in to the program by the White House."

I thought that was a misstep at the White House for at least three reasons. First, I felt it was important that Americans were assured that the lawyers at the Department of Justice making important judgments about the war on terror, especially in those turbulent days following the attacks on our nation, were not operating arbitrarily but were consistent with professional standards. The OPR oversight helped provide that assurance.

Second, although I was confident of John's work, it had evoked strong disagreements. Jack Goldsmith and Pat Philbin had questioned some of John's opinions, for example. So if there was a problem with anything John had worked so hard to accomplish under extremely difficult circumstances due to the highly charged atmosphere following 9/11, we ought to address it. This was not to second-guess whether John's work was reasonable based upon the circumstances, nor was it necessary to agree with John's conclusions. It was simply to assure the quality of those early opinions met basic professional standards.

Third, I thought it was unwise and absolutely wrong to put the president in a position where it would appear he was blocking a Department of Justice investigation of officials in his own administration. There was no way his critics would let that alone.

I instructed Kyle Sampson to talk with the White House about these matters, but we couldn't get any movement. Finally, I asked to see the president personally. I met with him, along with the new chief of staff, Josh Bolten, and new White House counsel Harriet Miers, in the Oval Office, and laid out my reasons why he should consider reading Marshall Jarrett, head of

OPR, into the surveillance program so he could examine the Yoo legal opinions undergirding our actions.

The president listened carefully, but I could tell by his manner that he had already made up his mind, and his answer was going to be no. Perhaps he and Harriet had already come to that conclusion before I arrived; he didn't say. Nor did he refuse my request during the meeting.

Harriet called me later and said, "The president is not going to read Marshall Jarrett into the program."

I was disappointed and worried about the political fallout to the president—and to me—if his decision became public. Sure enough, in almost no time, the president's detractors picked up the issue. His critics in Congress sent me a letter questioning why the investigation had been blocked. Their letter carried a what-are-you-hiding tone and an implicit, second question: "Did the president block the investigation to protect you, Al Gonzales?"

Stories quickly circulated in the media suggesting the president had blocked an investigation to protect me in regard to my involvement with the surveillance program.[2] There was even some suggestion that I had *requested* the investigation be blocked. The news stories were totally upside down. I was the one who had *encouraged* the president to allow the investigation.

The stories soon morphed into the completely untrue "Al Gonzales is blocking the investigation!" I was getting clobbered in the press, accused of acting unethically and unprofessionally to protect myself or because of my friendship with the president. None of that was true.[3]

Perhaps motivated by the negative media attention, the president eventually reconsidered and allowed Marshall Jarrett to be read in to the program, and the investigation went forward. But by then the damage to me had been done.

Certainly, the president was within his right to refuse clearance into Stellar Wind. He may have possessed information to which I was not privy, and he was certainly right to be more concerned about damage to our national security than damage to my reputation. Nevertheless, his initial refusal hurt me publicly, the false stories impugned my professionalism, and cast further aspersions on my own ethics and morality.

John Yoo's opinions, signed by Jay Bybee of OLC, were examined thoroughly by OPR. That investigation concluded Yoo and Bybee committed intentional, professional misconduct. On review, by then associate deputy attorney general David Margolis, the DOJ declined to adopt OPR's findings of professional misconduct and concluded that Yoo and Bybee exercised poor judgment. From my perspective, they did a commendable job of examining very difficult issues and providing legal justifications for US actions in the war on terror under horribly stressful circumstances.

Nevertheless, the criticism over my role added to a developing narrative that questioned my integrity.

CHAPTER 31

SEARCHING FOR JUSTICE

I kept busy during my early months at DOJ, getting comfortable with the job and the people. Having served as White House counsel, I already knew many of the main players and many of the major issues with which we were dealing, so the transition was relatively easy, yet still time-consuming.

I continued to meet with the small group screening potential Supreme Court nominees. In the spring of 2005, our selection committee ramped up our work to be ready for a vacancy at the end of the Supreme Court term in June. Harriet Miers was now counsel to the president, so she joined Vice President Cheney, Andy Card, Karl Rove, and me in reviewing potential Supreme Court candidates. While we had to be prepared for any contingency, we primarily worked with an eye toward filling the seat of Chief Justice William Rehnquist, given his decling health.

In April, we informed the president that our top four choices for the chief's seat were Fourth Circuit judge Michael Luttig, Fourth Circuit judge J. Harvey Wilkerson, Second Circuit judge Samuel Alito, and DC Circuit judge John Roberts. President Bush instructed us to interview the four candidates and report back to him. All were marvelous, extremely competent candidates. I had talked with several of them privately over my four years in the White House, and I believed any of the four would perform admirably as chief justice.

Harriet and I took the lead in questioning the four candidates. In our interviews with potential justices, we did not ask about specific cases or how the individual might rule on a particular case, because if the person was later confirmed, he or she likely would have to recuse himself or herself if such a case ever came before the court. Furthermore, if we had asked those questions on the record, the Judiciary Committee could then explore those same issues. Instead, the questions stayed closer to how the nominee would interpret the Constitution, US laws and regulations, as well as whether they appreciated the value of restraint and of deferring, when appropriate, to the elected branches of government. Rather than the outcomes of cases, I was more interested in the process a potential nominee would use to reach a decision. In my judgment, this was much more indicative of how a future Supreme Court justice would discharge his or her duties on the court.

Second Circuit judge Sam Alito responded brilliantly during the interview process. He was several committee members' number one choice. His answers were crisp, precise, clear, and to the point. He had a wealth of experience, having been on the Court of Appeals for more than fifteen years, and there was no question about his conservative credentials. Oddly, Judge Alito had not done particularly well when I had met with him in the White House early in President Bush's first term. He had appeared nervous and a bit nerdy, but when we interviewed him at the vice president's residence, Judge Alito was stellar.

Fourth Circuit judge Mike Luttig was another favorite. Intelligent, articulate, and thoroughly conservative in his views and his legal opinions, Mike's only drawback was he was almost *too* conservative. I liked Mike and admired him, and his nomination would surely fire up the conservative base. I knew, however, that to nominate him would stir up a lot of liberal opposition. Based solely on my private conversations with the president, I questioned whether he wanted to take on the fight that a Luttig nomination would surely create.

A well-respected Southern gentleman, Fourth Circuit judge J. Harvie Wilkinson III had been on the bench a long time, had a lot of experience, and was a distinguished jurist. The downside was that he was older, had a long paper trail, and some of the things he had written were sure to be viewed by liberals as controversial and challenged.

DC Circuit judge John Roberts was young, but he was brilliant. He had been on our radar since 2003, and seemed to have a solid grasp of the Constitution combined with an impeccable, almost photographic memory of past legal cases. His relative lack of experience on the bench meant he had less of a paper trail to attack, and he had a charming, easygoing manner that masked a ferocious intellect.

Because we did not want the world to know who we were interviewing, we held the discussions at Vice President Cheney's residence at the Naval Observatory. Our selection group met with Judges Luttig and Roberts on May 3 and Judges Wilkerson and Alito on May 5. All four candidates were impressive. Following the interviews, members of the selection group had a much better appreciation for who they might recommend to the president in the event of a vacancy.

In early June, our selection committee met again, and Andy Card advised us that the president was unhappy with only four options. The president wanted some diversity on the final list. Our committee refocused our efforts to examine diverse candidates that included women, Hispanics, and African Americans. Believing that our committee was now looking for a replacement in the event of an O'Connor vacancy, on June 21, our committee quietly interviewed two female federal circuit court judges in a conference room in the basement of the West Wing. We did not reach a consensus on a candidate to recommend to President Bush, but I felt better prepared in the event of a vacancy.

We waited until July 1, when Harriet called to inform me we had news of a vacancy on the court—and it was not as we had expected. When I arrived at the Oval Office, I was met by President Bush and members of the selection committee, except for Andy Card, who joined us by phone.

Associate Justice Sandra Day O'Connor, the first woman ever to serve on the US Supreme Court, had announced her resignation. Appointed by President Reagan, Justice O'Connor had served for more than a quarter century. On the closely divided court, Justice O'Connor's vote often carried the day. She was widely viewed as a moderate conservative justice, although some conservative groups believed she was too liberal on social issues. I was an admirer of Justice O'Connor, and I had asked her to administer my ceremonial oath of office as attorney general. I thought it fitting that the first female Supreme Court justice should swear in the first Hispanic attorney general in US history.

Justice O'Connor's resignation came unexpectedly, but we were ready nonetheless. This was the opportunity we all—especially President Bush—had been anticipating, the chance to nominate another conservative to the US Supreme Court.

On the morning of the O'Connor announcement, our small selection group met with the president to discuss the selection process and the timing of the announcement of his nominee. At the conclusion of the meeting, the president asked me to stay behind, along with Vice President Cheney. For more than four years, there had been serious speculation about my appointment to the Supreme Court. Now there was a vacancy. That morning, however, the president told me, "I'm not going to put you on the court." He said that I was doing a great job as attorney general, and while he was confident I would do great work on the court, he wanted me to stay with his team. The news was bittersweet. Despite the obvious obstacles and strong headwinds from some conservative groups the president would have encountered by appointing me, I must admit I was still somewhat disappointed. I loved my job as attorney general, and I never would have lobbied for a position on the court. But I would have served had I been asked.

I told the president, "I owe you everything. You owe me nothing. I'm proud and grateful for the appointment as attorney general." I returned to the Department of Justice and began putting together the team that would prepare the nominee for a confirmation hearing.

While having dinner at a restaurant that evening, I said to Becky, "I have two important things to tell you."

Her interest was piqued. "Yes?"

"First, I won't be going to the Supreme Court." Although Becky shared some of my disappointment, she was relieved and immediately caught the unspoken part of my statement: we could leave Washington at the conclusion of my service. Supreme Court appointments are for life, so had the president nominated me and had I been confirmed, we'd have to continue living in Washington. The media was already reporting that I was a leading candidate. So another benefit of my conversation with the president was that I could concentrate on doing my job.

"And second, I'm going to Iraq." I was headed there to confer with my Iraqi counterpart, visit with wounded soldiers in the hospital, and meet with DOJ employees and thank them for helping draft Iraq's constitution and design a new legal system. For security reasons, I had limited the number of people who knew about the trip.

"When?"

"Tomorrow."

Although Becky was always anxious about my safety when I traveled, I think she was more comfortable with me going to a war zone than the Supreme Court.

In the first few weeks after the O'Connor announcement, our committee had even more serious discussions about possible nominees. The clear signals from Harriet and Andy were that President Bush wanted to fill the O'Connor vacancy with a diverse nominee. A majority of our committee, however, worried that this may be the president's only opportunity to nominate a strong conservative. I, too, urged the president to nominate the best candidate, irrespective of race or gender. Eventually the president decided to meet with the finalists identified by the selection committee.

During the afternoon of July 18, we had several discussions with and without the president regarding potential Supreme Court nominations. The president made it clear that he wanted someone who would lead the court and move the court to the right. I told the president he needed to go with his gut. Who did he feel most comfortable standing with and introducing as his nominee? He told me he had decided on John Roberts. He felt Roberts had the right personality. He had been told by Senate minority leader Harry Reed that there were red lights for Luttig and others, but Roberts seemed acceptable to the Democrats, whose votes would be necessary to confirm the new justice. Andy Card called me later to let me know that the offer had indeed been made to John Roberts and he had accepted the nomination.

On July 19, 2005, the president announced that he was nominating John Roberts to fill the O'Connor seat as the next justice of the US Supreme Court. A team of lawyers at the Justice Department immediately got busy helping to get Judge Roberts prepared for his hearing before the Senate Judiciary Committee. Then fate threw us a curve. On September 3, while the Roberts nomination was still pending, eighty-year-old Chief Justice William Rehnquist passed away after losing his battle against thyroid cancer. Suddenly, we had not one but two opportunities to influence the Supreme Court.

Following Rehnquist's death, Vice President Cheney suggested that Antonin Scalia be elevated to chief justice. The selection team knew that elevating Scalia would evoke a fight with the Judiciary Committee, and I understood that President Bush did not want to have a brutal battle over Supreme Court nominations. He depended on us to provide him with qualified, conservative nominees who could be confirmed without jeopardizing the president's legislative agenda.

I knew there would be a fight simply to get one conservative confirmed, so I asked why we would willingly ask for another battle with the Judiciary Committee when we could just as easily avoid it by selecting a new chief justice?

The vice president pushed hard at first, but eventually he got comfortable with the possibility of John Roberts as chief justice. Moreover, we had heard through various sources that Justice Scalia himself believed that John Roberts was the best advocate who had ever appeared before him on the Supreme Court. Wrong or not, we regarded that as a signal he was okay with John Roberts as chief justice.

Nevertheless, all options were on the table. In one meeting, President Bush asked me, "What do you think about Miguel Estrada as chief justice?"

"I don't think that is a good idea," I said. "It would be a historic pick, but you need someone who has some gravitas within the legal community and would immediately have the respect of the older members of the court.

Miguel is smart, but he is young. He does not have the influence you want. If you are serious about putting him on the court, you should elevate Scalia and then bring in Miguel behind him. But I can guarantee you that you will have two major fights if you do that."

The president decided that wasn't worth it.

On September 6, President Bush withdrew his nomination of John Roberts to replace Justice O'Connor, and instead nominated him to the Rehnquist seat as the new chief justice. Six days later, Roberts was seated in front of the Senate Judiciary Committee, and he negotiated the gauntlet with relative ease. He was confirmed by the full Senate as chief justice by a vote of 78 to 22.

Following the nomination and confirmation of Roberts to fill the Rehnquist vacancy, our selection committee found itself in the same position as we were on July 1, that of having to fill the O'Connor vacancy. Since the president had already nominated a white male to the court, it became obvious to me that President Bush intended to select a diverse nominee for this second seat—particularly because the person was to fill the O'Connor seat. Complicating the situation was the media buzz that I was a leading candidate for the vacant seat, as well as the very public opposition to me from some conservative groups.

The selection committee continued the consideration of various diverse candidates, but I and others on the committee believed the president should nominate the best candidate available. We had replaced one conservative for another in the chief's seat, but the O'Connor seat represented an opportunity to move the court to the right. To that end, I thought Judge Alito and Luttig were the best options.

I arrived at the White House for our committee meeting in late September, along with Vice President Cheney, Andy Card, Karl Rove, and, I assumed, Harriet Miers to discuss names for the O'Connor seat. But Harriet was not at the meeting; instead, her deputy was there in her place.

I was puzzled, but as he reported on Harriet's record as a lawyer and expressed his views on Harriet's political philosophy, I realized she was absent because the president wanted us to consider her as a potential nominee.

I thought, *What? What has happened?*

I couldn't help but feel blindsided that the president might want to nominate Harriet Miers to the Supreme Court, but not because she wasn't qualified. She clearly was by virtue of her training and legal experience. But for nearly five years, more than a dozen highly intelligent and politically savvy lawyers and I had been involved in the study and vetting of potential Supreme Court nominees, examining the legal careers and the opinions and beliefs of hundreds of people as possible nominees. Harriet's name had never appeared on our lists. In fact, if the president thought so highly of her as a potential justice, I have to admit I was a little embarrassed that her name hadn't appeared on any of our lists.

While everyone in the White House and the Justice Department admired Harriet as a smart lawyer and a devout Christian, and her conservative credentials were beyond question, she had no judicial experience and little academic scholarship beyond her time at Southern Methodist University law school. I worried that her background would not be a plus when trying to sell Harriet to the Washington Federalist Society elite. Granted, because of her legal experience, her service as Texas State Bar president, her past leadership within the American Bar Association, and her many professional accolades, she would probably be rated qualified for the position by the ABA, but was she the president's best available nominee? I worried how she would be viewed by the conservative base.

Immediately after the White House meeting, I met privately with Andy Card. "Andy, what's going on here? What happened?"

"The president is seriously considering Harriet," Andy replied.

I understood that I was not entitled to know this information, but it bothered me that I was not even told about this new direction, even though I had led the work to develop the short list of potential nominees for the president from as far back as the transition in 2000. Some people later suggested that the reason I was not told may have been because my name was still on the president's short list. Perhaps so, but given the extraordinary efforts to identify diverse options for President Bush, by this time, I had concluded that I had no shot at a nomination.

Regardless, I expressed my surprise and a bit of frustration to Andy that as much as we all loved Harriet, if the president nominated her, we would not be going with our strongest choice. "She's good," I said, "but this may be the president's last chance to put somebody on the court. He should go with the strongest candidate who can be confirmed."

Andy didn't disagree, but he didn't agree either. Apparently Andy had always been open to the idea of nominating Harriet, and Karl was definitely a fan of Harriet's, as were Dan Bartlett and Ed Gillespie—all of whom apparently had told President Bush that Harriet would be a sound political choice.[1]

Because of our friendship and the outside speculation about my potential nomination, this was a delicate spot for Andy. He suggested, "You should talk to the president directly if you believe he is making a mistake on this."

I knew Andy was right, but I was reluctant to talk with the president about the matter. It would be terribly awkward. Anything I said now would be viewed as an attempt to protect my own shot at the court by hurting my friend Harriet, the person I understood had recommended me as general counsel to Governor Bush after he was first elected as governor of Texas.

Even more than the nomination itself—which was worrisome enough—I was concerned that the president was bucking his own allegiance to process. President Bush was at his best when he relied on a process for making decisions. That allowed him to be consistent in his actions, reduced the possibility of arbitrary choices, and shielded him from accusations that his decisions were based solely on politics. Relying on a process worked well for him, especially when he faced controversial or gut-wrenching decisions such as executions. As long as he relied on his established processes, he normally arrived at an outcome in which he felt he had made the right decision.

We had a good, disciplined process in place to analyze and evaluate potential Supreme Court justices and to help the president avoid putting another Souter on the court. That process had provided four quality finalists and the ultimate selection of John Roberts. But now President Bush was deviating from the process. There was no interview of Harriet by our committee and no evaluation of her speeches or writings by the selection committee, only an accelerated vetting by her deputy. I worried about the outcome and reaction, but how could I tell the president that? Harriet was our good friend and I respected her.

I went back to the Department of Justice and informed my senior staff about what was going on over at the White House. "I think the president is going to nominate Harriet." All of them were surprised, and some were deeply disappointed. Rachel Brand, the assistant attorney general who had helped prepare and shepherd John Roberts's nomination, was incredulous. Rachel, like several of the people on my staff at DOJ, had come over with me from the White House counsel's office, and she had been involved in the selection process for several years. She was proud of the list of excellent potential nominees we had assembled, and she was equally well aware that Harriet had never been on any of our lists.[2]

My chief of staff agreed with Rachel. Kyle Sampson believed he had a good pulse on how conservative leaders would react, and he urged me to intervene with the president. "You owe it to the president to discourage him from making this pick," Kyle said. "Give him your best advice, and let him know that if Harriet hasn't shown up on any lists in the past four years, that says something."

I wrestled over what I should do. Finally, I decided I couldn't worry about what others thought. I was morally obligated to give my best advice to the president.

On September 29, I went back to the White House to present my concerns to President Bush. It was one of the most uncomfortable meetings I'd ever had with him. We sat down in his office, and he began by telling me that he was looking at Mike Luttig, Sam Alito, Priscilla Owen, Harriet, and me. I told him that I was not there to talk about me, that I did not want to be considered. I felt I needed to say that to establish credibility about the advice I was about to give him. As awkward as it was, I gently but as clearly as possible attempted to candidly lay out all the reasons why Mike Luttig or Sam Alito would be a wiser choice than anyone else he had mentioned, including our friend Harriet.

I told him that a Luttig or Alito pick would be a brave and bold choice.

I reminded him that he told the cabinet to play "big ball," not little ball, and a Luttig or Alito nomination would be the big choice. He said there were other considerations, and then he asked, "So you are in the camp that believes we should go with the best athlete?"

"Yes," I responded.

We spoke for about half an hour, and he never once mentioned me going on the court. To the contrary, we talked about my future plans for the DOJ, which told me that I was not a real candidate for the court. I knew the president, and early in the conversation, I sensed that he had already made up his mind.

So I said in conclusion "If you nominate Harriet, I will support her and I will go out and fight for her confirmation," I said. "But my job is to tell you what I think."

President Bush thanked me, but I could tell what he was going to do. He was going to nominate Harriet. I didn't argue with him, because he was the one elected to make these decisions, and he undoubtedly had other factors to consider. In my mind, Harriet was qualified to serve on the court, but I disagreed that she was the president's strongest choice, and a nominee who could best cement the president's legacy.

I went back to my staff at the DOJ and told them, "Okay, I told him. But I think it is a done deal. I think he is going to nominate Harriet."

Sure enough, four days later, on October 3, President Bush nominated Harriet Miers to fill the O'Connor seat on the US Supreme Court. At the announcement, President Bush said, "I've known Harriet for more than a decade. I know her heart. I know her character."[3] The media did not seem to care about Harriet's heart, only her lack of experience. Some reporters and political pundits openly derided Bush's decision. Since Harriet's position prior to becoming White House counsel had been White House staff secretary—an important but little known role—many people were confused about her responsibilities.

"Bush nominated his *secretary* to the Supreme Court?" was typical of the derisive nature of the comments. While not unexpected, the remarks about the president and Harriet angered me.

Karl and others in the White House were convinced that conservatives would trust the president's judgment and rally around Harriet Miers. Many didn't. Even conservative members of the media such as Charles Krauthammer and George Will opposed Harriet's nomination.[4] Harriet was unknown in most conservative legal circles, so I wasn't surprised that they didn't support her.

In hindsight, the nomination of Harriet Miers should not have come as a surprise to me. The decision was vintage Bush. He really wanted to put another woman on the Supreme Court. Harriet had been his personal lawyer; she was a close friend, and she had been loyal to the president. More important, even though she had no judicial record, the president believed (and so did I) she was capable of doing the job by virture of her education, training, and experience. He now wanted to honor her, much as he had honored me when he had appointed me attorney general, or Condi as secretary of state, and Margaret Spellings as education secretary. I should, however, have been more aggressive in pointing out to the president the challenges represented by a Miers nomination, and why Harriet's nomination was likely to run into strong headwinds—but I wasn't. I was so concerned about appearing self-serving or self-aggrandizing, I failed to do my job. That was a mistake.

I failed to appreciate the difficult challenges created by the nomination of a former or current White House counsel. The US Senate would want to see Harriet's internal memos, as well as sensitive documents she had reviewed. They would be interested in knowing her legal advice to the president. Such a nomination sets the White House on a collision course with the Senate over access to documents the president would want to protect as privileged.

I also truly worried whether the Washington legal elite would support a Texan and a Southern Methodist University graduate, rather than an alumnus with an Ivy League background. Additionally, because Harriet was not a constitutional scholar, she would need extra time to prepare for a tough confirmation hearing, time that she did not have because of her many significant duties as White House counsel. Her confirmation hearing was already scheduled for November 7.

Indeed, as Harriet worked to prepare for what was sure to be a grilling by the Senate, she came over to DOJ for hours. Our lawyers ran her through a refresher on the Constitution, a tutorial on important constitutional cases and discussions about the role of the courts in our system of government, then loaded her with heavy binders filled with material she needed to know. Harriet's own diligence and conscientiousness worked against her. She attempted to study this massive amount of material while still going into work as counsel every day, then studying at night. The material is simply too difficult to attempt to master on a part-time basis.

Besides all the other challenges, Harriet had the misfortune of following John Roberts, whose abilities were outstanding and whose performance at his confirmation hearing had been remarkable. She couldn't simply be good; she had to be great.

Finally, as we neared the scheduled confirmation hearings, my staff members who had been working with Harriet came to me, and one of them said, "She is not going to be ready enough."

"She has to be ready."

"She will not be."

I did not want my friend Harriet to be embarrassed. Nor did I want one of President Bush's nominees to be rejected by the Senate. I also worried that Democrats would use Harriet's nomination to demand access to sensitive documents involving high-level discussions—perhaps even presidential communications—on matters such as detainee interrogations and surveillance.

I went to Andy Card and told him honestly, "Andy, my team tells me Harriet is not going to be ready, and I am worried about the demand for internal documents we are likely to get from the Senate. Harriet needs to quit as White House counsel and commit all of her time to getting prepared, and we need to develop a response to the requests for documents."

On October 27, 2005, Harriet withdrew her name from the nominating process and continued her job as White House counsel. Four days after Harriet withdrew her nomination, President Bush nominated Judge Sam Alito, whose impeccable credentials and formidable intellect stymied even the staunchest Democrat's opposition, including that of the first-term senator from Illinois, Barack Obama. On January 31, 2006, Judge Alito was confirmed in the Senate, becoming—along with John Roberts—part of President Bush's greatest contribution to America.

In the end, the president placed two excellent jurists on the Supreme Court. Nevertheless, I felt some responsibility for the failed Miers nomination. It is never a good thing for a president when a Supreme Court nominee withdraws or fails to receive confirmation. But in light of George and Laura Bush's friendship with Harriet, and the president's loyalty and commitment to diversity, there was probably little that I—or anyone else—could have done to avoid what happened.

Was I ever a serious contender to go on the court? Probably not. Too many conservatives would have opposed me because of my votes in the Texas parental notification cases and how they perceived my role in the Michigan affirmative action cases. Liberals would doubtless have opposed me because of what they believed my role had been in controversial terrorism policies such as surveillance, interrogations, and Guantanamo Bay. I had no real loyal base of support other than the president. Had I been advising the president about a potential nominee with my history, I probably would have cautioned against my nominations, as I did Harriet's, especially if there was a strong alternative.

During my years working with President Bush, I questioned his decisions only a few times. The nomination of our dear friend Harriet Miers was one of them. It would not be the last.

CHAPTER 32

MONEY IN THE FREEZER

When Democratic congressman William Jefferson, Louisiana's first African American representative since the Civil War, was suspected of demanding payments to help businesses receive contracts in Africa, I knew it would be a volatile case. But I could not have imagined how the corrupt congressman's actions would influence so many lives, including my own.

In March 2005, the US attorney's office in the Eastern District of Virginia began investigating Jefferson for taking bribes in exchange for his influence in various overseas business ventures. The investigation was led by US attorney Paul McNulty. Jefferson was seen on videotape accepting $100,000 in cash at the Ritz-Carlton Hotel in Arlington, Virginia, just across the Potomac River from the Capitol. The money ostensibly came from a businessman purported to be interested in landing lucrative contracts in Africa, but was actually delivered by an FBI informant.[1] When investigators searched Jefferson's home in August 2005, they found $90,000 of the original $100,000 cash stashed in the congressman's freezer.

Two of Jefferson's cohorts, one a Kentucky businessman and the other a former Jefferson aide, pled guilty, but the eight-term congressman denied any wrongdoing and vowed to remain in office to battle the investigation. The case dragged on into May 2006, when my staff brought the matter to me. In the meantime, the greater New Orleans area—represented by Jefferson—was decimated by Hurricane Katrina. That exacerbated the situation even further, since it appeared we were now pursuing a beleaguered representative whose home state had already taken a huge hit. Of course, the investigation against Jefferson had begun long before the levees at Lake Pontchartrain gave way. But that made no difference to many people. Jefferson was reelected in the middle of the investigation.

Our case against Jefferson was strong, the investigators explained, but it seemed the congressman was willing to do almost anything to stall the investigation and discredit the prosecution. Consequently, Paul McNulty, who had been sworn in as deputy attorney general two months earlier, and the prosecution team wanted to build an ironclad case against Congressman Jefferson.

They told me that they believed Jefferson was concealing important evidence relevant to their case in his congressional office in the Rayburn House Office Building on Capitol Hill. Specifically, the investigators hoped to obtain notes, telephone records, faxes, ledgers, computer files, and other communications showing Jefferson's suspicious overseas travel and meetings. The prosecutors wanted to conduct a search of Congressman Jefferson's office.

The planned raid would be the first time FBI agents had ever searched a sitting lawmaker's Capitol Hill office. McNulty and other members of my DOJ staff wanted to make sure that I was comfortable with their intended course of actions.

I was not.

Surprising as it might seem to some people, the US attorney general is not usually involved in decisions regarding the execution of search warrants by a US attorney's office. But an FBI raid on Jefferson's office would be no ordinary search.

I questioned the prosecutors, "Why do we do we need to do this? After all, we have Jefferson on tape accepting a bribe. We found the $90,000 in his freezer. And two individuals have already pled guilty in connection with the bribery scheme."

The prosecutors responded that they liked their chances of a prosecution with the evidence they already had, but the case would be even stronger if they could get the information they believed was located in Jefferson's office.

"Have you exhausted all other means? Is there any other way to get this information?" I asked.

"Jefferson is unwilling to cooperate," the investigators told me. "And the House of Representatives counsel has also refused to assist in the investigation. They say the documents belong to Jefferson so the House has no authority to provide access."

"What about working out some sort of accommodation with the House?" I asked, still not convinced a raid was our best option.

"We've tried that as well, to no avail. Besides, any agreement would still require the approval of Congressman Jefferson because the documents belong to him, not the House."

"Will this search be lawful?" I asked, voicing the question that all of us knew we'd have to address sooner or later if we went through with the raid. Just because the FBI does it doesn't necessarily mean it will stand up in court as a lawful raid. In fact, our Constitution provides that members of Congress must have great freedom to study and discuss issues pertaining to our country and in the legislative process; that "speech and debate" is considered privileged material.[2] The Constitution safeguards the communications and written materials that members of Congress produce or use while fulfilling their duties.

Even if the search were successful in procuring the desired items from Jefferson's office, I worried that the investigators might view other materials concerning the congressman's duties that would come under the protections of the speech and debate clause. When I voiced my concern to Steve Bradbury, the acting head of the Office of Legal Counsel (OLC), he reminded me the Supreme Court had ruled that the speech and debate clause covered activities such as voting, committee hearings, and reports, but did not protect members of Congress when they were engaged in nonlegislative activities.

I remained uncertain. A wily congressman could tie virtually anything to some legislative activity. How would we ensure that the prosecution team searching Jefferson's office would not peruse privileged materials, whether intentionally or accidentally?

The answer the department developed included a set of special search procedures, designed specifically for the raid on Jefferson's office. We decided to take along a "filter team," consisting of two Department of Justice attorneys who were not involved in the prosecution work and one FBI agent who had no role in the investigation. These objective observers would accompany the team of FBI agents who would conduct the search.

The filter team would examine the documents seized and would return any irrelevant items immediately to Congressman Jefferson. For any potentially privileged documents, the filter team could provide a log and copies of the documents to Jefferson within twenty days of the search. The filter team would submit any questionable documents to a judge for determination of privilege. I felt more comfortable with the search if it could be conducted with these safeguards. At least if we were challenged—as we quite likely would be—we could credibly say that we had made a valiant attempt to protect congressional privilege while conducting an important investigation.

I really did not believe that the framers of our Constitution intended that an uncooperative member of Congress should be above the law and immune from searches. Nor did I believe that Capitol Hill should be a safe haven to hide potential evidence of wrongdoing. But when I inquired further, I could find no precedent for searching the Capitol Hill office of a sitting member of Congress. I found precedents for searching a lawmaker's home or car. I assumed that many members had offices in their homes where they might have files or documents pertaining to their work, and those were subject to search. Even a judge's chambers were subject to search. Why should members of Congress be any different?

Nevertheless, I wondered how Speaker of the House Dennis Hastert might react to a search of a congressman's office, irrespective of the legality. The Speaker was a proud man. Would he regard such a raid as an assault on his institution? I understood that. When I had served as White House counsel, I had fought fiercely to protect the institution of the presidency. For instance, I had worked carefully with the 9/11 Commission to help them get information they needed while not encroaching upon the president's constitutional prerogatives.

I didn't know Speaker Hastert well. We'd met, of course, and had been together on numerous occasions when the president was signing a bill, but the Speaker and I were not close friends. He was, however, a Republican Speaker of the House who owned the good graces of the president, and although he was probably not a fan of Jefferson's, a Democrat, I had little doubt that if Hastert felt his territory was being encroached upon, he'd push back and likely cry foul to the White House.

My gut instincts told me that it would be wise to give the House leaders and the White House a heads-up—letting them know in advance that the raid was going to happen. But how could we do that without jeopardizing the investigation? The Justice Department did not clear investigations with the White House, much less Congress. This was Washington, after all, where self-interest often resulted in leaks of sensitive information.

The safe decision would have been to override McNulty and his team and tell them to either get the information some other way, or go to court with the solid evidence they already had in hand. On the other hand, the experience of Paul McNulty and his prosecution team, coupled with OLC's Steve Bradbury's view that the search was legal, weighed heavily toward my taking the risk.

If I second-guessed the judgment of my own deputy attorney general and the director of the FBI, and discounted the opinion of the OLC, some people at the Justice Department would wonder if I was simply appeasing President Bush. They would see me as not wanting to buck Speaker Hastert, because the president needed him to carry the water for his legislative agenda in the House of Representatives. The question of my allegiance to the law or to Bush had popped up during my confirmation hearings as attorney general: Because of my friendship with the president, could I be objective about investigating any potential wrongdoing, especially if it touched upon White House or Republican interests? Now, if I nixed the Jefferson search, would I be branded as another political tool?

I stood at the desk in my office overlooking the Washington Monument as I wrestled with the decision. Armed with the OLC advice that the search would be constitutional, and the collective judgment of senior DOJ prosecutors and the FBI that the search was necessary, I approved the search despite my concerns, because one of the top priorities for the Justice Department was prosecuting public corruption. The prosecutors approached a DC federal judge, Thomas Hogan, and obtained a search warrant based on probable cause that evidence of a crime existed in Congressman Jefferson's Capitol Hill office. To minimize publicity about the search—to the extent that it's possible to downplay a number of FBI agents hauling boxes out of a Capitol Hill office—I agreed with the FBI that it should occur during a weekend, when House offices were closed.

———

On Wednesday, May 17, 2006, I departed on board an FBI G5 Learjet from Andrews Air Force Base, traveling to Dallas for a round of meetings with the Mexican attorney general, Daniel Cabeza de Vaca, and John Walters, US director of the Office of National Drug Control Policy. When I boarded the plane later that night, we flew to Houston, my hometown, where the next day, I gave a speech to the Houston Forum, a well-respected community group; I then met with the *Houston Chronicle* editorial board, and participated in a roundtable discussion regarding hot-button immigration issues. Later that evening, I got a chance to fulfill a dream: throwing out the first pitch at a Houston Astros baseball game.

All the while, back in Washington, FBI investigators readied themselves for the raid on Congressman Jefferson's office. As I was recognized by Leadership Houston at a black-tie dinner on Saturday evening, May 20, the FBI search party entered the office, not allowing anyone else in the area while they were inside. Just before the raid commenced, investigators notified the White House, the House of Representatives, and Jefferson's lawyers, to avoid them first hearing about it on the news, but we did not allow anyone else to be present while the FBI scoured the office. The search concluded eighteen hours later, early Sunday afternoon, and the investigators left with a cache of documents.

Explosive repercussions ensued almost immediately—and not merely from Jefferson or his lawyers. On Sunday, May 21, I left Houston at 2:00 p.m., heading back to Washington. During the flight, one of my staff members informed me that White House chief of staff Josh Bolten wanted to discuss the Jefferson search. Josh had replaced Andy Card when Andy left the administration in 2006, the longest-serving presidential chief of staff in fifty years.

It had been a busy weekend and I was tired. Besides, I had not yet received all the details of the raid and the materials seized, so I had little new information. "Ask him if it can wait till I get back to Washington," I responded. The staffer dutifully passed along my question and quickly returned.

"It can't."

When I took the call in the plane, I quickly realized why. It was not merely Josh on the phone; also on the call were White House counsel Harriet Miers; David Addington, counsel to the vice president; and Joel Kaplan, Josh's deputy.

Harriet began by telling me they had concerns about the search. David was more direct. "It is a clear error," he said, "a mistake you must correct."

David and I had worked together through many difficult situations. We were colleagues and friends. So I was somewhat taken aback by his brusque tone, which sounded almost patronizing to me. I was instantly irritated by his challenge. I disagreed with him and I told him so. "This is a unique case with unique circumstances," I continued. "It's important that this case move forward." I briefly sketched out the reasons. I concluded by questioning why we would give members of Congress special treatment not afforded to judges, state legislators, or ordinary citizens.

Addington remained skeptical. "I've spoken to McNulty, and he was unable to confirm whether Jefferson was about to destroy evidence," David said. "So where's the urgency?"

Josh interrupted to say that the president wanted to discuss the matter of the search at 7:45 a.m. the following day.

"Of course; fine. I'll be there," I replied.

As the call concluded, David Addington asked rhetorically, "Does the seizure of the documents, by itself, violate the speech and debate privilege?" Apparently David believed it did. I did not.

David is a brilliant lawyer and the type of person you want on your side in any legal fight. During the six years I had been in Washington, I had witnessed him taking on other outstanding lawyers many times, but this was the first time he had ever directly challenged me in front of others.

After being picked up by my FBI security detail—protection afforded every attorney general—and taken home, I greeted Becky and the boys before directing a conference call that included Kyle Sampson, Paul McNulty, Steve Bradbury, and McNulty's chief of staff, Mike Elston. Paul had already spoken with Dennis Hastert's chief of staff, Scott Palmer, and, apparently it had not been a friendly conversation. The Speaker felt blindsided by the search and wanted to know why they had not received advance notice. As I had suspected, the Speaker's concerns were over the institutional interests of the House, not any particular fondness for Congressman Jefferson.

During the conference call, Steve assured me that we were "right on the law." I certainly hoped so, because we now knew that not only Jefferson would contest the search, but the Speaker of the House was upset by it, and so was the White House—that catchall, ambiguous, amorphous term used to describe a consensus that might include everyone from the president to the senior staff.

From my call during the flight home, I knew that at least some officials in the White House believed the documents seized in the search should be returned immediately, so I raised that possibility during the conversation with my team. To a person, they opposed returning the documents. They suggested at least four good reasons why we should *not* return the seized items.

First, these were documents in an ongoing criminal investigation. To return the documents could jeopardize the prosecution of a crime. Second, returning the documents could create a chain of custody challenge over the authenticity of the documents—who had the rights to what? Third, conceding that the speech and debate privilege applied in this case, and to completely cut off any search would certainly inhibit future congressional investigations, and might even make it impossible to search Congress members' homes or vehicles. Finally, my team was convinced that if we returned the documents, we would not get them back—at least not intact. We'd been unable to enforce a grand jury subpoena because the House counsel was unwilling to cooperate. And if we returned the documents to Jefferson, we'd probably never see them again.

We all understood the risks that comity could break down between the executive branch of government and the legislative branch. Congressional leaders would be outraged—not because they believed Jefferson was innocent, but because they regarded the incursion into his House of Representative's office as a violation of speech and debate privilege, and therefore of congressional privilege.

At the conclusion of the conference call, I asked Steve Bradbury to call Harriet Miers to inform her of OLC's views. I believed it was important that Harriet hear other expert legal voices on the matter in addition to David Addington's.

The next morning, I met with President Bush in the Situation Room, along with Josh, Joel, Harriet, David, and Candi Wolff, the assistant to the president for Legislative Affairs. Participating by means of the secure video conferencing feature in the Situation Room was Vice President Cheney.

I explained the reasons for the search and the special circumstances surrounding it. I also informed the president of the Department of Justice's position on the legality of the search, but I emphasized that the decision to act was mine and that I was responsible.

President Bush listened intently. On the conference screen, the vice president suggested that we not be so definitive on this question. The legal issues, he said, were not that clear, so why shouldn't the legislature have the opportunity to decide whether privilege applied? "Why should the executive branch answer this question?" he asked.

I reminded Vice President Cheney that the question would not be answered solely by the executive branch. After all, a federal judge had issued the search warrant, so a federal judge would be involved in verifying whether the search was constitutional.

The vice president seemed undeterred. "The White House often asserts privilege," he said. He expressed concern about how the DOJ's search of a congressional office might impact the White House's assertions of privilege in the future. On that point, he was probably correct.

As I listened to him, I thought, *Addington has certainly armed the vice president well—as a good lawyer should for his client.*

After listening to the discussion, the president weighed in. "I don't want the attorney general to be undercut," he stated. He then turned to me and said, "Talk to Speaker Hastert this morning, before I see him later."

"Yes, sir." The president's response had not been one of rousing support, but at least he had not ordered me to return Jefferson's documents. I considered that a win.

Following the meeting, I traveled to Allentown, Pennsylvania, to participate in an anti-gang event. I also met with Hispanic leaders and spoke to a group of high school students. It was a busy day, but I repeatedly placed calls to Speaker Hastert's office at every opportunity. Each call was rebuffed. "He's busy," I was told. After a number of calls, his staff informed me, "The Speaker will call you later today."

He never called.

The raid of Jefferson's office had made the news by now, so later that afternoon, while still in Allentown, I made my first public comments about the search. "The Department of Justice took a unique step in response to a unique set of circumstances," I said.

By the end of the day, the story had escalated in the media, prompting harsh comments from House members. Hastert had still not returned my calls.

I returned to Washington, and later than evening, I received a call from Harriet at my home, warning me that the situation seemed to be spiraling out of control. The House leadership was furious and the president wanted this matter resolved—now. We talked it over, and although it was already past 9:00 p.m., I agreed to immediately send a team from DOJ up to the Hill to work with members and their staffs pursuant to the president's instructions. Harriet scheduled a meeting for 10:00 p.m.

She advised me not to include Paul McNulty in the group because the White House viewed Paul as too close to the decision to proceed with the search, since the case had originated when he was a US attorney. I was disappointed with that perception, but I sent Alice Fisher, the head of the DOJ Criminal Division, instead. Along with Alice was Will Moschella, our legislative director, and Steve Bradbury from OLC.

Prior to the meeting on the Hill, I convened another conference call with my team. We agreed to offer two accommodations to the House that could easily resolve the dilemma. First, the documents would be returned to Jefferson on the condition that the House agreed it would immediately honor the DOJ subpoena for the documents. This would, of course, require Jefferson's cooperation. He was unlikely to acquiesce, but that was the Speaker's problem.

As a second possibility, we would agree to place the documents with the court as custodian for Jefferson and the prosecution as we worked through the issues.

The team assembled on Capitol Hill, but around midnight I received a report that little had been accomplished in the meeting. It had been tough and intense, with the House staff casting plenty of criticism, but offering little else.

Just prior to my morning national security briefing at the FBI headquarters the following day (Tuesday, May 23), I called the president around 7:00 a.m. to give him a report. He seemed to appreciate my update, but before concluding the call, he cautioned me, "You're in the middle of a storm, Fredo, and you need to get it worked out."

"Yes, sir. We made some progress last night, and I'll continue to work at it."

Later that morning, Josh Bolten called me and suggested that he, Harriet, Paul McNulty, and I get together before the president's afternoon meeting with Hastert. I readily agreed and passed along the information to Paul.

Paul was delayed, so that gave me a chance to talk privately with Josh before the meeting. Josh told me candidly that there was a strong view in the White House that the Jefferson documents should be returned.

I was surprised. I could feel the rug being pulled out from under me. As

I listened to Josh, regardless of the way he artfully posed his points, I could tell the real question he was asking was whether I would stand with the Department of Justice or abandon my prosecutors because of the request by the White House.

"I will not voluntarily return the documents," I told Josh quietly. I wasn't being stubborn or obnoxious. I had made my decision based on the recommendations of knowledgeable, senior DOJ officials. I did not want to lose credibility with the entire Justice Department over this issue. "If the White House wants the documents returned," I reiterated to Josh, "the president will have to order me to do it."

My words were carefully calculated. As White House counsel, I had repeatedly cautioned the White House against interfering with an investigation by the Department of Justice. I hoped they had learned the lesson and would back off.

When McNulty and Miers arrived, we plunged headlong into the discussions of possible options for resolving the controversy before it became a full-blown political firestorm. Harriet proposed that we simply return the documents to Jefferson and then get another search warrant, but that we should give the House the opportunity to contest the search before collecting any documents again. Her suggestion troubled me and smacked of silly gamesmanship, but worse yet, I feared that as a longtime friend of the president, she was expressing his preferences, expecting me to read between the lines. In any event, I was not about to follow that suggestion.

Nor was McNulty, who pushed back during the meeting. He reiterated our position, that it made no sense to return documents to a suspected criminal in the middle of an investigation—congressman or no congressman. Part of the reason we were in this situation was because Paul had so adamantly recommended that we sieze the documents from Jefferson's office, so I appreciated that Paul stepped up.

As the meeting continued, it sounded to me that the White House wanted the documents returned, but was unwilling—at least for now—to order the FBI to do so. That made for an awkward tension. I had expected the White House to support my decision. In the Situation Room, the president had stated that the White House would not undercut me. Apparently that position was shifting. I left the meeting discouraged and returned to my office at the DOJ. Although I did not believe that the White House was attempting to obstruct justice, this was the first time since coming to Washington that I worried I could not count on the Bush administration for support on a law enforcement matter.

Around 1:30 p.m., Josh called, requesting that he and I get together again that afternoon. "I'm sorry, Josh," I said, "my afternoon is packed with meetings here at DOJ."

"Well, I'd be willing to come over there," he suggested.

That signaled to me that whatever Josh wanted to discuss was serious. "No," I replied. "I'd better come over there. Let me see what I can do." I knew that nobody would consider it unusual for the attorney general to go to the White House to meet with the president's chief of staff, but if Josh came to our offices, the entire Justice Department would notice. His presence would send a worrisome signal throughout the building.

That afternoon, just before I attended a telemarketing fraud press conference, I had a brief, open segment in my schedule, so I went to see Josh in his White House office. It was another awkward meeting—with Josh hinting that the White House wanted the documents returned and with me outlining the reasons why that wasn't a good idea. I well understood that the president needed Hastert to be happy so he could press through his legislative agenda in the House. I also understood that we were still immersed in the war on terror, and the president needed united support in the House and the Senate. I wasn't surprised that we couldn't work out a deal between DOJ and the House. It was obvious the House leaders believed that in the end, we would acquiesce because the White House needed the House's support and would order us to return the documents.

I reminded Josh of the president's remark in the Situation Room a few days ago, when he said he did not want me to be undercut. Now, contrary to that assurance, it seemed the White House wanted to do precisely that.

Josh agreed that I was being undercut, but he disagreed that if we returned the documents, I would lose respect, credibility, and influence at the Department of Justice. "You are beloved over there," Josh said with a hint of a smile. "You'd be fine."

"Well, give us a chance to reach an accommodation with the House that will also satisfy DOJ concerns," I suggested. I reminded Josh that we were convinced Jefferson had broken the law; the FBI and the prosecutors believed the seized documents were important to their case, and OLC said the search was legal.

Josh understood but suggested that it might look better for me if we returned the documents without President Bush ordering me to do so.

I disagreed. "In fact," I said, "if the president is leaning toward directing me to return the documents, I would like to speak to him privately."

"Of course," said Josh.

Later that afternoon, Josh called me at my office to let me know that Candi Wolff, the White House legislative director, was setting up a meeting on the Hill at 3:30 p.m. to resolve the impasse. This thing had dragged on far too long. To lighten the moment, it seemed, Josh shared with me that the president had asked him whether, in the course of our discussions, he had reminded me that the president loved me. Josh told me, "I said, 'No, Mr. President. The L-word never came up.'"

Josh and I both laughed. We understood how much the president cared about the people close to him, and we realized that the Jefferson incident strained his relationships in ways that some people could not even imagine.

Not surprisingly, that same day during my press conference about telemarketing fraud, questions popped up about the Jefferson search. I stuck to the usual scripted sort of answers. "This is an ongoing investigation. The Department of Justice considers it a valid search. We will continue to work to allay the concerns of Congress."

Paul McNulty, Will Moschella, Alice Fisher, and Steve Bradbury attended the 3:30 p.m. meeting on Capitol Hill, at which I authorized them to present two further possible accommodations to the House. The first, suggested by Kyle Sampson, was to place the documents in the custody of the House sergeant at arms, during which time the House and the DOJ would share custody. This would allow the documents to be "returned," and the House could announce that they "had the documents back," yet still allow DOJ access to them as we worked toward a better solution.

The second offer, proposed by Alice Fisher, called for the department to return the original documents to Congressman Jefferson, but the department would keep a copy.

Paul called me around 5:00 p.m. to report that for the first half hour of the meeting the House staff had whined and complained, but by the end of the meeting, they seemed intrigued by the new proposals. Another meeting was scheduled for 8:00 p.m. that night. I took that as a hopeful sign.

Unfortunately, around 7:00 p.m. Paul called again, this time to report that the later meeting had been canceled by the House; "they needed more time to discuss our proposals" and would get back to us in the morning.

Really? More time? The president himself has stated that he wants this thing settled and you need more time to consider two quite simple proposed solutions? But the House staff also said they wanted to discuss a plan that could include House Democrats.

Hmm, maybe that is a good thing. Yes, and perhaps global peace is possible.

Regardless of my skepticism, I remained hopeful. I should have known better.

The following morning, Wednesday, May 24, 2006, I went to the White House to give the president his Homeland Security briefing. While waiting outside the Oval Office, I spoke to Fran Townsend, the Homeland Security advisor, and Michael Chertoff, the secretary of Homeland Security. Both Fran and Mike were former federal prosecutors. They were surprised that the Jefferson search had even become an issue.

Following the security briefing, I remained behind in the Oval Office to speak with the president about the Jefferson matter. He pressed me hard again to find a resolution. I reminded him that it was best that the White House stay out of this matter.

"Well, I'm worried for you," the president said.

"Oh, I'm not worried," I replied.

"I know you are not worried, but I am," he said with a hint of a grin. I could tell President Bush was troubled by this situation. Josh had already informed me the president was concerned that Speaker Hastert might push for my resignation. Congress could also "punish" me through incessant investigations and subpoenas. Worse still, Congress held the power of the purse; they could easily defund certain programs that as attorney general I had been spearheading. Indeed, because financial appropriations begin in the House, they could slash our entire department's budget.

I acknowledged the seriousness of the situation and expressed my appreciation. I told him we were still waiting to hear how the House might respond to our latest offers but that we'd keep working on it.

I waited patiently all morning long, but still no answer came from the House of Representatives. We checked with Candi Wolff, and she reported that she'd heard nothing either, but that Scott Palmer, Dennis Hastert's chief of staff, was holed up on the Hill working through our options.

Meanwhile, Congressman Jefferson's attorneys filed a motion with Judge Hogan, demanding the documents be returned.

That afternoon, I attended a three-hour-long meeting at the White House with other cabinet officials regarding hurricane preparedness measures. That was nothing new; the government had conducted such exercises long before Katrina, but the devastation of that storm reminded all of us that our time was not being wasted.

Around 4:00 p.m., while I was still at the Old Executive Office Building across from the White House, I received an urgent call from Kyle Sampson. He told me that Speaker Hastert and Nancy Pelosi had just issued a joint public statement demanding the seized Jefferson documents be returned to the congressman, and that the search warrant must be vitiated and no member of the search team could be a part of the prosecution team.

I was stunned. First, because their public demands were outrageous, but even more so because we had been blindsided. At Justice, we had been trying to play fairly, thinking that the House leadership was using this time to evaluate our proposals and would come back with suggestions for resolution. That was not the case at all. They had been using the time to line up allies on the other side of the political aisle who obviously would join forces with the Republicans to protect their fellow Democrat. The political gamesmanship angered me.

I returned immediately to the DOJ, where I was again informed that the congressional leaders demanded the seized documents be returned.

I refused.

McNulty was already in his conference room, along with Kyle Sampson, Mike Elston, Bill Mercer, Alice Fisher, and Will Moschella. Their mood was somber and their discouragement almost palpable. We had to develop another plan.

I knew it was only a matter of time before Josh called on behalf of the president. What I did not know was that earlier that afternoon, Paul McNulty and Scott Palmer had engaged in another heated conversation over the Jefferson matter. Paul had urged Palmer to think about the long-term ramifications of what the House was asking the FBI and the Justice Department to do.

Then at some point in their conversations, Paul insisted that nobody wanted another Saturday Night Massacre, alluding to the DOJ resignations during the Watergate investigation. Candi Wolff had been on the call as well, and apparently she reported the threat of DOJ resignations to the White House. That was not good. The president and I had lived through resignation threats over the Stellar Wind surveillance program, and they were abhorrent to us then. I knew he would not be happy to hear that the resignation issue had resurfaced at DOJ.

Not surprisingly, Josh called shortly thereafter. The tone of his voice was different than it had been during our previous calls. Now he sounded less friendly, more businesslike, more of the authoritarian tone of a chief of staff.

I knew this was difficult for Josh. He and I were friends; moreover, he knew that the president and I were friends. But I had made a decision that had infuriated one of the White House's most important allies in the political/legislative realm, and I understood that Josh had to protect the interests of the president and the institution of the presidency.

I suspected that the president wanted the documents returned. This whole incident had become an unnecessary irritation. Yet I assumed two roadblocks prevented the president from ordering me to return Jefferson's documents. First, this *was* an ongoing criminal investigation. I hoped that the White House would be reluctant to order prosecutors to do something that would interfere with an investigation of a member of Congress. I understood that the White House did not want the documents returned simply to protect Jefferson. Nor did they intend in any way to obstruct justice. White House lawyers simply believed the search was questionable.

Second, I guessed that my long relationship with the president, as well as the White House staff, caused them to pause and might have bought the DOJ some time. But obviously that clock was ticking too.

Josh probed the resignation issue. "I've heard some disturbing reports about resignations," he said, "and I hope that is not true. But if it is, I hope you will tell me first." Ever the master of understatement, Josh continued, "It appears things are not moving in a positive direction."

I tried to reassure Josh that I was not aware of any serious discussion of mass resignations at DOJ. "Paul's comment was unfortunate, but it does not reflect the feelings of the department." That seemed to ease Josh's mind slightly, but it did nothing to soften his response. Without actually saying the words, Josh signaled to me that the president would order that the documents be returned. He was careful not to give me that order over the phone, but it was clear that he was doing everything but speaking the words. Perhaps Josh was hoping that I would fall on my sword and as attorney general, order that the FBI return the seized documents.

I could not do that, and I would not. If I backpedaled from the DOJ position at this point, the political appointees and the career lawyers in the department would regard it as capitulation to the White House. I told Josh that unless there was some evidence of wrongdoing by the prosecution team that had conducted the search, I could not voluntarily return the documents to a defendant in the middle of a criminal investigation. I did not understand the urgency to return the documents when the question regarding the legality of the search was now in the courts.

I reiterated to Josh, "The president could certainly order the documents to be returned, but I hope that he won't." As the former White House counsel, and as the president's friend, I emphasized that I thought it was unwise for the White House staff to have the president involved in decisions about a criminal prosecution.

After Josh and I hung up, I thought further about McNulty's regrettable comment about resignations. The president had been on the receiving end of similar threats during the tense discussions regarding Stellar Wind, and I recalled how angry he had been that his subordinates were trying to force his hand. I guessed that these latest veiled threats from DOJ were eliciting the same sort of response.

Walking over to Paul's office, I stopped by the office of David Margolis. David was a career Department of Justice employee with more than forty years of experience in the DOJ. His office was like a museum, filled with everything from baseball cards to Justice memorabilia, posters, and pictures. I often stopped in, and if he was not there, I left him notes, facetiously questioning why he was not at his post. I liked David and respected his judgment.

Margolis was aware of the Jefferson situation and we talked briefly about the recent developments. "What I don't understand," David said thoughtfully, "was how your advisors allowed you to get into this position."

I nodded and told him that the decision had ultimately been mine, and I had made it. Nevertheless, David's point registered with me.

I visited with FBI director Bob Mueller for his views on Jefferson's seized documents. "Your instincts are correct," he told me. "You should not voluntarily turn over the documents to Jefferson or to the House." We talked briefly about what might happen. "It would be better for you and for the department if you were ordered by the president to return the documents." Bob was reaffirming my position.

He then said something that I had never consciously considered, but the possibility troubled me. The director of the FBI said that even if the president ordered the documents be returned, the documents were with him, and he wasn't sure he could, as a matter of principle, comply with such an order. "I might have to resign," Bob said.

The director's comment hit me hard. He might have simply been expressing support for the DOJ position in the case, but as I looked at the strong-jawed, former marine, I had little doubt that he would seriously consider resigning rather than returning the documents confiscated by the FBI.

For the first time since the matter began, I accepted the real possibility that should the president order the documents returned, and Mueller as the head of the FBI responded by resigning, as Mueller's boss, I'd have few options other than to resign as attorney general.

Kyle Sampson reported that after another tough call with Joel Kaplan, the White House deputy chief of staff, he'd been asked to meet that night at 7:00 p.m. As a parting word, I told Kyle to remind Joel that the president should never negotiate with subordinates in the executive branch. He was in charge. If the president ordered that the documents be returned, I would ensure that the order was carried out.

I felt strongly that nobody at DOJ should act in an insubordinate manner by *threatening* to resign. If you disagree with a policy and you cannot live with it, fine, resign, but don't attempt to hold the chief executive hostage by threatening to resign.

I did not discuss possible resignations with Kyle, but as the evening wore on, with no resolution, I found myself thinking more about those scenarios.

I was still working in my office when around 10:00 p.m., Paul McNulty reported to me that Scott Palmer, the Speaker's chief of staff, had suggested a thirty-day stand down, to allow Congress to pass legislation that could deal with congressional search issues such as the Jefferson case. I was encouraged by Palmer's calmer idea, especially since it was consistent with our earlier proposals.

The tide of public opinion was incrementally swinging in favor of the Department of Justice. News stories critical of the Speaker and the House's position appeared in the press. Even some members of Congress questioned publicly whether the House position made good sense.

Complicating matters, unfortunately, was that some of the press coverage was distorted. For instance, *ABC News* ran a story claiming that Speaker Hastert was under investigation. The story angered me because I worried that the Speaker might conclude that DOJ had leaked it in retaliation for his going public. That had not happened, and I ordered that we deny the story, which we did. Palmer asked McNulty to issue additional public denials, and we did that too.

It was nearly 11:00 p.m. by the time Kyle Sampson returned from his White House meeting and the news was not good. Our team met in McNulty's conference room, and Kyle delivered the message from Josh Bolten: the president wanted the documents returned. I was surprised, given my earlier, encouraging conversations with Josh.

"What are you going to do?" several members of our team asked me, perhaps gauging their own responses according to mine.

"I don't know," I responded honestly. "Right now I'm just going to go home and talk with my wife." Although Becky had been ready to return to Texas for a couple of years now, this was not the exit plan we had envisioned. Nevertheless, there was a real possibility that tomorrow might be my last day as attorney general, so I wanted to talk it through with her.

I arrived home at nearly one o'clock in the morning, and Becky was still waiting up for me. I was tired and dispirited. "I think the end is near," I told her disconsolately. "I'm probably going to receive an order from the president in the morning, and as a result, I will probably have to resign." I briefly explained the issues surrounding the search of Congressman Jefferson's office.

Becky didn't ask too many questions about the details of the case. She simply said, "It will be their loss." She hugged me and said, "I'm with you whatever you decide to do."

I admitted to her that I was disappointed at the lack of support I had received from the White House on the Jefferson matter. That stoked the fires in Becky's eyes too. "I'm angry that nobody in the White House is strongly advising President Bush to let the prosecution run its course and let the chips fall," she said.

I shrugged. I agreed with her, but there was nothing left for me to do. It was hard to maintain faith, but we prayed together, asking God for wisdom. I went to bed thinking about what I might say in my resignation letter.

CHAPTER 33

WRONG EVEN WHEN RIGHT

W hen my alarm clock went off on Thursday morning, May 26, I rubbed the sleep out of my eyes. I'd been in bed a few hours. Nevertheless, I felt alert and ready to get back in the office by 6:00 a.m. I figured, *This might be my last morning as attorney general. I'm going to make the best of it.* When I arrived at my office, I penned my resignation letter to the president, informing him that I would see that his orders were carried out, but I had to resign. It was not an easy letter to write. President Bush had been good to me, and I knew my resignation might raise difficult issues for him.

Kyle came into the office sometime around 7:00 a.m., and we talked briefly about what the day might bring. I then called Bob Mueller to give him a heads-up that the president was likely to direct the Department of Justice to return the seized documents to Congressman Jefferson.

"I'm surprised it has come to this," Bob said. "I'll talk to Josh Bolten after the 7:45 a.m. national security briefing with the president."

"Okay, good," I said. "I won't be there."

"I'm not sure I can return the documents," the FBI director told me. "I might have to be fired."

By now, the tide of public opinion had swung clearly in our favor. News commentators, scholars, and more members of Congress questioned

Speaker Hastert's position. I felt vindicated, but it appeared too little too late.

At 8:25 a.m., Josh Bolten called me to tell me that the president would be available to speak to me privately at either 8:35 a.m. or 10:50 a.m. "I have a National Missing Children's Day event coming up later this morning," I told Josh. "I'll be right over." I placed the resignation letter in my inside coat pocket and climbed into the waiting black Suburban along with the FBI Security Detail. Sitting in the back right passenger's-side seat, I gazed out the window as the detail driver whisked us through the Washington traffic and over to the White House.

When I arrived, I met Bob Mueller in the West Wing basement as he was returning to the FBI building. Bob informed me that he had just talked with Josh Bolten and had emphasized that returning the documents in the middle of an investigation would be a terrible miscalculation. It would embarrass the Department of Justice and set a bad precedent. Mueller told me that he had informed Josh that should the president demand the documents returned, as a matter of principle, as the FBI director, he was not sure he could carry out such an order. He might have to resign.

I didn't say anything to Bob about his statement, but I really regretted that he had raised the resignation possibility directly to the chief of staff. I heard echoes of 2004 DOJ resignation threats related to Stellar Wind in my mind again. I felt strongly that the president should never be threatened by subordinates, and both Bob and I served at the pleasure of the president.

As I walked into the Oval Office, Vice President Cheney, Steve Hadley, and Josh walked out. The president remained alone, sitting at his desk, so I sat in a chair near his desk.

"We've been through a lot together," I reminded the president.

He laughed and said, "Yes, but this is the worst one yet."

"It doesn't have to be," I responded.

It struck me odd that he could think this was the worst issue we had dealt with together. The dispute with the Speaker involved a legal question—a delicate matter, to be sure, but still, a relatively easily solvable issue, compared to the many major legal questions we had faced together regarding the war on terror. Moreover, it would probably be solved in the courts, so there was no constitutional crisis in play.

"I believe that part of my job is to not create problems for you," I said. "The decision to search was right and necessary," I explained, "but I know it created an awkward situation between you and the Speaker. For that, I am sorry."

The president waved his hand. "Don't worry about that," he said.

I went on, "When we met earlier this month in the Situation Room, you said you would support me."

The president nodded at my reminder but did not respond, so I continued. "But the White House has undercut me. At the very time you urged me to work out a solution with the House leadership, the House had no incentive to agree on a deal because they knew the White House would eventually order the documents returned. This has been very disappointing."

"Well, Fredo, I have to take into consideration more than law enforcement. I have to also consider comity between the three branches of government."

I assured him that we had tried to consider such matters as well. Nevertheless, we were undercut by his people in the White House. "My judgment was being questioned by people in the White House," I said, "and that really bothered me."

The president seemed to understand my perspective, and did not attempt to correct my assumptions that I had been undercut by people in the White House. He moved on to the matter of resignations, mentioning the possibility before I did.

"I don't want you to resign," he said to me, looking me right in the eyes. "It makes no sense." He paused as though thinking about that possibility, then said, "Besides, we are in the middle of fighting a war on terror. You need to stay." He reassured me that I would continue to be effective at Justice. "I will make it clear that you still have influence at the White House," he said.

I said nothing, but my resignation letter was burning a hole in my coat pocket.

The president continued talking about McNulty's subtle threat of resignations. That made him look weak, he stated. He also complained about

Mueller possibly resigning. "Bob is stubborn and has threatened to resign before," the president said.

How well I remembered!

All the talk of resignations put the president in a box he did not appreciate. I remained silent, except to agree that subordinates should not threaten to resign; if they are unhappy or disagree over something, they should simply resign. My own resignation letter in my coat pocket now seemed ready to pop out.

"I can't have mass resignations," the president said. "Did you know about Bob's position?"

"Yes," I said. "We talked yesterday and this morning." I told the president that Bob was beloved in the Justice building, and as the FBI director and a former US attorney, if he resigned over an order from the president to return documents seized during a high-profile criminal investigation, then I would have to resign as well, irrespective of what I thought about the president's decision. It would be wrong for me to continue on as attorney general if the director of the FBI resigned as a matter of principle. If Bob resigned and I stayed, I'd be ineffective anyhow, as my credibility would be gone as far as my coworkers were concerned.

As soon as I said the words, I had regrets. While not couched as an ultimatum followed by a threat to resign, my comment signaled just that. It was not right. I needed to keep an open mind about what I would do if Mueller resigned.

I quickly added, "I believe you deserve to have your orders carried out, even ones I disagree with. After all, there's nothing illegal about returning the documents." I then explained to the president how we had offered various compromises to the House leadership—good, viable options, in my opinion—but they had all been rejected, presumably because the White House had undercut the Department of Justice.

My conversation with the president lasted about half an hour. It was an emotional and straightforward discussion, and at no point did the president order me to return the seized documents to Congressman Jefferson. As I started to leave the Oval Office, the president walked to the door with me and patted me on the back. "You know that I think of you as a brother," he said, his hand still on my back.

"Yes, sir," I replied. "Thank you."

"Well, hang in there," he said.

"I will."

I felt a wave of relief flow over me as I walked out of the White House and climbed into the waiting Suburban for the brief ride back to Justice. As we turned down Constitution Avenue, I felt that I had stated my case to the president, and I thought about how I would respond if, after all, he ordered the documents returned. If that happened, I decided I would first do my best to convince Mueller to follow the order and to remain as director of the FBI. If Mueller agreed, then having him by my side, if I decided to stay, would deflect some internal criticism from career DOJ employees who would feel that we had kowtowed to the political pressure from the White House.

On the other hand, if Bob Mueller balked and refused to return the documents, or even if he did return them but resigned as FBI director, I'd face the difficult decision about whether I could stay on as attorney general.

I asked Paul McNulty and other senior DOJ officials to join me for lunch in the attorney general's dining room. We didn't often eat together, and this might well be the last opportunity.

As we sat down for lunch, we received some good news. The jury on the Enron case had returned with fraud and conspiracy convictions for the company's chairman, Ken Lay, and CEO Jeff Skilling. The Enron scandal had rocked the economic world in December 2001, when the Texas-based energy company declared bankruptcy, taking with it the pensions and life savings of more than twenty thousand of its employees and investors. The FBI discovered that the mighty fall had taken place due to cheating investors and sham accounting practices that allowed the leaders of the company to enrich themselves. Enron's collapse triggered the demise of giant accounting firm Arthur Andersen, which had collected fees of more than $25 million from Enron the previous year.[1] The company's chairman, Ken Lay, had been a Bush supporter, so naturally, the focus turned toward that relationship.

But as it turned out, fully three-quarters of the US Senate had received cash from Enron, both Republicans and Democrats.[2]

The FBI investigation involved more than forty-five agents in Houston and Washington. They carted out more than five hundred boxes of evidence from the fifty-story Enron headquarters. The five-year investigation had finally led to the convictions of the top Enron officials.

I had known and worked with Ken Lay early in my Houston law career, helping with various community projects. He seemed like a decent man, so the news of his conviction was bittersweet. I was saddened for Ken and his family, but happy for the prosecution team, and glad that the many people who had lost their livelihoods, health insurance, and retirement savings would at least have the consolation of knowing the perpetrators of the fraud would be punished for it. It was a great win for our prosecution team and a highly visible example of the president's commitment to punish corporate wrongdoing.

The irony was not lost on me that the convictions came on the day when congressional wrongdoing with far less money and far fewer lives involved might end the careers of many of us who had been guiding the Enron investigation. Nevertheless, the verdict lifted our spirits.

During lunch, Josh Bolten called, so I went to my office to take the call. The message Josh conveyed surprised me. "The president is going to order that we seal the documents for forty-five days under the custody of Solicitor General Paul Clement," Josh said. "To provide time to work something out."

I was pleased and concerned at the same time—pleased that the president was not ordering us to return the documents to Jefferson, yet worried that he was inserting himself into a criminal investigation. To Josh, I questioned the wisdom of involving the president in an ongoing criminal investigation. "As attorney general, I could order a stand-down for forty-five days," I suggested.

"No," Josh replied. "The White House wants it public that the president is stepping in to resolve the crisis." Although Josh did not say so, I suspected that the president's decision was also intended to show Speaker Hastert that this would be the extent of President Bush's help on this matter.

I thanked Josh and walked back into the dining room, no doubt unable to mask my relief. I announced the president's decision to our team, and they responded with a quiet, subdued, but heartfelt cheer and a few fist-pumps. I immediately ordered that we comply with the president's order and turn the documents over to the solicitor general.

I walked back to my office and breathed a sigh of relief.

The next morning, President Bush called me around 7:00 a.m. "How are you feeling?" he asked.

"Great," I replied. "How are you feeling?" Both of us knew that we were not inquiring about the other's physical health. I thanked the president and told him he had made a good decision regarding the Jefferson documents.

"Well, it was hard watching you agonize over this. That caused me to agonize," he said. He then told me to use the forty-five days to work out a solution.

I understood and I urged him to limit the White House's involvement. There were already grumblings from law enforcement because he had interjected himself.

"Yeah, imagine if I had ordered the documents returned," he said. "The grumbles would turn into a rumble!" We both laughed, and then the president was back to business. While he noted that the tide of public opinion had shifted in our direction, he emphasized that we needed to give the House and Dennis Hastert a noble way out.

I understood. Comity was important. Damage had to be assuaged; egos had to be soothed. The president needed the House Republicans to further his agenda.

He concluded the call by saying, "All right, brother. Talk to you later."

I appreciated his call. I sensed that it was his way of saying, "I hope you are okay now; all is well between us." He did not have to do such a thing, but it was part of his character. With the myriad matters on his desk each morning, it was especially thoughtful that he would take the time to make such a call. When people later wondered why I and others on his team were so intensely loyal to President Bush, moments like these came to mind.

The following day, true to form, the *New York Times* and the *Washington*

Post got part of the story right and part of the story wrong. Both newspapers reported that Mueller and I had threatened to resign over the documents issue. That was false. Although I had carried my written resignation in my coat pocket during my meeting with the president, I never threatened to resign. I well might have resigned had he ordered me to return the documents, but I did not—nor would I—*threaten* to resign. I regretted my inadvertent signal because I believed then, as I do now, that subordinates should not attempt to influence the president's decisions by threatening to resign. If a government official is unhappy about the chief executive's lawful orders, he or she should either accept it quietly or simply resign. Threat of resignation should not be a weapon used against the president.

———

While the president's decision gave us forty-five days to find a solution, the legal questions remained: Was the search of Jefferson's office constitutional? And more specifically, what is the scope of the speech and debate clause?

On July 10, 2006, we received our initial answer. Judge Hogan—an experienced and well-respected jurist—held that the search was lawfully conducted, ruling that members of Congress who are under criminal investigation deserve no more protection under the law than ordinary citizens. Judge Hogan concluded that Congressman Jefferson's interpretation of the speech and debate privilege would have the effect of converting every congressional office into a taxpayer-subsidized sanctuary for crime. The possibility that some legislative material might have been "inadvertently captured" by the FBI did not make the search illegal. It was a sweet victory for the Justice Department; the judge had agreed with us.

Unfortunately, the decision did not stand. A year later, the DC Circuit Court reversed Judge Hogan's decision and ordered that all privileged documents should be returned to Jefferson. The court said that the FBI should not have viewed documents in Jefferson's office without first giving Jefferson the opportunity to say which materials did not involve legislative business.

Although we were pleased that all the documents did not have to be returned, the court's ruling effectively prevented any future searches of congressional offices on Capitol Hill and threatened to impede searches of lawmaker's homes, vehicles, or even briefcases. The US Supreme Court declined to hear the Justice Department's appeal of the DC Circuit Court's decision. As a result, the perfect place to hide evidence of a crime is now in the office of a congressman or senator in our nation's Capitol.

The privileged documents were returned, and the Justice Department successfully prosecuted Congressman Jefferson without them. He was found guilty on eleven of sixteen counts of money laundering and conspiracy to bribe, and received a thirteen-year sentence.

In hindsight, I should have listened to my better judgment and not authorized the search of Jefferson's office. It was a close legal conclusion, but according to a panel of circuit court judges, my decision was a mistake; I had made the wrong call.

After this incident, Speaker Dennis Hastert and I never again met or even spoke to each other for the remainder of my time in Washington. While the Jefferson saga boosted my standing at the Justice Department, it hurt me with the House leadership. Jefferson was not the only big loser. His fate had already been sealed by the evidence, but the search of his office and the residual anger on Capitol Hill meant the loss of goodwill and political capital for me.

CHAPTER 34

HUNTING SEASON

Shortly after I was appointed attorney general in 2005, Harriet Miers became White House counsel and suggested that the Department of Justice replace the nation's ninety-three US attorneys located throughout the country. Her suggestion was not improper. A US attorney is a presidential appointee whose term of office is by statute four years, after which he or she may be held over until a successor is appointed.

While the work of the US attorney is expected to be above politics, the appointment of a US attorney is often quite political, and the removal of a US attorney can be partisan as well, all part of the political patronage system. Some members of Congress even regard these appointments as *theirs*, a way to reward party loyalty. Home-state senators expect to weigh in on US attorney appointments, although the final selections are made by the White House.

Federal prosecutors work as part of the Justice Department and report to the attorney general, but they know they serve at the pleasure of the president. They can be removed from office by the president at any time, for political or other reasons, or frankly, for no reason at all. The president has wide latitude to make such changes. The only inappropriate removal would be one made to impede an investigation or an ongoing case. Even under these circumstances, however, a removal of a US attorney would not likely affect an investigation or case because these are normally supervised by career attorneys whose jobs are protected by civil service laws.

The president, of course, does not usually make a decision to remove a US attorney arbitrarily, but would ordinarily do so with the advice of or at the suggestion of the leadership at the Justice Department, including the attorney general. Nevertheless, US attorneys serve at the pleasure of the president, not the attorney general. Because they are presidential appointees, they cannot be appointed or removed without the concurrence of the White House. Consequently, at Harriet's prompting, I instructed my then deputy chief of staff, Kyle Sampson, to coordinate a high-level review of all ninety-three US attorneys across the country.

Kyle was ideally suited to gather the views of DOJ senior leadership and help assess personnel. He had been involved since the transition days in 2000 and 2001 in evaluating and vetting lawyers for highly responsible positions throughout the Bush administration, including the deputy attorney general, the solicitor general, and the heads of DOJ divisions such as tax, antitrust, and criminal law. He knew generally the responsibilities of the US attorneys. In fact, he had participated in screening interviews of many of the sitting US attorneys, and his evaluation played a role in their appointments.

Beyond that, Kyle knew the type of individuals the president and I wanted as US attorneys—straight arrows, tough, and responsible. I expected him to consult with Mike Battle, the director of the executive office for US attorneys, our liaison with the US attorneys, and Deputy Attorney General Paul McNulty to get their perspectives about our prosecutors across the country. Mike and Paul had both previously served as US attorneys and knew well these people, their qualifications, and reputations. I also expected Kyle's reviews to be completed in a reasonable amount of time.

Unfortunately, because of pressing DOJ business and other priorities at the White House, the evaluations took nearly two years. Kyle kept me generally aware of his progress, and I assumed that he was consulting with both White House and DOJ senior leadership throughout the review process. It was only much later that I discovered that Kyle did most of the review work on his own, while consulting only periodically with McNulty, Battle, and David Margolis, an associate deputy attorney general and the highest ranking career attorney in the department.

On November 27, 2006, I met with Sampson, McNulty, Battle, and others to discuss the US attorney removal plan. After subsequent conversations, a list of seven names was finalized: Kevin Ryan (Northern District of California), Carol Lam (Southern District of California), John McKay (Western District of Washington), Paul Charlton (Arizona), David Iglesias (New Mexico), Dan Bogden (Nevada), and Margaret Chiara (Western District of Michigan). No one among the senior leadership of the Department of Justice who had knowledge of these individuals—not McNulty, Battle, Sampson, or Margolis—raised an objection to these removals at the time or subsequently. This was a consensus recommendation at Justice. Likewise, there was no objection or concern expressed by the White House as far as I knew at the time.

The reasons for the removals varied. Kevin Ryan and Margaret Chiara were asked to leave because of mismanagement of their respective offices and low morale. Carol Lamm was removed because of DOJ concerns about the low number of gun and immigration prosecutions in her district. Paul Charlton was asked to leave because of his actions relating to a death penalty case and unilateral implementation of an interrogation policy. John McKay was asked to leave because of a disagreement with the deputy attorney general over an information-sharing program. David Iglesias had lost the confidence of the senior senator from New Mexico, so he, like Dan Bogden, was asked to leave to make a change.[1] Whether anyone disagreed with these reasons or not, it was not inappropriate to remove a US attorney who served a full statutory term; all served at the pleasure of the president and could be removed for any of the above reasons.

There was no suggestion that these removals would be improper by impeding a case or an investigation. In the years since the removals, following several investigations by Congress and the DOJ inspector general and the office of professional responsibility, not even a shred of evidence suggests the removals were improper because they were intended to impede an

investigation or an on-going case. In fact, FBI director Bob Mueller testified under oath that he was not aware of any case or investigation adversely
affected by the removals.[2]

In December 2006, I accepted the suggestions from the DOJ senior
leadership, believing changes would strengthen the department, and had
them presented as my recommendations to the White House, where the
decisions were approved. These were, after all, presidential appointees, so
the final decision whether the US attorneys would be replaced rested in the
White House.

It is not unusual to see turnovers in US attorneys' positions during a
president's term in office. Sometimes appointees choose to leave to pursue
higher office or work in the private sector. Some leave for family or other
personal reasons. Occasionally a US attorney may be asked to leave because
of misconduct, mismanagement of the office, or insubordination. Others
may simply be asked to step aside to provide an opportunity for someone
else to serve. Such departures over the course of a president's term would
not be considered uncommon or inappropriate. Asking seven US attorneys
to transition at once may have evoked questions, but should not have raised
accusations of wrongdoing. Moreover, why would Democrats care that a
Republican president was dismissing Republican appointees?

The first sign of trouble came when I met with California senator
Dianne Feinstein prior to a Senate Judiciary Committee oversight hearing
in January 2007. She raised questions about the dismissal of two US attorneys in California—Kevin Ryan in San Francisco and Carol Lam in San
Diego. Respecting the service of Ryan and Lam, I declined to share specifics
about the removals, but I assured the senator that our actions were to ensure
the best individuals were serving the citizens of California.

At the January 18 hearing, Senator Feinstein again questioned the dis-
missals and asked whether the new appointees would be brought to the
Senate for confirmation—or would they be appointed under the PATRIOT
Act, allowing the attorney general to make an interim appointment without
Senate confirmation?

I understood her concerns. Senators want a say in who serves as US attorney in their states. Further, the power of confirmation is something the Senate zealously guards.

Nevertheless, I questioned Feinstein's concerns. It was common knowledge within the senior leadership of the Justice Department that the San Francisco US attorney's office had serious morale and mismanagement issues; Kevin Ryan had lost the respect of senior leaders in his office. In San Diego, Carol Lam had failed to deal adequately with immigration and gun prosecutions—both of which were priorities for a border-state US attorney. Senator Feinstein had even written the DOJ complaining about the work of the San Diego office, so I wondered why she was questioning and making it sound as though she was troubled by the dismissals.

What had changed? When the review process began in 2005, the Republicans controlled the US Senate and the House of Representatives. Following the midterm elections in 2006, that was no longer the case, and in January 2007, the Democrats took over power in the Senate. Democrats had been explicit in their 2006 election campaigns to win back control of the Senate and thus provide oversight of the Bush administration and rein in Bush policies. They now controlled the legislative calendar and the power to conduct investigations. They were looking for a political issue with which they could damage the Republican brand and, in particular, hammer the White House. The US attorney dismissals supplied them with a rallying point.

My questions about Senator Feinstein's motivation notwithstanding, I assured the Judiciary Committee that I did not intend to use my new appointment powers to select the successors. Those powers in the PATRIOT Act were intended to be used in situations of a national security emergency in which there was precious little time to have a confirmation hearing. I emphasized my belief that a Senate-confirmed US attorney is in a stronger position to deal with state and local officials, as well as other federal agencies, and better able to handle the challenges that accompany the position. I declined to get into the specifics of the dismissals out of respect for the people the president had removed from office, but I repeatedly assured the Judiciary Committee that there was nothing improper about the dismissals.

I had no reason to suspect that anyone at the White House had improperly influenced the Department of Justice regarding the dismissals—and even if they had asked that someone be removed, that would not be an issue, since US attorneys can be replaced by the president at any time for any reason other than the obstruction of justice. Based on what I knew, nothing improper had happened in the case of the seven US attorneys.

Indeed, if I had been looking at the dismissals strictly through a political lens, we certainly would not have proceeded with them after the Democrats won the midterm election in 2006 and took control of the Senate. But we were not thinking in political terms—the dismissals were not a political hatchet job—so in our estimation at Justice, the replacement of the US attorneys was nothing extraordinary. Certainly, the dismissals were significant in the lives of the seven individuals affected, but they all understood the reality that they served at the pleasure of the president.

I had two objectives in making the changes: one, to strengthen the Department of Justice; and two, to ensure that the president had the type of US attorneys he wanted.

Nevertheless, to put an end to the speculations about the reasons for the dismissals, on February 6, 2007, Deputy Attorney General Paul McNulty testified in a Senate Judiciary Committee hearing chaired by New York Senator Charles Schumer. I had encouraged Paul to be straightforward with the committee, but to avoid disparaging the reputations of the dismissed US attorneys by giving specifics about their questionable performances.

I was traveling in South America during that time, meeting with my foreign justice counterparts and addressing such issues as human trafficking and drug prosecutions. When I heard about Paul's testimony, I was disappointed. I felt he had gone too far in blaming the dismissals of the US attorneys on their poor performances. My concern was twofold: one, I certainly did not wish to publicly disparage the reputations of US attorneys who had served our country; and two, most US attorneys are not docile, passive individuals. I knew that if their performances came under scrutiny, they would defend themselves. I certainly would. That could unnecessarily open a can of worms and was almost certain to beg for more questions. Even though there had been nothing improper about the dismissals, I worried that partisan Democratic members of the Senate Judiciary Committee would play politics with the issue.

I was right. The speculations and accusations about the removal of the seven US attorneys continued, igniting a fire under the Democrats, now a majority in the Senate, as though someone had tossed a match into a gasoline-soaked batch of deadwood.

Paul's testimony was damaging. Once he acknowledged that the removals were based on poor performance by the US attorneys, that became the narrative, and if we could not provide facts to support that narrative, then we would be seen as being untruthful. Democratic attacks that the removals were improper had no legitimate basis in view of the president's almost unlimited power of appointment and removal; it simply could not be sustained and they knew it. Lying to Congress, on the other hand, was a much more serious charge and more difficult for us to fight.

In hindsight, we should have said from the beginning that the removals were personnel decisions and we would not talk publicly about them. That would have forced the Democrats to prove the removals were made to obstruct justice by impeding an investigation or prosecution—which, of course, we knew they were not—or drop the issue. Hindsight, of course, is always perfect.

I do not blame Paul for his testimony, nor others in the department for the removals, or for the explanations provided to defend the removals. I was the head of the department, and I was responsible for the actions of my subordinates as well as my own. Paul was simply testifying to the truth as he believed it. Nevertheless, his testimony provided Democrats with a far easier path of attack in questioning my integrity.

On Valentine's Day, I met with President Bush about the DOJ's investigations of two border patrol agents who had shot a drug dealer from behind and then had tried to cover up the shooting. Johnny Sutton, US attorney for the Western District of Texas, was leading the investigation. Sutton was a no-nonsense prosecutor and had worked as criminal policy advisor for Bush when he was governor.

Yet Sutton was being publicly second-guessed by conservatives because he was prosecuting two so-called "heroes who were only doing their jobs to protect Americans." That simply wasn't the truth.

I explained to President Bush that Sutton felt certain these agents had broken the law and should be prosecuted. When Sutton asked me whether he should move forward with the case, I told him that he should do the right thing and I would stand behind him. President Bush agreed, and said that he trusted Johnny Sutton and would stay with him.

It was then that I spoke to the president for the first time about the US attorney dismissals. He viewed the media speculation and the rumblings in the Senate as typical Washington political gamesmanship. "This is no big deal," he said. "I trust your judgment. Don't worry about it." Both of us acknowledged that he and I had more important matters on which to focus.

As I turned to leave, the president stopped me. "Fredo, are you going to stay on until the end of my administration?"

"I'd like to," I replied, "but as you know, Becky is concerned about our financial situation."

The president brushed aside those concerns with a wave of his hand. "Within a year out of public service, you'll recoup everything you have sacrificed," he assured me. "I hope you will stay on."

I went back to work and, over the next few weeks, spent little time worrying about the attorney removals. There were simply too many other important issues that required my attention.

Some Democrats, however, apparently believed they had discovered an opportunity to hurt President Bush and openly speculated that the dismissal of the seven US attorneys was due to their failing to prosecute Democrats, or attempting to prosecute Republicans. Without waiting for actual proof of their claims, they launched a whisper campaign purporting that I had "politicized the Department of Justice."

Keep in mind: the removal of US attorneys cannot happen without White House approval. So if it could be shown that the removals were intended to obstruct justice or impede an investigation or if there was active concealment by the Justice Department with respect to the dismissals, the

Democrats might be able to reach all the way to the president—or at least to his friend, the attorney general.

Both Karl Rove and I regarded the removal of the US attorneys as clearly within the authority and discretion of the president. We failed to anticipate that the Democrats would use their recently gained control of the Senate to initiate a political witch-hunt. It seemed their primary intention was to damage the president's credibility.

The media picked up on the questions and innuendoes and asked me about them. Early on, I responded to questions in a low-key, relaxed manner, assuring the American public that nothing improper had occurred by our replacing the US attorneys. We had nothing to hide because we had done nothing wrong.

March 6, 2007, was a day packed with events, including a phone call with Mexican attorney general Eduardo Medina-Mora, a speech before the National Association of Attorneys General, and a meeting of the Judicial Selection Committee at the White House. In between events, I managed to see portions of a Senate Judiciary Committee hearing concerning the US attorney removals that included the testimonies of Carol Lam, David Iglesias, John McKay, and H. E. "Bud" Cummins. I wondered why Cummins was even at the hearing, since the decision to replace him in Arkansas had been made the previous June, months before the other seven US attorneys had been asked to leave, and after serving his full four-year term.

Obviously, the Democrats wanted to perpetuate the narrative that the Bush administration was removing US attorneys for political motives. Cummins had been asked to leave earlier in the year to make room for Tim Griffin. Griffin had worked in Rove's office inside the White House and had served in various legal positions in the Justice Department, including work with our DOJ team in Iraq. Cummins had not been asked to leave as a result of the Sampson review process. That fact notwithstanding, Democrats desperately attempted to link the Cummins removal to the Griffin appointment and thus tie Karl Rove to the removals, even though the Cummins situation was totally unrelated to the seven removals at the end of 2006.

Regardless of the real reasons behind their dismissals, these former US attorneys came across during the hearings as innocent victims and hardworking public servants betrayed by their supervisors at the Department of Justice. I understood their desire to defend their reputations, yet on the other hand I was disappointed that they allowed themselves to be used. Their testimonies gave the Democrats what they wanted—faces to a scandal. While Carol, John, David, and Bud all acknowledged that as presidential appointees they served at the pleasure of the president, and they understood he could remove them at will, their appearance nonetheless played right into the hands of the Democrats on the committee and helped perpetuate the myth that they had been wrongfully terminated.

During the weekend of March 3, I tried to focus on my boys' basketball games. Meanwhile, the drumbeat over the dismissals intensified as the Democratic senators pointed to the Evaluation and Review Staff Reports of US attorneys' offices (known as the EARS evaluations). For most of the US attorneys who had been dismissed, the EARS evaluations were generally positive. What critics failed to point out was that an EARS evaluation is *not* a direct report on the US attorney's effectiveness. It is a peer review of the US attorney's office, which the US attorney can influence to some degree, but it is primarily an assessment of career prosecutors. The evaluation is a report on the entire office as a whole over a period of time, which may or may not coincide with the tenure of the US attorney.[3]

Nevertheless, the Democrats claimed that the positive EARS evaluations demonstrated that the US attorneys were not removed for poor performances. On the one hand, they argued that these fine prosecutors had been removed for political reasons. Of course, there would have been nothing improper about removing these US attorneys for political reasons. They were, after all, political appointees. On the other hand, Democrats argued that these prosecutors had been removed to impede an investigation or prosecution. Again, their allegations were absolutely false, but once reported in the media, that didn't seem to matter. Many in the public assumed the US attorneys had been fired because I, as a friend of the president, had recommended their dismissal for improper reasons.

Senior aides at the White House were growing concerned about the story being blown out of proportion, so I met with the senior leadership at the Department of Justice and decided to get my voice into the narrative by writing an op-ed piece for USA Today. Kyle Sampson, now my chief of staff, prepared the initial draft. Meanwhile, members of my team called members of Congress to reassure them that nothing improper had been done in the dismissal of the US attorneys.

When I reviewed Kyle's work on the op-ed piece, I was unhappy with language that characterized the dismissals as a "tragically overblown personnel matter." It was indeed a personnel decision, but asking seven US attorneys to step down was no insignificant matter to the seven individuals involved. I had no interest in publicly criticizing their performances and further disparaging their reputations.

Later that evening, I walked down from my office on the fifth floor at the Department of Justice to the first floor "press shop," the DOJ media center. My communications team, led by Tasia Scolinos, was scrambling to answer media questions. Ironically, we were experiencing a problem with our computers, so Kyle Sampson was on the phone, calling in my article to USA Today.

Standing in the pressroom, I read the final draft of the article and my eyes widened. I took the article to Tasia. "Have you seen this?" I asked.

"No, sir," she responded. "I haven't read that yet."

As Tasia listened, I read aloud the new conclusion regarding the dismissed US attorneys: "They simply lost my confidence. I hope this episode ultimately will be recognized for what it is: an overblown personnel matter." Not only had Kyle kept the "overblown" language, he alluded to the US attorneys' poor performance issues by stating that they had lost my confidence.

I went to Kyle and questioned him about the conclusion. "How could you have included this? You know I would never say publicly that the seven had lost my confidence."

"Well, the senior leadership in the department had included the seven on the dismissal list," he said. "Obviously, if the seven had lost the confidence of DOJ's senior leadership, they had lost the AG's confidence as well."

I sighed and shook my head. I was frustrated with Kyle, but there was no point in discussing this with him; Tasia confirmed that it was too late.

The editorial was already in the hands of a national newspaper and would hit the press in a few hours. The damage was done.

I went back to my office, packed up my briefcase, took the elevator down to the waiting FBI Suburban, and headed home. I sat in sullen silence as the security detail drove out Pennsylvania Avenue. *Oh, Lord*, I prayed. *Where is this going?* I knew the article would set the wrong tone, and rather than alleviate concerns, it would be like throwing red meat to hungry wolves. The Democrats would pounce on it.

The op-ed ran on March 8, and evoked the expected reaction. Senator Patrick Leahy, chairman of the Judiciary Committee, demanded DOJ documents and access to DOJ officials. When I heard about Leahy's contorted calls for answers to contrived questions, I thought he might indirectly be providing us an opportunity to be proactive. After all, we had done nothing wrong and we had nothing to hide. What better way to take the air out of the dark balloons Leahy and others were floating than by offering to fully cooperate and share information with Congress?

I decided to give the inquisition what it wanted—access to written documentation and to personnel. My decision carried significant risks. After all, I had not personally investigated the US attorneys we had dismissed. My staff had done the bulk of the work, and had assured me that making changes in these offices would improve the work of the department. I knew of nothing improper about these recommendations. But in agreeing to allow them to talk to the Judiciary Committee about the dismissals, while I was expressing confidence in our staff, I had no certainty about the questions they might be asked, or how they would answer.

Moreover, my decision invoked institutional issues between the legislative and executive branches of government. I had offered to turn over to Congress DOJ documents, some of which might be privileged information. Normally, institutional interests had to be considered and precedents respected regarding the protection of certain communications within the executive branch.

Nevertheless, I felt that I had to do something dramatic. Full cooperation would show the American public that the Department of Justice was not simply a political arm of the president. If we invoked executive privilege, the Democrats would claim we were hiding something, and the story would continue to escalate and distract from President Bush's efforts in other areas. This was now a distraction for me, and I had so many other important issues that deserved my attention, everything from fighting terrorism and public corruption to the protection of America's children from predators.[4]

The contrast between my willingness to be forthcoming with Congress and what the Obama administration DOJ did a few years later regarding the "Fast and Furious" operation—in which firearms flowed illegally into the hands of the Mexican drug cartel—could not be more stark. When Congress attempted to investigate the Fast and Furious scandal, the Obama administration refused to turn over documents, citing "executive privilege."

Instead of invoking executive privilege, fighting contempt citations, and forcing delay through litigation, I chose to do none of those. Rather, I wanted to demonstrate that we had done nothing wrong.

Later that afternoon, I headed to the Hill to meet with Chairman Leahy, and Senators Specter, Schumer, and others to discuss what information I was willing to provide to the Judiciary Committee. The senators were bringing one staff person, and I was permitted to do the same, but I chose to go alone. As White House counsel, I had often met with senators in their offices unaccompanied by staff, and I quickly discovered that the one-to-one meetings were usually more effective and more productive. I was also conscious of appearances, that it was better to approach with humility rather than an entourage.

Walking in, I suddenly recalled the biblical account of Daniel in the lions' den. I hoped for a relatively brief, cordial meeting in which I could agree to be cooperative. I assumed the senators would be pleased at what I planned to offer them. Upon my arrival, I quickly realized that I had misjudged the senators' goodwill. Senator Specter was late, so the meeting began with Leahy, Schumer, and their staff members, who sat with pens and paper, ready to record every word. Clearly, this was not going to be the comfortable, cordial conversation I had hoped.

Getting straight to the point, I told Chairman Leahy that we had nothing to hide and I would voluntarily testify in an open hearing, but as a cabinet official, I would not sit for a private interview with his staff. I would, however, permit DOJ personnel that had been involved in the US attorneys' decisions to appear at a Judiciary Committee hearing or meetings with the senators' staffs and answer any relevant questions. I also offered to provide the committee with all DOJ documents related to the removals. My only request was that junior staffers, who had no authority in this matter, not be required to testify.

I was not required to be so generous to the Judiciary Committee, and could potentially tie them up in knots for months by slow-walking our search for documents, vigorously contesting the relevancy of documents and fending off requests for access to my staff. I could also urge the president to exert executive privilege. Barely acknowledging my offer of cooperation, Leahy demanded that all junior staffers be available for questioning before a hearing, too, although he conceded that as the attorney general of the United States, I would not be required to spend my time in private interviews.

When Senator Specter arrived, the senators pushed for specifics as to why each of the seven US attorneys had been asked to leave. Keep in mind that as presidential appointees, the US attorneys serve at the pleasure of the president and could be dismissed for any reason whatsoever, even political reasons, provided the removal was not intended to obstruct justice.

I declined to provide much information, not because I intended to obstruct their investigation; I simply was unsure of all the reasons my senior team had for recommending the dismissals. I had decided not to talk to my team about these reasons for fear the Senate might later accuse me of trying to influence potential witnesses. I had not anticipated having to answer specific questions now about the removals. I had understood this meeting to be one in which we would discuss access to information and witnesses. This was a tactical mistake on my part. I had come in good faith to meet with them, and they wanted to turn the occasion into a mini-hearing.

I gave them brief, deliberately careful answers, without getting into any specifics. The senators were unsatisfied.

Senator Specter, the lone Republican in the room besides me, was no help at all. Indeed, right in front of the other committee members and their staffers, Senator Specter criticized me about the *USA Today* article. The comment about this being little more than an overblown personnel matter angered him, he said. "You are wrong. This is much more than just a personnel matter," he said.

I looked back at him in anger. Yes, those words were unfortunate and never should have been included but, *Whose talking points are you reading?* I wondered. Rather than encouraging and supporting me—the attorney general appointed by his Republican president—Senator Specter sounded more like the Democrats.

I left the meeting feeling ambushed, mad that I had been treated so disrespectfully, and angrier at myself for foolishly trusting the people involved. Their attitudes had been consistent with their past overtly partisan actions, but I had hoped that we could work together to calm the situation and avoid wasting any more time, money, or energy on the perfectly legal and proper dismissal of the US attorneys. Apparently that was not the intention of the people I met with in that room.

Afterward, the Senate staffers informed my staff that I had "performed poorly" at the meeting because I had been unable to defend the removals of the US attorneys. My inability—or perhaps unwillingness—to explain the dismissals raised suspicions even higher.

The comments further angered me. This was a political witch-hunt, and the people perpetrating it knew that. Later, a Democrat staffer described their efforts as a pride of lions culling out the weakest member of a herd on which they hoped to prey. Similarly, members of the Democratic caucus would target one cabinet official and target that person for destruction. In this situation, they targeted me. Now understanding the nature of the adversary, my staff and I called various members of Congress that night, hoping to calm the waters, line up allies, and inform them of the potential bad press to come.

During the course of those calls, I learned about what might portend a much worse problem: Paul McNulty had testified to Congress that the White House involvement in the removal of the US attorneys had been "minimal," in fact, nonexistent prior to October 2006. That was not accurate.

I had assigned Kyle Sampson to head up the review of the US attorneys shortly after I became attorney general in 2005, and part of his responsibilities included keeping the White House informed. Paul, apparently, was unaware of Kyle's reports. Nor was Paul aware that the White House had initially suggested that we remove all ninety-three US attorneys at the beginning of President Bush's second term.

The White House *had* been involved in discussions about the US attorneys, and there was nothing improper or unusual about that. Indeed, if the White House had *not* been involved, that might be more of a concern, and given Paul's experience, I was a little surprised he had not known that. The US attorneys across the country were, after all, presidential appointees. Nevertheless, the key point was that Paul's statement before Congress was inaccurate.

This misstatement gave Democrats a reason to expand their investigation to determine whether we had lied. Now the investigation would be less about the substance of the US attorney removals and more about a possible cover-up. This greatly complicated matters for me, forcing me to defend my credibility and integrity. It became a far more difficult environment for the nation's chief law enforcement officer to have to prove that he was credible and truthful.

When I spoke to Paul by phone, he was angry that Kyle had not informed him prior to his testimony about the White House involvement. McNulty had been a House staffer, and he had numerous friends on the Hill. The goodwill that he had accrued over many years in Washington could easily disappear if people thought he had purposely misled Congress—or worse still, given false testimony.

Under ordinary circumstances, Paul's faulty testimony would simply be attributed to poor preparation, but in the hypercharged atmosphere in Washington following the Democrats retaking control of the Senate in 2006, it was like adding more fuel to the already burning fire.

I spoke with Tasia Scolinos in our communications department, and she told me that most reporters had already filed their stories for the day, but they would be hot on the trail. Mere suspicion that the deputy attorney general had given misleading testimony to Congress would create a media frenzy. I asked Tasia to call Kyle for his response to Paul's testimony.

To his credit, Kyle was up front about it. "I simply missed it," he told Tasia. "I should have better prepared Paul for his testimony."

When Tasia called me at home late that night and told me Kyle's explanation, I shook my head and sighed. This latest slip stirred a sense of foreboding within me. I had no reason to disbelieve Kyle, but to let McNulty go before Congress unprepared was inexcusable. It felt like death by a thousand cuts. Little, relatively minor mistakes or misstatements were accumulating to create a seemingly false narrative. There was nothing improper about the dismissals, but for the first time, I realized that it might not matter. We were failing at a spectacular level in getting the true story to the public.

Before making another round of congressional calls the following morning, I met with Kyle in my office. He readily admitted that he had failed to inform Paul that the White House had been informed about his reviews of the US attorneys since 2005.

I had known Kyle since I first came to Washington at the beginning of President Bush's first term. He had worked for me in the White House and the Justice Department. I knew him as a man of integrity, a solid family man, a person of strong faith in God, basically a good man. I trusted Kyle. I didn't believe that he had intended to deceive anyone or ignore his responsibilities. Most likely, McNulty's prep session focused more on the reasons for the removals than the removal process itself.

Our meeting was brief, but serious. It ended with Kyle offering to resign. I felt sadness for Kyle and for our entire department. In our many travels together, Kyle and I sometimes sat alone in the forward cabin of the FBI aircraft, discussing what we hoped we might do after leaving public service in the Bush administration. I had never imagined this scenario.

I did not accept Kyle's resignation, but I did not refuse it either. "I want to think about this over the weekend," I told him. I knew that the media and the Democrats would regard Kyle's resignation as ammunition. They would claim that Kyle Sampson was the scapegoat, that I had offered up his resignation to deflect attention from something or someone else—namely, the president or me. Certainly, that was not true, but in Washington it is the *perception* of truth that trumps all.

As Kyle stepped toward my office door, I stopped him. "Kyle, that *USA Today* op-ed piece hurt me."

He nodded. There was little more we could say.

CHAPTER 35

BEWARE THE IDES OF MARCH

With each passing hour, there seemed to be another story questioning the dismissals and the reasons behind them. I was discouraged
by the accusations that we had improperly removed the US attorneys. I
had willingly offered to cooperate fully with the congressional investigation. I had recused myself from any decisions regarding the production of
DOJ documents, and now Steve Bradbury, the head of the Office of Legal
Counsel, and a team of lawyers shared that responsibility. What bothered
me even more than the media frenzy over the dismissals were the allegations
the Department of Justice was a mess, operating without leadership. In fact,
the department was functioning at its usual high level. We continued to pursue terrorists and their supporters, bringing them to justice. Using reforms
included in the Adam Walsh Act, we intensified efforts to protect children
against sex offenders. Through Project Safe Childhood, we combatted child
exploitation over the Internet. Working with state and local officials, we
continued our fight against drugs and gangs.

While I had always been a person of prayer, these events intensified my
prayer life. I prayed for understanding, wisdom, and patience. Although I
didn't realize it at the time, God was preparing me. I was about to enter the
greatest tribulation of my life.

On Sunday, March 11, Senator Chuck Schumer and Senator Joe Biden, both members of the Senate Judiciary Committee, called publicly for my resignation as attorney general. These two longtime members of the nation's most important committee concerning justice apparently decided to circumvent our country's long-standing principle of "innocent until proven guilty." The Justice Department had not even completed supplying Congress the DOJ documents; congressional staffers had not completed their public hearings of DOJ employees; moreover, my own scheduled testimony before the Judicial Committee was still more than a month away. Yet Schumer and Biden had the audacity to declare me guilty and sentenced.

Bad enough that the Democrat members of the Judiciary Committee knew that the dismissal of the US attorneys was totally permissible, it was outrageous that these so-called proponents of the "rule of law" would rush to judgment before even hearing my testimony or seeing all the evidence. In one of the great ironies of my service, members of the powerful Senate Judiciary Committee shifted the burden onto me to prove my innocence. With no evidence to support their claims of improper dismissal of the seven US attorneys, they said the burden was on *me* to prove that nothing improper had happened.

Think about it. These same Democrats and their ilk had been arguing for more than five years that Bush policies had denied *terrorists* suspected of killing American citizens their fundamental rights in military commissions—including the presumption of innocence. Yet they publicly denied this same consideration to the attorney general of the United States. It was a mockery of their positions on the Judiciary Committee and an insult to me and my office.

Ridiculous or not, the actions by Senators Schumer and Biden fueled further speculation on Monday that I might resign. Amidst the mayhem, I continued to maintain my normal busy schedule of meetings and appearances, including a session with the Judicial Conference Executive Committee and a meeting on immigration at the White House.

My wife, Becky, and I even had time to enjoy a quiet lunch when she came to the Justice Department that day to review television ads with my staff for Project Safe Childhood, one of my signature programs protecting children from predators. Seeing the needs of those kids helped me remember what really mattered about my job.

Monday morning, however, began with an early, somber meeting with Kyle Sampson. Although Kyle had offered to resign, and though I had purposely not accepted his resignation at the time, as I worked through the weekend, I concluded it was best that Kyle step down. So when Kyle informed me on Monday that he was, in fact, resigning as chief of staff, I made no attempt to dissuade him. Still, I was sad for Kyle and his family.

As soon as news of Kyle's resignation became public, as expected, critics portrayed Kyle as the scapegoat, sacrificed to protect others. The calls for my resignation escalated.

Several of my advisors at the Department of Justice urged me to hold a press conference to address some of the issues being raised by Kyle's resignation as well as others mentioned in the media. I agreed, and on the afternoon of March 13, 2007, I scheduled a statement in the attorney general's conference room. Before the media gathered, however, I hosted a conference call with all the remaining US attorneys to express my regrets about how all this had unfolded, to assure them that I would address the situation, and to urge them to stay focused on doing their jobs.

When the members of the media assembled in the conference room, I stated clearly and unequivocally that I had done nothing wrong. Moreover, to the best of my knowledge, nobody else at the department had done anything improper regarding the removal of the seven US attorneys. I emphasized that to reassure the American citizens that we were cooperating fully with the inquiries by Congress. In reference to the purposefully planted rumors of my resignation, I reminded the media that I was not a quitter and I would continue to serve my country and our president. I then fielded a few questions, mostly about my role in the firings of the US attorneys, the process we followed, as well as Kyle's resignation. The entire press conference totaled little more than nine minutes.

Nevertheless, I later thought about some of my answers in that brief encounter. I realized that I was not precise with some of my responses regarding the nature and frequency of my discussions with Kyle and others about the US attorney removals. Given the political nature of the congressional investigation, I considered it imperative to correct the record.

Consequently, I decided to accept requests to appear on the morning network news shows. I made my rounds from one media outlet to the next, beginning with Hannah Storm on the CBS Early Show at 6:30 a.m., then at 6:40 a.m. I appeared with George Stephanopoulos on Good Morning America. At 6:50 a.m. I was talking live with Gretchen Carlson on Fox and Friends, then at 7:05 a.m. I discussed the situation with Miles O'Brien on CNN American Morning, and then I was on at 7:30 a.m. with Alex Witt on MSNBC. If you've ever wondered how the "talking heads" can appear on so many network shows in such a short amount of time, it is because they are all located in the same Washington building complex.

Following my television romp, I gave an extended interview to Pete Williams, correcting any misimpressions I might have left as a result of my press conference the previous day.

There; it was done. As humbling as it was to admit that I hadn't done a great job during the initial press conference, I was glad the media had given me the opportunity to put out the correct information.

Unfortunately, certain Democratic members of Congress and the media willfully chose to emphasize my original statements in the March 13 press conference, and almost totally ignored the corrected statements I made to the media the following day. When Kyle Sampson later testified under oath before the Senate Judiciary Committee, even he acknowledged that I had misspoke at the March 13 press conference, but he also testified that I had clarified my remarks.

I had hoped the press conference and media interviews would calm the waters. I needed to focus on leading the Department of Justice, and there was much work to be done. Following the morning interviews on March 14, I received a positive briefing on the department's efforts in Iraq in promoting democracy and the rule of law. Afterward, I met with an Egyptian delegation and then participated in a judicial selection committee meeting at the White House.

Of course, by this time, having recognized flaws in our process, I had set about trying to address them, beginning with ideas for a series of reforms. One suggestion was the establishment of a task force of US attorneys and DOJ officials to develop a system to regularly review the performance of US attorneys. Second, create a policy of reporting contacts between local and state officials and US attorneys regarding ongoing cases. Third, establish a protocol involving the Public Integrity Section of the Criminal Division to ensure that the discipline or removal of a US attorney is not inappropriately connected to a public corruption case.

Just prior to a scheduled lunch in the attorney general's dining room with Democratic senator Sheldon Whitehouse on March 14, I received a call from President Bush, who was traveling aboard *Air Force One*. He told me that he planned to tell the press that he had talked with me about the US attorney dismissals, and I had promised to take corrective actions, which I had already outlined to Paul McNulty. We weren't going to rehire the seven fired US attorneys, but we would do a better job in the future in handling any dismissals.

I assured President Bush that the Department of Justice was working as hard as possible to be responsive to Congress. He seemed satisfied with that.

The involvement of the eighth US attorney, Bud Cummins, who served the Eastern District of Arkansas and had been asked to speak at the hearing before the Judiciary Committee, along with three of the US attorneys who had been removed, continued to bother me. His case was quite different from the other seven. Bud had served his full four-year term, so in June 2006, the White House chose to replace him, and under my interim appointment power granted to the attorney general by the PATRIOT Act, I appointed Tim Griffin.

My goal was to get Griffin in place immediately so he could establish himself and show the people of Arkansas that he could do the job, and then get him nominated by the president and confirmed by the Senate. Although the PATRIOT Act provision allowed the attorney general to appoint US attorneys for an unlimited duration, I preferred all the US attorneys carry the added authority associated with a presidential appointment and a Senate confirmation. It gave both the public and the US attorney added confidence.

I knew, however, even to get Tim Griffin a hearing with the Judiciary Committee, he needed the support of at least one of the two Democratic senators from Arkansas, either Blanche Lincoln or Mark Pryor.

Pryor was one of the few Democrats who had voted for my confirmation as attorney general. I liked him, and I thought he respected me. A former state attorney general, he understood the challenges of the office, and he could be a key vote in the Senate on a number of administration law-enforcement issues. I initiated a dialogue with Senator Pryor about supporting Griffin and told him that I intended to recommend the president nominate Griffin.

Pryor remained suspicious and made it clear that he had problems with Griffin. I couldn't understand why, but some in the White House believed that Pryor regarded Griffin as a potential political rival for his Senate seat, thus explaining his reluctance to see him receive any presidential appointment. Pryor did not tell me that, so I urged him to at least give Griffin a chance. "I will appoint Griffin on a temporary basis, and then you and I can both evaluate his work for possible nomination and hopefully confirmation," I told Senator Pryor.

Although Senator Pryor assured me that he would be open-minded about Griffin, in my judgment he never gave Tim a fair shot. Shortly after I had appointed Tim on an interim basis, Senator Pryor informed me that he would not support Griffin.

I felt the senator was wrong about Tim, but I remained true to my word. Just as I had promised Pryor, I called Tim Griffin and informed him that I would not recommend him to the White House for a presidential appointment because he could not be confirmed without Pryor's blessing, and I wanted a Senate-confirmed US attorney.

After this, an e-mail between Kyle Sampson and an associate counsel at the White House was uncovered among the DOJ documents freely turned over to Congress. In the e-mail, Kyle discussed his thoughts about a plan to appoint Griffin under the attorney general's interim authority, and then allow him to serve indefinitely without Senate confirmation until the end of the president's term in 2008. Kyle had not discussed that plan with me. He may have hoped that we might go that route, but if so, it was nothing more than wishful thinking. That was never my intention.

The disclosure of the e-mail elicited a prompt response by Pryor. On March 15, he went on the Senate floor, called me a liar, and demanded my resignation. He said, "I feel lied to. And the truth is, I was lied to, because I was told that the attorney general—and he not only said it to me; he said it to the Senate Judiciary Committee and he said it to the world—[that he] wanted a Senate-confirmed US Attorney in every slot. That is absolutely not true in Arkansas, based on the e-mail from the Justice Department."[1]

Pryor made his statements while I was working on strategies to make US neighborhoods safer and meeting with senior government officials from Sri Lanka.

I was stunned. Without even the courtesy of calling me—which Pryor easily could have done—he had gone on record in the United States Senate and called me a liar, with no opportunity to explain or rebut his disparaging remarks. Although the senator's statement was blatantly false—I never lied to Pryor, nor would I—his comments on the Senate floor reinforced claims that we had removed the seven US attorneys so we could install our own nominees without the scrutiny of a Senate confirmation. Nothing could have been further from the truth.

The new provision in the PATRIOT Act contemplated the interim appointment of a US attorney by the attorney general during an emergency period when the Senate could not act to confirm the US attorney. The Senate never intended to give up its power to review and confirm US attorneys. What I intended to do with Griffin was in keeping with the law—to appoint him on an interim basis and then have the president nominate him to the Senate for confirmation.

Ironically, that was why I had initiated conversations with Pryor in the first place. Had I simply wished to appoint an interim US attorney indefinitely, I had the full authority of the law to do so. As with the confirmation process for judges, however, the home-state senators are almost always considered. Since Griffin would be serving in Pryor's state, I felt it only courteous to engage him in the process. That made his attack on me even more disappointing.

Months later, when the Department of Justice inspector general looked into the US attorney dismissals, the IG noted, "Our investigation did not find evidence that Attorney General Gonzales ever supported the idea to appoint Griffin to an indefinite term to avoid the Senate confirmation process."[2]

Under oath, Kyle Sampson testified that I had never supported the idea. Kyle was subjected to grueling and repeated questioning by senators who appeared almost desperate to get him to confess that I had misled Senator Pryor and the Judiciary Committee. Nevertheless, Kyle stood tall, and I was proud of him for telling the truth. In response to the same question, asked in a variety of ways, Kyle said three times that the idea of interim appointments to avoid Senate confirmation was never adopted by the attorney general. He answered four times that I had rejected the idea and that I had been unwilling to consider it.

According to transcripts, handwritten notes, e-mails, and other documents relating to the testimony of Harriet Miers, and released by the House Judiciary Committee on August 11, 2009—nearly eight months after President Obama had taken office—Harriet Miers testified that she spoke with me about the Griffin appointment and that I had told her that I did not intend to bypass the Senate. Harriet stated that no decision was made to use the PATRIOT Act appointment authority in the manner Kyle Sampson had described in his e-mail.

Of course, when I testified before Congress, I emphasized those same points.

It seems the only person who doubted my intentions was Senator Pryor of Arkansas. In fact, my decision to inform Griffin that I could not recommend him for appointment because Pryor opposed him actually did not sit well with the White House at the time. That was, after all, a decision about a presidential appointment, so it was really their call. Griffin later confided to the inspector general that Karl Rove had informed him that some people in the White House were unhappy I had decided Griffin would not be a presidential appointee. I understood that, but I had made a promise to Pryor and I had kept my word.

Pryor's inflammatory, false comments further damaged my standing as the US attorney general. His accusations made it more difficult to obtain the support of Senator Pryor's colleagues, even Democratic senator Ken Salazar, whom I was proud to have introduced me at my confirmation hearing in 2005.

Despite the media's frenzied speculation that I might resign—they had already begun naming potential replacements—I was still the attorney general, so I wanted to take positive steps to get past the scuttlebutt. By this time, I had asked the department's Office of Professional Responsibility and the DOJ's inspector general to conduct their own independent investigations, so Congress and the American people could be 100 percent assured of the facts. I hoped this would show I had nothing to hide. Why would I offer up internal DOJ documents, and offer myself and other DOJ personnel to testify and give interviews, as well as request an internal OPR and IG investigation, if I had done something wrong?

To ensure the independence and integrity of these internal investigations as well as those of Congress, I purposely did not talk to any of the DOJ employees who had played a significant role in the removals and had been interviewed by congressional staff members. Consequently, I was not able to answer many questions posed later at my hearing. I had no basis to refresh my memory. So my decision to order internal investigations may have helped shield the DOJ, but it indirectly hurt me.

I met with Chuck Rosenberg, a career prosecutor, a US attorney, and formerly Jim Comey's chief of staff, and I asked Chuck to come on board temporarily as my chief of staff until I could find a permanent replacement for Kyle. Chuck agreed. His appointment was intended as a clear statement that I refused to politicize the Department of Justice.

I also hoped that by having Chuck as chief of staff, it might calm concerns among other US attorneys around the country. To that end, I held a conference call the afternoon of March 16 with the more than eighty remaining US attorneys. I repeated my personal regret that the dismissals of some of their colleagues had created a distraction interfering with all of us doing our duties. I reassured them that the firings were not intended to obstruct justice, and I informed them that future removals would be handled differently. I encouraged them to do their jobs, to follow the leads in their investigations regardless where the evidence might take them.

That evening, I hosted a wonderful event at the Justice Department Great Hall for wounded soldiers and their families. I had been discouraged due to the developments of the past few weeks, but when I saw those brave, young, wounded soldiers and witnessed their indefatigable spirits, my own spirit lifted as well. Yes, my character and reputation had been attacked, but my problems seemed trivial as I met and talked with these heroes. I went home that night grateful to God, buoyed by the experience, and better able to put my own troubles in proper perspective.

The president called me about 7:15 on Tuesday morning, March 20. He was hopeful that the worst fallout from the US attorney case was over. "Let's move on," he said. We talked briefly. "Hang in there and fight, Fredo," he encouraged me. He joked that at least the US attorney firings had diverted attention from the department's inspector general's report on abuses relating to the FBI's use of National Security Letters. Then he repeated what he had often said before: "This is just another example of Washington at its worst."

The president told me the White House would inform Congress that they would release documents between the White House and Department of Justice, and certain staff members would be able to sit for private interviews. He was not willing to let the White House staff testify regarding the US attorney dismissals because it would set a bad precedent.

I agreed with the advice that Fred Fielding, now White House counsel, had given to the president.

The president reassured me that he fully supported me. But even as he said those words, I questioned how these events might possibly impact him. On the other hand, I was no quitter, and I certainly did not wish to reward the despicable conduct of the political hacks. Most importantly, I knew that I had done nothing improper.

"I will stay on and fight if you want me to, sir," I told him, "but I worry that there may come a time when you need to do something different. If that time comes, we should do it." Without stating it, we both knew that we were talking about my leaving the administration. "I love my job, I love my country, and our family loves you," I told him, "but I'm willing to do whatever needs to be done."

"The White House will produce their documents," the president said, "and then we will all see where matters stand." He needed to assess the situation then, he said.

That same morning, I attended a terrorism briefing with the president at 8:25. The entire Homeland Security briefing team was present, and President Bush made a point of telling everyone that we were going to fight these attacks on the Justice Department. He told me that on his recent trip to Mexico, the Mexican president had offered to defend me. President Bush thanked him but said, no, he would defend me.

As the briefings began, President Bush paused, looked at me, and said quietly, "One day we will be sitting on a porch in a pair of rocking chairs somewhere in Texas and laughing about all this nonsense."

When the briefings concluded, we all turned to leave. President Bush winked at me and said, "Go get 'em, Fredo!"

The president's strong support in front of my colleagues was encouraging in the face of the numerous stories in the press predicting my imminent departure from the administration. The White House did its best to knock the air out of such stories. Aboard *Air Force One* on the way to Kansas City, White House press secretary Tony Snow confirmed to the traveling press corps that the president had called me at 7:15 a.m. to reaffirm his support. "It was a very strong vote of confidence," Tony explained.

White House deputy press secretary Dana Perino also confirmed the president's call and emphasized that I still had the president's backing despite the controversy. When pressed, Perino stated straightforwardly that rumors of a search for my replacement were "untrue."

In the days and weeks that followed, I met in person with as many US attorneys as possible. I traveled around the country on what I referred to as "The Listening Tour," expressing my regrets but also listening to the concerns of our US attorneys. I explained to them in person what had happened in regard to their dismissed colleagues, allowed them to ask questions, and encouraged them to continue their good work. Most of the US attorneys were quite appreciative of my efforts, even if they disagreed with the way the dismissals had been handled.

In one of several meetings that I hosted with our prosecutors to explain the removals, Tom Moss, the US attorney from Idaho, spoke straightforwardly. Tom was slightly older and more experienced than many of our other US attorneys, and I valued his opinion. Tom admitted that the dismissal of his former colleagues was painful for him because they were friends. He believed, however, the removals were not inappropriate, and he was angry about the scurrilous accusations repeatedly hurled at me suggesting that certain removals were motivated to obstruct justice. Tom offered encouragement in the form of a metaphor, comparing the Justice Department as a castle under siege. "You are the moat surrounding the castle," he told me. "You need to stand firm and defend the department and the employees from this attack." I appreciated Tom's support, and I needed it.

Regardless of where I went, the firings dogged me at every event. Whether I was reporting progress on fighting the meth epidemic, child predators, or identity theft, the media inevitably regurgitated the Democrats' talking points regarding the US attorney dismissals and my future plans.

For now, my plans were to continue as attorney general as long as President Bush wanted me to do so. I hoped and prayed that was God's plan as well. Nevertheless, many in the media speculated that my future depended on my performance at my hearing before the Senate Judiciary Committee—an event now only a few weeks away.

CHAPTER 36

TOO SAD FOR A COUNTRY SONG

As the controversy over the US attorney dismissals dragged on, President Bush encouraged me to hang in there, and I was more than willing to do that, but I worried about the continued suggestions that the Department of Justice had suffered under my leadership. I knew the facts would confirm that the US attorney removals were not improper, but how could I defend myself against attacks that morale was low at DOJ? When events heated up in March 2007, White House press secretary Tony Snow was tremendously helpful in coming to my defense. Tony was a highly respected former journalist and newscaster, and also known as a person of impeccable character. If Tony told you something, you could believe it. And Tony was telling the reporters hovering over the US attorney story that there was nothing improper there and the president fully supported me as attorney general.

While I wrestled with issues related to guns and violence on our borders with Mexico, and worked with the Iraqis on a new constitution, Kyle Sampson was testifying on March 29. He clarified that keeping Tim Griffin in place indefinitely as US attorney in Arkansas without Senate confirmation was not my plan. That helped, although some of Kyle's other statements played into the hands of the Democratic senators who seemed intent on ascribing political motivations to us.

Referring to my March 13 press statement, Kyle told the Senate Judiciary Committee, "I don't think the attorney general's statement that he was not involved in any discussions about US attorney removals is accurate." He also stated that White House counsel Harriet Miers and I had made the final decisions about whom to fire. Technically Kyle was correct; in my statements on March 13 I said I'd had no such discussions. I had, however, clarified my statement on March 14 in media interviews, confirming that I had engaged in some discussions. But there was no final decision until Kyle presented the final recommendations to me and then presented them to the White House.

My hearing before the Senate Judiciary Committee was set for Tuesday, April 17, so during the week of April 2, I made additional calls to some members of Congress seeking their advice. Most were helpful and supportive. Senator Mitch McConnell asked, "Where is the scandal here? There's not a scintilla of evidence to support a scandal."

"I've been through this kind of thing before," Senator Trent Lott said. He reminded me that we were approaching Easter, the season of forgiveness and resurrection. "It is a time of redemption," he said. That was a tremendously hopeful message to me. Senator Lott also expressed displeasure that the individuals who had been removed had allowed themselves to become political pawns. "The US attorneys ought to have their fannies spanked!"

Senator Joe Lieberman provided a subtle warning to me. "Everything in this town is partisan," he told me. He implied that I could expect intense opposition from Democrats. Senator Orrin Hatch was angry on my behalf. He was a true warrior for me, and he encouraged me to stay strong. Congressman Chris Cannon was adamant that I did not need to kowtow. "Apologize for what?" he asked. "This whole thing is upside down. The president and the AG make these decisions, not the attorneys."

CNN commentator Ruben Navarrette Jr. saw through the smoke, noting "Gonzales' critics aren't after the truth. They're after him."[1]

The advice from members of Congress ran along consistent lines: Be tough. Be open. Be forthright. Be humble. Remind the committee that President Clinton fired all ninety-three US attorneys, not seven or eight.

Admit the dismissals could have been handled better but nothing about the removals crossed any lines of impropriety. Acknowledge that you should have been more involved, despite your trust in your staff's expertise in this area.

Indeed, nearly two years later, when the inspector general issued a report on this incident, the strongest admonition was that Paul McNulty and I should have provided Kyle Sampson more oversight. In retrospect, I agree; I did not meet the standard I expected of myself. Yet at the time, I trusted these men to do their jobs, and based on their past experience with personnel issues and their knowledge of the department and of our US attorneys, I just didn't feel it necessary to micromanage them.

As perhaps the most important hearing of my professional career loomed ahead of me, in early April I traveled to Pennsylvania to attend the funeral service of FBI special agent Barry Lee Bush, who had been killed in the line of duty. I arrived back home in time to attend our son Gabriel's soccer practice. The range of emotions I experienced that day was remarkable.

On Sunday, April 15, just days before my scheduled hearing, Senator Schumer issued a press release that was essentially a hit piece, stating that my upcoming testimony "will be make or break for him. Alberto Gonzales is a central figure in this investigation. The burden of proof is now on Alberto Gonzales."[2]

Schumer focused on the misstatements I made on March 13, and chose to ignore the clarifications I presented the following morning. Schumer repeatedly accused me of lying. "He said the US attorneys were dismissed for performance reasons," Schumer said. "We now know they received outstanding performance evaluations."

Schumer was referring to the EARS evaluations, which were more about the work of the entire office personnel than the US attorney. It is quite possible for a US attorney's office to have a good EARS evaluation, even if the US attorney is not performing adequately.

"He also told us that he would never make a US attorney change for a political reason. It is clear now that he did."

No, I did not. While the Democrats claimed that complaints by Republican senator Pete Domenici had led to the dismissal of David Iglesias, these hypocrites would have been furious had I ignored their complaints about the performance of a US attorney in their states. Furthermore, they chose to ignore Senator Feinstein's complaints about the performance of US attorneys in the San Diego and San Francisco offices. No one was dismissed to obstruct justice by impeding an investigation or prosecution, as was later confirmed by the DOJ inspector general.

"Now the attorney general has said that he was not involved in discussions about the firings, but his former chief of staff [has] said that was an inaccurate statement."

Again, Schumer was referring to when I had misspoken in the press conference saying that I had no discussions about the firings. I did indeed have a handful of discussions with Kyle over a period of time, and I had clarified that point in my interviews the next day. Moreover, I was the one who had assigned Kyle the responsibility of reviewing the US attorneys, so of course I had some limited discussions about the matter. But the Democratic caucus clearly wanted to give the impression that we were in collusion with the White House and were discussing reasons for dumping the US attorneys that included the obstruction of justice. That was blatantly false.

Schumer's press release confirmed that I was not voluntarily appearing at a hearing to provide helpful information so we could lay aside the issue once and for all; I was walking into a snake pit. *This is going to be a tough hearing*, I thought. I had suspected that the hearing was more for political theater—as many congressional hearings are—rather than a genuine quest to uncover the truth. I knew then the hearing had already devolved into a partisan witch-hunt.

Later that same day, on Sunday, April 15, I was in my office preparing for the hearing and studying binders of information about potential questions I might be asked when I received a telephone call from a former high-ranking DOJ official whose judgment I trusted. He told me that a senior Republican member of the Judiciary Committee had contacted him and warned that the Democrats on the committee were setting a perjury trap for me. "They're going to come after you," he said. He advised me to hire a lawyer and take counsel with me to the hearing. "I have the names of a couple of good defense lawyers I'd recommend," he offered.

I was stunned. I had no reason to doubt my friend. I knew he was concerned for me. Nevertheless, I was the attorney general; I was the chief law enforcement officer in the country. What message would it send if I were to take a lawyer with me during my testimony? Moreover, I had encouraged people at the Department of Justice to cooperate with the congressional investigation. How could I expect others to cooperate with the investigations if I refused to answer questions on the advice of counsel? I wasn't going to "lawyer up" just because of the antagonistic attitudes of some senators on the Judicial Committee.

"Thanks, but I can't do that," I said. "I've done nothing wrong."

The call, while well intentioned, bothered me. I had planned to fully cooperate with the congressional investigation and sincerely wanted to answer any questions and explain what I knew about the dismissal of the US attorneys. The danger, of course, was that I did not know what I did not know. Prior to the hearing, I reviewed some documentation, but I dared not talk to other witnesses and risk charges of tampering with the congressional investigation or the internal OPR/OIG investigation.[3] I also did not know what information may be hidden in memos or the documents and e-mails turned over by the DOJ, nor did I have a good recollection of the meeting in which I had accepted the unanimous recommendations of the department's senior leadership. My perceptions of the events might differ from those of Kyle, or Paul McNulty, or even those of Mike Battle, the director of the executive office for US attorneys, to whom fell the task of informing the removed attorneys that their service was no longer required.

Schumer and Leahy and their colleagues were on a destructive mission. They had, indeed, culled me from the herd. If I could be tricked into answering the same questions in different ways, or in a manner inconsistent with sworn public testimony or private interviews with others involved, they would say my misstatements were intentional and that I had committed perjury.

I understood the need for being careful with every word of my testimony. To do otherwise would not merely imperil my standing as attorney general, but that kind of legal jeopardy could devastate my family. Becky and our sons had made tremendous sacrifices so I could serve our nation, and I was not about to risk their futures by foolishly falling into an intentionally set perjury trap.

I prayed about this. With the stakes so high, I decided that if I had the slightest doubt about an answer, if I did not have accurate recollection about any facts the interrogators might ask, I would qualify my answers or state that I did not recall or that I did not know the specific details. I understood that I would sound defensive and would be castigated for parsing words, or appear that I was attempting to hide something. I could no longer give the Democrats the benefit of the doubt, or assume that their questions were intended to learn the truth. They already knew the truth. This was not about *truth*; it was about raw politics.

The hearing was scheduled for Tuesday, April 17, but on Monday, a tragic shooting occurred at Virginia Tech University, with a lone gunman killing thirty-two students and teachers and wounding seventeen others on the Blacksburg, Virginia, campus. Chairman Leahy called immediately after the first reports and asked to reschedule on Thursday, April 19. I said, "Of course."

———

As my security detail drove up Connecticut Avenue on Thursday, we passed the protestors outside the Hart Senate Office Building, where the hearing was to take place. There were always protestors, it seemed, anywhere it was announced that I was to speak, thanks to the mistaken belief that I had advocated the torture of detainees and was responsible for the president's electronic surveillance program, and every other controversial Bush policy. Walking into the building, I felt as though I were walking into a judgment hall. I thought, *I really don't want to do this. Why, God?* I prayed. *Why this?*

I assumed the hearing was going to be difficult; that was to be expected, but the fact that I would not be able to definitively answer the committee's questions because of a poor memory and because of my concerns that an answer contrary to what had already been provided to the committee would affect every response I made. But I had to do this. It was not merely about me. I stood for the department and 105,000 employees. This was about them, too, and the entire Bush administration.

My wife, Becky, came to the hearing along with Elizabeth Law, a friend from Becky's Bible study group. Becky was even more apprehensive about the hearing than I was. Although I didn't know it at the time, Elizabeth and Becky prayed for me before they entered the hearing room that morning.

As I did before every congressional hearing I attended, I greeted each senator cordially before we all took our seats. The senators sat at the bench and I sat at a table at the front of the room, surrounded by spectators, media, and protestors. The chairman encouraged people to crowd closer so more could come inside. The atmosphere was charged, as though people were anticipating a great sporting event. I knew the tenor of the meeting would change quickly once the questioning began.

Indeed, I provided few answers during the hearing and repeatedly answered, "I don't recall" or "I don't remember" to scores of questions. That was frustrating for me and exasperating for the senators, but it was what I had to do to protect myself.

The hearing began around 9:30 a.m. and continued for more than five hours. I sought to present a careful defense of the firings, apologizing for the way they were handled, but defending them as the right decision. "While the process that led to the resignations was flawed, I firmly believe that nothing improper occurred," I said. "It would be improper to remove a US attorney to interfere with or influence a particular prosecution for partisan political gain. I did not do that. I would never do that."

In his opening statement, Senator Specter opined, "I believe you have come a good distance from the day you said that this is an overblown personnel matter in the USA Today article." It irritated me that he just could not let that go. Specter went on to say, "So this is as important a hearing as I can recall, short of the confirmation of Supreme Court justices, more important than your confirmation hearing. In a sense, it is a reconfirmation hearing." With leadership like that, I wondered whether the other Republicans on the committee would come to my defense.

Much of the discussion focused on the meeting held at the Justice Department on November 27, 2006, in which the recommendations for the dismissals—recommendations that I believe reflected the consensus of the Justice Department's senior leadership—were discussed. I had a full schedule of meetings and events that week including a trip to Mexico, so this meeting was simply one of many. Further, replacing seven of ninety-three US attorneys who had served their full terms at the pleasure of the president was not improper. When Kyle presented the recommendations, believing that he and our staff had been working on it for some time, I trusted they had conducted a thorough review and I relied on their conclusions. In truth, I could not recall the full details forming the basis for each of their recommendations.

That put me at a disadvantage as I attempted to answer the senators' questions, because I had not talked to other witnesses about each dismissal. I knew, however, that the US attorneys could be dismissed for any reason or no reason other than obstruction of justice, so the fact that we were making changes was not improper. Nevertheless, the senators grew increasingly irritated when I repeatedly answered, "I don't recall" or "I don't remember" to their questions about what was discussed at that November meeting.

I was not being coy, just careful. I could not remember the specifics of that meeting. Rather than pretend, I honestly admitted that I did not recall the details of the discussions, but acknowledged that I had accepted the recommendations that we inform the White House the seven US attorneys should be removed. The decision to recommend their removal was mine. That sent the inquisitors into a collective frenzy, with several making derogatory, insulting public statements about me and my leadership. Ironically, had I lied, I might have easily negotiated the inquiries.

In a subsequent conversation I had with Senator Jeff Sessions, himself a former Alabama attorney general and a former US attorney, Senator Sessions drawled, "It sure would be good if you could recall that meeting."

I, too, wished that I could recall that meeting, if for no other reason than that it would hopefully soothe the anger of some of the US attorneys removed subsequent to that meeting. What happened there affected their lives as well, and I'm sure they wanted to think it was important enough that I would remember it.

In addition to the November meeting, many of the questions centered on my role in the process. I testified that my role was limited. Yes, there were periodic questions or conversations about individual US attorneys. But I assumed there were numerous ongoing, substantive sessions among my senior team evaluating all of our US attorneys. Certainly, there were meetings and discussions that did not involve me. I had directed an evaluation and I expected that was being done, so I testified that over the course of two years, my involvement in the process was limited. I stand by that statement.

The Democrats on the Judicial Committe were brutal, but Republican ranking member Arlen Specter was no help. He pontificated, "We have to evaluate whether you are really being forthright in saying that you, quote, should have been more precise, close quote, when the reality is that your characterization of your participation is just significantly, if not totally, at variance with the facts."[4]

Republican Lindsey Graham said, "Mr. Attorney General, most of this is a stretch. I think it's clear to me that some of these people just had personality conflicts with people in your office or at the White House and, you know, we made up reasons to fire them. Some of it sounds good. Some of it doesn't. And that's the lesson to be learned here . . . at the end of the day, you said something that struck me: 'That sometimes it just came down to these were not the right people at the right time.' If I applied that standard to you, what would you say?"

I responded, "Senator, what I would say is, is that I believe that I continue to be effective as the attorney general of the United States. We've done some great things."[5] But that was not the message the senators wanted to hear.

Senator Tom Coburn said, "But to me, there has to be consequences to accepting responsibility. And I would just say, Mr. Attorney General, it's my considered opinion that the exact same standards should be applied to you in how this was handled. And it was handled incompetently. The communication was atrocious. It was inconsistent. It's generous to say that there were misstatements. That's a generous statement. And I believe you ought to suffer the consequences that these others have suffered." Coburn then caustically suggested, "And I believe that the best way to put this behind us is your resignation."[6] Senator Coburn's staff had warned mine in advance that he would ask for my resignation, but that didn't soften the blow.

I basically responded that I intended to stick around, address the problems, work with the Senate, and continue the fine progress of the Department of Justice.

At the end of the hearing, Senator Specter said, "I think we have gone about as far as we can go." Then to emphasize his disdain, Specter added, "We have not gotten really [sic] answers."[7] Apart from avoiding a charge of perjury, I did myself little good that day.

During this time of turmoil, of course I worried about my future. I worried even more, however, how these hearings and media stories would affect the work of the Department of Justice. Fortunately, in a Senate Judiciary Committee hearing on March 27, 2007, when asked whether the dismissal of the US attorneys had impeded ongoing investigations, FBI director Bob Mueller answered firmly that they had not.[8]

Although my hearing had been brutal, I chose not to dwell on it. It was time to move on. I had to concentrate on my job as well as my family. For example, two days later, I joined my sons in participating in a volunteer cleanup of the Anacostia River. Even there, however, reporters lurked nearby us. That evening, I attended the black-tie White House Correspondents' Dinner. Usually a festive occasion, when most attendees let down their guard for a few hours, I nonetheless felt that all eyes of the media were on me. My press hosts for the evening admitted that they had wondered if I would even attend, speculating that my absence might be the signal that I was resigning.

I told them straightforwardly, "I am here, and I am not resigning."

Following my testimony in April, the Democratic senators redirected the thrust of their attacks beyond my decision to recommend that President Bush dismiss seven US attorneys to my competence as attorney general. They portrayed me as too inept to lead the department. By late April and on into early May, various senators, including several so-called conservative voices in Congress, abandoned me and joined the chorus calling for me to resign.

It was a tough time for my family and me, but I maintained my focus on serving the American people. There were 105,000 DOJ employees counting on me. The president was counting on me. And my family was counting on me. While Becky read every word of the criticisms, I did not. The accusations were not true so I ignored them. The strength to do so came not from political sources but from my faith, bolstered by continued prayer with my wife.

The chorus soon took on even more vitriolic tones. Critics hurled insults saying I had lied about the Terrorist Surveillance Program and that I had politicized the Justice Department; they trumpeted their misrepresentations repeatedly, cumulatively creating a snowball effect. The snowball continued to grow and became a mountain of false accusations, with my critics and even some of my so-called political friends excoriating me for my overall failures as the attorney general, rather than pointing to any actual evidence of my failures.

By this time, I had asked Kevin O'Connor, the US attorney from Connecticut, to serve as my interim chief of staff. He served in both positions for the remainder of my tenure as attorney general. Kevin was bright and outgoing, and well respected by his peers. Over time, he became more than my chief of staff; he became an advisor and a friend.

I sat for another hearing on May 11, 2007, this time with the House Judiciary Committee, chaired by Michigan Democrat John Conyers Jr. The questions were much the same, as were my answers, but the Republican members of the House were much more supportive and more protective of me than had been their counterparts in the Senate.

Several congressmen didn't bother to ask any questions at all about the dismissed prosecutors, and others disdained the Democrats' pursuit of the topic.[9] Lamar Smith of Texas, the ranking Republican on the committee, suggested that it might be time to end the investigation. "If there are no fish in this lake, we should reel in our lines of questions, dock our empty boat and turn to more pressing issues," Smith said.[10]

Amen! I thought. I went back to work with renewed vigor, concentrating on matters such as immigration, border violence, the rule of law in Iraq, and the increasing Islamist radicalization in our prisons.

On May 15, 2007, former deputy attorney general Jim Comey, now in the private sector prior to being selected in 2013 as FBI director under President Obama,[11] testified before the Democratic members of the Judiciary Committee and Senator Specter regarding the dismissal of the US attorneys. But the real agenda became clear when the senators questioned Comey about Stellar Wind. Before getting to Comey, however, the acting chairman, Senator Schumer, presented a caustic opening statement, misrepresenting facts or casting them in the worst possible light.

Schumer went on to say that Comey "has contradicted other DOJ officials by testifying that most of the fired US attorneys performed well."[12] Interestingly, when Schumer finally got around to asking Comey about the US attorneys—after Schumer questioned him for more than twenty minutes about the visit to John Ashcroft's hospital room—the former deputy attorney general was much more vague than Schumer had implied. That seemed to matter little to Senator Schumer.

Although I was not at the hearing, Schumer tipped his hand early—the hearing was not nearly so much about the dismissal of the US attorneys as it was about me, and specifically, Schumer's intent to oust me as attorney general. Unfortunately, other Republicans on the committee were not in attendance, and the only Republican there to defend me was Senator Specter—and he didn't. Specter quickly piled on with his future Democratic colleagues.

Anyone who has testified before Congress or served in the federal government would find it hard to believe that Jim Comey had not been warned in advance that in a hearing about the removal of US attorneys, the committee would inquire in detail about Stellar Wind and the visit to former attorney general John Ashcroft in the hospital. Comey had been the US attorney in Manhattan, so he obviously had a relationship with New York senator Schumer. But an even more important relationship may have been the one between Comey and Preet Bharara, who served as chief counsel and staff director of the Senate Judiciary Committee's Subcommittee on Administrative Oversight and the Courts. Mr. Bharara worked under Comey when he was US attorney in New York. A former assistant US attorney in the Southern District of New York, Mr. Bharara helped lead the Senate Judiciary Committee investigation regarding the removed US attorneys.

While debriefing Jim Comey prior to his testimony, Bharara learned about the hospital visit. He took that information to Schumer. Years later, in an interview with the *New Yorker*, Bharara acknowledged his prehearing collusion with Comey and Schumer. According to writer Jeffrey Toobin, "In the days leading up to the hearing, Bharara and Schumer told no one about the revelation that was coming. 'I was afraid that if the story got out of what Jim was going to say the Bush Administration would figure out a way to prevent him from testifying,' Bharara said. 'We needed to preserve the element of surprise.'"[13]

One might wonder whether Preet Bharara's role in ambushing the Bush administration was a factor in his appointment as a US attorney in Manhattan.

When I found out from our DOJ legislative liaison that Comey was testifying, I was surprised. *What? What is he testifying about?* I wondered. Jim had been away from Washington for several years, so why would he be called upon to testify about the US attorneys? It was also odd that we had received no notice at DOJ regarding the appearance of one of the former members of our leadership team at a Senate hearing. I called White House counsel Fred Fielding, and Fred confirmed that he had no prior notice of Comey's testimony either. I was disappointed that the man who had been given so much in his legal career—appointed by President Bush as a US attorney and then as deputy attorney general—did not even notify the White House or me in advance of his testimony. It felt to me that Jim's loyalty was more to his friend Preet Bharaha and to Chuck Schumer.

As the hearing was taking place on Capitol Hill, I was with President Bush. May 15 is also observed as Peace Officers Memorial Day, a day honoring fallen police officers sponsored by the Fraternal Order of Police. As the nation's chief law enforcement officer, this event meant a lot to me, and I attended every year I was attorney general. So late that morning, President Bush and I sat together on the platform at the ceremony, along with other law enforcement officials and congressional leaders.

Typically, at most events, President Bush and I engaged in friendly banter of some sort, but not on this occasion. We were not yet aware of what was said at the hearing, and had not yet had an opportunity to study it or react to it with each other. Still, we were painfully aware that the media would be glued to our every expression, looking for a reaction to the former deputy attorney general's testimony. Consequently, other than a brief greeting, neither of us said a word to each other during the entire program, and we exited quickly at the conclusion.

Comey's testimony for nearly the first hour of the hearing had nothing to do with the US attorneys, as first Schumer and then Specter questioned him about Andy's and my visit to John Ashcroft's hospital room. In what some would later describe as a passionate recollection of that night, he gave the impression that Andy and I were trying to take advantage of a dying man, to force him to sign the authorization for Stellar Wind.

Later when I learned of the testimony, I felt sadness. What would my wife think? What would my two young sons think? Would their friends make fun of them because of their dad?

To his credit, when asked, Comey acknowledged he did not suffer any recriminations as a result of his opposition to the disputed aspects of Stellar Wind, not from the president, not from Andy Card, not from DOJ, and not from me. In fact, he and I continued to work together for another sixteen months after that unusual incident, until August 2005, when he left to go to work in the private sector.

When the senators finally got around to asking Comey for his impressions of the seven dismissed US attorneys, he basically said that he thought they were all doing a good job, that he had a positive sense about several of them, and that he had no personal knowledge of why they were asked to resign. He did say that the EARS evaluations were a top-to-bottom review of the US attorney's office, although he clearly did *not* say the EARS report analyzed the performance of the US attorney.[14] Apart from that, he added nothing to the discussion of the dismissals. Also to his credit, when Senator Specter asked him about his interactions with me, Comey answered, "In my experience with Attorney General Gonzales, he was smart and engaged.

And I had no reason to question his judgment during our time together at the Department of Justice. We had a good working relationship. He seemed to get issues. I would make a recommendation to him. He would discuss it with me and make a decision . . . I did not have reason to question his judgment as attorney general."[15] Nevertheless, Comey's testimony hurt me, more than I realized at the time.

The next day, in San Antonio, I had an opportunity to reinforce my support of our US attorneys at their national conference. Nevertheless, the assaults on my integrity, competence, and character continued throughout the month. I stayed focused on my job, working with Secretaries Spellings and Levitt on gun violence at schools following the tragic incident at Virginia Tech, highlighting the plight of missing children, developing strategies to deal with corrupt online pharmacies, as well as attending a G8 Justice and Interior Ministries meeting in Munich. Becky, however, bore the brunt of it; she continued to read every word of the negative press, and it hurt her deeply. From time to time, the president gave me a reassuring word and encouraged me to hang in there. On May 29, I was at the White House for a Homeland Security briefing. Following the meeting, the president and I walked back to his private dining room.

"I'm concerned about how you are getting beat up," he said. "How are you doing?"

"I'm fine," I told him, "but this is hard. I'm trying to stay focused on doing my job as attorney general."

"How's the department doing?" he asked.

"We're all trying to stay focused," I said.

"Well, I want what is best for you," he said.

I expressed my appreciation and went back to work, determined to fend off the attacks against me.

In early June, the president traveled overseas to a G8 conference. Upon his return, I went to the White House again for another Homeland Security briefing on June 12. The president appeared tired, but we had a lively session. While the president had been away, the Democratic senators had attempted to drive through a no-confidence vote on my continuation as attorney general. They had failed to get enough votes to invoke cloture, so the motion was dropped. With a twinkle in his eye, the president whimsically congratulated me on the failed cloture vote.

He told me that he had been asked about the vote by the media while he was in Albania. "I told them that I didn't care what the Senate did," he quipped, "the vote wouldn't matter to me."

On June 22, Becky and I attended the Academy of Achievement awards banquet. Every year at their International Summit conference, the academy inducts new members based on their outstanding achievements in business, politics, sports, entertainment, academia, or public service. I was honored to have been selected in 2006, so Becky and I attended the 2007 edition of the black-tie banquet in Washington.

As past honorees, Education Secretary Margaret Spellings and I were asked to present country music superstars Brooks & Dunn, two of the inductees for 2007.

Before the banquet, Margaret and I were visiting with Kix Brooks and Ronnie Dunn. I was a longtime fan of the country music duo, so I was excited to meet them. During the course of our conversation, I was surprised to learn that they were aware of me and my recent troubles. I jokingly suggested that they should consider writing a song about me, that events surrounding me might make a great country song.

"Oh no," quipped Dunn. "That's too sad for a country song."

CHAPTER 37

A SLOWLY TURNING TIDE

On July Fourth, Becky and I attended the president's birthday party, hosted by the First Lady at the White House. For a few hours, we dismissed our troubles as we celebrated the president's birthday and our nation's independence.

By mid-July, I felt the worst was over regarding the fired US attorneys, but I continued to get beat up badly in the media. Despite the fact that there was no evidence of wrongdoing and no smoking gun in the documents produced by the Department of Justice and the many hours of testimony before Congress, my detractors only increased their speculation about my future. When the White House chose to invoke executive privilege, based on institutional considerations, to exclude certain high-level White House communications over the US attorneys' flap, the Democrats insisted the Bush administration was hiding something. The Democrat-led drumbeat demanding my resignation incessantly pounded away.

Although I had been part of the Bush administration for seven years, and had witnessed firsthand the vindictiveness of those vying for power inside the Washington Beltway, I still had a naïve optimism that the truth would win out, and that everything would work out. As my father had often told me, "It has to work out."

Some Hispanic groups suggested the abusive treatment I had received was nothing short of racism. Many of my Hispanic friends wondered whether the opposition to me, as the highest-ranking US government official with a Hispanic ethnic background, was an effort to undermine President Bush's hopes of immigration reforms or to block me from ever going on the Supreme Court.

As the nation's chief law enforcement officer, I had wanted to help lead the way to develop genuine, workable immigration reforms. As the first-ever attorney general with Hispanic roots, I believe I would have been an effective spokesperson to address what was wrong with our broken immigration system and to offer viable alternatives, but the controversies swirling around me rendered my views and suggestions almost useless. It was frustrating for me and for my many Hispanic friends who had come to America legally.

Several friends encouraged me to resign, warning that I was sabotaging my own future and that of my family by staying and enduring the almost daily false accusations. Tim Flanigan, my former deputy in the White House, called me a couple of times during this period and said, "Get out of there. You're getting killed. This is going to ruin you professionally. Get out of there!" I'd also heard that the president's counsel, Fred Fielding, had mentioned to several people in the Washington legal community, "Al needs to get out of there." At times, I wondered if it might be better for the Justice Department and for the president, as well as for me, if I simply resigned. But my friend, the president of the United States, had asked me to stay on and fight. So I did.

I was now one of the few Bushies who had come from Texas and was still working together with the president. Most others had moved on or moved back to Texas. I understood that; with each passing day, I felt more and more isolated and alone in Washington. After a while, it seemed I was standing all by myself, abandoned by everyone except the president. Most days, I kept my chin up. I had to because of my job. But increasingly I went home discouraged, feeling as if there was nobody to whom I could turn. The more I pondered the situation, the more I was confused. I prayed for understanding, but found none. I tended to internalize my frustrations and concerns. I didn't even try to talk with Becky about the matters with which I was dealing. It was simply too painful.

Becky and I coped with the pressures differently. I clammed up and kept everything inside, while she vented to her Bible study group. We found that it was actually easier not to talk to each other about what was happening, so Becky often cried alone. She tried not to let me see her tears because she didn't want to put more of a burden on me. We simply put our heads down and tried to get through each day.

Even normally happy, good times somehow came with a sour twist. On a Sunday afternoon in July, my family and I attended a T-ball game held on the South Lawn of the White House, commemorating the sixtieth anniversary of Jackie Robinson's career in Major League Baseball. We sat in the stands along with other members of the president's cabinet, Housing Secretary Alphonso Jackson and Interior Secretary Dirk Kempthorne. As he usually did, President Bush stood at home plate to welcome everyone. Before the game, the president acknowledged Alphonso and Dirk, but he had not seen me, so he failed to note my presence.

Later, when he returned to the stands and saw me, he waved and was apologetic for not mentioning me. I didn't give it a second thought.

A few days later, the president confided in me that First Lady Laura Bush had expressed concerns that the president had not mentioned me at the T-ball game. "Laura said that the reporters would be buzzing because I failed to mention my friend," he said with a laugh.

"Oh no; please tell Laura that it was okay," I said. "It was just a T-ball game. I didn't expect you to make a big deal about me."

The president said, "I know, but Laura brought it up several times throughout the game."

The First Lady's instincts proved correct. The next day, the *Washington Post* wrote a story expressing the very questions that had troubled the First Lady—implying that the fact that the president had not mentioned me, even though I had been at the game, indicated trouble in paradise.

Some members of Congress continued to call for my resignation, but both the president and I had made it clear that I was not going to resign over the US attorney firings. Still determined, the Democrats launched a second front. On July 24, 2007, I sat before the Senate Judiciary Committee again as a witness from 9:30 a.m. to 1:30 p.m.

This time the Democrats said that I had committed perjury in my previous testimony regarding Stellar Wind. They said that I had intentionally misled them, contending that I had mischaracterized the scope and source of the opposition from DOJ, specifically that of the deputy attorney general, as well as OLC lawyers Jack Goldsmith and Patrick Philbin.

In this hearing, I discussed for the first time under oath the events surrounding Andy Card's and my 2004 visit to John Ashcroft's hospital room. During the four-hour hearing, the senators continued to probe the reasons for the disagreement over the legal basis for the program. Once again, I was guarded about some of my answers because whether they were doing so intentionally or not, certain senators asked questions about parts of the Stellar Wind program that remained classified. I emphasized that the dispute was not over the Terrorist Surveillance Program, or TSP, itself (Basket I content collection of certain international calls), but about "other intelligence activities."

The president called later that afternoon and encouraged me. We had a good discussion and he repeated several times, "Hang in there."

"I will, sir," I said. "You hang in there too."

Two days later, the House Judiciary Committee called FBI director Bob Mueller to testify about the same intelligence matters. In response to a rather rambling, convoluted question by Texas Democrat Sheila Jackson Lee, the director's answer seemed to contradict my testimony.

"I had an understanding that the discussion was on a[n] NSA program," Mueller said in answer to the question from Representative Lee.

Asked whether he was referring to TSP, he replied, "The discussion was on a national NSA program that has been much discussed, yes."[1]

The following day under the headline "FBI Chief Gives Account at Odds with Gonzales's," the New York Times reported that Mueller's testimony was a serious blow to me. The director's testimony immediately raised questions among my critics that perhaps my testimony had not been accurate. Apparently that was exactly what the Senate Judicial Committee was hoping to hear. They renewed their efforts to force my resignation, and Democratic senators Russell Feingold, Dianne Feinstein, Charles Schumer, and Sheldon Whitehouse sent a letter to Paul Clement, the solicitor general, asking him to appoint a special counsel to investigate whether I had committed perjury in my testimony about the surveillance programs. At best, it reflected a basic misunderstanding because of their ignorance of classified activities. At worst, it was more political grandstanding and chicanery.

Because Mueller's nebulous testimony raised questions anew, DOJ spokesperson Brian Roehrkasse issued a statement that same night stating that I had indeed testified truthfully. He emphasized, "Confusion is inevitable when complicated classified activities are discussed in a public forum where the greatest care must be used not to compromise sensitive intelligence operations."[2]

He further stated, "The disagreement that occurred in March 2004 concerned the legal basis for intelligence activities that have not been publicly disclosed and that remain highly classified."[3]

To counteract the charges by the senators, I attempted to get a letter from Mike Hayden, former NSA director and now director of the CIA, explaining why my statements about the NSA surveillance program were accurate without revealing the still classified details. Mike was out on vacation, so the director of national intelligence, Mike McConnell, confirmed that the president had indeed authorized multiple activities, not simply the content selection under Stellar Wind. Neither McConnell nor I had the authority to disclose that the disagreement that had occurred in March 2004 concerned the collection of certain metadata.

I also wrote a similar letter to Congress, approved by Steve Bradbury at OLC, and we had the letter cleared by Mueller and his general counsel for accuracy. We didn't want to be blindsided again by the FBI director. Not surprisingly, those clarifications never gained traction in Congress or in the media.

On August 4, 2007, the House passed the FISA Modernization Act, making surveillance even more expansive than it had been in 2004 when it had been so disputed. Based on the new act, we could now pursue surveillance of a broad spectrum of terrorist organizations. I had wanted to be actively involved in pushing the legislation to modernize FISA, since that was the key law governing the collection of electronic surveillance, but because of the controversies surrounding me, I was not as effective as I had hoped to be.

I was scheduled to leave at 11:00 p.m. for my third trip to Iraq on August 9 to visit with DOJ personnel working with the Iraqis, helping them solidify their new government. Before leaving, I certified the new FISA authorities so the DOJ could begin using them. Mike McConnell signed them as well. By then, the personnel and hiring issues at DOJ that had fueled the public criticism and prompted congressional hearings contending that I had politicized the department had been addressed. I selected Craig Moreford, a well-respected career prosecutor, as acting deputy attorney general, and life was getting back to normal.

I went on to Iraq and met with General David Petraeus and other military leaders about the challenges the Iraqi leaders had to overcome as they attempted to set up their fledgling government. We had Department of Justice personnel there, so I went to encourage them to continue working with Iraqi leaders to develop a constitution and establish the rule of law. The last time I traveled to Iraq, I was able to visit briefly with my nephew Anthony, who was serving with our troops outside of Baghdad. Seeing him and his commitment to liberate Iraq and help keep Americans safe touched me deeply. I returned from Iraq tired, but inspired.

After visiting with our dedicated troops working for the cause of freedom under extremely difficult and dangerous circumstances, I thought, *If the president wants me to keep fighting, I can do nothing else.* What I didn't know, however, was that others in the White House had different views.

CHAPTER 38

GOD MUST HAVE A
SENSE OF HUMOR

Shortly before 1:00 p.m on August 24, 2007, one of my security agents received a phone call from Josh Bolten, requesting to speak to me. I knew immediately that something important was up, otherwise the president's chief of staff would not be calling me during the last few hours of my weeklong family vacation. We were in Austin, Texas, shutting down the rental house where we were staying, packing up, and getting ready to head to the airport to fly back to Washington, DC. Whatever it was that Josh wanted to talk to me about was important enough that it couldn't wait a couple of hours until we were back in our nation's capital.

I was riding alone in the FBI Suburban when I picked up the phone. Josh conveyed the gravity of his call through his tone of voice. "Al, we've had serious conversations about you here at the White House; we're worried about you, and we think this might be the time for you to resign."

At first, I couldn't believe what Josh was saying. I had stayed on the job at the president's request. I had endured months of demeaning and debilitating attacks, but I had survived. Beyond that, I'd been at DEFCON 1 for so long, thoughts of disarming were foreign to me. The soldier in me instinctively was ready to fight on.

Josh was still talking, but I only half heard him. "The controversy over the US attorney firings and the allegations from some members of Congress that you intentionally misled them about the NSA surveillance program make it difficult for you to continue to serve the Department of Justice and meet the president's law enforcement priorities."

I could hear the tension in Josh's voice as he struggled to explain the reason for his call and how difficult the conversations had been with our friends in the White House. Josh was a friend, and shortly after he had become chief of staff, I had told him that because of my friendship with the president, there might come a day when he would need the courage and strength to tell me it was time to go. Apparently that day had come.

"Is the president aware of this call?" I asked, although I knew the answer to my question before I voiced it.

Josh responded with little hesitation, "Yes."

I knew what that meant.

I had served in the White House for four years and almost three years at Justice. I knew how things worked at the White House. Josh would not be making this call if the matter had not already been hashed out and if the decision had not already been made; it was a done deal with the president.

I hung up with Josh and immediately put in a call to the president who was at home on his ranch in Crawford, Texas. I then returned to the rental house to continue packing while I awaited his return call.

I told Becky that I had received a call from Josh. Seeing the look on her face, I guessed that she instantly comprehended this was no ordinary call. Becky had been urging me for months to step down. She knew that I wanted to finish out the term, if possible, so she held her tongue about leaving sooner. She never said the words, "I want us to leave now." The congressional allegations of wrongdoing and the continual flood of media stories speculating about my resignation pummeled my reputation and made life in Washington almost unbearable for her. Nevertheless, I had refused to quit when I knew I had done nothing wrong and while the president encouraged me to stay and fight, so she had stood strong with me.

Along with our FBI security detail, we loaded our suitcases and other belongings into the SUVs and headed toward the airport. I told the lead agent to put the president through to me the moment he called.

As soon as President Bush came on the phone, I directed the agents to pull over into a parking lot just off Highway 71, a short distance from the airport. I instructed the FBI detail to take our sons Graham and Gabriel out of the vehicle while the president was on the phone.

President Bush got straight to the point, letting me know that it was time for me to step down, yet he seemed more concerned about me. "This is what I want for you," he said.

Just hearing him say those words, I felt the heavy burden lift off my shoulders. In many ways, and for many reasons, I felt relief. Yet with Becky at my side, I also felt sadness as I talked with our friend. From the time I first went to work for George W. Bush, he always had treated me well. Although he did not have to do so, he had watched out for me, and he seemed to be doing so even now. On this call, unlike so many others we had shared previously, there were no words of encouragement about my continued service, no admonitions to "Hang in there, Fredo," no urging me to stay and fight.

"The Democrats are after you," he said. "They want to bring criminal charges against you, trying this perjury charge again. I do not want to see that happen."

I didn't challenge what he was saying. I didn't ask him to reconsider. I well understood that I, too, served at the pleasure of the president and for the benefit of his presidency and the good of our nation. If he felt it was time for me to go, that was all that mattered. The decision was irrevocable; the die had been cast.

Certainly, had he given me a choice, I would have chosen to remain at the helm of the Justice Department until the president completed his term of office. Even after all the abuse, I could leave the office with my head held high, knowing that I had served our country to the best of my ability. Besides, I had been so beaten up for so long, there was little more the opposition could do to me. I would have gladly stayed on and served.

But he didn't offer me that choice, and I knew better than to ask for special favors or reconsideration of his decision. Once President Bush reached a decision point, his mind was made up.

"Thank you for giving me the opportunity to serve," I said sincerely. "I'll call Josh back and work out the details." It was one of the most emotional calls of my entire life—a candid conversation between two friends who had endured so much together.

The president then talked with Becky for a few minutes, offering her comfort and assurance through her tears that all would be well. We said good-bye to my boss and looked at each other, a bit shell-shocked. After thirteen years of riding the George W. Bush roller coaster, we had come to an abrupt, screeching halt. The ride was over.

We gathered our children to us. The guys in the security detail may have suspected what was happening, because rather than teasing with the boys, as they were sometimes prone to do, they continued in somber silence the rest of the way to the airport.

As we pulled up to the Signature Terminal, Becky and I looked at each other and smiled. This was where it had all begun for us that night so long ago, back before the 2000 presidential election, when we had stood at this same terminal and welcomed home then governor George W. Bush as he returned from his last campaign stop before the election. Surrounded by thousands of friends and supporters that night, we basked in the joy and optimism of anticipating a remarkable journey ahead. And it had been that—an incredible trip, more amazing than a boy from Humble could have ever dreamed.

Now we were back at the airport, relatively alone. Firmly believing that God had directed my steps from childhood to the US attorney general's office, I had witnessed and been part of American history. Like many who participated in such monumental moments, I had endured public persecution while attempting to maintain high standards of integrity within government. With my faith sorely tried, my reputation smeared in the media, my family under stress, and controversy swirling all around me, my wife and I realized we had come full circle figuratively and geographically. Becky saw the irony clearly. She mused aloud, "God must have a sense of humor."

We arrived back in Washington late that afternoon and attempted to pretend that everything was normal. In follow-up conversations with Josh, I decided to announce my resignation on Monday, August 27, but not actually leave office until September 17, so we could have an orderly transition.

The president indicated that he wanted to see me before I announced my resignation, so on August 26, Becky and I flew to Crawford to have a private lunch and spend some time alone with the president and Mrs. Bush. It felt bittersweet as we boarded the FBI jet; this would be my last trip to Crawford, Texas, as a member of the Bush administration.

It was a perfect, blue-sky day when we landed back in Texas. The president and Mrs. Bush greeted us with smiles and hugs when we arrived at their ranch. They were both dressed casually, the president wearing blue jeans and cowboy boots.

"Is this going to be a funeral or a celebration?" Bush asked as he hugged Becky and me. We all laughed.

"A celebration," I responded.

But even as I said the words, a profound sadness enveloped me. I felt like I had failed. I had been fighting for so long, at war with critics and fending off their attacks, that it was hard to put down my shield, hard to accept that this dream was over.

Mrs. Bush and Becky went inside, and the president and I sat on the front porch to talk alone for a few minutes.

"I always believed we could ride out the controversy," he began. "I really thought we could survive this. But two things hurt you. One was Comey's testimony about the surveillance program, and his version of you and Andy visiting Ashcroft in the hospital, and the other was Mueller's testimony." Comey had convinced certain senators that Andy and I had tried to take advantage of General Ashcroft when he was sick, all for a nefarious purpose. Mueller's answer convinced my critics in Congress that I had intentionally misled them about the disagreement between the White House and the leaders in the Department of Justice over Stellar Wind. People respected Mueller, so when word got out that Mueller's testimony seemed to contradict mine, it was a mountain too high to climb.

As we talked through the ridiculous set of events, the president shook his head as though irritated or frustrated, or perhaps in disbelief. But none of that mattered at that point. It was over.

He and I joined our wives inside. The president and Laura were so gracious and encouraging to Becky and me; he offered several times to help us, and repeatedly reassured us about the future. Then Laura, Becky, the president, and I climbed into the president's pickup truck and he drove us around the sprawling property, giving us a tour of the ranch. The Bush ranch at Crawford has both areas of rugged landscape and untamed brush, as well as beautiful patches of wildflowers and serene streams. The natural scenes reminded me in many ways of our hosts. The president enjoyed pointing out various trees and wildflowers as he drove, and we enjoyed listening to him.

After the tour, we sat down to lunch in their beautiful ranch home, followed by one of the Bush family's favorite activities—working on a complex wooden jigsaw puzzle. We sat in the large, open living room, talking casually about a range of issues—everything from baseball to immigration to Iraq. Occasionally, the president punctuated a sentence with a statement about my loyalty. "I know you stayed on and fought because of my spoken and unspoken encouragement," he said. "Like friends who communicate without talking."

All too soon, it was time for us to head back to Washington. We all hugged good-bye. "If I were you," President Bush said before we left, "I wouldn't watch the news for a few days."

We nodded, understanding.

"In three days," he said, "the news value will be over and the media will move on."

The president and Mrs. Bush walked us outside where Karl Rove, who himself had announced his resignation on August 13, barely two weeks earlier, had pulled up to the ranch house in a white pickup truck, ready to give us a ride back to the airport.[1] As we slowly drove away from the ranch, I waved good-bye and the president gave me a salute.

We talked with Karl about our futures on the way to the airport—Karl planned to stay on till the end of the month—but mostly I was thinking about what we had just experienced. Becky and I were content, relieved, and proud. We had sacrificed so much to serve our country during a difficult period of world history. Now after thirteen years in public service, we hoped a brighter future lay ahead of us.

We did not even tell our closest friends or colleagues about my conversations with the president. Because reporters were hovering like vultures over a dying animal alongside the road, I told a few key people who asked that weekend that I had not resigned—which technically was true, as I had not yet done so officially.

The following morning, I called for a 10:30 a.m. news conference at the Justice Department Press Room. I met first with my senior staff in the spacious attorney general's conference room on the fifth floor of the Robert F. Kennedy Building and informed them of my decision prior to meeting the media. Speculations about my resignation had been bandied about for so many months, nobody in our inner circle at Justice paid much attention anymore to press rumors and innuendoes regarding my imminent departure. Perhaps that's why some of my staff members were stunned when I announced my resignation. Following the senior staff meeting, as I walked out of the stately conference room, I glanced at the portraits of some of my predecessors hanging on the walls. I wondered how they felt at the end of their tenure.

During my formal announcement in the press room later that morning, I told everyone, "I often remind our fellow citizens that we live in the greatest country in the world and that I have lived the American dream." I felt my voice crack slightly as I said, "Even my worst days as attorney general have been better than my father's best days." I had much for which I could be thankful, and I was.

Still in Texas, President Bush commented upon my resignation, saying that he had accepted the resignation reluctantly. He spoke of me as "a man of integrity, decency, and principle" and remarked about the "months of unfair treatment" that preceded my resignation.[2]

"It's sad," President Bush said, "that we live in a time when a talented and honorable person like Alberto Gonzales is impeded from doing important work because his good name was dragged through the mud for political reasons."[3]

I purposely kept the announcement brief, and I took no questions from the press. They already had their slants on the story, so there was nothing I could say that might alter their perspectives.

I tried to keep a normal schedule of meetings that day—after all, I wouldn't actually be leaving the job for several more weeks, and there was a lot of work to be done before that time. There was a meeting with Native American tribal leaders, photos with Presidential Rank Award recipients, and my monthly meeting with our inspector general. Nevertheless, as the day progressed, I found myself becoming emotional as I thought of the many fine employees with whom I had worked at the Justice Department. We had made great strides in fighting corporate and political corruption; we had continued working through the complex legal issues surrounding the war on terror; we had made remarkable progress in prosecuting child predators; and we had done so many other good things that would have lasting impact on our country. I would miss working with the dedicated people at the department. I was grateful for their work, and I was proud to have been their boss.

The following day, I received an envelope from the president. In a handwritten letter to me, written the day of my announcement, President Bush wrote in part:

> As you and I discussed on the ranch, Washington is a treacherous place. Ambition and pettiness often displace statesmanship and service. And when that happens, individuals are treated unfairly. This happened to you.
>
> During the last months, you have maintained your composure and dignity. Your class shined brightly. Your inner soul was strong.
>
> As you move on, I know you will do so with head high and spirit solid. You and Becky are dear friends to Laura and me. The past months have pained me, but not nearly as much as those closest to you and those who love you most. I was heartened to hear Becky say that the toils have strengthened your bonds. I feel the same way. I honor my friend and appreciate all that you have done.

News of my resignation brought out anonymous critics within the administration who accused me of being incapable of standing up to the likes of David Addington and John Yoo. The truth is, the advice I gave was always mine. Other critics claimed then and now that I could not be objective when it came to George W. Bush. They are wrong. The strongest evidence of my loyalty to the president was doing my job, irrespective of the consequences. That is what he expected of everyone in his administration and that is what I demanded of myself.

I continued working through the first few weeks of September. Shortly before my last day on the job, White House counsel Fred Fielding scheduled a meeting of the Judicial Selection Committee, the group that had been gathering regularly since my early days in the administration to discuss potential federal judicial appointments. When I arrived at the Roosevelt Room in the White House, I discovered that we had no candidates to consider and no real agenda for the meeting. "What are we doing here?" I asked Fred.

"We just wanted to meet in your honor one more time," Fred said. It was a thoughtful and much appreciated gesture from my friends and colleagues.

The DOJ held a formal farewell ceremony in the Great Hall that gave me an opportunity to say good-bye to the senior leadership and general staff. My attorney general staff of about twenty people held a more intimate going away event in my conference room. I was moved by the remarks of those who knew me best at the department, especially those of Kevin O'Connor, my acting chief of staff, who said, "No matter how difficult or stressful things may have been for the judge, those of us privileged to work on his staff never suffered from it. We all knew what he was going through had to be incredibly difficult for both him and his family, yet he never once took it out on us, or let it impact our work. He was fully engaged at all times and he continued to encourage and motivate us to do our jobs in the way that would best serve the department and the American people. Frankly, I remain absolutely amazed at the dignity he displayed in the face of such unfair criticism and public pressure."

My assistant, Carrie Nelson, and several others helped pack the many photos and memorabilia I had in my office. Since I was not moving to another job, all of my furniture and belongings were moved to a storage unit. I took a last bike ride along with my security detail as my time as attorney general drew to a close.

Peter Keisler, a highly respected attorney from Maryland and head of the DOJ's civil division, was selected as the interim attorney general. Peter was one of the early choices I had recommended for appointment as a federal judge, but the Democratic Maryland senators had shot down his nomination, so I was glad to see him finally receive some well-deserved recognition. Federal judge Mike Mukasey, from New York, was sworn in as the eighty-first US attorney general on November 9, 2007, and he served well and honorably throughout the remainder of George W. Bush's presidency. I was (and remain) grateful for his support and friendship.

On my final Sunday afternoon as attorney general, Becky and I went to the White House and walked through the historic building and around the picturesque grounds for the last time. As the daylight turned to dusk, I asked my security detail to take us to the Lincoln Memorial. Becky and I climbed the steps to the top and stood between the pillars in front of the large nineteen-foot-high statue of one of the most maligned presidents in American history—and one of the greatest. The artist, Daniel Chester French, depicted Lincoln sitting in a large chair during the Civil War, contemplating how he could hold the country together while still championing the cause of freedom and liberty for every person.

We looked at the panorama of the National Mall, from the Reflecting Pool extending back to the majestic Washington Monument and the US Capitol. It was impossible for me not to be overwhelmed at the sight any time, but on this evening, I felt a magnificent sense of wonder and accomplishment. I had served as the counsel to the president and had been the attorney general of the United States, the only lawyer in our nation's history to have held both positions. Amazing. *Thank You, God, for taking us further than we could have imagined.*

On Monday morning, September 18, I awakened early, as always, and looked out my window. No black SUV sat waiting for me in our driveway; no FBI detail was watching our home. I was no longer the attorney general, so they were gone.

The good news was: the media trucks and television cameras that had staked out in our neighborhood were gone as well.

With no pressing government business, and nowhere I had to be, I decided to drive Graham and Gabriel to their school bus stop. It was an unusual, almost surreal feeling. I had not been able to do something so mundane in a long time. I thought, *This is good; I like this!*

The boys didn't say much about the price they paid simply for being my sons, but Becky and I learned indirectly of the fallout from the negative press about me that landed on Jared, Graham, and Gabriel. For instance, one evening a mom of one of Gabriel's classmates called Becky and asked, "Is Gabriel okay?"

"Yes, why?" Becky asked. "What happened?"

"Well, my son came home from school and said that the teacher had been talking about Al in class, and had spoken in a very derogatory manner about your husband, with Gabriel right there in the room." Gabriel hadn't said a word about the teacher's comments to us, but unfortunately, the teacher's outlandish actions had not been an isolated incident.

Becky and I didn't even attempt to explain the chaotic events that had led to my driving the boys to the school bus each morning. It wasn't that they wouldn't be interested or wouldn't care about something that meant so much to me, but I think what mattered most to them was that their dad loved them and was now more available to them. In a way, they were just glad to have their dad back. From my perspective, the silver lining behind all the dark clouds was that I now had more time to spend with my wife and our teenage boys, and I relished every minute with them.

During my time working with George W. Bush, he had been wonderfully kind to our family. When we left his administration, our youngest sons wrote him cards of thanks. Fifteen-year-old Graham wrote:

Dear Mr. President,

Thank you so much for everything you've done for my dad and family. When we moved to Virginia (I was in third grade), I hated it with no friends and I had no idea why I could never see my dad. Then, slowly I started to see things in the news and began to understand what he did and who he worked for. I've taken a lot of stuff from people about my dad's job, but I knew he was working with you to help our country. Thank you so much for everything you have offered to our family and the opportunities and experiences. If my dad had not taken this line of work, I wouldn't have the same friends, and I wouldn't be the same person. Thank you for everything.

Sincerely,

(Alberto) Graham Gonzales

Thirteen-year-old Gabe wrote a shorter note, reflective of his age:

Dear Mr. President,

    Thank you so much for all you have done. Thank you for letting my dad have so many chances to work with you. And I thank you for the fun times with you.

Sincerely,

Gabe G.

Over the years, I collected many personal notes from the president, and he was especially good at presenting special gifts to those of us who worked closely with him. One of the most meaningful presents given to every cabinet secretary was a leather-bound copy of prayers. A little-known aspect about the Bush administration was the frequent acknowledgment that we needed and sought God's help to lead the country well. For example, before each cabinet meeting, one of the members would lead in prayer. The president had the prayers preserved and printed, creating a priceless treasure, and a testimony of our faith in God. That faith saw me through even the toughest of times.

Shortly after leaving office, I received wise advice from former secretary of state James Baker, who encouraged me to focus my energies on the investigations that still continued hanging over me. Although I knew I had done nothing wrong, I set up a legal defense fund, managed by my former colleagues David Lietch, Tim Flanigan, Reginald Brown, and Jim Carroll, to fight the allegations. Many of my friends contributed, and I was able to hire my friend and a former deputy attorney general George Terwilliger to represent me.

All of the issues involving me were thoroughly investigated by Congress and the Justice Department's Office of Professional Responsibility and by the DOJ inspector general. Despite the allegations against me, Congress made no referral to the Department of Justice indicating that a crime had been committed. Nor did the inspector general ever make a referral, leading to the obvious conclusion that, while I had made errors in judgment, the investigations by Democrats in Congress were primarily politically motivated by people opposed to me, and ultimately opposed to President Bush. When the inspector general's report came out, I was exonerated of all supposed perjury allegations relating to Stellar Wind, and of any criminal wrongdoing in the firing of the US attorneys. Ironically, after dozens upon dozens of stories in the media about my so-called politicizing of the Justice Department, the media barely mentioned my complete exoneration. The *Wall Street Journal* compared the investigations to much ado about nothing, asking the proverbial question, "What do you say when a tree falls in the forest, and there's no one there to hear it?" The *Journal* rightly described the investigations as nothing more than political machinations attempting to discredit President Bush and me. "If a Washington 'scandal' ends long after it can be milked for a political gain, and it turns out there was nothing to it, does anyone notice? Consider the whimpering end to the once ferocious controversy over the firing of nine U.S. Attorneys . . . The Justice Department informed Congress . . . that a special investigator in the case found no evidence of wrongdoing . . . The findings of investigator Nora Dannehy confirm that this fiasco was always a political dispute, not a criminal one."[4] I accepted that, but the poignant question once posed by Ronald Reagan's secretary of labor, Ray Donovan, now haunted me: "To which office do I go to get my reputation back?"

CHAPTER 39

THE PRICE OF SERVICE

During a private conversation after I left office, my friend and Treasury Secretary Hank Paulsen told me that I would never have another job as rewarding, as challenging, and as fulfilling as my work as attorney general. He was right. The decompression of going from a pace of one hundred miles per hour to zero was an abrupt jolt.

For a period, I floundered in a dark netherworld following my departure from the Bush administration. I was a Hispanic with a Harvard Law degree, a former partner with one of the most prestigious law firms in Texas, a former Texas secretary of state and supreme court justice, a former counsel to the president of the United States, and a former US cabinet secretary, yet job headhunters told me I was considered radioactive—an unwanted, unemployable pariah, burdened with too much negative press. At first, prospective employers used the pending investigtations as an excuse not to hire or associate with me. But not even the reality of an exoneration could remove the stain on my reputation.

Even before I had resigned as attorney general, several major law firms in Texas had reached out to me, indicating an interest in having me come on board. Those offers didn't pan out, and others disappeared following my resignation.

I traveled to a southern state to visit with the CEO and the general counsel of a Fortune 500 company to discuss being on their board of directors. I thought the position was a real possibility until I was told, "Sorry, you're too controversial. The other board members don't want you."

Perhaps most disappointing, my former law firm, Vinson & Elkins, at which I had been a partner in Houston, declined to take me back. Over the years, when lawyers from the firm had visited Washington, I had hosted them in the White House. Again and again, Becky and I had heard, "Don't forget that we are your family, and you will always have a place with us at V&E when you are done here." Now I was done, but there were no offers of employment or words of encouragement. If the people at the firm who knew me best did not want me, why would any other firm take a chance on me? Granted, while I had been attorney general, the DOJ had prosecuted Ken Lay and Jeff Skilling of Enron, and V&E had been closely intertwined with Enron; the demise severely hurt the firm both financially and by reputation. Although I had been recused, the investigation likely had created some ill will. I was grateful V&E had employed me in the early days of my career and promoted me to partner, but hurt by the firm's unwillingness to hire me back.

I had always thought that I would be welcomed back to Houston with open arms. I had worked there for so many years, and I had built strong relationships within the legal community, as well as with various civic and Hispanic groups. Houston was our home.

But nobody wanted me. I talked with some professors about teaching at Rice University, the school that had once honored me as a distinguished alumnus. The department chairman said, "I'll go talk to the university president. Let me see if I can make it happen." He couldn't.

Although Becky and I really wanted to get our family back to Texas, I spoke with several prestigious DC law firms, but they, too, regarded me as damaged goods. "It's not the right fit; it's not the right time," they said.

Fickle friends fled but true friends stayed close to Becky and me. Don and Joyce Rumsfeld, for example, stayed in touch with us and continued to encourage us. They had been through two Bush administrations, and knew how quickly people tended to forget their "friends" and move on in their relationships.

David Leitch and his wife, Ellen, and Tim Flanigan and his wife, Katie, stuck by us and never gave up trying to help. Clay and Anne Johnson and Alphonso and Marcia Jackson continued to encourage us, as did Jim and Sharla Thompson and Larry and Heidi Dreyfuss. Kerry Cammack and Harriet O'Neill as well as Bill and Mary Sweeney, longtime Texas friends, went the extra mile to help Becky and me. Several people (including a prominent Dallas businessman who I didn't even know) offered us money, when Becky and I were struggling to make ends meet financially. Throughout that period, God surrounded us with good people who cared about us for who we were, not for what we could do for them.

Our pastor at the Falls Church, John Yates, invited me to join a small group of men from our church who met weekly to study the Bible and to simply encourage one another. The group was comprised of a couple of businessmen and a few former government officials. At first, I was reluctant to accept the invitation, but eventually I said yes. The group turned out to be a lifesaver for me, a safe place where I didn't have to be the former attorney general; I could just be Al, one of the guys trying to grapple with the pressures of life and finding spiritual strength for each new day. We didn't pretend to be Bible scholars, but each week, John Yates would ask us to identify key passages in the Bible, and then we would talk about how they applied to our situations.

Our pastor and friends from church remained constant sources of spiritual support, encouraging me to keep trusting God to bring good out of the difficult situations with which I was dealing. I found my faith in God returning even more robustly. Of course, I sometimes wondered, *Why, God? Why have these things happened? I was trying to serve You by serving our country. I tried to do the right things. Why, why, why?* Some of the opposition I experienced still made no sense to me, but I accepted the truth that God used it all—even the ugly, hurtful things—for good in my life. I realized that in the midst of the rancorous rhetoric hurled at me and about me, the realities of my faith were refined by fire. Though sorely tested, the verities and values I believed still stood strong, despite intense pressures to fold. God had never left me or forsaken me; indeed, He had been there all the time.

Ever gracious, in late October 2007, the president and Mrs. Bush hosted a small farewell gathering for Becky and me, to which they encouraged us to invite four other couples to join them for a private dinner in the residence. Having lived in Washington since 2001, Becky and I had numerous people we might have invited, but we chose Tim and Katie Flanigan, who had been there from the beginning with us; Kevin and Kathleen O'Connor, because Kevin had played such a key role helping me through the US attorney controversy; my former deputy in the White House counsel's office, David Leitch and his wife, Ellen; and Jim and Sharla Thompson, from Houston. Jim was a lawyer at Vinson & Elkins.

It was a memorable evening with the president and Mrs. Bush in their home. The conversation was lighthearted, relaxed, and wide-ranging, covering the gamut from baseball to life in the White House. We talked about anything but government business or politics. There were no speeches, toasts, or tributes offered, although throughout the evening, the president said numerous kind things about me, comments that were even more meaningful in front of the lawyers with whom I had worked. We were grateful for the kindness and love shown to us that night.

Mrs. Bush led a tour of the private quarters, giving us an intimate feel for their lives within the White House. She had just returned from the Middle East, so she retired earlier than the president, who gathered our group in the Oval Office for more conversation and insight. Although I had met with him countless times in his office, I was nonetheless fascinated as he regaled our friends with details about the décor of the room, everything from the portraits on the wall to why he chose the yellow carpet—for optimism. The entire evening was truly meaningful and memorable.

For months, I searched for a regular, full-time legal job. We had no steady income, but all the same expenses, so I accepted some corporate mediation work, hired on as a legal mediator in a complicated patent case in Texas. I did some other mediations in cases around the country. I also struck a deal with Greater Talent Network, a first-rate speakers bureau, and accepted some paid speeches—and that's how we survived financially for nearly two years after leaving the administration. During the down time, I often rode my bike along the Potomac River. Now I rode alone—without a security detail—and I was content with that, just me and my thoughts.

It was a humbling period, but looking back, I now see it as a time of reflection and growth. Moreover, I needed that time for the wounds to heal.

Although I rarely spoke with President Bush while we remained in Washington, Becky and I received an invitation to the White House senior staff Christmas party in 2008. The senior staff party had been one of our favorite activities when I had served in the White House. It was an intimate dinner party with a small group that included senior staff members, spouses, and guests, and I was surprised to even receive the invitation, since I was no longer part of the administration. When we walked into the East Room of the White House, I received another surprise to find that I was seated at the president's table.

I sat next to Fran Townsend, the president's Homeland Security advisor, a woman of grace and strength. At some point during the evening, Fran and I were talking about the past and my future plans when she said something that revealed a great deal to me about President Bush. She said, "You know, Al, during those times when you were getting killed in the press, when we'd meet at Camp David, the president would agonize over you." I appreciated Fran telling me that, and it raised my appreciation and affection for the president even higher. He cared for all his friends and for his staff.

In another gesture of kindness, President Bush invited me to join him and Mrs. Bush along with his father and mother, and several other Texas Bushies, including Karl Rove, Dan Bartlett, Margaret Spellings, Clay Johnson, Don Evans, Karen Hughes, and Alphonso Jackson, for their return home to Texas. On January 20, 2009, after an emotional farewell ceremony at Andrews Air Force Base, the former president and Mrs. Bush boarded *Air Force One*, designated for the trip as "Special Air Mission 28000," and we flew together across the country. Along the way, I thought about my first flight to DC, during the presidential transition in 2000. We had traveled so far since then. There were a few tears, but most people on board celebrated a job well done.

Late that afternoon, we landed at Midland and attended an emotional and boisterous rally at Centennial Plaza. Repeatedly, former president Bush expressed his heartfelt thanks to his supporters: "I could not have done this without you."

Afterward, we visited the president's boyhood home, and later had one last intimate dinner with staff members and spouses. It was a bittersweet farewell, and the following morning, I flew back to Washington.

———

A short time later, I was at Texas Tech University in Lubbock to speak at a Hispanic event. The chancellor's chief of staff was Jodey Arrington, who had worked with Bush in the governor's office in Austin and also in Washington. While in Lubbock, I talked with Jodey and said, "I'd really like to get back to Texas. Do you think Tech would be interested in having me to teach?"

Jodey talked with Chancellor Kent Hance, the only person who had ever defeated George W. Bush in an election, for a seat in Congress. Kent not only wanted me to come, I was given an opportunity to work with the Office of Institutional Diversity to help recruit and retain Hispanic students, and to teach a political science class. Kent privately expressed high hopes that I could become dean of the law school at Tech.

I appreciated Kent being willing to take a chance on me. I had been an adjunct professor earlier in my career, and I loved teaching. He hired me to begin on August 1, 2009, but I didn't exactly receive a hero's welcome. In late July, more than forty of Tech's current and former faculty members signed a petition opposing my being hired at Tech, some for political reasons, others because they felt it was inappropriate for the chancellor to be hiring faculty. Regardless, it was an awkward first day on the job, but things soon calmed down.

To accept the job at Texas Tech, of course, required a move to Lubbock, a small city of about 300,000 residents in West Texas. To some people, Lubbock may not seem like their dream destination in which to relocate. For our family, however, Lubbock was the Lord's ideal place for us to decompress after Washington; it was a great place to raise our younger boys, a small, safe city where we could catch our breath and regroup.

Nevertheless, it was a bit of a shock to our systems after living in the Washington, DC, area for more than seven years. At first, Graham and Gabriel were not happy about moving from Langley High School in McLean, Virginia, one of the wealthiest public schools in the nation, to a blue-collar, diverse, and relatively poor school in Texas. Graham especially hated it at first since it was his junior year. Gabriel was a freshman. Speaking of our time in DC, I told our boys, "Don't be sad that it is over; be glad that it happened." The next adventure was ready to start.

Worse, since we hadn't yet sold our home outside DC, Becky remained behind in Virginia with our dog, Sasha, while Graham, Gabriel, and I relocated to Texas so the boys and I could begin school on time. We lived initially in an apartment, and I spent a lot of time with my sons during those first six months, fully appreciating what wonderful young men they were becoming. Jared, Graham, and Gabriel all give us such great joy. The Texas transition was difficult and for the first few weeks, Graham and Gabriel were unhappy, but they grew to love Lubbock. When we moved from Lubbock to Nashville a few years later, the boys didn't want to leave.

On the first day of school at Texas Tech, I received a phone call from former president Bush. "Hey, professor, how are you doing?" he asked. It was good to hear his voice. I had not talked with him regularly after leaving Washington, so I was surprised that he even knew that I had taken the teaching job.

I didn't really know if the president was aware of my activities until a few years later. On November 16, 2012, Becky and I attended the ground breaking for the George W. Bush Presidential Center on the campus of Southern Methodist University near Dallas. While there, I spent some time with Tobi Evans, President Bush's general counsel at the Bush Foundation. Tobi is married to Evan Young, a lawyer who served as one of my special assistants at the DOJ. Speaking to Becky and me, Tobi said, "The president reads everything he sees about you, Judge. Anything that is reported about you, he reads. He knows what you're doing." How typical that he would keep up with those who had served with him.

Because of the controversies surrounding my government service, the law faculty at Tech were opposed to my becoming the dean of the law school. So I continued working with Kent Hance and Juan Muñoz, a talented educator, and taught a few political science courses.

The hearty people of Lubbock, however, embraced our family and made us feel welcome and respected, a nice change after the final years in Washington. One day, the boys and I were having dinner in a local Lubbock restaurant when I noticed a stout man staring at us. After a few moments, the man got up and came over to our table.

"Are you Alberto Gonzales?" he asked.

"Yes, sir, I am," I responded a bit cautiously.

"I thought so," the man said. He extended his hand in my direction. "I just want to thank you for your service to our country."

"Thank you, sir," I replied as I shook his hand. "We did our best."

I've never been much for self-promotion. I didn't expect pats on the back; nor did I expect everyone to agree with the many tough decisions we had to make during the Bush administration. But if someone can appreciate the sacrifices we made and accept the truth that we were honestly trying to do our best, that's good enough for me.

When our son Graham began looking at colleges, one of the schools on his list was Belmont University, a small, Christian-oriented university in Nashville. I made a trip with Graham to Nashville and visited the campus, a beautiful, stately academic environment just off Nashville's famous Music Row. We were impressed with the school and the city.

Shortly after our visit, Jeff Kinsler, the founding dean of the new Belmont University College of Law contacted me and asked if I'd be interested in teaching. At the time, I was content in Texas, but Belmont connected me with some law firms that might be interested in hiring me. One of those was Waller Lansden Dortch & Davis, one of the most established and prestigious law firms in the Southeast. Being able to educate Graham and Gabriel at Belmont, while teaching at the law school and working at Waller, made the decision to move to Nashville quite easy.

My arrival on the Belmont campus, however, produced much the same response as when I first showed up at Texas Tech, with a number of faculty members writing to the president of the university voicing concerns. Others more overtly protested my hiring due to my past associations with the Bush administration. I also had a few protesters show up in my classroom early in the semester, yelling about torture and Gitmo. Many of the protestors were not enrolled at Belmont, so one of my older students stood up and railed at them, "We paid for this education; you need to leave!"

After the police ushered the protesters out of the building, I whimsically told my class, "These guys are amateurs. I've been protested by the best, and these guys are slouches. This is nothing. If you want to pursue a career in government, get used to it."

My students laughed and appreciated my keeping a sense of humor about it. The protests died down quickly, and I enjoyed being at Belmont, eventually teaching classes in constitutional law, separation of powers, First Amendment law, and national security law. One of the benefits of teaching has been the opportunity for my students to discover the dichotomy between the narrative of "Al Gonzales as portrayed by the media" and who I am as a person. One of my students summed it up succinctly at the end of the first semester: "You're nothing like what I thought you would be." I think that was supposed to be a compliment.

In June 2014, I was named dean of the school. Because the American Bar Association requires law school deans to be full-time, I had to sever my ties with Waller, but the decision proved worthwhile for me and the law school.

Becky decided to return to college and finish her degree, which she did. She graduated from Belmont in the spring of 2015, and then graduated from the University of Tennessee with her master's degree in the spring of 2016. Graham graduated from Belmont in December 2015, and Gabriel is on track to graduate from Belmont in 2017.

Our fledgling law program quickly caught up with its competitors. In 2015, our law school graduates earned the highest bar passage rate (94 percent) in Tennessee for first-time test takers at ABA accredited schools. Our job placement rate for our first two graduating classes has been equally impressive, given our relatively small alumni base. On the strength of our strong record, the law school received full ABA approval in 2016. We are off to a good start, but much work remains.

While fully committed to the work of the law school, I give speeches across the country and often write columns and do media interviews about current events. Today, I am often asked about my views on America and whether my time in Texas and Washington was worth it. I am quick to say yes, but the total story has yet to be told.

History, I believe, will reveal the great accomplishments of our efforts, not the least of which was keeping the American people safe by preventing terrorist attacks. Will there be more attacks on American soil? I believe the correct question is not *if* there will be future attacks, but *when*. But I am thankful to say they did not happen on our watch, and I am hopeful future presidents will discover, as President Obama did, that the Bush policies were necessary to retain and effective in helping to safeguard our nation.

Beyond the threat of terrorism, I have serious concerns regarding the direction of our country. First, I believe in the significance, both from a biblical and a national security perspective, of our relationship with Israel. It pains me to see the deterioration of the friendship with our ally, and our cozying up to Iran, who has sworn to destroy Israel and considers the United States "the great Satan."

Second, I am dismayed at the assault on the Christian church and our religious liberties. The rhetoric today may be for neutrality, but in reality, the goal appears to be something more sinister, such as the elimination of religion from our national discourse. Opponents of religion expect unequivocal tolerance from Christians on virtually all matters, yet many are intolerant of our religious beliefs. While I understand our government's position regarding the separation of church and state, and I am willing to be persecuted for my belief in Jesus, I fear we are witnessing the systematic elimination of religion in America, specifically Christianity.

Third, I believe in the importance of families, and I worry about the deterioration of the family unit. I believe it is critical for a mom and a dad to be a loving and consistent presence in the lives of their children. I wish it were within my power to make all parents love and provide for their children, and teach them values regarding right and wrong, and personal responsibility.

Fourth, I believe in education; it represented freedom for me. I know that not everyone is able to afford college, nor is it a good fit for everyone. Certainly we need skilled individuals who can build, invent, and manufacture products. The key is for each person to find work in which he or she can be productive. Historically, that has been the American way, and the American Dream can *still* be achieved with education.

The treachery of Washington politics and the subtle prejudices against outsiders, can be disillusioning. Washington can be a brutal place, a place where careers and reputations are tainted with impunity simply so a particular person or political party has an advantage in the next election cycle. It is possible to survive with your integrity intact in our nation's capital, but it is not easy. I'm sometimes asked, "Do you think you were treated unfairly?"

Of course. But so what? Everyone, at some point, believes life is unfair, but you must learn to accept and overcome adversity, put your trust in God rather than human beings, and move on. I harbored resentment for a time against Democratic senators and staffers who attacked me, and against Republicans who abandoned me. Now I see that while they sought to do evil to me, God used it for good. And indeed, I am in a good place with my family, my career, and my God.

To thrive in such a cutthroat, often anti-Christian culture as Washington, it is important to know what you believe, and to define yourself rather than letting others do so in a way that serves their interests. The importance of true friends, family, and your faith are invaluable—especially when you are under attack.

It is no secret that life is filled with adversities; events happen that are hard to understand. During an especially difficult period while I was the attorney general, one of my former colleagues in the White House, a woman of strong Christian faith who was aware of my tenacious efforts to apprehend child predators, surprised me by her insight. "You are engaged in a battle between good and evil," she said. "Your cause is just, but there are evil forces at work against you." She helped me realize that opposition to me was not merely political, but spiritual.

The lesson I took away from that conversation was that I was engaged in something much bigger than me. Consequently, I have tried hard not to personalize the attacks on my character or competence nor whine that I was treated unfairly. I knew I represented the president, my department, and the entire administration. I also sensed that my response to all this would form an impression in some minds about Hispanics in leadership positions. I knew people of my ethnic background were watching carefully how I conducted myself under pressure. At the risk of being presumptuous or overly pious, I knew that as a Christian I also represented Jesus Christ and his teachings. God had placed me in the positions I held, so I wanted to walk worthy of Him, in integrity and dignity, believing always that someday, somehow, the truth would triumph.

Today, I tell young people who wish to engage in political battles, "Step into the arena with your eyes open and your armor securely attached. Be bold and take risks. Never fear criticism; you will not be treated fairly; accept the fact that you will be criticized no matter what you do, so do *good* anyway."

My critics claimed that as attorney general, I attempted to align the Justice Department too closely with the White House. Those who believe I made decisions to curry favor with the White House do not know me or my values, nor do they understand my personal relationship with the president. Yes, one of my responsibilities as a cabinet official in the Bush administration was to promote and carry out the president's law enforcement priorities. I make no apology for that. As long as those policies were lawful, I had a duty to carry them out.

Unlike other cabinet members, however, as attorney general I also had a duty—indeed, my primary responsibility was to prosecute crimes and to provide advice on the legality of administration policies. Several of our terrorism policies raised difficult legal issues that resulted in significant disagreement among administration lawyers.

I listened carefully to competing views and weighed the arguments before rendering a legal opinion. Sometimes my decisions did not align with the interests of the White House, but I always worked hard to see that they aligned with the Constitution.

When I stood to take the oath of office as US attorney general, I repeated these words: "I, Alberto R. Gonzales, do solemnly swear that I will support and defend the Constitution of the United States against all enemies, foreign and domestic; that I will bear true faith and allegiance to the same; that I take this obligation freely, without any mental reservation or purpose of evasion; and that I will well and faithfully discharge the duties of the office on which I am about to enter. So help me God." That was not a new commitment for me. In a sense, *true faith and allegiance*—faith in God and allegiance to my family and to my country—have been the guiding principles of my life. I have not always succeeded in living up to those standards, but as I stepped into the arena, that was my aim.

It has been an honor to serve my country, and I would do it again in a heartbeat. Despite the difficulties and adversities I experienced, I am happy and content. I have a loving family and a meaningful career helping to shape the legal minds who will guide America in the future. I have accomplished the American Dream. I have journeyed from Humble beginnings to one of the most powerful offices in the world, and beyond.

My story is not over. The trials and tribulations have made me stronger and wiser. I possess a renewed sense of mission, and although I have no idea where God will lead me, or how He will use me, I know I have more chapters yet to write. I live each day with the awareness that there is much more for me to do, and I'm ready for every challenge.

ACKNOWLEDGMENTS

There are far too many people who played a role in this remarkable life of mine to acknowledge by name. Whether our lives touched for a short time or you have been by my side for much of my journey, I am grateful and I thank you. A few individuals, however, deserve special recognition.

I wish to first acknowledge the work of my talented collaborator, Ken Abraham. Ken and I began working on this project two years ago. We spent countless hours together reviewing original handwritten drafts, recorded interviews, talking over ideas and writing and rewriting drafts of the manuscript. Ken is a true professional who now knows perhaps as much about my life and experiences as anyone except my wife, Rebecca. I appreciate Ken's help and counsel. Rebecca and I are grateful for our friendship with Ken and his wife, Lisa.

I also want to thank Thomas Nelson (HarperCollins Christian Publishing) for their confidence in me and for their patience and guidance. Webster Younce and my excellent editor, Heather Skelton, along with the rest of the Thomas Nelson team, have successfully brought my story to life. I appreciate their counsel while giving me the flexibility to tell my story, my way, and in my voice.

A significant part of this book is based on my memories, notes, and outside sources and materials. However, I also relied on friends and former colleagues to help get the story right. Special thanks to Andy Card, Kevin O'Connor, Jim Haynes, Mike Hayden, and Bill Sweeney for their insightful comments and suggestions to make the book more readable and more accurate.

I served in the White House during one of the most historic events in our nation's history—the September 11, 2001, attacks. I honor those members of the Bush administration on duty during this tragic period. In particular, I want to say thanks to those in the counsel's office. You stood tall during challenging times, and I was fortunate to have you by my side. I consider you part of my family.

Lawyers who held the rank of special assistant to the president and/or attended morning staff meetings in the counsel's office during my tenure at the White House include David Addington, Christopher Bartolomucci, Bradford Berenson, John Bellinger III, Stuart Bowen, Rachel Brand, Reginald Brown, Jim Carroll, Robert Cobb, Grant Dixton, Charles Duggan, Courtney Elwood, Timothy Flanigan, Leslie Fahrenkopf Foley, Noel Francisco, Dabney Friedrich, Brett Kavanaugh, David Leitch, Jennifer Brosnahan McIntyre, Edward McNally, Thomas Monheim, Jennifer Newstead, Benjamin Powell, Nanette Rutka, D. Kyle Sampson, Theodore Ullyot, Helgi Walker, and Raul Yanes. (My apologies to anyone I may have inadvertently omitted.) I honor all of you for your service to our country.

Tim Flanigan and David Leitch, my two deputies, deserve special mention, as does David Addington, who was, at the time, Vice President Cheney's counsel and whom I welcomed in my morning staff meetings. These remarkable men are brilliant and courageous, and they remain trusted colleagues and friends.

The White House legal team could not have properly served the president without the support of a terrific team of energetic, young lawyers, paralegals, assistants, and staff including Hana Brilliant, Elizabeth Bingold, Patrick BuMatay, Charlotte Montiel Davis, Michael Drummond, Tracy Lucas Eddy, Libby Camp Elliott, Laura Flippin, Jonanthan Ganter, Brent Greenfield, Jenny Kim, Heather Larrison, Lori Lorenzi, Ann Loughlin, Morgan Middlemas, Elizabeth Neumann, Colin Newman, Grant Nichols, Allison Riepenhoff

Ratajczak, Emory Rounds, Carolyn Nelson Spurlock, Raquel Cabral Terry, Ansley Tillman, Jason Torchinksy, and Katie Crawford Yarger.

During my tenure as attorney general at the Department of Justice, there were many significant law enforcement achievements. I am grateful for the tireless work and dedication of the 105,000 DOJ employees who report to work every day to see that justice is done without regard to politics or personal agendas. In particular, I wish to honor my predecessor, John Ashcroft, and my successor, Michael Mukasey, for the courtesies they extended me and for their courage to step into the arena of public service. I also want to thank the three men who served as my deputy attorney general, James Comey, Paul McNulty, and Craig Morford. These men served during challenging times for the department, and I appreciate their courage and candid counsel. I also wish to thank the FBI special agents who were members of the attorney general's protective detail and who watched over my family and me during my tenure in office.

I also wish to acknowledge Dr. Bob Fisher and Belmont University for supporting my family and me. Special thanks to Doyle and Barbara Rogers for their kindness and friendship.

I often say that George W. Bush gave me several once-in-a-lifetime opportunities that fundamentally changed the trajectory of my life. He took a chance on me, and I am grateful to him. President Bush has my deepest respect and affection.

Finally, I acknowledge the love and guidance of my mother, Maria, father, Pablo, and my brothers and sisters. My parents taught me love, courage, and the subtle balance between pride and humility. My brothers and sisters give me never-ending support and the comforting reminder of who I am and where I come from.

Through the highs and lows of my life, my wife, Rebecca, and our sons, Jared, Graham, and Gabriel, have been by my side. They are my love and inspiration and the reason I strive to be a better man and continue to work to make a difference in the lives of others. I wrote this book primarily for the boys to better understand the people and events that helped to form my values and shape my life.

NOTES

CHAPTER 1: THE 911 EXPERIENCE
1. Author's interview with William James Haynes II, June 25, 2015.

CHAPTER 8: THE DEATH CASES
1. George W. Bush, *A Charge to Keep* (New York, NY: William Morrow and Company, 1999), 145.

CHAPTER 11: WEST WING POSSIBILITIES
1. Mimi Swartz, "The Outsider," *Texas Monthy*, July 2010, accessed March 7, 2016, www.texasmonthly.com/politics/the-outsider/.

CHAPTER 12: WHITE HOUSE BOUND
1. www.highbeam.com/doc/91G1–68139760.html, accessed April 12, 2016. Also: George Kuempel, Dallas Morning News, December 18, 2000.

CHAPTER 14: THE CALM BEFORE THE STORM
1. Dick Cheney, *In My Time* (New York, NY: Threshhold Editions/Simon & Schuster, 2011), 292.
2. Donald Rumsfeld, *Known and Unknown* (New York, NY: Sentinal/The Penguin Group, 2011), 312.

3. Ibid., 314.

4. Condoleezza Rice, *No Higher Honor* (New York, NY: Crown Publishing Group /Random House Publishing, 2011), 48.

5. George Tenet, *At the Center of the Storm* (New York, NY: Harper/Perennial, 2008), 144.

6. Rice, 66.

7. Tenet, 150.

8. Karen Hughes, *Ten Minutes from Normal* (New York, NY: Penguin Books, 2004), 230.

9. Vicente Fox, *Revolution of Hope* (New York, NY: Viking Penguin, 2007), 229.

10. Ibid., 230.

CHAPTER 15: THE NEW PRIORITY: DEFEATING TERRORISM

1. Hughes, 246–47.

2. Ibid., emphasis mine.

3. Tenet, 105.

4. Tenet, 178.

5. Ibid.

6. Rumsfeld, 359.

7. Authorization for Use of Military Force, Pub. L. No. 107-40, 115 Stat. 224 (2001).

8. Address to a Joint Session of Congress and to the American People, September 20, 2001, edition.cnn/2001/US/09/201 gen.bush.transcript/.

9. Ibid.

10. Ibid.

11. Ibid.

CHAPTER 16: BATTLES ON THE HOME FRONT

1. Tommy Franks, *American Soldier* (New York, NY: HarperCollins, 2004), 284–85.

2. Ibid., 285.

3. Rumsfeld, 387.

4. Ibid.

5. *New York Times*, October 8, 2001, accessed April 12, 2016, www.nytimes.com /2001/10/08/news/08iht-text_ed3_0.html.

6. Bill Frist, *A Heart to Serve* (New York, NY: Center Street/Hachette Book Group, 2009), 214.

7. Ibid., 215.

8. George W. Bush, *Decision Points* (New York, NY: Crown Publishers/Random House, 2010), 153.

9. Ibid.

10. Rumsfeld, 559.

11. House of Commons Foreign Affairs Committee, visit to Guantanamo Bay, Second Report of Session 2006–07, 27, paragraph 85. The report concluded that the Geneva Prisoners of War provisions "lack clarity and are out of date."

12. John Yoo, *War by Other Means* (New York, NY: Atlantic Monthly Press, 2006), 43. See also: Robert K. Goldman and Brian D. Tittemore, "Unprivileged Combatants and the Hostilities in Afghanistan: Their Status and Rights Under International Humanitarian and Human Rights Law," The American Society of International Law Task Force on Terrorism, December 2002.

CHAPTER 17: THE ULTIMATE CLUB FED

1. Military Order of November 13, 2001—Detention, Treatment, and Trial of Certain Non-Citizens in the War Against Terrorism, 66 Fed. Reg. 57, 833 (November 16, 2001).

2. Rumsfeld, 566. See also: Karen J. Greenberg, *The Least Worst Place: Guantanamo's First 100 Days* (Kindle edition), 119–53.

3. Memorandum from Patrick F. Philbin, Deputy Assistant Attorney General, and John C. Yoo, Deputy Assistant Attorney General, to William J. Haynes, General Counsel for the Department of Defense, December 28, 2001, accessed March 17, 2016, http://nsarchive.gwu.edu/NSAEBB/NSAEBB127/01.12.28.pdf.

4. Yoo, 46.

CHAPTER 18: BRINGING TERRORISTS TO JUSTICE

1. Yoo, 217. See also: Jennifer K. Elsea, *The Military Commissions Act of 2009: Overview and Legal Issues*, 19–20.

2. Jack Goldsmith, *The Terror Presidency* (New York, NY: W. W. Norton & Company, 2007), 49–50.

3. Ibid., 50.

4. Memorandum from Franklin D. Roosevelt to Francis Biddle on June 30, 1942, as cited in David D. Danelski, *The Saboteurs' Case*, 1 J.S. CT HIST. 61, 65 (1996).

5. Goldsmith, 49.

6. Military Order of November 13, 2001—Detention, Treatment, and Trial of Certain Non-Citizens in the War Against Terrorism, 66 Fed. Reg. 57, 833 (November 16, 2001).

7. Rice, 106.

CHAPTER 19: THE BRITISH REBELLION

1. Secretary Rumsfeld ultimately appointed two individuals with judicial experience and two former cabinet secretaries, including an attorney general, to serve on the review panel. These individuals could hardly be accused of being biased and closed-minded.
2. Yoo, 212.
3. Rumsfeld, 587.
4. Ironically, Congress later passed the Military Commissions Act, which included many of the provisions requested by Lord Goldsmith. In hindsight, I wished I had agreed with him and the United States would have been able to move forward with military commissions with the blessing of two of our nation's strongest allies.

CHAPTER 20: INTERROGATIONS FOR INTELLIGENCE

1. Tenet, 241–42.
2. Ibid.
3. Convention Against Torture and Other Cruel, Inhumane or Degrading Treatment or Punishment, December 10, 1984, S. Treaty Doc. No. 100-20 (1988), 1465 U.N.T.S. 85.
4. US Department of State Summary and Analysis of the Convention Against Torture, Senatorial Advice & Consent Function, Section 2, 295.
5. Ibid., 297.
6. Convention Against Torture: Hearing on S. Treaty Doc. No. 100–20 Before the Senate Foreign Relations Committee, January 30, 1990. Prepared statement of Abraham D. Sofaer, Legal Advisor, US State Department, 299.
7. Ibid., 300.
8. *County of Sacramento v. Lewis*, 523 US 833 (1998).
9. Senator John McCain, an American hero whom I respect greatly, would later insist that waterboarding was torture.
10. Memorandum for John Rizzo, Acting General Counsel of the Central Intelligence Agency, August 1, 2002, US Department of Justice, Office of Legal Counsel, Office of the Assistant Attorney General, Washington, DC, 1–2.
11. A military officer was convicted for ordering waterboarding during the Spanish-American War, but in that case, there were none of the precautions and safeguards required by the OLC opinion, nor did the US anti-torture statute exist at that time.
12. Scott Shane and David Johnston, "U.S. Lawyers Agreed on the Legality of Brutal Tactic," *New York Times*, June 7, 2009, accessed June 1, 2016, http://

www.nytimes.con/2009/06/07/us/politics/o7/lawyers.html?_r=l&ref=global
-home&pagewanted=print.

13. Cheney, 359.

14. Rumsfeld, 578.

15. Ibid., 553.

16. Hearing before the Committee on the Judiciary, *DOJ Oversight: Terrorism and Other Topics,* June 8, 2004, Serial No. J-108-79, United States Government Publishing Office, accessed March 7, 2016, www.gpo.gov/fdsys/pkg/CHRG -108shrg98625/html/CHRG-108shrg98625.htm.

CHAPTER 21: RACE TO THE COURTHOUSE

1. "Gonzales's Racial Quota Test," *Wall Street Journal* editorial, January, 2, 2003, accessed March 4, 2016, www.wsj.com/articles/SB10414711152811279993/.

2. Dana Milbank, "White House Split on Taking Affirmative Action Stance," *Washington Post,* December 18, 2002, www.stgate.com/politics/article/white -house-split-on-taking-affirmative-action-2745053.php.

3. *Grutter v. Bollinger*-No. 011516–05/14/2002; Appeal from the United States District Court for the Eastern District of Michigan at Detroit.

   No. 97–75928—Bernard A. Friedman, District Judge.

   Argued: December 6, 2001

   Decided and Filed: May 14, 2002; Dissenting opinion by Judge Julian Boggs, dissenting, 796–797, accessed March 9, 2016, http://diversity.umich .edu/admissions/legal/grutter/gru-ap-op.html.

4. Ron Fournier, Associated Press, January 16, 2003, accessed March 8, 2016, http://www.heraldextra.com/news/world/bush-affirmative-action-program -unconstitutional/article_46d4885e-3524–500f-9597–892fb3dc58bd.html.

5. Neil A. Lewis, "Angry Groups Seeking a Justice Against Affirmative Action," *New York Times,* June 24, 2003, accessed March 4, 2016, www.nytimes.com /2003/06/24/politics/24/CONS.html.

CHAPTER 22: "CASUS BELLI"

1. Cheney, 365.

2. Authorization for Use of Military Force Against Iraq Resolution of 2002 (Public Law 107-243), October 16, 2002.

3. The principals committee consisted of all members of the National Security Council with the exception of the president.

4. From a declassified report by the Central Intelligence Agency, "Key Judgments,"

National Intelligence Estimate: Iraq's Continuing Programs for Weapons of Mass Destruction, October 2002.

5. President George W. Bush, speech to the United Nations General Assembly, September 12, 2002.

6. Rumsfeld, 440–41.

CHAPTER 23: DANCING WITH A DEVIL

1. Tenet, 322.

2. Ibid., 333.

3. Ibid., 323.

4. Ibid., 327.

5. Ibid.

6. CIA, "Key Judgments."

7. Tenet, 328.

8. Ibid., 338.

9. John Kerry, statement, "Authorization of the Use of United States Armed Forces Against Iraq—Continued," 107th Cong., 2d sess., Congressional Record, vol. 148, no. 132, October 9, 2002, S10174.

10. Senator Joseph Biden, in an interview with Tim Russert, *Meet the Press,* NBC News, August 4, 2002.

11. Hillary Rodham Clinton, statement, "Authorization of the Use of United States Armed Forces Against Iraq," 107th Cong., 2d sess., Congressional Record, vol. 148, no. 133, October 10, 2002, S10288.

12. Hans Blix, statement to the United Nations Security Council, January 27, 2003.

CHAPTER 24: FOR THE SAKE OF PEACE AND SECURITY

1. George Tenet, 373.

2. Colin Powell, speech before the United Nations Security Council, New York, NY, February 5, 2003.

3. Ibid.

4. Ibid.

5. Senate Select Committee on Intelligence, *Report on Postwar Findings About Iraq's WMD Programs and Links to Terrorism and How They Compare with Prewar Assessments,* 109th Cong., 2d sess., September 8, 2006, 93–94.

6. Rumsfeld, 451.

7. President George W. Bush, Address to the Nation, March 17, 2003.

8. Franks, 431.

CHAPTER 25: LISTENING TO THE ENEMY

1. Glenn Greenwald, "NSA Collecting Phone Records of Millions of Verizon Customers Daily," *The Guardian*, June 5, 2013.

2. Yoo, 107.

3. Cheney, 348.

4. Interview with General Michael Hayden, *Frontline*, PBS-TV, accessed February 22, 2016, www.pbs.org/wgbh/pages/frontline/government-elections-politics /united-states-of-secrets/the-frontline-interview-michael-hayden/.

5. Ibid.

6. Ibid.

7. Cheney, 350.

8. Hayden, *Frontline*.

9. Ibid.

10. *Report on the President's Surveillance Program*, Volume 1, July 10, 2009, 60–66, prepared by the Offices of Inspector General of the Department of Defense, Department of Justice, the Central Intelligence Agency, the National Security Agency, and the Director of National Intelligence, Report No. 2009-0013.A, accessed March 8, 2016, https://oig.justice.gov/reports/2015/PSP-09-18-15 -vol-1. Pdf.

11. Ibid.

12. Goldsmith, 71.

13. Ibid.

14. Ibid., 73–74.

CHAPTER 26: STUNTING STELLAR WIND

1. Interview with Mike Hayden, *Frontline*. Hayden later commented on the inception of the program during a nationally televised PBS interview:

We have the dialogue with the president, the vice president, director of Central Intelligence. We get the order from the president. My lawyers look it over, and I had three really good operational lawyers, really good, really operational. And all three of them serially, independently said, "the president has the authority to authorize this."

Again, we hadn't done it before. In fact, we had rejected an approach a little bit like this during the Millennium Weekend. Remember the threats there? But we had no authority to do it, not presidential authorization.

With this program, we did.

And they all three agreed that it was within the president's Article II authorities. Now, there's been a grand debate about what justifies this, the raw commander in chief authorities from Article II or the AUMF, the Authorization for the Use of Military Force? Justice has frequently argued AUMF. My lawyers never went there. My lawyers said, "Raw Article II commander in chief authorities." And I think appellate courts have kind of upheld that.

There have been two FISA appellate court decisions; both of them contained the language: We take as a given that the president has inherent constitutional authority to conduct electronic surveillance without a warrant for foreign intelligence purposes. So we had that meeting.

But then we had a workforce. We had a workforce that's very cautious, very conservative, that drilled into it, on an annual basis—and they have to certify the training—"thou cans" and "thou cannots." This was going to be something they had never been previously authorized to do. So we took the small team, probably several dozen, into my large conference room at Fort Meade.

I went in there, explained the broad outlines to the program with my ops and legal team right there. Explained the broad outlines of the program to the folks there. Said that it was different but lawful, and that we were going to do this, and we were going to do it very, very well. In fact, I recall saying, "We are going to do what the president has authorized us to do, and not one electron or one photon more."

2. The thought occurred to me that the DAG had conferred with Ashcroft and was speaking for him. But he never said that. Perhaps the DAG did not want to put additional stress on the attorney general by telling him that his previous legal advice to the president was being second-guessed. If the DAG had spoken with the attorney general while he was hospitalized and in a weakened condition, no doubt he would be subject to the same sort of criticism that Andy Card and I would later receive: attempting to influence a sick man.

CHAPTER 27: JOINING FORCES WITH CONGRESS

1. Bush, *Decision Points*, 172.
2. Ibid.
3. Cheney, 351.
4. Hayden, *Frontline* interview.

CHAPTER 28: THE INFAMOUS HOSPITAL VISIT

1. Anticipating that the congressional leaders might later publicly say something at odds with their private support in the meeting, the president asked me

to memorialize the discussions, which I did in a handwritten summary. My handwritten notes later became the subject of an IG investigation in 2007 because I had included the name of the classified program, Stellar Wind. The IG concluded that when I moved from the White House to the DOJ, I improperly stored the notes. The IG ultimately concluded my actions were not knowing or intentional. (Report of Investigation Regarding Allegations of Mishandling of Classified Documents by Attorney General Alberto Gonzales, Department of Justice Office of the Inspector General, September 2, 2008.)

2. Bush, *Decision Points*, 173.

CHAPTER 29: RESIGNATION THREATS

1. Ibid.
2. Ibid.
3. Ibid.
4. Ibid.
5. Ibid.
6. Cheney, 353.
7. Bush, *Decision Points*, 176.

CHAPTER 30: GET YOUR UNIFORM ON

1. In *Hamdi v. Rumsfeld*, Yaser Esam Hamdi, a Saudi national born in Louisiana, and thus a US citizen, was captured in Afghanistan. The Supreme Court held that the president on his own could not declare an American citizen an enemy combatant without a civilian criminal charge. The court ruled that Hamdi, as a US citizen, was entitled to a notice of charges and enabled to contest his designation as an enemy combatant. The court also overturned *Hamdan v. Rumsfeld*, in which Salim Hamdan, a Yemeni detainee at Guantanamo Bay, was granted the right of habeas corpus, holding that Common Article 3 of the Geneva Conventions applied to the conflict with al-Qaeda and Gitmo detainees.

2. An example of the flagrantly vindictive and mistaken journalism was: Murrey Waas, "Aborted DOJ Probe Probably Would Have Targeted Gonzales," *National Journal*, March 15, 2007, accessed May 31, 2016, http://warisacrime .org/node/19696.

3. In response to suggestions that the president or I blocked the investigation to protect me, Assistant Attorney General Richard Hertling informed Congressman John Conyers on March 22, 2007, "The president made the decision not to grant the requested security clearances to OPR staff. Judge

Gonzales did not ask the president to shut down or otherwise impede the OPR investigation." Judge Gonzales "recommended to the president that OPR be granted security clearances." (Letters from R. Hertling, Acting Assistant Attorney General to Rep. Conyers, March 22, 2007; see also: DOJ000748–63, letter from R. Hertling to Sen. Feingold, Sen. Schumer, Sen. Durbin, Sen. Kennedy, Rep. Hinchy, Rep. Lewis, and Rep Woolsey, DOJ 000772.)

CHAPTER 31: SEARCHING FOR JUSTICE

1. Jan Crawford Greenburg, *Supreme Conflict* (New York, NY: Penguin Books, 2008), 263.
2. Ibid., 266.
3. Ibid., 270.
4. Rove, 422.

CHAPTER 32: MONEY IN THE FREEZER

1. Garrett M. Graff, *The Threat Matrix* (New York, NY: Little Brown/Hachette Publishing Group, 2011), 509.
2. Section 6, Article 1 of the Constitution provides this protection, and the US Supreme Court has held that the speech and debate clause protects activity that is an integral part of Congress's deliberative and communicative processes with respect to the consideration of legislation or other matters within their jurisdiction. *Gravel v. United States*, 408 US 606 (1972).

CHAPTER 33: WRONG EVEN WHEN RIGHT

1. "The Real Scandal," *The Economist*, January 17, 2002, accessed February 22, 2016, www.economist.com/node/940091.
2. Ibid.

CHAPTER 34: HUNTING SEASON

1. US DOJ IG and OPR, "An Investigation into the Removal of Nine U.S. Attorneys in 2006," September 2008.
2. Indeed, later FBI director Mueller would testify that he was unaware of any case that had been compromised or adversely affected because of the US attorney removals. Some time later, the OIG/OPR report found no evidence that the removals were intended to obstruct justice, nor was there any finding that the manner in which I cooperated with Congress and answered questions were

intended to obstruct justice. There were improper political considerations by some junior staffers at the DOJ in the hiring of individuals for the Summer Honors Program, but no evidence the department was used for political reasons to affect a specific case. Contrast these events with President Bill Clinton's granting of a pardon to Mark Rich, a fugitive from the law. Rich was granted a pardon with the support of the Department of Justice; later, Rich's wife made a sizable donation to the Clinton library.

3. DOJ officials Will Moschella and Monica Goodling both testified under oath that EARS evaluations are office-wide reviews; they are not reviews of the US attorneys themselves. See: Will Moschella, House Judiciary Committee Testimony, March 6, 2007, 8 and 15; Monica Goodling, House Judiciary Committee Testimony, May 23, 2007, 14.

4. Ernie Allen, president of the National Center for Missing and Exploited Children, spoke in glowing terms about my efforts on behalf of children. In a *USA Today* article, "Gonzales Concentrates Outrage on Child Abuse," December 14, 2006, he described my example in raising this issue to prominence as a "clear profile in courage."

CHAPTER 35: BEWARE THE IDES OF MARCH

1. Senator Mark Pryor, accessed March 8, 2016, https://books.google.com/books ?id=utWm7XbC784C&pg=PA6486&lpg=PA6486&dq=Congressional+ Record,+March+15,+2007+US+Senate&source=bl&ots=vq9J1K7B-B&sig =hSVRSFziYWLwnqimtZJZjVyhqKE&hl=en&sa=X&ved=0ahUKEwjHiY Hem7LLAhWlkoMKHSN5C7UQ6AEIPDAF#v=onepage&q=Congressional %20Record%2C%20March%2015%2C%202007%20US%20Senate&f=false. See also: Meet the Press, April 1, 2007, MTP Transcript for April 1, 2007, accessed March 8, 2016, http://www.nbcnews.com/id/17857501/ns/meet_the _press/t/mtp-transcript-april/#.Vt9evenvaJU.

2. US Department of Justice, An Investigation into the Removal of Nine U.S. Attorneys in 2006; US Department of Justice Office of the Inspector General /US Department of Justice Office of Professional Responsibilities, September 2008, accessed March 8, 2016, https://oig.justice.gov/special/s0809a/final.pdf.

CHAPTER 36: TOO SAD FOR A COUNTRY SONG

1. Ruben Navarrette Jr., "Gonzales' Persecutors Blinded by Rage," CNN Commentary: March 22, 2007, accessed May 31, 2016, www.cnn.com/2007/US /03/22/navarrette/index.html?ereff=rss_latest.

2. David Johnston and Neil A. Lewis, "'Nothing to Hide,' U.S. Attorney General Insists," *New York Times*, April 15, 2007, accessed March 8, 2016, http://mobile .nytimes.com/2007/04/16/world/americas/16iht-web-0416attorneys.5301215. html?_r=0.

3. I did have a conversation with Monica Goodling, a liason between the DOJ and the White House, about events leading up to the dismissals. The OIG report (pages 342–44) concluded that I did not speak to Ms. Goodling to influence her testimony, but rather to comfort her after she displayed serious emotional and personal problems. Additionally, the OIG report (page 352) concluded that Ms. Goodling committed misconduct in failing to disclose important information to DOJ officials and failing to correct DOJ officials when she knew they were giving false information to the public and Congress.

4. Statement by Senator Arlen Specter, US Senate Judiciary Committee: *Preserving Prosecutorial Independence: Is the Department of Justice Politicizing the Hiring and Firing of US Attorneys?*, accessed March 9, 2016, https://www.gpo .gov/fdsys/pkg/CHRG-110shrg35800/html/CHRG-110shrg35800.htm. See also: CQ Transcripts, "Gonzales Testifies Before Senate Panel," *Washington Post*, April 19, 2007, accessed March 9, 2016, http://www.washingtonpost.com /wp-dyn/content/article/2007/04/19/AR2007041902035.html.

5. Dan Eggen and Paul Kane, "Senators Chastise Gonzales at Hearing," *Washington Post*, April 20, 2007, accessed March 9, 2016, http://www.washingtonpost.com /wp-dyn/content/article/2007/04/19/AR2007041902935.html?hpid=topnews.

6. Ibid.

7. David Johnston and Eric Lipton, "Gonzales Endures Harsh Session with Senate Panel, *New York Times*, April 20, 2007, accessed March 10, 2016, http://www .nytimes.com/2007/04/20/washington/20gonzales.html?_r=0.

8. Testimony by Robert Mueller, US Senate Judiciary Committee, "FBI Investigation Oversight," broadcast archived on C-SPAN, March 27, 2007, accessed February 22, 2016, www.c-span.org/video/?197355–1/federal-bureau-investigation-oversight.

9. Andrew Zajac, "Gonzales Gives Little to House," *Chicago Tribune*, May 11, 2007. Online version reprinted by *The Baltimore Sun*, accessed February 22, 2016, http://articles.baltimoresun.com/2007–05–11/news/0705110348 _1_gonzales-conyers-attorney-general.

10. Ibid.

11. At the time of the announcement of Jim Comey as President Obama's pick as FBI director, the *Wall Street Journal* noted, "Obama's FBI nominee has a record of prosecutorial excess and bad judgment," Review & Outlook, "The Political

Mr. Comey," *Wall Street Journal*, June 24, 2013, accessed May 31, 2016,. http://www.wsj.com/articles/SB10001424127887323728204578515650309268038.

12. Ibid.

13. Jeffrey Toobin, "The Showman," *The New Yorker*, May 9, 2016, accessed May 5, 2016, http://www.newyorker.com/magazine/2016/05/09/the-man-who-terrifies-wall-street?mbid=rss.

14. Testimony by James B. Comey, former US Deputy Attorney General, Senate Judiciary Committee, *Preserving Prosecutorial Independence: Is the Department of Justice Politicizing the Hiring and Firing of US Attorneys?*—Part IV, May 15, 2007, accessed March 9, 2016, https://www.gpo.gov/fdsys/pkg/CHRG-110shrg35800/html/CHRG-110shrg35800.htm.

15. Ibid.

CHAPTER 37: A SLOWLY TURNING TIDE

1. David Johnston and Scott Shane, "F.B.I. Chief Gives Account at Odds with Gonzales's," *New York Times*, July 27, 2007, accessed February 22, 2016, www.nytimes.com/2007/07/27/washington/27gonzales.html?_r=0&pagewanted=print.

2. Ibid.

3. Ibid.

CHAPTER 38: GOD MUST HAVE A SENSE OF HUMOR

1. John D. McKinnon, "Karl Rove to Resign at the End of August," *Wall Street Journal*, August 13, 2007, accessed February 22, 2016, www.wsj.com/articles/SB118698747711695773.

2. Steven Lee Myers and Philip Shenon, "Embattled Attorney General Resigns," *New York Times*, August 27, 2007, accessed February 22, 2016, www.nytimes.com/2007/08/27/washington/27cnd-gonzales.html?_r=0.

3. Dan Eggen and Michael A. Fletcher, "Embattled Gonzales Resigns," *Washington Post*, August 27, 2007, accessed February 22, 2016, www.washingtonpost.com/wp-dyn/content/article/2007/08/27/AR2007082700372.html.

4. Review & Outlook, "General Pinata's Exoneration," *Wall Street Journal*, July 23, 2010, accessed May 31, 2016, http://www.wsj.com/articles/SB10001424052748703467304575383192738893092.

ABOUT THE AUTHOR

Alberto R. Gonzales was the eightieth attorney general of the United States and the first Hispanic to lead the nation's largest law enforcement agency. He served as counsel to President George W. Bush from 2001–2005. Prior to his service in the White House, he served as general counsel to the Texas governor, as Texas secretary of state, and as a justice on the Texas supreme court.

Gonzales is an air force veteran and attended the US Air Force Academy. He is a graduate of Rice University and Harvard Law School. Presently, he is dean and Doyle Rogers distinguished professor of law at Belmont University College of Law.

He and his wife, Rebecca, have three sons, Jared, Graham, and Gabriel. They currently reside outside Nashville, Tennessee.

INDEX